LEGAL PROFESSIONAL PRIVILEGE: LAW AND THEORY

Legal Professional Privilege: Law and Theory

JONATHAN AUBURN
LL.B, BCL, D.Phil (Oxon.)
Barrister, Middle Temple

·HART·
PUBLISHING
OXFORD – PORTLAND OREGON
2000

Hart Publishing
Oxford and Portland, Oregon

Published in North America (US and Canada) by
Hart Publishing c/o
International Specialized Book Services
5804 NE Hassalo Street
Portland, Oregon
97213-3644
USA

Distributed in the Netherlands, Belgium and Luxembourg by
Intersentia, Churchillaan 108
B2900 Schoten
Antwerpen
Belgium

Hart Publishing Ltd is a specialist legal publisher based in Oxford, England.
To order further copies of this book or to request a list of other
publications please write to:

Hart Publishing Ltd, Salter's Boatyard,
Folly Bridge, Abingdon Road, Oxford OX1 4LB
Telephone: +44 (0)1865 245533 or Fax: +44 (0)1865 794882
e-mail: mail@hartpub.co.uk

British Library Cataloguing in Publication Data
Data Available
ISBN 1 84113–101–6

Typeset in Sabon 10pt
by Hope Services (Abingdon) Ltd.
Printed in Great Britain on acid-free paper
by Biddles Ltd, Guildford and King's Lynn

Foreword

The rules of legal professional privilege occupy an important part of the structure of civil litigation as a whole. The fundamental changes to the civil justice system brought about by Civil Procedure Rules 1999 and anticipated by the Human Rights Act 1998 will undoubtedly impact on the traditional view of privilege as a right arising in the context of litigation. The importance of the subject is beyond doubt. Lord Taylor, CJ in the House of Lords in R v Derby Magistrates [1996] AC 487 at p. 507 described it as the cornerstone whereby justice is achieved. The Civil Procedure Rule Committee was recently reminded of the undesirability of tampering with legal professional privilege when it sought to interfere with legal professional privilege without express Parliamentary authority (see General Mediterranean v Patel [1999] 3 All ER 673).

This book therefore offers a timely examination of the fundamentals of this important area of civil law. Through careful scrutiny and constructive criticism of the rules of legal professional privilege, Jonathan has set out a careful and well-argued analysis of the current position. I congratulate him on the production of a text which I am sure will come to be essential reading for all those interested in this subject.

The Right Honourable Lord Woolf
Master of the Rolls

Preface

Lawyers and judges often have an overwhelmingly confidence in the capacity of the privilege to achieve its aims. Practitioners are often surprised by the suggestion that the privilege should be weakened in any manner. The usual responses to such suggestions come in the form of high-minded statements about the importance of the privilege. However this approach by practitioners contrasts disturbingly with the absence of anything apart from their own experience to support these assumptions about the practical efficacy of the rule. The privilege relies heavily on assumed patterns of client behaviour. It is dependent on the premise that client confidence will be maintained only with an extremely strong privilege; a rule with few and narrow exceptions. Yet all the evidence we have tells us that this assumption is questionable.

There are many reasons to believe that the extension of existing exceptions to the privilege or the recognition of new ones may not significantly affect the operation of legal communications. Chief among these is the structure of the privilege. The privilege is qualified by a large number of different exceptions which exist to give effect to competing values and to ameliorate some of the unfairness generated by a strict application of the rule. Some of these exceptions depend upon clear and certain criteria, while other exceptions employ criteria which are less well defined. We should see the privilege not as a near monolithic rule, but as a complex rule with many derogations and sub-rules. Part of the reason we currently regard the privilege as having very few exceptions is that most of the existing ones are all lumped together and called "waiver", thereby giving the impression that they are all part of the same sub-rule. Once the privilege is viewed in the manner suggested in this book, an overly strict application of the rule becomes difficult to justify. There is room for greater flexibility, and the accomodation of interests in the disclosure of evidence to a court or to an agency of the executive.

This book is intended to present a slightly different way of viewing the privilege as a whole, giving greater weight than is usually accorded to the values underlying the need for the disclosure of evidence, with a belief that in the past the demands of confidentiality have been overstated. This approach is then applied to the main common law privilege derogations. The general approach, except where stated otherwise, is to examine the common law across the Commonwealth as a whole. This book is not intended to be a comprehensive treatment of all the rules of legal professional privilege. Rather, it is an attempt to present some new ideas and new ways of looking at the privilege. The aim is more to generate questions rather than to provide answers.

This work arises out of research which began life as a BCL thesis, then grew into a D.Phil. thesis. Through this all my supervisor Professor Colin Tapper has been extremely generous with his time over many years, reading and commenting on countless drafts of this work in its varied forms. I have been fortunate to have benefited from his wisdom and knowledge over this time. I am also grateful to my D.Phil. examiners, Roderick Bagshaw and Paul Roberts, for their very helpful comments on my work; to Dr Katharine Grevling for the important role she played as my College supervisor during my postgraduate studies; to John Toohey for his help in pursuing my further studies and his constant encouragement; and to the staff and postgraduate students of Magdalen College, Oxford for their support, assistance and good humour. The research which formed the basis of this book would not have been possible without the generous financial support of both the British Council and the Hackett Foundation. Finally, and most importantly, I owe the greatest debt to my parents, without whom this would not have been possible.

JONATHAN AUBURN

Contents

Works Frequently Cited

CLEARY, E., *et al.* (ed.) McCormick on Evidence (3rd edn. West Publishing, St Paul, Minn., 1984)

COMMENT, "Developments in the Law—Privileged Communications" (1985) 98 *Harv. LR* 1450

DESIATNIK, R.J., *Legal Professional Privilege in Australia* (Prospect Media, Sydney, 1999)

MCNICOL, S.B., *Law of Privilege* (Law Book Co., Sydney, 1992)

NEWBOLD, A.L.E., "Inadvertent Disclosure in Civil Proceedings" (1991) 107 *LQR* 99

NOTE, "Functional Overlap Between the Lawyer and Other Professionals: Its Implications for the Privileged Communications Doctrine" (1962) 71 *Yale LJ* 1226

NOTE, "The Attorney–Client Privilege: Fixed Rules, Balancing, and Constitutional Entitlement" (1977) 91 *Harv. LR* 464

NOTE, "Attorney–Client and Work Product Protection in a Utilitarian World: An Argument for Recomparison" (1995) 108 *Harv. LR* 1697

PASSMORE, C., *Legal Professional Privilege* (CLT, Sutton Coldfield, 1998)

PHIPSON, S.L., HOWARD, M.N., CRANE, P., and HOCHBERG, D.A., *Phipson on Evidence* (14th edn., Sweet & Maxwell, London, 1990)

SOPINKA, J., LEDERMAN, S.N., and BRYANT, A.W., *The Law of Evidence in Canada* (Butterworths, Toronto, 1992)

STRONG, J.W. *et al.* (eds.), *McCormick on Evidence* (4th edn. West Publishing, St Paul, Minn., 1992)

TAPPER, C., *Cross and Tapper on Evidence* (8th edn., Butterworths, 1995)

WIGMORE, J.H., and MCNAUGHTON, J.T., *Evidence in Trials at Common Law* (Little, Brown & Co., Boston, 1961) viii

WRIGHT, C., and GRAHAM, K., *Federal Practice and Procedure* (West Publishing, St Paul, Minn, vol. 23 1980; vol. 24 1986; vol. 25 1989; vol. 26A 1992)

ZACHARIAS, F.C., "Rethinking Confidentiality" (1989) 74 *Iowa LR* 351

Table of Cases

Table of Legislation

INTERNATIONAL CONVENTIONS

NATIONAL LEGISLATION

Australia

Canada

Statutory Instruments

United States

1

Conceptual and Historical Introduction

PLACE OF THE PRIVILEGE

This book is concerned with the structure of the rule of legal professional privilege. In different jurisdictions essentially the same rule goes by different names, such as "attorney–client privilege" in the United States, and "client–legal privilege" under the Australian federal Evidence Act 1995. The rule, as it is found in varying forms across the Commonwealth and United States, will be referred to as "the privilege".[1]

The privilege is a derogation from the general rule that all relevant evidence is both admissible and compellable before a court or tribunal. The standard application of the privilege means that both the lawyer and client concerned are still generally competent to testify, but that certain communications may not be compellable from them, in either oral or documentary form. The relevant communications are still considered to be admissible, but not compellable. However even these basic concepts are subject to challenge, as will be shown below.

The privilege is a rule relating to the confidentiality of legal communications. There are other rules which also affect this, such as the equitable doctrine of breach of confidence, and ethical rules concerning client confidentiality. In some areas the privilege has a troubled relationship with these other rules. This will also be discussed in parts of the book below. For now it is worth noting the very important point that the privilege is not a branch or variant of any over-arching confidentiality doctrine, and is sometimes driven by goals which are slightly different from these other rules.

[1] The term "legal professional privilege" has been criticised as a misnomer as the privilege belongs to the client, not to the lawyer: e.g., see *Waugh* v. *British Railways Board* [1980] AC 521 at 531 (HL); *Baker* v. *Campbell* (1983) 153 CLR 52 at 85 (HCA); D.L. Mills, *Legal Professional Privilege: Its Application in New South Wales* (Law Foundation of New South Wales, 1975) para. 2.1. The word "privilege" comes from the Latin *privata lex*, a prerogative given to a person or to a class of persons. It may be odd that a rule which, on the utilitarian theory, exists for the benefit of all rather than for an individual's benefit, should be called a "privilege".

DATING OF THE PRIVILEGE'S ORIGIN

The origin and early history of the privilege were set out by Wigmore in his imposing treatise.[2] Wigmore's view of the privilege's history revolves around two important propositions: first, that the privilege was an immediate and natural exception to testimonial compulsion; secondly, that the early rationale for the privilege was a respect for the status or honour of the lawyer.[3] Since Wigmore first published his work on the history of the privilege this has been the generally accepted view of its history and origin in Anglo-American law.[4] In fact, it is difficult to find academic opinion to the contrary.[5] However there are a number of strong reasons to doubt the Wigmorean analysis of the early history of the privilege. In particular, there are two important misconceptions conveyed by this currently accepted view of its history: first, that the privilege has always been an important part of the law of testimonial compulsion; secondly, that non-instrumental theories have from the very start played a role in rationalising the privilege and that therefore utilitarian reasoning has never been the only or most important rationale.[6]

The first misconception relates to the dating of the privilege's origins. Wigmore argues that legal professional privilege had the earliest possible starting point: the rule "appears to have commended itself at the very outset as a natural exception to the then novel right of testimonial compulsion".[7] Wigmore's thesis on the origins of the privilege can be broken down into the following three propositions[8]: first, that common law testimonial compulsion first developed in the middle of the sixteenth century and owes much to section 12 of the 1563 Perjury Act,[9] which provided a penalty[10] for failure to testify after service of

[2] J.H. Wigmore and J.T. McNaughton, *Evidence in Trials at Common Law* (Little, Brown & Co., Boston, 1961) viii, 542–5.

[3] Note also the equally flawed theory of A.L.E. Newbold, "Legal Professional Privilege", unpublished Ph.D thesis (University of London, 1990) 17–18 that the Elizabethan rule regarding lawyer–client communications was a rule of confidentiality, not a rule of non-compulsion. The comparison between the treatment of lawyers and, say, the treatment of peers or other noblemen, shows the error in this approach. The Elizabethan rule was indeed a rule of non-compulsion, or "privilege" in the modern sense.

[4] E.g. W.S. Holdsworth, A *History of English Law* (3rd edn. Methuen & Co., London, 1944) ix, 201–2; Comment, "Developments in the Law—Privileged Communications" (1985) 98 *Harv. LR* 1450 at 1455.

[5] One notable exception is G.C. Hazard, "An Historical Perspective on the Attorney–Client Privilege" (1978) 66 *Calif. LR* 1061 at 1070 ("invitation for reconsideration").

[6] E.g. see Developments (1985), n. 4 above, 1502–4, under the heading "The Utilitarian/Non-Utilitarian Schism".

[7] Wigmore (1961), n. 2 above, 543.

[8] Note that Wigmore did not actually deconstruct his argument in this way.

[9] 5 Eliz. C.9 sect.12. Wigmore rather unhelpfully refers to this provision as the "Statute of Elizabeth". This title is unhelpful as the provision Wigmore describes as a "Statute" is only one section in a statute which ostensibly deals with a different subject (namely perjury). The designation "of Elizabeth" is hardly a useful point of reference when there were many hundreds of statutes enacted in the reign of Elizabeth I.

[10] Of £10 and compensation to the aggrieved party.

process; secondly, that the privilege itself was first recognised around the 1570s; thirdly, that because of the first two propositions, it is most likely that the privilege arose in response to the then novel right of testimonial compulsion.

However Wigmore's argument is flawed as it fails to distinguish properly between compulsion and privilege in Chancery as compared with the common law courts. His first premise listed above, that testimonial compulsion began in the middle of the sixteenth century, relates to the common law courts only, and not to Chancery or ecclesiastical courts. Later in his text Wigmore acknowledges that compulsion in Chancery began in the late fourteenth century.[11] Thus his statement that the privilege "commended itself at the very outset"[12] is puzzling. Even on Wigmore's own version of the history, which itself is debatable, it is the supposed advent of testimonial compulsion in the common law courts only[13] which prompted the recognition of the privilege shortly after in Chancery courts only.[14] It is difficult to see how these two events have a direct causal link.

Despite this fundamental problem, this aspect of the Wigmorean version of the rule's history has been adopted by virtually all writers after him,[15] who present this point in more certain terms than Wigmore himself presented it with.[16] These later writers often completely miss the distinction between compulsion in Chancery and that at common law. [17]

THE ORIGINAL REASON FOR THE PRIVILEGE: HONOUR THEORY?

The second aspect of the almost universally accepted Wigmorean history of the privilege referred to above relates to the rule's founding rationale or purpose. Wigmore says that the original rationale for the privilege stems from a sixteenth century regard for the honour of the lawyer:

[11] 1375 to be precise. See Wigmore, n. 2 above, 65 n. 19 and 68 n. 28, though it is doubtful whether compulsion was widely employed this early on. It probably started to gain widespread use only around the middle of the 15th century.

[12] *Ibid.*, 543

[13] "Only" in the sense that this development (i.e. compulsion) was new only to common law courts, as Chancery already had it.

[14] All of the 16th-century cases relate to Chancery: see the cases listed at n. 25 below. There are no similar cases to be found in the reports of common law courts.

[15] Relying either on Wigmore, or on Holdsworth (who in turn took this straight from Wigmore), or on both writers.

[16] E.g. see Developments (1985), n. 4 above, 1456

[17] For example, the great American evidence academic Edmund Morgan said: "[t]he origin of the lawyer–client privilege is easily explained. There was no compulsory process for witnesses in England until the time of Elizabeth" (Morgan, E.M., "Suggested Remedy for Obstructions to Expert Testimony by Rules of Evidence" (1943) 10 *University Chicago LR* 288). Similarly, the editors of the *Harvard Law Review* said: "[e]vidential privileges arose with the imposition of compulsory process in Elizabethan England [citation to Wigmore] . . . The first evidentiary privilege to be recognized was that protecting the attorney–client relationship; cases upholding the attorney–client privilege appear as early as 1577, in virtual coincidence with the advent of compulsory process." (Developments (1985), n. 4 above, 1455–6)

> a concern for *the oath and honor* of the attorney rather than for the apprehensions of his client . . . If the "point of honor" was to be recognised at all as a ground for exemption, then surely the attorney fell within this exemption. And no doubt this was, in the beginning, and so long as any countenance was given to that general doctrine, the theory of the attorney's exemption.[18]

People writing after Wigmore have usually adopted his honour theory without question[19] and the theory has taken on a rigidity and a greater certainty than perhaps Wigmore ever intended.[20]

One important way in which Wigmore's theory has been conveyed by later American writers is that they have cast the honour rationale as a specifically status-based exception. For example, the editors of the *Harvard Law Review* begin the history section of an article with:

> The attorney–client privilege was originally justified as a vindication of "the oath and honor of the attorney" [citation to Wigmore]. Derived as it was from the status of the attorney as a professional . . . It announced a broad value of high-mindedness and seemliness ostensibly inherent in the business of lawyering.[21]

There are innumerable other such examples.[22] This interpretation of the honour rationale stresses the status of the lawyer almost to the exclusion of that of the client. For example, a leading Canadian evidence text describes this theory as "the oath and honour of the solicitor, as a professional man and a gentleman . . . the client benefited from it only incidentally".[23] This is typical of the treatment of Wigmore's theory in subsequent American writings and in English writings.[24] Wigmore's treatise is ambiguous as to whether the honour theory was a purely

[18] Wigmore (1961), n. 2 above, 543 (emphasis in original).

[19] E.g. Holdsworth, *A History of English Law*, n. 4 above, 202; Developments (1985), n. 4 above, 1494; H.L. Ho, "History and Judicial Theories of Legal Professional Privilege" [1995] *SJLS* 558 at 561; E.M. Morgan "Suggested Remedy for Obstructions to Expert Testimony by Rules of Evidence" (1943) 10 *Uni. Chicago LR* 285 at 288; M. Radin, "The Privilege of Confidential Communication Between Lawyer and Client" (1928) 16 *Calif. LR* 487 at 487; *Solosky* v. *The Queen* [1980] 1 SCR 821 at 834 (SC).

[20] E.g. Morgan, n. 19 above ("the attorney . . . should not be compelled to take the role of a witness and violate the code of honor of a gentleman"); Developments (1985), n. 4 above, 1502 ("Dean Wigmore posited . . . that the privilege originally derived from notions of 'honor among gentlemen' ").

[21] Note, "The Attorney–Client Privilege: Fixed Rules, Balancing, and Constitutional Entitlement" (1977) 91 *Harv. LR* 464 at 465 (hereafter "Note (1977)").

[22] E.g. M. Rosenfeld, "The Transformation of the Attorney–Client Privilege" (1982) 33 *Hastings LJ* 495 at 496 (privilege "conceived to safeguard the 'oath and honor of the attorney' in a society predicated on the inequality of rank"); S. Saltzburg, "Privileges and Professionals: Lawyers and Psychiatrists" (1980) 66 *Virginia LR* 597 at 604 ("[h]istorically, the primary purpose of the privilege was to promote and preserve the honor of the attorney"); R.A. Sedler and J.J. Simeone, "The Realities of Attorney–Client Confidences" (1963) 24 *Ohio St LJ* 1 at 4 ("[h]istorically, it is said to have existed because of the 'exalted' status of the barrister"); Note, "The Lawyer–Client Privilege" (1961) 56 Nw ULR 235 at 235 (hereafter "Note (1961)") (privilege arises from status of the lawyer "as a professional man and a gentleman . . . professional dignity"); R.W. Nashtoll, "The Lawyer's Allegiance: Priorities Regarding Confidentiality" (1984) 41 *Washington and Lee LR* 421 at 426.

[23] J. Sopinka, S.N. Lederman and A.W. Bryant, *The Law of Evidence in Canada* (Butterworths, Toronto, 1992) 635–6.

[24] E.g. R.G. Toulson and C.M. Phipps, *Confidentiality* (Sweet & Maxwell, London, 1996) 200 ("its rationale was the honour of the professional man").

status-based exception. However that is the way his work has been consistently interpreted by later writers.

If one wishes to examine the original rationale for the privilege then one must first look to the original privilege cases decided in the Chancery court in the 1570s and 1580s. There are over a dozen such cases,[25] which clearly establish the privilege for counsel and possibly also for attorneys and solicitors.[26] Analysis of these cases yields two important results. First, that lawyers were not actually exempt from being called and examined.[27] Rather, when the privilege was invoked, they were discharged from their obligation to depose to certain matters only. Thus the privilege was unlikely to have been a rule of incompetence. Secondly, the privilege was tightly restricted to matters arising from the lawyer's involvement in the case at hand.[28] Lawyers were not exempt from being examined in their personal capacity, in relation to matters not arising from their professional work.[29] For example in *Kelway* v. *Kelway*[30] the plaintiff's solicitor appeared but refused to be examined. The court ordered that he be examined but not asked about any matter "which he knoweth as solicitor only".

These principles make it less likely that the privilege was originally founded on some respect for the special status of the lawyer. The lawyer's status was not sufficient to prevent him from being called in the first place, and was also insufficient to shield him from questions unrelated to the particular matter in issue in

[25] The authorities are scattered around the various writings covering the history of the privilege. Each commentator cites a few of them, but no two authors get the same combination. As no-one has yet managed to compile a comprehensive list of 16th-century privilege cases, it may be useful here to set out one possible list: *Lee* v. *Markham* (1569) Monro 375, Tothill 48; *Breame* v. *Breame* (1571) Tothill 48; *Windsor* v. *Umberville* (1574) Monro 411; *Berd* v. *Lovelace* (1577) Cary 62; *Austen* v. *Vesey* (1577) Cary 63; *Hartford* v. *Lee* (1577) Cary 63; *Kelway* v. *Kelway* (1579) Cary 89; *Dennis* v. *Codrington* (1579) Cary 100; *Creed* v. *Trap* (1579) Choyce Cas 121; *Havers* v. *Randoll* (1581) Choyce Cas 149; *Strelley* v. *Albany* (1583) Choyce Cas 163; Monro 519–20 (*quaere* whether this is the case described in M. Birks, *Gentlemen of Law* (Stevens & Sons Ltd, London, 1984) 98); *Cutts* v. *Armiger* (1585) Monro 544; *Cotton* v. *Kynersley* (1589) Monro 588. As all of these reports, except for Monro, can be found in vol. 21 of ER, the separate ER references will not be cited here. Monro's reports are found in C. Monro (ed.) *Acta Cancellariae* (London, Benning, 1847).

[26] The extent to which different branches of the profession benefited from the privilege is contentious. Given the very mixed nature of the profession in the late 16th century, with the practice of young people working as attorneys or soliciting to earn money during their training as barristers at the Inns, the debate is perhaps not particularly instructive to the immediate issue of the origin of the privilege. Therefore the neutral term "lawyer" will be used throughout this section, though admittedly this term may be over-inclusive as a description of those benefiting from the privilege.

[27] E.g. *Lee* v. *Markham* (1569) Monro 375, Tothill 48 ; *Austen* v. *Vesey* (1577) Cary 63. In *Cotton* v. *Kynersley* (1589) Monro 588, attachment was awarded against an attorney who failed to appear upon a *subpoena ad testificandum*. However it is not clear whether or not he had ever acted for one of the parties to the litigation.

[28] E.g. *Lee* v. *Markham* (1569) Monro 375, Tothill 48 ("which shall touch or concern the discussing of the title"); *Breame* v. *Breame* (1571) Tothill 48 ("case at hand"); *Berd* v. *Lovelace* (1577) Cary 62 ("knowledge touching the cause at variance"); *Hartford* v. *Lee* (1577) Cary 63 ("solicitor in the cause"); *Dennis* v. *Codrington* ("touching a matter in variance, wherein he hath been of counsel").

[29] E.g. *Creed* v. *Trap* (1579) Choyce Cas 121 ("[b]ut for any other matter it shall be lawful for the plaintiff to examine him"); *Havers* v. *Randoll* ("not any thing concerning his clyents title"); also see W.J. Jones, *The Elizabethan Court of Chancery* (Clarendon Press, Oxford, 1967) 319.

[30] (1579) Cary 89.

the litigation. If the only concern evident from these cases is the secrecy of the information relating to the very issue at trial, it is difficult to see the link between this and the oath or honour of the lawyer.

It is true that status, as evidenced by financial wealth or title, was generally important in determining the role of witnesses at this time. For example, jurors could be challenged on grounds of not having sufficient freehold.[31] However this did not necessarily transfer to the use of status as a ground for exemption from compulsory process in the manner used in relation to legal professional privilege as it then operated. This much was made clear in the *Countess of Shrewsbury's Case*.[32] In that case the Countess refused to answer questions put to her by the King via his Lords of the Council. She defended the subsequent contempt charge on the ground that she had a "privilege of nobility, to answer only when she was called judicially before her peers".[33] The court listed all the privileges afforded to nobility before the courts,[34] but held that such privileges did not include a refusal to answer questions.

When "honour" was invoked in the sixteenth century in the context of witness testimony, it meant an alternative basis for the taking of evidence, i.e. that evidence should be taken on one's word or in writing, rather than on the strength of the oath.[35] It did not mean that evidence should not be taken at all. This amounted only to the adoption of a different procedure for the taking of evidence.[36] The relevant evidence was still required. A witness could not invoke his status or honour to refuse to give evidence altogether. If the honour of the defendant proved insufficient to secure their reply or attendance, then a subpoena would be issued as a matter of course.[37] If an "honour exception" in this more limited sense were being applied to lawyers in the sixteenth century then we would expect to find that their honour removed the need for compulsion by issue of subpoena and that they were still required to answer questions. However the reverse was true: they could be compelled to attend, but were then excused from testifying. Thus the privilege for lawyers operated in the opposite way to the "honour exception" for people of high status. The concept of "honour" has a set meaning in the language of sixteenth-century evidence law, and this has nothing to do with legal privilege whatsoever.

31 J.B. Thayer, *A Preliminary Treatise on Evidence at the Common Law* (Little Brown & Co, Boston, 1898) 124.

32 (1613) 12 Co. Rep. 94, 77 ER 1369.

33 (1613) 12 Co. Rep. at 95, 77 ER at 1370.

34 E.g. special procedure where a party pleads that a noble person is not so titled; not subject to arrest in a private suit; not to be tortured; not to be sworn in assises, juries or other inquests

35 Macnair, M., The Law of Proof in Modern Equity (Unpublished PhD thesis, Oxford University, 1991) 37, 271. The most famous case on this issue is probably *Dacres* v. *Lord Dacre* (1564) Monro 353

36 "Instead [of a subpoena], the Chancellor wrote to inform [the 'honoured' person] that a charge had been brought against him and requested that he return an answer. If this letter was ignored, the Court reverted to more stringent measures and issued a subpoena or, if warranted, an injunction". M.L. Cioni, *Women and Law in Elizabethan England with Particular Reference to the Court of Chancery* (Garland Publishing, 1985) 45.

37 E.g. as in *Countess of Westmoreland* v. *Earl of Westmoreland* (1564) Monro 348.

NEED FOR HISTORICAL REVISION

It will never be possible to come to a conclusive answer to the origin of and early rationale for the privilege because the decisive pieces of information, the reasoning underlying the first reported cases and precise knowledge of pre-Elizabethan Chancery procedure, are simply not available. The best that can credibly be done with the information we have is to describe the trends and directions in the law of testimonial compulsion and privilege at the time, and from that give an opinion on what was most likely. The distrust of strangers that underlay the maintenance rule[38] had largely fallen away by the middle of the sixteenth century. Conversely, the law was coming to regard interest and bias in a negative manner. By the latter part of that century there had developed an extensive set of rules to guard against the problem of bias.[39] These two trends also occurred against the backdrop of the relatively new incompetence of the parties and the recent major expansion of common law testimonial compulsion.

In this environment of change and the redefinition of fundamental principles the development of an important rule on such a narrow, aggrandising rationale as the honour of a single profession seems oddly out of place. This is particularly the case when some ranks of that profession were not enjoying wide admiration from either the populace or the judges making the relevant rules. Attitudes and concerns towards the legal profession and litigation procedure were not as different four centuries ago as Wigmore would have us believe. Testimonial compulsion was a vital issue then as now. It is likely that such a large exception to this principle was recognised for more important reasons than the status and honour of lawyers.

The Wigmorean view of the origin of the privilege is flawed, both in regard to the original rationale for the privilege and in seeing it as an immediate reaction to testimonial compulsion. The privilege was not so obviously important that it immediately commended itself as a natural exception to compulsion. It may have arisen gradually, and some time after the advent of compulsion, as a rule grounded more on practicality and the apparent illogicality of having a lawyer testify to matters his client could not have spoken of.

Contrary to Wigmore's view of the origins of the privilege, it is most likely that it has always been an important part of the law of testimonial compulsion, and there is little evidence from which to suggest that non-instrumental theories played an important role in the early development of the privilege.[40] The privilege is more accurately seen as having been one of many rules in the large mass of law relating to testimonial compulsion. It was not unimportant, but also not

[38] E.g. see Fortescue (writing in 1476 and quoted in Thayer (1898), n. 31 above, 131), disapproving of "unknown witnesses . . . strangers, untrustworthy, or those whose condition or hostility is unknown".

[39] See Holdsworth (1944), n. 4 above, 194–5.

[40] E.g. see Developments (1985), n. 4 above, 1502–4, under the heading "The Utilitarian/Non-Utilitarian Schism".

of special or greater importance than other rules. Also, it may from the start have been grounded on fairly straight-forward considerations of practicality that are closer to the modern instrumental rationale than anything else. The time has come for careful re-examination of the supposed non-instrumental origins of the privilege which Wigmore first claimed for it and writers following him have keenly adopted.

BOOK THESIS: BALANCING AND ABSOLUTENESS

An important concept within the common law privilege is the notion of absoluteness. This is the idea that, apart from the doctrine of waiver, the privilege is an absolute rule from which no derogation should be allowed. It will be shown that Commonwealth courts have placed great weight on this view, and that it has had a significant effect on the development of the common law rule. The notion of absoluteness has led courts to some very harsh results; maintaining the privilege when the interests of justice would seem to point strongly to its displacement.

It will be argued that the structure of the privilege should be re-examined in the light of a more realistic view of the goals of the rule, and the resultant degree of "absoluteness" actually required for the attainment of these goals. This book will be divided into two parts. The first part will outline the key concepts which go to determine the structure of the privilege. It will examine in detail the modern rationale for the rule, both at common law and under the European Convention of Human Rights, and then attempt to evaluate the two basic elements of the privilege equation: the need for confidentiality for the purposes of the privilege, and the need for the disclosure of the evidence which the privilege withholds. The purpose of this part is to show that the usual approach of the courts to date has favoured the values of confidentiality too much and the values of disclosure too little. A new reformulated balancing may provide greater scope for the displacement of the privilege. Chapters 6 and 7 will look specifically at the structure of the privilege and will argue that the current approach of some Commonwealth courts to this issue is flawed, particularly in their insistence on an "absolute" privilege and their refusal to engage in a process of rule balancing to recognise new derogations from it.

The second part of this book will apply this broad analysis to some of the main common law derogations. Separate chapters will be devoted to the crime-fraud exception, the treatment of criminal exculpatory evidence (which some Commonwealth courts have expressly decided does not give rise to a derogation, while the position in other jurisdictions remains in doubt) and secondary evidence, and the many derogations from the privilege usually classed as "waiver". Statutory abrogations from the privilege, such as section 1 of the Children Act 1989 (UK), will not be examined other than in passing, as the purpose of this book is to consider the common law approach to the privilege. The litigation privilege will not be separately considered, as this rule may rest on different concerns which may require a different approach to the issue of absoluteness.

It must be stressed that this book does not advocate the abolition of the privilege. It simply seeks a re-evaluation of the goals, needs and structure of the privilege. It is believed that once this is done it will be clear that the privilege is not, and does not need to be, as "absolute" as many believe.

PART A

THEORETICAL FOUNDATIONS

2

Emerging Common Law Right

INTRODUCTION

The scope and application of the privilege have both expanded considerably in the second half of this century, particularly as a result of new forms of executive investigation. This has rightly called into question the rationale for the privilege. Generally it has been assumed that these new applications of the privilege require a new rationale. For example, note the tone in which one commentator phrases the issue:

> The courts in all these countries have . . . encountered the same basic problem: how do you apply a legal concept that is the product of an outmoded rationale and a flawed philosophy to situations which are the product of new socio-political realities? Do you adapt the concept to meet the demands of a changing world by adding patches to its worn and faded fabric, stretching and stitching it in ways unimagined by its original designer? Or do you fashion the material anew, tailoring it precisely to fit the exigencies of fresh demands?[1]

This chapter will analyse the privilege's rationale in light of the developments in the common law rule this century. It will examine the advent of rights-based arguments in the common law. First though, it is necessary briefly to outline the state of the privilege prior to this, when the rule was almost universally regarded as giving effect to non-rights based instrumental goals or, as it is often described, a utilitarian view of the privilege.

NON-RIGHTS INSTRUMENTALISM AND UTILITARIANISM

Instrumental justifications for the privilege first appeared, at the latest, early in the nineteenth century, and possibly some time before. The origins and development of the theory are outside the scope of this work. The rationale posits that absolute confidentiality in legal communications is necessary for the maintenance of good lawyer–client relations; a goal taken to be important for the effective administration of justice. There are broadly three steps in this reasoning[2]: first, that the law is so complex that people need lawyers to manage their

[1] A. Paizes, "Towards a Broader Balancing of Interests: Exploring the Theoretical Foundations of Legal Professional Privilege" (1989) 106 *SALJ* 109 at 128.

[2] Taken from J.W. Strong *et al.* (eds.) *McCormick on Evidence* (4th edn., West Publishing, St Paul, Minn., 1992) 120–1. Compare the reasoning in C. Wright and K. Graham, *Federal Practice and Procedure* (West Publishing, St Paul, Minn., 1986) xxiv, 80–4.

affairs and disputes[3]; secondly, that lawyers are unable to discharge this function without the fullest possible knowledge of the facts of their client's situation[4]; thirdly, that the privilege encourages the flow of this information from the client to the lawyer.[5] Most dispute surrounds the last of these steps. The correctness of this final assertion will be analysed in detail in Chapter 4 below. The rationale is concerned with many benefits beyond those accruing to the client. Society benefits through, for example, increased compliance with the law,[6] greater efficiency for attorneys in the adversary system,[7] an easing of the burden on courts and, arguably, greater accuracy of fact-finding.[8]

There is no doubt that the overwhelming majority of cases in the nineteenth century and first half of the twentieth century proceeded solely on the basis of this rationale. However it still may be said that the debate in this area has been skewed by Professor Wigmore's devotion to this theory, and almost everyone else's devotion to Wigmore. Praise for Wigmore's treatise has come from almost all of the great American evidence scholars of this century, and is often effusive.[9]

[3] See especially *In re Grand Jury Subpoena* 406 F Supp. 381 at 388 (SD NY 1975) ("[t]he privilege is . . . born of the law's own complexity"); also see *Greenough* v. *Gaskell* (1833) 1 My & K 98 at 103, 39 ER 618 at 621; *Russell* v. *Jackson* (1851) 9 Hare 387 at 391, 68 ER 558 at 559–60; R. v. *Cox and Railton* (1884) 14 QBD 153; *Grant* v. *Downs* (1976) 135 CLR 674 at 685 (HCA); R. v. *Bell, ex p. Lees* (1980) 146 CLR 141 at 152 (HCA). The best examination of this aspect of the lawyer–client relationship is by C. Fried, "Two Concepts of Interests: Some Reflections of the Supreme Court's Balancing Test" (1976) 85 *Yale LJ* 1068–75. Also see E.A. Dauer and A.A. Leff, "Correspondence" (1977) 86 *Yale LR* 573; C. Fried, Correspondence, (1977) 86 *Yale LJ* 584 ; E.M. Morgan, "Suggested Remedy for Observations to Expert Testimony by Rules of Evidence" (1943) *Uni of Chicago LR* 288.

[4] *Anderson* v. *Bank of British Columbia* (1876) 2 Ch. D 644 at 649 (CA); *Baker* v. *Campbell* (1983) 153 CLR 52 at 66, 94 (HCA). though this has been doubted: see C. Wright and K. Graham, *Federal Practice and Procedure*, vol. 24 (West Publishing, St Paul, Minn., 1986) at p. 82.

[5] *Pearce* v. *Foster* (1885) 15 QBD 114 at 119–20 (CA); *Baker* v. *Campbell* (1983) 153 CLR 52 at 93, 108; *Waterford v The Commonwealth* (1987) 163 CLR 54 at 62 (HCA); *Attorney-General (N.T.)* v. *Maurice* (1986) 161 CLR 475 at 487.

[6] *In re Grand Jury Subpoena (Marc Rich & Co)* 731 F.2d 1032 at 1036–7 (2nd Cir., 1984); Comment, "Developments in the Law—Privileged Communications" (1985) 98 *Harv LR* 1450 at 1506–7.

[7] M. Rosenfeld, "The Transformation of the Attorney–Client Privilege" (1982) 33 *Hastings LJ* 495 at 508 n. 77.

[8] F.C. Zacharias, "Rethinking Confidentiality" (1989) 74 *Iowa LR* 351 at 358.

[9] E.g. J.H. Beale, "Book Reviews: A Treatise on the System of Evidence in Trials at Common Law" (1905) 18 *Harv. LR* 478 at 478, reviewing Wigmore's 1905 4-vol. work ("the most complete and exhaustive treatise on a single branch of our law that has ever been written"); Z. Chafee, "Book Reviews: A Treatise on the Anglo-American System of Evidence in Trials at Common Law" (1924) 37 *Harv. LR* 513 at 521 ("[i]t has created law."); M. Radin, "The Privilege of Confidential Communication between Lawyer and Client" (1928) 16 *Calif. LR* n. 487 at 11 ("[t]here is no fuller or better discussion of the subject . . . It is inconceivable that where there are lawyers there is no copy of Wigmore. *Chi non ha Wigmor[o], non vada al foro*"); E.M. Morgan, "Book Review: A Treatise on the System of Evidence in Trials at Common Law " (1940) 20 *Boston Uni. LR* 776 at 777, 793 ("the best, by far the best, treatise on the Law of Evidence"); J. Ritchie, "John Henry Wigmore: A Centennial Tribute" (1963) 58 *NW U LR* 443 at 443 ("unrivalled as the greatest treatise on any single subject of the law", *per* Justice Frankfurter); McCormick (4th edn. 1992), n. 2 above, 121 ("the great champion and architect of the privilege"); for further discussion of Wigmore as law, see W. Twining, *Theories of Evidence: Bentham and Wigmore* (Weidenfeld & Nicolson, London, 1985) 111 and R.D. Friedman, J.H. Wigmore, and D.P. Leonard, *The New Wigmore: A Treatise on Evidence* (Little Brown & Co., Boston, 1995) xxvi. For discussions of the importance of Wigmore's work see the articles collected in Ritchie (1963) supra.

Criticism of his work is less common.[10] Privilege writers in the latter half of this century, particularly those in the United States, often tend to rely virtually exclusively and without question on Wigmore's analysis of the rationale.[11] However Wigmore greatly downplays opposition to the privilege.[12] He exaggerates the importance and acceptance of the instrumental argument,[13] and the revision of his work by McNaughton ignores the views of important evidence writers such as Morgan[14] and McCormick.[15] Wigmore's misleading presentation of the instrumental rationale as having near universal acceptance has been adopted by other writers without comment.[16]

This rationale for the privilege is often described by writers and judges as a "utilitarian" one. It is not necessary for present purposes to examine the nature and theory behind utilitarianism in its many forms.[17] This is because the traditional theory as considered below does not in fact depend on the doctrine of utilitarianism. Those that employ this rationale are only describing a rule which exists not for the intrinsic value of the immediate result (being the secrecy of the instant legal communication), but for the promotion of other broader goals (being the confidence reposed in legal advisers). The term "instrumentalism" adequately captures this latter concept, and so will be used in this book in preference to the term "utilitarianism". Unfortunately though the terminology of utilitarianism has been adopted virtually without question over the last

[10] E.g. see D.W. Louisell, "Confidentiality, Conformity and Confusion: Privileges in Federal Court Today" (1956) 31 *Tulane LR* 101 at 111; L. Kaplow and S. Shavell, "Legal Advice About Information to Present in Litigation: Its Effects and Social Desirability" (1989) 102 *Harv. LR* 565 at 606–8; Wright and Graham, xxiv (West Publishing, St Paul, Minn., 1986) at p. 87.

[11] E.g. see V.A. Alexander, "The Corporate Attorney–Client Privilege: A Study of the Participants" (1989) 63 *St John's LR* 191 at 216 and D.W. Shuman and M.S. Weiner, "The Privilege Study: An Empirical Examination of the Psychotherapist–Patient Privilege" (1982) 60 *North Carolina LR* 893 at 904–5; R.A. Kasting, "Recent Developments in the Canadian Law of Solicitor–Client Privilege" (1978) 24 *McGill LJ* 115 at 115–16. For a stunning example of how, in the USA, all references lead to Wigmore, see Note, "Attorney–Client and Work Product Protection in a Utilitarian World: An Argument for Recomparison" (1995) 108 *Harv. LR* 1697 at n. 11.

[12] "Rarely indeed has any question been made of the soundness of the privilege . . . Bentham, . . . Lord Langdale and Chief Justice Appleton [are] the only eminent names enrolled in our annals in strong opposition to the privilege", J.H. Wigmore and J.T. McNaughton, *Evidence in Trials at Common Law* (Little, Brown & Co., Boston, 1961) viii at 549.

[13] D.W. Louisell, "Confidentiality, Conformity and Confusion: Privileges in Federal Court Today" (1956) *Tulane LR* 101 at 111.

[14] E.g. E.M. Morgan, "Foreword" in American Law Institute, *Model Code of Evidence* (American Law Institute, 1942) 27.

[15] E.g. C.T. McCormick, *Handbook of the Law of Evidence* (West Publishing, St Paul, Minn., 1954) 182, heavily criticising the fundamental operation of the privilege.

[16] E.g. see C.A. Miller, "The Challenges to the Attorney–Client Privilege" (1963) 49 *Virginia LR* 262 at 262 ("[e]xcept for . . . Bentham, the privilege has not seriously been questioned for several centuries") and C.J. Cooper, "The Attorney–Client Privilege in Alabama" (1977) 28 *Alabama LR* 641 at 643–8.

[17] E.g. see D. Lyons, *Forms and Limits of Utilitarianism* (Clarendon Press, Oxford, 1965); J.J.C. Smart and B. Williams, *Utilitarianism: For and Against* (Cambridge University Press, Cambridge, 1963); R. Hare, *Freedom and Reason* (Clarendon Press, Oxford, 1963).

century,[18] and now dominates both the academic literature and the case law to such an extent that it is unlikely to be abandoned.

RIGHTS

As will be seen, many judges have asserted that the common law rule of legal professional privilege is, or should be treated as, a "right". It is not the aim of this chapter to engage in a jurisprudential discussion of the nature of rights, or the use of a rights discourse in general. Rights terminology is discussed in this chapter because it is descriptive of the terminology used in those particular common law cases.

Where a human rights instrument expressly provides for, or has been interpreted as providing for, a right to legal professional privilege, or some other form of professional secrecy which is capable of overriding compulsion by a court or agency of the executive, then the privilege may rest on a constitutional or statutorily entrenched right, and the scope of this constitutional or statutory protection may be determined largely by reference to the provision establishing the right and its associated jurisprudence. Where there is no such constitutional or statutory provision establishing a right to legal communications, the basis of the privilege is determined by the common law. In addition, in human rights documents that purport to protect, or have been interpreted as protecting, legal communications, there are bound to be large gaps in the coverage which may fall to be considered by the common law.

There are numerous dicta in most Commonwealth jurisdictions stating that the privilege at common law gives effect to or safeguards rights, fundamental rights or human rights.[19] Most of the cases concern the applicability of the privilege to search warrants and other forms of executive compulsion. Many cases which use a rights rationale (such as *S* v. *Safatsa*[20]) do so by reliance on the main Commonwealth search warrant authorities (in this case, *Baker* v. *Campbell*). This has led some commentators to talk of the demise of the "utilitarian" rationale and the rise of rights-based theories.[21] Such discussions are problematic because the extent to which a rights-based privilege is also designed to give effect to instrumental concerns is not clear, and has received little attention. It may be useful therefore to examine the advent of the common law "right" to legal professional privilege, particularly in the context in which this development has taken place.

[18] As an examination of just about any of the academic articles referred to in this chapter will illustrate.

[19] No distinction appears to have been drawn between these various formulations. The terminology used in expositions of this area of the law is often imprecise and vague.

[20] [1988] 1 SA 868 (AD).

[21] E.g. Paizes, n. 1 above 124 ("fall from grace of the utilitarian rationale").

CONTEXT

Before embarking on a voyage across the Commonwealth in an attempt to determine the basis of the common law privilege, it may be useful to first note the context in which this issue is often discussed. The change has largely been prompted by the rise and pervasive spread of powers of executive compulsion. The common law never recognised a general power to compel the production of information or documents outside legal proceedings.[22] The limited common law power to authorise compulsory search and seizure by means of search warrants was exercised only to search for stolen goods.[23] The advent of legislation giving executive bodies such as police and administrative tribunals the power to compel testimony or the production of documents raised a novel problem for the common law of privilege:[24] was the law a principle of courtroom admissibility only, or did it have a wider application?

When the power to compel information first arose outside the courtroom, the response in most jurisdictions was that the privilege was only a "rule of evidence", and therefore had no application in such circumstances.[25] The one exception was New Zealand, where in *IRC* v. *West-Walker*[26] the privilege was held to apply to a request for information by the Commissioner for Inland Revenue. When judges were faced with the problem of whether to apply the privilege outside the curial realm, they felt the need to reconsider the rationale. In doing this many judges employed the terminology of rights. It will be argued below that this re-evaluation of the rationale was not required to resolve the issue at hand, and in some cases has proceeded upon dubious authority. At the same time all of these Commonwealth jurisdictions, with the exceptions of Australia and (until the Human Rights Act 1998 (UK) comes into force) England and Wales, enacted into law human rights legislation, which was effectively imposed over the top of the common law privilege. The way in which the common law privilege doctrine fits in with this new rights framework has never been adequately settled.

[22] *Ibid.*, at 116.

[23] E.g *Baker* v. *Campbell* (1983) 153 CLR at 60–1, 123; also see D. Unterhalter, "Notes and Comments: Professional Privilege and the Proof of Innocence" (1988) 105 *SALJ* 291 at 317

[24] Paizes, n. 1 above, at 116 says that "it took many years for these powers to collide with the privilege, probably . . . because the nature of things for which the warrant authorised a search to be made . . . made it unlikely they would be found in a solicitor's office". This is a dubious proposition, as the 1980s tax investigations which *Baker* v. *Campbell* were a part of illustrated. A better historical account is that Paizes is simply wrong and the matter did indeed come up. Paizes fails to cite the earlier Commonwealth authority dealt with below.

[25] England—*Parry-Jones* v. *Law Society* [1969] Ch 1 at 9 (CA); Australia—*Brayley* v. *Wilton* [1976] 2 NSWLR 495 (NSW SC, Eq. Div.), *Crowley* v. *Murphy* (1981) 34 ALR 496 (Fed. Ct.) and *O'Reilly* v. *State Bank of Victoria Commissioners* (1983) 153 CLR 1 (HCA); Canada—*R.* v. *Colvin* [1970] 3 OR 612 at 617 (Ont. HC); South Africa—*Andresen* v. *Minister for Justice*, 1954 (2) SA 473 (Witwatersrand LD).

[26] [1954] NZLR 191 (CA).

The following discussion may give the impression that judgments considering the extra-curial application of the privilege can be neatly divided into those advocating rights-based and non-rights-based rationales, or that the rights-based rationale, being somehow different from the traditional rationale, does not employ an instrumental justification for the privilege. However, contrary to the views of some commentators, many of the cases in which the basis for the privilege is discussed can be read as supporting both rights-based and non-rights-based rationales together, as well as both instrumental and non-instrumental reasoning together. The distinctions between a rights-based and a non-rights-based rationale, and between instrumental and non-instrumental reasoning, are irrelevant to the question underlying most of these cases, which concern the interpretation of statutory search warrant provisions. This issue requires no more than the recognition of an important common law doctrine. Both rationales may give rise to a doctrine of this nature.

Further, it should be noted that there are many other theories which seek to explain the common law privilege. Unfortunately there is not the space in this book to look at these, though they may briefly be noted here. The early honour rationale[27] discussed in the previous chapter[28] is often presented as being non-instrumental in nature. There are also more modern justifications which are relatively close to this honour rationale, such as the dignity theory[29] and the treachery theory[30] of the privilege. One of the most influential alternative theories this century is the privacy rationale. Finally, there are other theories which do not even attempt to defend or justify the place of the privilege, such as the power theory[31] and the image theory.[32]

With this brief introduction out of the way, it is now time to examine that state of the privilege across the Commonwealth, starting with the jurisdiction that has had perhaps the most influence on the common law of the others.

[27] E.g. see J.H.Wigmore and J.T. McNaughton above at n. 12, paras. 2286, 2290; M. Radin, "The Privilege of Confidential Communication between Lawyer and Client" (1928) 16 *Calif. LR* 487; J. Gardner, "A Re-evaluation of the Attorney–Client Privilege" (1963) 8 *Vill LR* 279; Developments (1985), n. 6 above, 1494.

[28] See "The original reason for the privilege: honour theory?" in Chap. 1, above.

[29] See M. Frankel, "The Search for Truth Continued: More Disclosure, Less Privilege" (1982) 54 *U Col. LR* 51 at 55; L.W. Wolfram, "Client Perjury" (1963) 50 *S. Cal. LR* 809 at 838–9. For criticism of this theory see F.C. Zacharias, "Rethinking Confidentiality" (1989) 74 *Iowa LR* 351 at 368–9.

[30] See V.A. Alexander, "The Corporate Attorney–Client Privilege: A Study of the Participants" (1989) 63 *St John's LR* 191 at 218–19; J. Gardner (1963) above at n. 27, 307–8. For a rejection of this argument see L. Kaplow and S. Shavell, "Legal Advice About Information to Present in Litigation: Its Effects and Social desirability" (1989) 102 *Harv. LR* 565 at 608.

[31] C. Wright and K. Graham, *Federal Practice & Procedure* (West Publishing, St Paul, Minn., 1980) xxiii, 673–379; Developments (1985) above at n. 27, 1493–8.

[32] *Ibid*., 1498–1500.

CANADA

Legal communications receive some protection under the Canadian Charter of Rights and Freedoms. Section 10(b) of the Charter grants everyone a right "on arrest or detention . . . to retain and instruct counsel". To the extent that this provision affords a basis for the recognition of private lawyer–client communications and legal professional privilege,[33] that privilege is, to that extent only, the expression of a right. However this right is limited in nature. It relates only to criminal accused and applies mainly in the context of arrest and detention; the scope of the right to "retain" counsel prior to and during trial being the subject of much uncertainty. The status of the privilege in all other contexts is open to debate.

It may be that the Charter has had an effect on the surrounding common law.[34] The Canadian Supreme Court was the first court in the Commonwealth in the 1980s to analyse the relationship between the rationale and the scope of the privilege. This was done the same year as the Charter became law. In *Descôteaux* v. *Mierzwinski* the Supreme Court held that the privilege would have protected a form submitted for the purposes of applying for legal aid funding were it not for the fact that the document fell within the crime-fraud exception to the privilege. Lamer J, for the Court, held that the privilege was founded on a right to confidential lawyer–client communications.[35] This is a "personal and extra-patrimonial" right.[36] The rule of evidence appears to co-exist with this: "the right to confidentiality, which had long ago given rise to a rule of evidence, has also given rise to a substantive rule".[37] Lamer J expressly stated that the extension of the rule to documents of an administrative nature is a reflection of the rights rationale.[38]

However it was not necessary for Lamer J to develop the principle which he did. The instrumental rationale sufficiently supports the extension of the privilege that took place in *Descôteaux* v. *Mierzwinski*. Further, Lamer J's use of Canadian authority is open to question. Twice he clearly stated that the earlier Supreme Court case of *Solosky* v. *The Queen* ("*Solosky*") recognises this right to confidentiality.[39] This is not the case. While Dickson CJ in *Solosky* used the term "fundamental civil and legal right",[40] this basis for the privilege was posed

[33] For the scope of this see G. Beaudoin and E. Mendes (eds.), *The Canadian Charter of Rights and Freedoms* (3rd edn., Carswell, Toronto, 1996) 11–35; D.C. McDonald, *Legal Rights in the Canadian Charter of Rights and Freedoms* (2nd edn., Carswell, Toronto, 1989) 377–83.

[34] For an interesting discussion of the phenomenon of the "constitutionalisation" of the law of evidence, see D.M., "Charter Principles and Proof in Criminal Cases" (Carswell, Toronto, 1987) 3 *et seq*.

[35] *Descôteaux* v. *Mierzwinski* [1982] 1 SCR 860 at 870 (SC); also see 873 ("the privilege . . . being merely the earliest manifestation of the right to confidentiality").

[36] *Ibid*., at 871.

[37] *Ibid*., at 875.

[38] *Ibid*., at 876.

[39] *Ibid*., at 870 and 875.

[40] *Solosky* v. *The Queen* [1980] 1 SCR at 839.

as hypothetical only.[41] Dickson CJ clearly applied the instrumental rationale and expressly rejected the rights reasoning, saying that cases cited by counsel in support of such a proposition were all search warrant cases, and that these "can be rationalised as merely shifting the time at which the privilege can be asserted".[42] *Solosky* does not support the development of a new rights-based rationale, and Lamer J's invocation of it in *Descôteaux v Mierzwinski* is questionable. A better explanation for Lamer J's decision may be the particular statutory context of the case, in particular Article 9 of the Charter of Human Rights and Freedoms 1977 (Quebec), which provides a right to non-disclosure of all confidential professional communications, even when such information is required by a court.[43]

The same misreading of *Solosky* was made by the Supreme Court again in *Geffen* v. *Goodman Estate*.[44] Earlier Canadian cases do not support Lamer J's approach. Some of these cases may be read as favouring the recognition of an additional new rationale.[45] However most can either be read both ways,[46] or are neutral as to the issue of rationale.[47] Lower courts did not rush to embrace Lamer J's rationalisation of the privilege.[48] It is interesting to note that Canadian evidence texts, which give extensive treatment to the privilege, do not mention the Charter and its possible effect on the rule.[49]

AUSTRALIA

The Australian High Court decision in *Baker* v. *Campbell* is perhaps the leading Commonwealth authority on the rationale for the common law privilege. In

[41] "One *may* depart from the current concept of the privilege and approach the case on the broader basis that . . ." (*ibid.*, emphasis added). Surely if Dickson CJ had intended actually to change the basis of the law he would not have used the neutral tone in "current concept".

[42] *Ibid.*, at 837, also see at 836. Dickson CJ also insisted on an "evidentiary connection" for the privilege. Such a requirement is inconsistent with the rights analysis.

[43] See A.L.E. Newbold, *Legal Professional Privilege: Its Rationale and Exceptions*, Unpublished Ph.D thesis, University of London, 1990.

[44] [1991] 2 SCR 353 at 383 (SC).

[45] E.g. *Re Director of Investigation and Research and Shell Canada Ltd.* (1975) 55 DLR (3d) 713 at 723 (Fed. CA); *R* v. *Littlechild* (1979) 51 CCC (2d) 406 at 411–12 (Alberta CA); *Attorney-General (N.S.)* v. *MacIntyre* [1982] 1 SCR 175 at 179–80 (SC).

[46] E.g. *Re Director of Investigation and Research and Shell Canada Ltd.* (1975) 55 DLR (3d) at 721 supporting the instrumental rationale, but at 722 possibly favouring a wider basis; *Re Borden and Elliot* (1975) 70 DLR (3d) 579 at 583 (Ont. CA); also see R.A. Kasting, "Recent Developments in the Canadian Law of Solicitor–Client Privilege" (1978) 24 *McGill LR* 115 at 118–20.

[47] E.g. *Bell* v. *Smith* [1968] SCR 664 at 670 (SC); *In re BX Development Inc* (1976) 70 DLR (3d) 366 (BC CA); see Kasting (1978), n. 46 above, 121–2. Note the change made by Osler J between *R. v Colvin* [1970] 3 OR at 617 and *Re Presswood and Delzotto* v. *International Chemalloy Corporation* (1977) 36 CRNS 322 at 325 (Ont. SC). *In re BX Development Inc* similarly disapproved *R.* v. *Colvin.*

[48] Particularly the Ontario High Court: see *Re Gowling and Henderson* (1982) 136 DLR (3d) 292 at 302 (Ont. HC) and *Re Ontario Securities Commission and Greymac Credit Corp.* (1983) 146 DLR (3d) 73 at 80 (Ont. HC).

[49] E.g. Sopinka *et al.*, *The Law of Evidence in Canada* (Butterworths, Toronto, 1992) 635–676; R.J. Delisle, Evidence: Principles and Problems (4th edn., Carswell, Toronto, 1996) 641–52; H.J. Cox, *Criminal Evidence Handbook* (2nd edn., Canada Law Book Co., Toronto, 1991) 321–4.

answering a case stated, the court held by a majority of four to three that a legislative search warrant provision did not impliedly abrogate the common law privilege. The impetus for the Court's thorough analysis of the rationale was clear. The Court had granted leave to challenge the correctness of aspects of its own decision in *O'Reilly* v. *State Bank of Victoria Commissioners*,[50] which had been handed down just two months before the hearing in *Baker* v. *Campbell*.[51]

All of the majority judges held the privilege to be a substantive principle, and not a mere rule of evidence, and so was available before all forms of compulsory disclosure. Two of these judges (Murphy and Deane JJ) adopted the terminology of rights.[52] The other two majority judges (Wilson and Dawson JJ) expressly restricted themselves to the traditional instrumental reasoning,[53] as did all of the minority judges.[54] It is clear that foreign authority, particularly *Descôteaux* v. *Mierzwinski*, had a significant impact on the decision of the majority to reverse in part its very recent decision in *O'Reilly* v. *State Bank of Victoria Commissioners*.[55]

During the 1980s most Australian judges supported the instrumental rationale and paid little attention to the sort of rights arguments advanced by the Canadian Supreme Court.[56] Brennan J has been one of the strongest critics of rights reasoning, denouncing the "rhetoric of rights".[57] The one notable exception has been Deane J, who has constantly upheld the validity of his position in *Baker* v. *Campbell*.[58]

However in *Carter* v. *The Managing Partner, Northmore Hale Davy & Leake* ("the *Carter* case") McHugh J held the privilege to be a fundamental common

[50] Decisions prior to *O'Reilly* v. *State Bank of Victoria Commissioners* (1983) 153 CLR 1 favoured the overriding of the privilege but were not completely consistent. *Brayley* v. *Wilton* [1976] 2 NSWLR 495 followed *Parry-Jones* v. *Law Society* [1969] Ch. 1 and held that the privilege was a rule of evidence restricted to the courtroom. However *Morse* v. *Thompson* [1977] WAR 65 at 69–70, 73 (WA SC) expressly declined to decide the point. During argument in this latter case Ronald Wilson QC (for the Crown) conceded that the search warrant statute did not permit the seizure of privileged material. Seven years later Sir Ronald was the only judge on the High Court to change his mind between *O'Reilly* and *Baker* v. *Campbell* (1983) 153 CLR 52. In *Smorgon* v. *ANZ Banking Group* (1976) 134 CLR 475 at 488 (HCA) Stephen J expressly declined to decide between the conflicting authorities of *IRC* v. *West-Walker* [1954] NZLR 191 and *Parry-Jones* v. *Law Society* [1969] Ch. 1. In *Crowley* v. *Murphy* (1981) 34 ALR at 501, 519–20 the Federal Court followed *Parry-Jones* v. *Law Society* and *Brayley* v. *Wilton*, and disapproved *IRC* v. *West-Walker*.

[51] Note that Newbold describes *O'Reilly* as "decided by a lower court and overturned on appeal . . . [a] first instance decision": see Newbold above at n. 43, 8. This is wrong.

[52] *Baker* v. *Campbell* (1983) 153 CLR at 85, 116–71 and 118, approving statements in *AM & S Europe* v. *Commission* [1983] 1 QB 878 (ECJ) and *R.* v. *Uljee* [1982] 1 NZLR 561 (CA).

[53] *Baker* v. *Campbell* (1983) 153 CLR at 95, 128.

[54] *Ibid.*, at 67, 74–5,108, especially see Gibbs CJ ("the privilege exists for practical reasons, rather than to give effect to any basic principle").

[55] Especially see Wilson J at 93. Compare Brennan J's objection to re-opening *O'Reilly* v. *State Bank of Victoria Commissioners* (1983) 153 CLR at 106–7.

[56] E.g. *Attorney-General (N.T.)* v. *Kearney* (1985) 158 CLR 500 at 515–16, 522, 532; *Packer* v. *Deputy Commissioner of Taxation* (1984) 55 ALR 242 (Qld SC); *Federal Commissioner of Taxation* v. *Citibank* (1989) 85 ALR 588 at 596 (Fed. Ct.), though compare French J at 617–18.

[57] *Sorby* v. *Commonwealth* (1983) 152 CLR 281 at 314 (HCA).

[58] See *Baker* v. *Campbell* (1983) 153 CLR at 118, 120; *Attorney-General (N.T.)* v. *Maurice* (1986) 161 CLR at 490; *Waterford v The Commonwealth* (1987) 163 CLR at 82 (all *per* Deane J).

law right.[59] Deane J unsurprisingly took a similar view, without actually using the word "right".[60] The final majority judge, Brennan J, expressly rejected the rights-based rationale.[61] McHugh J held that the rights reasoning followed from the recognition of the privilege as a substantive rule of law. This argument is dealt with below. For authority McHugh J relied mainly on the Canadian decisions discussed above, including *Littlechild*, *Solosky*, *Descôteaux* v. *Mierzwinski* and *Geffen* v. *Goodman Estate*.[62] However it has been shown above that this line of Canadian authority is primarily based upon a misreading of *Solosky*, and should be read with care.

The rights rationale quickly gathered support following the *Carter* case. In *Ampolex* v. *Perpetual Trustee* Kirby J referred to the recent rise of rights and the division of opinion on the High Court, concluding that in his opinion the trend favoured the rights rationale.[63] This forecast proved to be accurate. In *Goldberg* v. *Ng* four out of the five judges adopted this rationale.[64] In the most recent case, *Australian Federal Police* v. *Propend Finance*, McHugh, Gaudron, Gummow and Kirby JJ all endorsed the rights rationale in strong terms and held it to be authoritative in Australia.[65] Brennan CJ held, in the third sentence of his judgment, that although this approach was not his preferred view, he was now bound to accept it.[66]

One caveat may need to be made in declaring the rights rationale supreme in Australia. That is that while it clearly seems to have found favour in the High Court, it is yet to be seen whether intermediate appellate courts[67] will understand and apply this change. There are signs that courts below the High Court may be oblivious to the additional new rationale.[68]

[59] *Carter* v. *The Managing Partner, Northmore Hale Davy & Leake* (1995) 183 CLR 121 at 160–1 (HCA). McHugh J had previously shown support for Deane J's formulation of the rationale: see *Gianarelli* v. *Wraith* (1991) 98 ALR 1 at 6–7 (HCA).

[60] *Carter* v. *The Managing Partner, Northmore Hale Davy & Leake* (1995) 183 CLR at 132.

[61] *Ibid.*, at 129.

[62] *Ibid.*, at 161 n. 177.

[63] *Ampolex Ltd* v. *Perpetual Trustee Co (Canberra) Ltd* (1996) 137 ALR 28 at 33 (HCA).

[64] *Goldberg* v. *Ng* (1996) 185 CLR 83 at 93–4, 121 (HCA). Toohey J did not express a view on the rationale.

[65] *Australian Federal Police* v. *Propend Finance* (1997) 141 ALR 545 at 574, 583–4, 593–4, 608 (HCA) (though query Kirby J's refusal at n.353 to disapprove *R.* v. *Ataou* [1988] QB 798 (CA) and *R.* v. *Craig* [1975] 1 NZLR 597 (SC)). Only Toohey J at 564 seemed to favour the instrumental rationale, though this is unclear.

[66] *Ibid.*, at 546.

[67] Such as state supreme courts and the Federal Court.

[68] E.g. *Somerville* v. *Australian Securities Commission* (1995) 131 ALR 517 at 525 (Fed. Ct.) *per* Lockhart J; also see *Newcastle Wallsend Coal Co.* v. *Court of Coal Mines Regulations* (1997) 42 NSWLR 351 (NSW CA).

SOUTH AFRICA[69]

South Africa appears to be the only remaining exception to the general acceptance of the application of the privilege to search warrants. In *Andresen* v. *Minister of Justice* Price J held that the relevant statutory search warrant provisions applied to privileged documents, although the privilege was not destroyed by the seizure of the documents. In doing so he held that privilege is a rule of evidence related only to litigation, and is not a substantive rule of law.[70] In accordance with this lack of enthusiasm for extending the privilege to the non-curial realm, Jansen JA in *Mandela* v. *Minister of Prisons*[71] held that the privilege is not a quasi-proprietary right protecting documents against seizure in general terms. This view of the nature of privilege was well established in South Africa many years beforehand.[72]

However in *S* v. *Safatsa* Botha JA adopted a fundamental rights analysis. He relied on *Baker* v. *Campbell*, saying that in that case, although the court split, all judgments recognised that the privilege is "a mere manifestation of a fundamental principle upon which our judicial system is based".[73] Botha JA quotes the South African case of *Euroshipping Corporation of Monrovia* v. *Minister of Agriculture*[74] to support his contention that the privilege is a fundamental right.[75] Botha JA was wrong to read all the judges in *Baker* v. *Campbell* as supporting such an approach.[76] His strong reliance on Dawson J's judgment is particularly concerning in this regard.[77] Zeffertt[78] doubts the value of the decision in *Andresen*. While the case was approved of in *Mandela* v. *Minister of Prisons*, its correctness was expressly doubted by Coetzee J in *Cheadle, Thompson & Haysom* v. *Minister*.[79] Coetzee J held that this issue was not necessary for him to decide, however he clearly stated that the authority of *Andresen* will have to be "carefully reviewed"[80] in light of the approach taken in Australia, New Zealand, the United States and Canada. With *Safatsa* the Appellate Division now has a more immediate motivation to reconsider *Andresen*.

The issue of search warrants aside, it appears that with the passing of the Constitution of the Republic of South Africa Act 1993 rights-based rationales

[69] For a thorough treatment of much of the South African case law on this issue, see D. Unterhalter, "Legal Professional Privilege: A Rule of Evidence or a Procedural Right?" (1986) 2 *SA Jo. of HR* 312; Paizes above at n. 1, 137–45.

[70] *Andresen* v. *Minister for Justice* [1954] 2 SA at 481D.

[71] 1983 (1) SA 938 at 957–8 (AD).

[72] E.g. see *Heiman Maasdorp & Barker* v. *Secretary for Inland Revenue* 1968 (4) SA 160 at 162D (Witwatersrand LD).

[73] *S* v. *Safatsa* 1988 (1) SA 868 at 885 (AD), quoting *Baker* v. *Campbell* (1983) 153 CLR 52.

[74] 1979 (1) SA 637 (CPD).

[75] *S* v. *Safatsa* 1988 (1) SA at 885G.

[76] Unterhalter (1988) 300; see the analysis of *Baker* v. *Campbell* (1983) 153 CLR 52 above at p. 21.

[77] See the analysis of Dawson J's judgment below at p. 30.

[78] D. Zeffertt, *The South African Law of Evidence* (4th edn., Butterworths, Durban, 1988) 257.

[79] 1986 (2) SA 279 at 283 (Witwatersrand LD).

[80] *Ibid.*

may find more support. For example, in *Jeeva* v. *Receiver of Revenue, Port Elizabeth*, Jones J said that, although the privilege does not have direct constitutional support, it is nevertheless a "fundamental right",[81] or a "method to protect individual rights".[82] He also explained the privilege on the basis of the traditional instrumental rationale.[83]

NEW ZEALAND

New Zealand was the first country to tackle the problem of the application of the privilege to search warrants. *IRC* v. *West-Walker* decided that the privilege might have such an operation. Three out of the four majority judges accomplished this without recourse to rights reasoning.[84] Only the final majority judge possibly adopted a rights-based approach.[85] The significance of this will be discussed in more detail below. *IRC* v. *West-Walker* was followed on this point by Davison CJ in *Rosenberg* v. *Jaine*.[86]

In *R.* v. *Uljee* Cooke J referred to "a fundamental right to professional advice".[87] While it is Cooke J's passage that is most often cited, the judgment of Richardson J actually gives more support to a rights-based rule. After discussing the right of access to counsel and the International Covenant on Civil and Political Rights, Richardson J goes on to say:

> the Courts have a responsibility for protecting the individual against the State . . . If society sets store on the right to legal services for (accused) . . . it must ensure the confidentiality of discussions between lawyer and client.[88]

Reference must now be made to the Bill of Rights Act 1990 (NZ). While this does not expressly provide for the privilege, it could be found indirectly through the right of access to a lawyer and the right to representation. However the Act also provides that rights not mentioned in it are not abrogated. As in Canada, New Zealand evidence texts do not mention the Bill of Rights Act in their treatment of the privilege.[89]

[81] *Jeeva* v. *Receiver of Revenue, Port Elizabeth* [1995] 2 SALR 433 at 453–7 (SE Cape LD).

[82] *Ibid*., at 456.

[83] *Ibid*., at 455.

[84] These were Fair J ([1954] NZLR at 205 (adopting a passage from *Bullivant* v. *Attorney-General for Victoria* [1901] AC 196)), Hay J ([1954] NZLR at 218, basing the rule in public policy) and North J ([1954] NZLR at 219 ("public policy") and 220 ("common law rule")).

[85] Gresson J [1954] NZLR at 212 (close to a rights argument) and 213 (mentioning the "common law right" three times). The sole dissenting judge, Stanton J ([1954] NZLR at 216) held the privilege to be a rule of evidence only.

[86] [1983] NZLR 1 at 12–13 (HC).

[87] R. v. *Uljee* [1982] 1 NZLR at 569.

[88] *Ibid*., at 572.

[89] E.g. D.L. Mathieson, Cross on Evidence—New Zealand Edition (looseleaf) (Butterworths, Wellington, 1998) 10.20–10.33.

ENGLAND

At the time of writing the most recent statement on the basis of the privilege in English common law is the High Court case of *General Mediterranean Holdings SA* v. *Patel*.[90] In this case Toulson J reviewed many of the developments across the Commonwealth described above and concluded, in relation to the common law, that the privilege had, irrespective of statutory human rights provisions, transformed over the last few decades into a substantive common law right.[91] It is often assumed that it is only relatively recently, with the warming effect of the European Convention on Human Rights, that English courts have considered the privilege as a "substantive rule", or as a right. However this doctrinal shift has earlier roots, and fits into the Commonwealth-wide common law movement outlined above.

The first English court expressly to consider the extra-curial application of the privilege took a narrow view of the rule. In *Parry-Jones* v. *Law Society*, decided in 1967, the Court of Appeal held that the privilege did not apply to defeat a notice from the Law Society to produce documents. The leading judgment, delivered by Diplock LJ, is widely quoted as supporting the "rule of evidence" approach. However Diplock LJ's judgment is still consistent with a rights analysis, albeit a right of limited scope. He describes the privilege as "a right to withhold from a court".[92] The fact that the rule is limited to the courtroom is only suggestive, not determinative, of the absence of a right. Little can usefully be drawn from this case as neither the original Chambers decision of Buckley J,[93] nor the Court of Appeal, discusses the reason for the rule in any depth. There was much dissatisfaction with the result in *Parry-Jones*.[94] The general issue of the privilege outside judicial proceedings does not appear to have been argued sufficiently.[95] Diplock LJ's statement was made in passing and without reference to the decided cases.[96] The judgment was not reserved and the case was argued by the appellant in person.[97]

In the 1970s there were conflicting decisions on the extra-curial application of the privilege. Swanwick J, in *Truman (Frank) Export Ltd* v. *Metropolitan Police Commissioner*,[98] applied the privilege to defeat a Forgery Act search warrant.[99]

[90] [1999] 3 All ER 673.

[91] Toulson J also determined the issue of whether the privilege would be protected as a right under the European Convention on Human Rights. This issue will be dealt with in the following chapter.

[92] *Parry-Jones* v. *Law Society* [1969] Ch. at 9.

[93] See [1968] Ch. 195.

[94] E.g. see *Baker* v. *Campbell* (1983) 153 CLR at 124.

[95] K. Lupton, "Legal Professional Privilege in Administrative Proceedings" (1985) 10 *Sydney LR* 614 at 618.

[96] *Ibid.*

[97] *Ibid.*

[98] [1977] QB 952 (QBD).

[99] S. 16(1) of the Forgery Act 1913 (UK).

He considered in detail the history of the use of the privilege in criminal proceedings.[100] However *Parry-Jones* was neither cited nor discussed and the relevance of the extra-curial context seems to have been missed.[101] *R.* v. *Peterborough Justices*[102] was a similar case, decided just four months after *Frank Truman.* In *Peterborough Justices* the Court of Appeal held that section 16 of the Forgery Act in fact overrode the privilege. However again the rationale and scope of the privilege were not adequately dealt with, and *Parry-Jones* was neither argued nor cited. Now the main search warrant provision is found in the Police and Criminal Evidence Act 1984, and the privilege is expressly preserved.[103]

In *R.* v. *Inland Revenue Commissioners, ex p. Taylor (No. 2)*[104] and, more recently *Applicant* v. *Inspector of Taxes*,[105] it has been held that the privilege does not apply to defeat compulsion by notices issued under section 20(1) of the Taxes Management Act 1970. It could be argued that these decisions represent a return to the narrow *Parry-Jones* approach; the first of these cases cited *Parry-Jones* with approval. However not too much should be taken from this line of cases on the issue of the rationale, as the relevant statutory provisions of the Taxes Management Act conferred the privilege in some situations but not others. The approach to statutory interpretation in the taxation cases must be viewed in light of the more rights-focussed approach in *General Mediterranean Holdings SA* v. *Patel*,[106] which has been discussed above. However it is not suggested that the legislative context of these cases is in any way comparable.

The decisions perhaps lending greatest support to the recognition of a common law right in England are the line of cases relating to the correspondence of prisoners, such as *R.* v. *Secretary of State for the Home Department, ex parte Leech (No. 2)*[107] and others.[108] This case was factually similar to *Solosky* v. *The Queen.*[109] It concerned the validity of regulations which empowered prison governors to open correspondence between a prisoner and his lawyer, the only exception being once a writ had been issued on behalf of or against the prisoner. The regulation was declared to be *ultra vires* the regulation-making power in the enabling statute. It has been suggested that this result indicates that lawyer–client communications are protected by a common law right.[110]

100 [1977] QB at 961–3.

101 Especially see *ibid.* at 965–6, assuming the application of the privilege.

102 *R.* v. *Peterborough Justices, ex parte Hicks* [1977] 1 WLR 1371, [1978] 1 All ER 225 (QBD).

103 See ss. 8(1)(d) and 9(2)(a); also see M. Zander, *The Police and Criminal Evidence Act 1984* (2nd edn., Sweet and Maxwell London, 1990) 30–3 and cases discussed therein.

104 [1990] 2 All ER 409 at 413–14 (CA).

105 [1999] STC (SCD) 128 at 133 (Special Commissioner).

106 [1999] 3 All ER 673.

107 [1994] QB 198 (CA).

108 *Raymond* v. *Honey* [1983] AC 1; *R* v. *Home Secretary, ex parte Anderson* [1984] 1 QB 778 (DC).

109 [1980] 1 SCR 821.

110 M. Hunt, *Using Human Rights Law in English Courts* (Hart Publishing, Oxford, 1997) at 178–80.

Looking to recent House of Lords authority, in *R.* v. *Derby Magistrates' Court, ex p. B* ("the *Derby Magistrates* case") all judges definitely used the instrumental rationale in their reasoning.[111] Lord Taylor also said that the privilege was "much more than an ordinary rule of evidence . . . It is a fundamental condition on which the administration of justice as a whole rests".[112] Lord Taylor appears to give support to those advocating a new basis for the privilege in human rights. However not all lower courts have been quick to pick up on this changed environment.[113] And in *In re L. (A Minor)*,[114] a case concerning litigation privilege, Lord Nicholls (albeit dissenting) described the privilege as reflecting the public interest in informed legal advice.[115]

Finally, as noted at the beginning of this section, in the recent case of *General Mediterranean Holdings SA* v. *Patel*[116] it was held that, considering comparable developments across the Commonwealth, the privilege had now become a substantive common law right. The same case also held that the privilege would be protected as a right under the European Convention on Human Rights. It is likely that, for significant parts of the privilege at least, this issue will be taken over by the Articles 6 and 8 of the Convention, once the substantive provisions of this treaty are incorporated into domestic law by the coming into force of the Human Rights Act 1998. This issue will be examined in more detail in the next chapter.

EUROPEAN COURT OF JUSTICE

The main European Court of Justice (ECJ) case is *A.M. & S. Europe* v. *Commission*.[117] The point of dispute in this case was the procedure for determination of the privilege, specifically whether the Commission could inspect a document to determine the privilege claim. The opinions of Advocates-General Warner and Slynn both discuss the privilege in a manner strongly supportive of the recognition of a new rights-based rationale.[118] This approach also finds expression in the judgment of the Court.[119]

However the European Court's recognition of the privilege should still be regarded as in a formative stage. In particular, the apparent restriction of the privilege to lawyers in independent practice, and not to in-house lawyers

[111] See the various judgments at [1996] 1 AC at 507D, 508H, 510A, 510D, 513C.

[112] *Ibid.*, at 507.

[113] E.g. *Kershaw* v. *Whelan* [1996] 1 WLR 358 at 370 (QB): "privilege is an aspect of the law of evidence and not of constitutional rights".

[114] For comment see A.A.S. Zuckerman, "Legal Professional Privilege—The Cost of Absolutism" (1996) 112 LQR 535; J. McEwan, "The Uncertain Status of Privilege in Children Act Cases: *Re L*" (1996) 1 *Evidence and Proof* 80.

[115] *In re L (A Minor)* [1997] AC 16 at 32 (HL).

[116] [1999] 3 All ER 673 (QB).

[117] [1983] 1 QB 878, ECJ.

[118] See Warner A-G, *ibid.*, at 895, 900 and Slynn A-G, *ibid.*, at 913.

[119] *AM & S Europe* v. *Commission* [1983] 1 QB at 941.

working for companies, is difficult to justify and will probably be the subject of further litigation.[120] In *Carlsen* v. *Council*[121] the Court of First Instance (CFI) held that legal opinions produced by the legal services of Community institutions were privileged and did not have to be disclosed to a Danish court, on the bases of maintaining the "legal certainty and stability of Community law" and ensuring that the Council is able to obtain independent legal advice.[122] The denial of the privilege to in-house lawyers, which appears to be a result of the *AM & S* case, was justified and the case distinguished on quite spurious grounds.[123] The state and scope of the privilege in European Community law following *Carlsen* v. *Council* is highly unsatisfactory and will surely need to be clarified.

UNITED STATES

Finally, it is worth noting the situation which prevails in the United States. The Supreme Court has clearly rested the privilege on instrumental concerns.[124] State appellate courts have from an early stage also used the instrumental rationale.[125] The language of rights is used occasionally, but the effect of casting the privilege as a "right" is never explained.[126] Federal courts have held that the Fifth and Sixth Amendments guarantee the right to effective legal communications, and that this prevents the state from eavesdropping by means of wiretapping[127] or by use of secret agents.[128] However these courts have not yet gone as far as saying that the privilege itself has the status of a constitutional right. This has not stopped numerous academics from attempting to rationalise the privilege as a constitutional right, either on the basis of the Fifth Amendment privilege against self-incrimination,[129] the Sixth Amendment right to counsel[130] or a

[120] See M. Dolmans, "Sauce for the Goose is Sauce for the Gander", *Euopean Counsel*, February 1999, 7–8.

[121] Case T–610/97, [1998] ECR II–485.

[122] *Ibid*., at paras 43, 46, 47.

[123] *Ibid*., at paras 51, 52.

[124] E.g. *Fisher* v. *United States* 425 US 391 at 403 (1976 SC); *Upjohn Co* v. *United States* 449 US 383 at 389 (1981 SC); *Swidler & Berlin* v. *United States* 118 S Ct. 2081 at 2086 (1998 SC).

[125] E.g. *Rochester City Bank* v. *Suydam*, 5 Howard's Practice Reports 254 at 258–9 (NY SC 1851) (but query Selden J's historical analysis of the privilege as an adjunct to the privilege against self-incrimination).

[126] E.g. *In the Matter of Kozlov* 398 A.2d 882 at 887 (NJ SC 1979) ("a well-defined relationship, recognised and defined over the centuries . . . to the essential rights of man").

[127] *Coplon* v. *United States* 191 F.2d 749 (DC Cir. 1950).

[128] E.g. *Caldwell* v. *United States* 205 F.2d 879 (DC Cir. 1959).

[129] E.g. H.I. Subin, "The Lawyer as Superego: Disclosure of Client Confidences to Prevent Harm" (1985) 70 Iowa LR 1091 at 1120–7; Note, "The Lawyer–Client Privilege" (1961) 56 *Nw ULR* 235 at 259.

[130] E.g. Note, "Government Intrusions Into the Defense Camp: Undermining the Right to Counsel" (1984) 97 *Harv. LR* 1143 at 1145; H.I.Subin, "The Lawyer as Superego: Disclosure of Client Confidences to Prevent Harm" (1985) 70 *Iowa LR* 1091 at 1127–34; Note above at n. 129, 258–9.

combination of both together.[131] Writers have also attempted to give other evidentiary privileges constitutional bases.[132]

ANALYSIS OF AUTHORITY

The stated approach in cases which decided the extra-curial applicability of the privilege was to look first to the privilege's underlying rationale, and then apply the rationale to the novel fact situation. However in reality the exercise was conducted the other way round. Courts decided that the privilege should apply to search warrants, and then fashioned a new rationale to justify this extension. The implicit logic advanced is that once the privilege applies beyond the threat of disclosure in court, then it must be a common law right.[133] For example in the *Carter* case McHugh J held that "[n]ow that this Court has held that legal professional privilege is not a rule of evidence but a substantive rule of law, the best explanation of the doctrine is that it is a practical guarantee of fundamental, constitutional or human rights".[134] Professor Paizes offers a more colourful description of this phenomenon:

> it is only relatively recently that the question arose whether the legal privilege was an answer to an authorized executive order of seizure or confiscation. And, when it did arise, it encountered the privilege in the process of one of its chameleonic colour-changes. Gone were the old hues which marked the privilege as a creature of adjectival law. Emerging, instead, were the colours of the substantive law, colours which, to lawyers steeped in the language of Bentham and Wigmore, seem strange and exotic, but which are, to human rights lawyers, instantly identifiable. But while the colour of the creature changed, its biological anatomy did not. The rules that gave it substance were, in large measure, left intact. . . . Not surprisingly, the nuances of these developments have not always been fully appreciated by the courts.[135]

However the extension of the privilege outside the courtroom can be adequately explained using only the non-rights based instrumental rationale, without resort to a rights-based rationale to supplement or possibly replace it. Even if the instrumental rationale is taken at its narrowest, to reflect only a concern

[131] E.g. Note, "The Attorney–Client Privilege: Fixed Rules, Balancing and Constitutional Entitlement" (1977) 91 *Harv. LR* 464 at 485–6; H.I. Subin above at n. 129, 1119–32; M. Rosenfeld, "The Transformation of the Attorney–Client Privilege" (1982) 33 *Hastings LJ* 495 at 511 ("in the context of American jurisprudence, existence of the privilege is mandated by constitutional considerations as a necessary bridge that spans the preservation of the individual's rights against self-incrimination and the right to counsel").

[132] E.g. T.G. Krattenmaker, "Testimonial Privileges in Federal Courts: An Alternative to the Proposed Federal Rules of Evidence" (1973) 62 *Georgetown LJ* 61 at 94–100; but compare *Branzburg* v. *Hayes* 408 US 665 (SC 1972) (the Constitution does not mandate a privilege for journalists).

[133] D. Unterhalter, "Legal Professional Privilege: A Rule of Evidence or a Procedural Right?" (1986) 2 *SA Journal of HR* 312 at 313.

[134] *Carter* v. *The Managing Partner, Northmore Hale Davy & Leake* (1995) 183 CLR at 161.

[135] Paizes above at n. 1, 116.

for the proper functioning of court trials,[136] then it can still be said that the prospect of disclosure to a non-curial body may affect lawyer–client communications, and in turn affect the administration of justice in court trials. As Dawson J held in *Baker* v. *Campbell*:

> As a matter of principle or practice it does not seem to me to matter whether the compulsion is at the hands of the executive or at the hands of the judiciary . . . the power to compel the disclosure in an administrative inquiry of professional confidences is as likely to destroy the freedom of communication.[137]

To similar effect, the Australian Full Federal Court, in their recent decision in *Adelaide Steamship Co Ltd* v. *Spalvins*, said that:

> even if there is not uniform agreement as to the policies informing, and the purposes of, the privilege . . . we can see no reason for ascribing different policies and purposes, and hence different attributes, to the privilege depending upon whether or not the privilege is claimed when evidence is being adduced at trial.[138]

The Supreme Court of the United States recently discussed the scope of the privilege in similar terms in determining that the privilege survived the death of the client.[139] The concern is for the faith of all clients in the privilege, and so the scope of the privilege should be determined primarily by the factors which affect client apprehensions. As discussed above, the very first case to recognise the extra-curial application of the privilege, *IRC* v. *West-Walker*, did this without recourse to rights arguments, and may be explained on the basis outlined in the above paragraph.[140] Many subsequent cases, particularly some of the Australian and English decisions dealt with above, may be similarly described.

This justification is not the same as the temporal extension argument put forward by Dickson CJ in *Solosky*.[141] This latter argument views the application of the privilege to search warrants as simply extending the concept of courtroom disclosure to cover compulsory revelation of materials that may possibly then be used at trial: "a step in the assembly of evidence intended for use in a prosecution".[142] Brennan J in *Baker* v. *Campbell* strongly criticised this view. He rejected the analogy between search warrants and civil discovery, concluding that "neither the issue nor the execution of a search warrant is in any sense a step in or incidental to those proceedings".[143] While the logical correctness of Brennan J's refutation of Dickson J's argument may be open to debate,[144] the

136 The more authoritative and more logical instrumental goal is the wider concern for "the proper functioning of our legal system" (per *Baker* v. *Campbell* (1983) 153 CLR at 128).

137 *Ibid.*, at 130–1.

138 (1998) 152 ALR 418 at 428; this was in the context of determining whether the same rules applied under the common law and the Evidence Act 1995 (Aust.).

139 *Swidler & Berlin* v. *United States* 118 S Ct. at 2086.

140 E.g. see North J at [1954] NZLR at 219; also see *Rosenberg* v. *Jaine* [1983] NZLR at 13.

141 *Solosky* v. *The Queen* [1980] 1 SCR at 836–7.

142 *Baker* v. *Campbell* (1983) 153 CLR at 99.

143 *Ibid.*,. at 100; also see *ibid.*, at 101–2.

144 Brennan J takes an overly technical approach to an argument that was presented only as an analogy.

temporal extension argument may best be dealt with by simply saying that it is unnecessary. The wide conception of the causes of the chilling effect supplies an adequate doctrinal basis for the application here of a rule based on the traditional instrumental rationale.

"MERE RULE OF EVIDENCE"

In analysing the privilege's rationale, judges frequently make the point that the privilege is not just a "mere rule of evidence",[145] but is a rule of substantive law.[146] For example, Lord Taylor CJ in the *Derby Magistrates* case said:

> Legal professional privilege is thus much more than an ordinary rule of evidence, limited in its application to the facts of a particular case. It is a fundamental condition on which the administration of justice as a whole rests.[147]

Similar terminology is used in the United States,[148] where the issue also has a practical application in the context of American diversity litigation.[149]

It is unclear exactly what is meant by such statements. There are a number of possibilities. First, some common law statements[150] are probably trying to make the point that the privilege is not just a rule governing trial evidence, and that it exists beyond the context of trials. However the concept of "evidence" always existed in a wider context. Search warrants apply to "evidence". Administrative and investigative proceedings still collect and review "evidence", even though not all the same admissibility rules apply to them. Thus it is hard to see what would be "mere" about the privilege being a rule of evidence. Another stream of common law cases seems to say that the privilege is more than a rule of evidence because it is a human right. However even if we accept the rights rationale, this does not alter the fact that the privilege is still a "rule of evidence". Other rules, such as the right to silence,[151] may be human rights, but are also considered to be rules of evidence.

The debate about whether legal professional privilege is a "mere rule of evidence" began in the context of determining whether to extend the privilege beyond trial and pre-trial procedures to investigative procedures, including the use of search warrants. The issue was a red herring then, but has carried on and

[145] E.g. *R* v. *Colvin* [1970] 3 OR at 617 (Ont. HC); *Solosky* v. *The Queen* [1980] 1 SCR at 836; *Baker* v. *Campbell* (1983) 153 CLR at 132; *Attorney-General (N.T.)* v. *Maurice* (1986) 161 CLR at 480, 490–1; *Carter* v. *The Managing Partner, Northmore Hale Davy & Leake* (1995) 183 CLR at 132–3, 161.

[146] E.g. *R* v. *Gray* (1992) 74 CCC (3d) 267 at 273 (BC SC) ("[w]hile the right to confidentiality or solicitor–client privilege was initially a rule of evidence, it is now clear that it is also a substantive rule of law").

[147] [1995] AC at 507.

[148] E.g. *McGranahan* v. *Dahar* 408 A.2d 121 at 125 (New Hampshire SC 1979).

[149] See D.W. Louisell above at n. 13, 102.

[150] Particularly Australian cases decided around the time of *Baker* v. *Campbell*.

[151] In countries where the right still exists in any meaningful form.

was picked up by recent cases claiming to follow the rights rationale. The issue has little more relevance decades later. The only meaning of privilege is with respect to its effect on the compellability of evidence. As such it is a "rule of evidence", albeit a strong one with a broad reach beyond the doors of the courtroom.

RATIONALE AND THE RULES OF PRIVILEGE

An important problem with the rights rationale is its inconsistency with many of the rules that go to make up the privilege. The rule that the privilege survives the death of the client[152] may possibly be justified on a rights-based rationale, but such a justification has not yet been offered, and some time ago Professor Louisell doubted that such justification might in fact be possible.[153] The privilege operates partly on the basis of clients' expectations of a legal relationship, rather than the reality of a relationship. For example, the rules regarding communications with laymen believed to be lawyers, and communications before a lawyer–client relationship is established, both support this broader notion of the scope of privilege protection. This view of the privilege is easily explained in terms of the instrumental rationale, but if these rules were to be considered within the framework of a rights rationale, then further justification would be called for.

The corporate privilege has greatly increased in importance over the second half of this century as corporations became more frequent litigating parties.[154] Non-instrumental rationales have been advanced for the extension of the privilege to corporations.[155] However it is clear that corporations have no claim to human rights[156] and that any privacy interests held by them are property rights.[157] The editors of the *Harvard Law Review* argue that the rise of corporate litigation has changed the balance between what they term the "utilitarian" and "rights" rationales.[158] This may be apparent in the United States, where in

[152] *Calcraft* v. *Guest* [1898] 1 QB 759 (CA); *Swidler & Berlin* v. *United States* 118 S Ct. 2081.

[153] D.W. Louisell above at n. 13, 113.

[154] For other problems in applying the privilege to corporations, see M. Rosenfeld above at n. 7, 513–31.

[155] V.A. Alexander, n. 30 above, 223 (privacy); C. Fried abvove at n. 3, 1076 (autonomy); A. Alschuler, "The Search for Truth Continued, the Privilege Retained: A Response to Judge Frankel" (1982) 54 *U Col. LR* 67 at 73 n. 29 (fairness). The privacy argument for corporations is rejected in Developments (1985), n. 6 above 1482 and C. Wright and K. Graham, n. 31 above, vol. xxiv, 79. The autonomy argument is rejected in E.G. Thornburg, "Sanctifying Secrecy: The Mythology of the Corporate Attorney–Client Privilege" (1993) 69 *Notre Dame LR* 157 at 185.

[156] Comment "Attorney-Client and Work Product in a Utilitarian World: An Argument For Recomparison" (1995) 108 *Harv LR* 1697 at 1703; S. Saltzburg, "Privileges and Professionals: Lawyers and Psychiatrists" (1984) 279–80; J. Gardner, n. 27 above, 498; Note (1984), n. 130 above, 484; M. Rosenfeld, n. 30 above, 515.

[157] E.G. Thornburg, "Sanctifying Secrecy: The Mythology of the Corporate Attorney–Client Privilege" (1993) 69 *Notre Dame LR* 157 at 185.

[158] Comment (1995) n. 156 above, 1703–4.

Upjohn v. *United States*,[159] the Supreme Court, in setting out the test for the corporate privilege, discussed the instrumental rationale only, without reference to non-instrumental rights-based arguments.[160] Rehnquist J (as he then was) made it clear that his explanation of the rationale covered the privilege generally, and was not restricted to the rule as it applies to corporations. However there may be problems with applying any instrumental rationale at all to the corporate privilege. It has been argued that corporations have the least compelling need for certainty in their legal relations.[161] As institutions, they are affected less by minor uncertainties.[162] Being "more deeply attached to current procedures and patterns, corporations are less likely than individuals to change their behaviour markedly in response to incremental departures from current privilege rules".[163] Corporations often have ongoing dealings with lawyers and an unavoidable reliance on them which removes much of the force of the instrumental reasoning.

One branch of the privilege rule that may be inexplicable on either a non-rights-based instrumental analysis or on a non-instrumental rights-based rationale is the application of the privilege to communications with third parties.[164] These communications hardly affect a client's state of mind in consulting a lawyer,[165] and "such information has to be gathered whether or not the party is represented by a lawyer".[166] However this aspect of the privilege rule is also hard to reconcile with rights reasoning. Litigation privilege, which includes the privilege over third party communications, may rest more simply on the unworkability of not having such a privilege. This is sometimes explained as the maintenance of the procedure for adversary litigation.[167] It is possible to conflate this rationale with the instrumental rationale for legal advice privilege. Under both rules protection from disclosure is essential for the proper conduct of litigation.[168] On this view:

> one is left with a broad rationale which furthers and promotes both the administration of justice and an effective adversary system of litigation. Legal professional

159 449 US at 389–90, 101 S Ct. at 682–3 (SC 1981).

160 *Ibid.*

161 Note (1984) n. 130 above, 474–5.

162 *Ibid.*, at 473–4.

163 *Ibid.*

164 Note though that in England the application of this rule to communications with experts has been significantly abrogated by Part 35 of the Civil Procedure Rules 1998. For an argument that this head does not exist (in Australia at least) see A. Ligertwood, *Australian Evidence* (2nd edn., Butterworths, Sydney, 1993) 160–1. Ligertwood's argument is met by S.B. McNicol, *Law of Privilege* (Law Book Co., Sydney, 1992) 50–1.

165 N.J. Williams, "Discovery of Civil Litigation Trial Preparation in Canada" (1980) 58 *Can Bar Rev* 1 at 39; S.B. McNicol n. 164 above, 48.

166 *Dingle* v. *Commonwealth Development Bank of Australia* (1989) 91 ALR 239 at 241 (Fed. Ct.).

167 Although it has been suggested that this aspect of the privilege could best be justified under a separate and narrower principle that a party is not bound to reveal to the court statements taken from witnesses for the purpose of the litigation.

168 E.g. see Brennan J in *Baker* v. *Campbell* (1983) 153 CLR at 108; but compare *Waugh* v. *British Railways Board* [1980] AC at 531.

> privilege is said to achieve both these objectives by, first, fostering candour and trust in the lawyer–client relationship, and secondly, protecting the information of each party to adjudication from disclosure to the other side.[169]

Therefore the two rationales are similar.[170] Sometimes there is a blending of rationales.[171]

One aspect of the privilege that may be better justified on the basis of a rights-based rationale may be the remedies available to protect against the disclosure of secondary evidence of privileged communications. In *Descôteaux* v. *Mierzwinski* Lamer J held that a rights rationale supports "preventive or curative remedies" that may not be otherwise available.[172] While the privilege as a rule of evidence could never prevent third parties disclosing secondary evidence of privileged communications, if the privilege is a substantive rule the judge must decide whether it is important to receive this evidence and whether there are any alternatives available.[173] However it should be noted that this is an extremely problematic area of law, and that the extent of the preventative or curative remedies available to courts, if any, are in great doubt. This whole area will be discussed in detail in a separate chapter below. The only point that needs to be addressed at present is the impact of the issue on the privilege's rationale. If preventive or curative remedies such as injunctions and the expunging of evidence are recognised as valid means of protecting the privilege from secondary evidence, then the only effect on the fundamental nature of the rule is that the privilege may have become a rule of inadmissibility rather than a rule of non-compulsion. However there is no *a priori* reason why a rule of inadmissibility must be supported by a right. The simpler explanation is that it is supported by an instrumental goal that is stronger than the one previously recognised.

CONCLUSIONS

It is clear that on current authority there is sufficient judicial support for the recognition of a common law right to privilege in most Commonwealth jurisdictions, but not in South Africa and not in some United States jurisdictions. Whilst the development of the privilege as a common law right is popular, it is sometimes based on dubious authority. *Descôteaux* v. *Mierzwinski* relied upon a questionable use of previous authority. The foundation Australian case of *Baker* v. *Campbell* did not take this approach but has been wrongly interpreted in both Australia and abroad as having done so. Constitutional rights documents, now enacted in all Commonwealth jurisdictions considered above

[169] McNicol n. 164 above, 48–9.

[170] Comment (1995), n. 156 above, 1699–1700.

[171] R.L. Marcus, "The Perils of Privilege: Waiver and the Litigator" (1986) 84 *Mich LR* 1605 at 1623–4.

[172] *Descôteaux* v. *Mierzwinski* [1982] 1 SCR 860.

[173] *Ibid.*, at 876.

except Australia, could potentially fill this gap in authority, but have not yet been used for this purpose.

Gardner says that "the rationale of the privilege cannot be settled by resort to authority, reason, history or convenience" and that "humanitarian values have first claim".[174] However one may have thought that if a legal rule has authority, reason, history and convenience on its side, there is probably little scope left for arguing against that rule. The same commentator links the rise of the rights rationale to the twentieth century experience of totalitarianism and a subsequent interest in humanitarian principles and human rights.[175] This is contrasted with Wigmore's "utilitarian" analysis,[176] which is seen as a product of nineteenth-century institutions and modes of thought.[177] This may be true of certain jurisdictions; especially Canada. However in Australia, South Africa, and possibly England and Wales, the rights rationale is inextricably bound up in the extension of evidentiary compulsion beyond the curial realm, and the need for courts to find a principle to justify the privilege's further reach.

174 J. Gardner n. 27 above, 285.

175 *Ibid.*

176 Note though that Wigmore did not actually use this term in his explanation of the policy of the privilege.

177 While Wigmore's most quoted work, the *Treatise*, was written in the 20th century, his ideas are seen as reflecting a typically 19th-century philosophy and set of priorities.

3

Privilege under the European Convention on Human Rights

INTRODUCTION

Apart from Australia, which has not implemented express human rights legislation, the United Kingdom[1] is one of the last large Commonwealth jurisdictions to face the merger of its common law privilege with over-arching rights legislation. Prior to the passing of the Human Rights Act 1998 (UK) there were numerous statements by judges of the view that UK privilege law may be changed in particular ways by the European Convention on Human Rights ("the Convention").[2]

The first English case to analyse the position of the privilege under the Convention is the High Court case of *General Mediterranean Holdings SA* v. *Patel*.[3] In the previous chapter it was noted that this case held that the privilege had, irrespective of statutory human rights provisions, developed into a substantive common law right. The case is also important for its express and considered ruling that the privilege would be protected as a right under the European Convention on Human Rights. The effect of these findings was that a provision of the Civil Procedure Rules 1998,[4] which empowered judges to override the privilege in determining wasted costs applications, and which had been in force for only three months at this stage, was *ultra vires* the empowering legislation[5] and therefore invalid.

English courts still have a significant amount of work to do to determine the effect of the Convention on the doctrine of legal professional privilege. It cannot be assumed that the Convention applies to all circumstances in which the privilege may be invoked. Further, it is not yet known what effect the Convention will have on the many exceptions and derogations to the privilege in English law.

[1] The implementation of the Convention is slightly different in each part of the United Kingdom; a matter which is beyond the scope of this book.

[2] E.g. *R.* v. *Derby Magistrates' Court, ex p. B* [1996] 1 AC at 507; *In re L (A Minor)* [1997] AC 16 at 32.

[3] [1999] 3 All ER 673.

[4] R. 48.7(3): "For the purposes of this rule, the court may direct that privileged documents are to be disclosed to the court and, if the court so directs, to the other party to the application for an order."

[5] Civil Procedure Act 1997, Sched. 1, para. 4: "Evidence—Civil Procedure Rules may modify the rules of evidence as they apply to proceedings in any court within the scope of the rules".

The provisions of the Convention which will have the most direct impact on the rule of privilege are Articles 6(1), 6(3)(c) and (d) and 8. These state in part:

Article 6 Right to a fair trial

1. In the determination of his civil rights and obligations or of any criminal charge against him, everyone is entitled to a fair and public hearing within a reasonable time by an independent and impartial tribunal established by law.

. . .

3. Everyone charged with a criminal offence has the following minimum rights:

. . .

(b) to have adequate time and facilities for the preparation of his defence;

(c) to defend himself in person or through legal assistance . . ."

Article 8 Right to respect for private and family life

1. Everyone has the right to respect for his private and family life, his home and his correspondence.

2. There shall be no interference with the exercise of this right except such as is in accordance with the law and is necessary in a democratic society in the interests of national security, public safety or the economic well-being of the country, for the prevention of disorder or crime, for the protection of health or morals, or for the protection of the rights and freedoms of others.

Other Articles, such as Article 10 (governing freedom of expression), may also have some relevance.[6]

SECTION I: ARTICLE 6

Scope and the Principle of Effective Access

Article 6(3)(c) clearly supports a right to be assisted by a lawyer.[7] The European Court of Human Rights (ECtHR) in *S* v. *Switzerland*[8] held that this brings with it some form of right to the confidentiality of legal communications:

> The Court notes that . . . the European Convention does not expressly guarantee the right of a person charged with a criminal offence to communicate with defence counsel without hindrance. That right is set forth, however, within the Council of Europe, in Article 39 of the Standard Minimum Rules for the Treatment of Prisoners.
>
> The Court considers that an accused's right to communicate with his advocate out of hearing of a third person is part of the basic requirements of a fair trial in a democratic society and follows from Article 6(3)(c) of the Convention. If a lawyer were unable to confer with his client and receive confidential instructions from him without such surveillance, his assistance would lose much of its usefulness, whereas the Convention is intended to guarantee rights that are practical and effective.[9]

[6] E.g. see *R.* v. *Secretary of State for the Home Department, ex parte Simms* [1999] 3 WLR 328 at 336–7, 341–2, 348–9; also see the CA decision which the HL overturned: [1999] 1 QB 349 at 361–2.

[7] *Murray* v. *UK* 22 (1996) EHRR 29 at 64–68.

[8] (1992) 14 EHRR 670.

[9] *Ibid.*, para. 48.

Article 6(3) is probably limited to criminal proceedings only. Article 6(1) has a wider potential reach, and may be the only part of Article 6 capable of applying in civil litigation. This provision appears on its face to be directed to the requirements of a fair procedure; however this does not limit it to events occuring during the trial itself. In *Imbrioscia* v. *Switzerland* the ECtHR said[10]:

> the primary purpose of Article 6 as far as criminal matters are concerned is to ensure a fair trial by a "tribunal" competent to determine "any criminal charge", but it does not follow that the Article has no application to pre-trial proceedings. The 'reasonable time' mentioned in paragraph (1), for instance, begins to run from the moment a 'charge' comes into being . . . the Court has occasionally found that a reasonable time has been exceeded in a case that ended with a discharge[11] or at the investigation stage.[12] Other requirements of Article 6—especially of paragraph (3)—may also be relevant before a case is sent for trial and in so far as the fairness of the trial is likely to be seriously prejudiced by an initial failure to comply with them.

One concept the ECtHR has developed in extending the reach of Article 6 is the principle of "effective access". The landmark case is *Golder* v. *United Kingdom.*[13] A prisoner sought to bring libel proceedings against a prison officer but was denied access to a solicitor. The Court found that both Articles 6(1) and 8 had been breached, and that there was no justification for preventing the prisoner from consulting a solicitor. The majority stated the principle of effective access thus:

> It would be inconceivable, in the opinion of the Court, that Article 6(1) should describe in detail the procedural guarantees afforded to parties in a pending lawsuit and should not first protect that which alone makes it in fact possible to benefit from such guarantees, that is, access to a court. The first, public and expeditious character of judicial proceedings are of no value at all if there are no judicial proceedings.[14]

The ECtHR extended the principle of effective access further in *Airey* v. *Ireland*[15] when it held that the denial of legal aid for the purposes of obtaining a judicial separation was a violation of Article 6. The complexity of the proceedings and their emotional nature meant that legal representation was essential, and the prohibitive cost of such representation meant this was an effective denial of access to a court. In *Campbell* v. *United Kingdom*[16] the right of access to courts protected legally privileged communications taking place via correspondence between a lawyer and a prisoner. The Court held that while security considerations can justify restrictions on prison visits, here the restrictions on correspondence were unjustifiable. The principle has also been applied to areas

[10] (1994) 17 EHRR 441 at 455.
[11] See *Maj* v. *Italy* (1991) 14 EHRR 405 at paras. 13–15.
[12] See *Viezzer* v. *Italy*, at paras 15–17.
[13] (1979–80) 1 EHRR 524 at 535–6.
[14] *Ibid.*, at para. 35.
[15] (1979–80) 2 EHRR 305.
[16] (1993) 15 EHRR 137.

as diverse as the cost of bringing proceedings,[17] decisions on whether to grant legal aid[18] and the adequacy of the representation provided by legal aid counsel.[19]

Effective Access and the Privilege

It is clear from the foregoing that Article 6 has an operation prior to the formal issue of proceedings. However the extent to which the principle can be applied outside the context of trial preparation altogether remains unclear. In *Golder* v. *United Kingdom* the legal communications protected by Article 6(1) were for the purpose of *starting* an action, and the Court's reasoning focussed on the effective impediment to the bringing of an action, rather than the need to safeguard access to legal advice *per se*.[20] Similarly, the advice protected in *Airey* v. *Ireland* was for the purpose of obtaining a *judicial* separation, that is, for the purpose of instituting a court action. The Court held that Article 6 may compel the provision of legal aid "when such assistance proves indispensable for an effective access to court". The cases on effective access also stress that proceedings must be such that legal assistance is required in order to utilise the courts. For example, in *Airey* the Court emphasised the complexity of the proceedings and the need to examine expert witnesses.

Article 6(1) will not cover all aspects of non-criminal litigation.[21] There is no such problem in Article 8. In *Campbell* the ECtHR said:

> Admittedly, as the government pointed out, the border line between mail concerning contemplated litigation and that of a general nature is especially difficult to draw and correspondence with a lawyer may concern matters which have little or nothing to do with litigation. Nevertheless, the court sees no reason to distinguish between the different categories of correspondence with lawyers which, whatever their purpose, concern matters of a private and confidential character. In principle, such matters are privileged under Article 8.[22]

However the same cannot necessarily be said of Article 6.[23] Article 6 has not been invoked to protect legal communications where litigation is not contem-

[17] *X* v. *Switzerland*, App. No. 9379/81 (1984), unpublished Commission decision discussed in P. van Dijk, "Access to Court" in R. St. J. Macdonald *et al.* (eds.), *The European System for the Protection of Human Rights* (Kluwer, The Hague, 1993) at 370–1.

[18] E.g. *Granger* v. *United Kingdom*, A 174 (1990) at paras. 44, 48.

[19] *Kamasinski* v. *Austria* (1991) 13 EHRR 36 at paras. 63, 65.

[20] N. 13 above. See the judgment of the majority at para. 26: "he intended 'taking civil action for libel'; it was for this purpose that he wished to contact a solicitor . . . the Home Secretary actually impeded the launching of the contemplated action".

[21] E.g. *X* v. *Germany* 32 CD 56 (entitlement to civil legal aid is outside Art. 6); *Atkinson* v. *United Kingdom* 67 DR 244 at 253 (journalists have no right under Art. 6 to report court proceedings).

[22] (1993) 15 EHRR 137 at para. 48.

[23] Note that in *Golder* the finding of a breach of Art. 8 was unanimous, whereas the finding of a breach of Art. 6(1) was made by 9 votes to 3. The Commission unanimously found a breach of Art. 6(1), but was split 7 votes to 2 on the issue of Art. 8.

plated and not likely. Therefore, it is questionable whether Article 6 would provide a basis for legal professional privilege where a solicitor was being instructed to draw up a will, or on a non-contentious conveyancing transaction.

The English common law draws a distinction between legal advice given when litigation is contemplated and advice given when it is not. Privilege is divided into two limbs: litigation privilege and legal advice privilege. The two limbs have different qualifying rules, and different scope. Article 6 may, on a restrictive reading, be seen as protecting litigation privilege only, as this is directed to "access to court". However the preferable approach would be to determine the scope of the application of Article 6 independently of this distinction, being a distinction developed by the common law for a different purpose, and without reference to the requirements of the Convention.

On the one hand it could be said that it is inherent in the nature of legal communications that they may ultimately result in litigation.[24] On the other hand there are many professions in which the work done by the professional may be proximate to litigation. Are these also to be covered by Article 6? Many people will regard this as stretching the effective access principle far past its limits. However what is the real ground for distinguishing between lawyers and other professionals whose work frequently leads to litigation, and may be essential for an action to come to the courts in the first place? For example, much of the work of an investigative journalist is proximate to potential court proceedings or other investigative compulsion. The House of Lords overturned a ban on contact between prisoners and investigative journalists in *R.* v. *Secretary of State for the Home Department, ex parte Simms*.[25] Interestingly, argument revolved around Articles 8 and 10, but not Article 6. The work of union officers may frequently result in employment law litigation. Even the work of psychiatrists is frequently done against a backdrop of possible litigation or administrative compulsion.[26] For example, in *W* v. *Egdell* counsel seeking to enforce confidentiality over a psychiatrist's report argued that this was necessary given the fact that such communications are made against the backdrop of tribunal review of the patient's case.[27] However Scott J gave little credence to this argument, saying:

[24] S. Bundy and E. Elhauge, "Do Lawyers Improve the Adversary System?" (1991) 79 *Calif. LR* 313 at 405–6; S.L. Phipson, M.N. Howard, P. Crane, and D.A. Hochberg, *Phipson on Evidence* (14th edn., Sweet & Maxwell, London, 1996) at 502 ("[i]t is in the nature of a lawyer's work that those who come for his advice may well be involved ultimately in litigation, and the more likely that is, the more the client will be aware of the possibility . . . This is simply untrue of medical advice. A medical adviser will equally require openness from his patients; but it will only be in highly exceptional cases that either doctor or patient would give any thought to the possibility of disclosure of what passed between them under compulsory process of law"). See pp. 61–3 below for a critique of this argument.

[25] N. 6 above.

[26] M. Guttmacher and H. Weihofen, "Privileged Communications Between Psychiatrist and Patient" (1952) 28 *Indiana LJ* 32 at 33–4; R. Slovenko, "Psychiatry and a Second Look at the Medical Privilege" (1960) 6 *Wayne LR* 175 at 187 ("it is obvious that the patient is likely to have the possibility of litigation in mind").

[27] [1990] 1 Ch. at 393. Evidence showed that independent psychiatric reports were used in about 80% of the cases reviewed by mental health tribunals.

> I do not think that this answer has much weight. The possibility of a lack of frankness must always be present when a psychiatric examination takes place. An experienced psychiatrist would, I think, expect to be able to detect it. And the lack of frankness itself would constitute material of interest to the psychiatrist.[28]

It must now be questioned whether this decision is compatible not only with Article 8, but also with Article 6.

If communications with lawyers which do not take place in the context of litigation can be protected by Article 6,[29] then it is at least arguable that communications involving other professionals whose work is proximate to, and facilitates, court proceedings may also be protected by Article 6. Of course such communications may also be protected by Article 8, as will be discussed below at pp. 46–53. However these two Articles have different scope, both in relation to their substantive rules and their derogations, such that the issue of additional coverage by Article 6 is not an empty question.

There may be good reasons for not extending Article 6 protection to legal communications not taking place in the context of trial preparation. The heading to the article, "right to a fair trial", firmly suggests the scope is limited to the trial context. This is supported by the opening words of Article 6(1): "[i]n the *determination* of his civil rights and obligations . . ." (emphasis added). This may be contrasted with Article 6(3), which has a different trigger, coming into operation upon a person being charged with an offence. Article 8 contains no such possible limitations.

Further, at the time *Golder* was decided it was a significant extension of the scope of Article 6. The interpretation given to Article 6 was not self-evident from the text or the drafting history of the provision; the ECtHR had to draw an inference from the text. The impugned state interference was a particularly egregious one; the state was completely preventing the prisoner from taking legal action against a public officer. There were also strong dissenting judgments, particularly those by Judges Zekia and Fitzmaurice, arguing that there was no basis for this implication from a provision securing the fairness of legal proceedings. All this is not to say that *Golder* may not be followed in the future; it clearly will. However it may have some bearing on the readiness of English courts interpreting the Convention to extend the principle of effective access enshrined in the line of cases beginning with *Golder*.

Finally, it must be noted that there are a number of limits on the ordinary scope of Article 6(1). One is the requirement that the proceedings be "directly decisive" of civil rights.[30] Thus the provision has been held not to apply to ancillary court proceedings such as applications for interim relief and the enforcement of a judgment,[31] an award of procedural costs as subsidiary issue,[32] the

[28] [1990] 1 Ch. at 393. But see p. 63 below for criticism of this case.
[29] And indeed even if they cannot.
[30] *Le Compte, Van Leuven and De Meyere* v. *Belgium* (1982) 4 EHRR at para. 47.
[31] X v. *United Kingdom*, App. No 7990/77, 24 DR 57, para. 4 (1981).
[32] *Alsterlund* v. *Sweden*, App. No 12446/86, 56 DR 229 at 232 (1988).

re-opening of a case[33] and an application for leave to appeal.[34] Does this mean that Article 6 protects legal communications made for the purposes of some forms of proceedings but not others? It must be remembered, though, that the ECtHR, and now English courts, will look to the issue of whether the overall procedure has been fair.

There are also strong arguments for extending the principle of effective access to cover legal professional privilege in all of its forms. The rationale underlying cases such as *Golder* and *Airey* is an implicitly expansive one; there are few obvious limits to the concept of what makes access to a court "effective". One of the leading English texts on the Convention does not see *Golder* as limited in any such way: "[i]t did not matter that . . . he might have made contact with his solicitor other than by correspondence, that he might never have instituted court proceedings at all or that the applicant would have been able to have written to his solicitor before his claim became statute barred after his release from prison".[35] This accords with the general approach to Article 6 stated above that the ECtHR will give a generous interpretation to the Convention rights and not become fixed on austere legalism. As the Court has stated: "[i]n a democratic society within the meaning of the Convention, the right to a fair administration of justice holds such a prominent place that a restrictive interpretation of Article 6(1) would not correspond to the aim and purpose of that provision".[36]

Access to privileged materials

As well as requiring the non-disclosure of material for the protection of legal professional privilege, Article 6 also requires access to relevant materials in certain circumstances. This falls within the general provision of Article 6 for a fair trial. The ECtHR has developed a principle of "equality of arms" which covers disclosure of evidence. This principle holds that each party must be afforded a reasonable opportunity to present his case under conditions which do not place him at a substantial disadvantage in relation to his opponent.[37] The principle derives from the notion of a fair hearing but does not exhaust the concept of a fair hearing,[38] being only one aspect of it.

One of the early cases on the non-disclosure of evidence to the defence is *Jespers* v. *Belgium*.[39] Referring to Article 6(3)(b), the Commision held that:

[33] X v. *Austria*, App. No 7761/77, 14 DR 171 at 173–174 (1978).

[34] *Porter* v. *United Kingdom*, App. No 12972/87, 54 DR 207 at 208 (1987).

[35] D.J. Harris, M. O'Boyle and C. Warbick, *Law of the European Convention on Human Rights* (Butterworths, London, 1995) at 197.

[36] *Delcourt* v. *Belgium*, A 11 at para. 25 p. 15 (1970).

[37] *Neumeister* v. *Austria*, A 8 (1968); *Kaufman* v. *Belgium* (1986) 50 DR 98 at 115; *Haes and Gijsels* v. *Belgium* (1998) 25 EHRR 1 at para. 53.

[38] *Delcourt* v. *Belgium*, A 11 at para. 28.

[39] App. No. 8403/78 (1981) 27 DR 61.

> the word "facilities" (French "*facilités*") is qualified by the adjective "adequate" (French "*nécessaire*"). Despite the slight difference in meaning between the adjective in the French text and the one in the English text it is clear that the facilities which must be granted to the accused are restricted to those which assist or may assist him in the preparation of his defence.
>
> In short, Article 6, paragraph 3(b) recognises the right of the accused to have at his disposal, for the purposes of exonerating himself or of obtaining a reduction in sentence, all relevant elements that have been or could be collected by the competent authorities. The Commission considers that, if the element in question is a document, access to that document is a necessary "facility" ("*facilité nécessaire*") if, as in the present case, it concerns acts of which the defendant is accused, the credibility of testimony etc.[40]

On the facts the Commission found no violation of Article 6(1) and (3)(b), despite what in its entirety seemed to be an egregious miscarriage of justice, and in which the prosecution did not disclose to the defence evidence which might have been exculpatory. The Commission doubted the value of some of the evidence, and discounted the non-disclosure of other evidence largely on the basis that the defence could have gained access to the relevant witnesses if they had sought to. In *Edwards* v. *United Kingdom*[41] a failure by the prosecution to disclose material evidence supporting the defence's case[42] was an infringement of Article 6, but in the circumstances was remedied by the consideration of this material by the Court of Appeal as fresh evidence.[43]

However neither Article 6(1) nor Article 6(3)(b) gives rise to a general rule requiring disclosure of all relevant material to the defence in every circumstance. The general approach of the Commission and Court has been to evaluate the denial of access to evidence in the context of the fairness of the trial as a whole.[44] "It is normally for the national courts to decide whether it is necessary or advisable to call a witness. There are exceptional circumstances which could prompt the Court to conclude that the failure to hear a person as a witness was incompatible with Article 6".[45] Considerations include the importance of the specific items of evidence to which the claim relates and the conduct of the defence in relation to this evidence. For example, in *Bricmont* v. *Belgium*[46] the failure to hear certain witnesses did not infringe Article 6 as one had died during the litigation and the evidence of the other had not been sought by the defence. However the failure to call a third witness did infringe Article 6(3)(d) as no reasons had been given for the decision.[47]

[40] App. No. 8403/78 (1981) 27 DR 61, at paras. 57–58.

[41] (1993) 15 EHRR 417.

[42] The fact that the victim, who purported to have seen her assailant during the crime, did not pick him out during a photograph identification.

[43] *Ibid.*, at paras. 36–7.

[44] *Ibid.*, at para. 33.

[45] (1990) 12 EHRR 217 at para. 89.

[46] *Ibid.*

[47] Also see *McGinley* v. *United Kingdom* (1999) 27 EHRR 1 (no breach as it was not established that documents existed, and applicant had not activated the special disclosure procedure available).

Further, the legitimacy of non-disclosure of confidential material in criminal proceedings has been recognised. In assessing restrictions on Article 6 rights, the ECtHR has held, over the course of numerous cases, that in order to be valid such a restriction must not impair the very essence of Article 6, must have a legitimate aim and must be proportionate to its objectives.[48] For example, in *Tinnelly & Sons Ltd & Others and McElduff & Others* v. *United Kingdom*[49] the conclusive nature of a public interest immunity certificate and lack of judicial scrutiny of the claim to an overriding national security interest were considered to be a disproportionate restrictions on the right of access to the courts, and therefore a breach of Article 6.[50] The ECtHR pointed out that in other contexts judicial procedures had been modified in a manner which safeguarded national security concerns and still accorded adequate procedural justice.[51] It is also worth noting that in interpreting Article 6(3)(d) the ECtHR has been prepared to balance the public interest in securing convictions with the public interest in adequate protection of the accused. It conducts such a balancing exercise even though the Convention does not expressly provide for it.[52]

It is not difficult to see, when looking at the operation of legal professional privilege, that there are many situations in which one party's right to confidential legal communications conflicts with another party's right to access to evidence for the purposes of ensuring a fair trial, especially as legal professional privilege operates on material that is "relevant", within the meaning given to this term by English law. One of the most common examples of the resolution of such a conflict in the civil sphere can be found in the rules relating to implied waiver of the privilege, and in particular the rule that requires a former client suing his solicitor for professional negligence to disclose the contents of the legal communications that previously passed between them under the retainer.[53] One of the most remarkable examples from the criminal sphere is the cases which establish that the privilege may not be overridden even when it may exculpate a criminal accused.[54] These will be returned to later, once Article 8 has been added to the equation.

[48] *Barbera, Messegué and Jabardo* v. *Spain* (1989) 11 EHRR 360, para. 77); *Golder* v. *United Kingdom* n. 13 above; *Tinnelly & Sons Ltd & Others and McElduff & Others* v. *United Kingdom* (1999) 27 EHRR 249 at para. 72.

[49] n. 48 above.

[50] (1998) 27 EHRR 249 at paras. 72–79.

[51] *Ibid.*, at para. 78; also see *Rowe and Davis* v. *United Kingdom* (1998) 25 EHRR CD 118, an admissibility decision in which the denial of evidence to the defence on the basis of a public interest immunity certificate may have breached Art. 6.

[52] Compare Art. 8(2).

[53] See J. Auburn, "Generalised Rules Of fairness in Evidence Law" (2000) 63 *MLR* 104; also see J. Auburn, "Evidential Issues In Professional Negligence Litigation" (1999) 18 *Civil Justice Quarterly* 283.

[54] See chapter 9 below.

In the *General Mediterranean* case Toulson J said:

> Article 6 gives every person a right to a fair trial, but I do not accept that it follows as a general proposition that this gives a right to interfere with another person's right to legal confidentiality. If that were generally so, the right to legal confidentiality recognised by the court would be useless, since its very purpose is to enable a person to communicate with his lawyer secure in the knowledge that such communications cannot be used without his consent to further another person's cause. In the absence of a general right under Article 6 to make use of another person's confidential communications with his lawyer, I do not see how solicitors have a particular right to do so under that Article for the purpose of defending a wasted costs application.[55]

It is worth briefly pointing out, in relation to this case, that the Commission has held in an admissibility decision that wasted costs orders do not relate to the determination of civil rights or obligations and thus do not benefit from the protection of Article 6(1), nor do they involve the determination of a criminal charge.[56]

In contrast to the views of Toulson J quoted above, it may be questioned whether the entire approach of the English law to privilege derogations complies with the Convention. The English common law has taken an extremely strict approach to the development of the privilege rule. English courts have frequently stated that the settled rule of legal professional privilege is itself the result of a balancing process, which was performed once and for all in the sixteenth century, and that such arguments were either presumed or considered and rejected in the course of the development of the common law. Therefore once the rule applies, no further balancing process need be carried out. This line of authority is analysed in detail in Chapter 7 below. English privilege law may now have approached the state of the common law of hearsay in 1965, following the House of Lords' declaration in *Myers* v. *DPP*[57] that it would not countenance new exceptions to the hearsay rule. Some other Commonwealth courts, particularly in Australia, have taken a similarly strict approach to privilege exceptions.[58]

The very strict line taken by English courts against privilege derogations should now be reviewed in light of the need for access to material evidence which Article 6 provides for. This will be the case not just in relation to the egregious injustice perpetrated by the *Derby Magistrates* case (i.e. denial of potentially exculpatory evidence to an accused faced with a murder charge), but also in a wider context of civil litigation, such as the implied waiver issue in *Paragon*

[55] N. 3 above, at 695.

[56] *B* v. *United Kingdom*, App. No. 10615/83 (1984) 38 DR 213 at 214–15 (a wasted costs order involved the imposition of a sanction on the lawyer, but involved neither a criminal charge nor a determination of his civil rights and obligations).

[57] [1965] AC 1001; see in particular Lord Reid at 1021; discussed below at pp. 138–42.

[58] E.g. *Waterford* v. *Commonwealth* (1987) 163 CLR 54 at 64–5, 74, 98–9; *Carter* v. *The Managing Partner, Northmore Hale Davy & Leake* (1995) 183 CLR 121 at 128–9, 133–4, 137; *Australian Federal Police* v. *Propend Finance* (1997) 141 ALR 545 at 592, 609.

Finance. I have already stated my views on this latter issue at length elsewhere.[59] English courts cannot ignore claims to access to evidence brought under the ægis of Article 6. An evaluation of the specific rule denying such access must be undertaken, and the court must be satisfied that the existing rule falls within permitted derogations from Article 6 or reaches an appropriate compromise with competing Convention rights. It is also worth noting that any reformulation of the opposition to the recognition or extension of privilege derogations championed in *R.* v. *Derby Magistrates' Court, Ex parte B* and *Paragon Finance Plc* v. *Freshfields* will also have to take account of the instrumental goals served by the privilege, and the possible effect that changes to the law may have on that. This difficult issue will be addressed below in relation to Article 8.

SECTION II: ARTICLE 8

The Protected Interest and the Problem of Instrumental Goals

The concept of "private life" under Article 8 is much broader than the Anglo-American concept of "privacy". It relates not just to the secrecy of one's own information, but also to the "right to establish and develop relationships with other human beings".[60] "Private life" is one of the least clear interests protected by the Convention. The boundaries are vague and uncertain. Not everything which affects a person's physical or moral integrity is necessarily protected by Article 8.

One important point that should be stressed when considering the application and importance of the right to private legal communications under Article 8 is the fact that this realm of privacy exists not just for the intrinsic benefits associated with private legal communications in the particular instance, but also with the role Article 8 plays in promoting the instrumental goals underlying privacy, being open and candid relationships. However the consideration of the instrumental goals of the privacy of legal communications is by no means a simple matter. If the privilege exists to foster candid legal communications, then the best way to do this is to protect the confidentiality of the relationship as it currently exists, in the hope that this will influence the future behaviour of clients. However there is no automatic reason why we must demand that confidentiality exists or continues to exist in the present communications at issue in order to protect the goal of confidentiality in all future legal communications in general. This is because the intrinsic and instrumental goals are reliant on slightly different things. The intrinsic goal may be satisfied simply by the instant communication remaining undisclosed. The instrumental goal, on the other hand, works differently. It is dependent on the appearance or expectation, rather than

[59] J. Auburn, "Generalised Rules of fairness In Evidence Law" n. 53 above.

[60] *Niemietz* v. *Germany*, A 251-b at para. 29 (1992); also see X v. *Iceland*, (1976) 5 DR 86 at 87; *McFeeley* v. *United Kingdom*, (1980) 20 DR 44 at 91.

the reality, of confidentiality. As will be discussed below, by offering apparent confidentiality and encouraging communications which are then disclosed the privilege could theoretically make more evidence available than would have existed in its absence,[61] thereby still reaping the same ultimate benefits of confidential legal communications, without the attendant loss of evidence normally associated with it. Put simply, if confidentiality is breached in the instant case, but few people ever hear about it (much less change their behaviour as a result), and clients continue to entrust their lawyers with their secrets as they have always done, then the intrinsic value of privacy in the instant case may have been frustrated, but the same cannot necessarily be said of the instrumental goal.

It is clearly unfair to induce a person to part with information in this way, and obtaining information by such a deception cannot be justified on the ground that it is useful. However the issue is not whether lawyers should go forth and deliberately attempt to induce the imparting of secrets using false promises of confidentiality. The issue to be addressed is the weight to be attached to the interest in private legal communications, particularly when this interest conflicts with the interest in gaining access to relevant evidence for the purposes of ensuring a fair trial under Article 6. Therefore when evaluating the Article 8 right to private legal communications, one should weigh up both the intrinsic and instrumental goals advanced by such privacy, but not assume the weight to be attached to the instrumental goal; it is contentious and it needs to be properly evaluated.

There is an important distinction in English law between confidentiality and privilege. The English breach of confidence doctrine protects against unauthorised use of communications imparted in circumstances of confidence. It applies, *inter alia*, when a party who has gained access to confidential materials seeks to make use of them as evidence before a court. However there is an important limit on the English doctrine of breach of confidence relevant to the present issue.[62] The doctrine cannot stand in the way of legal compulsion, whether such compulsion comes in the form of a search warrant or an order for discovery, or an order that a particular question be answered by a reluctant witness. As will be discussed in greater detail in Chapter 4 below, it is this distinction between confidentiality and privilege which provides the basis for the special status of legal communications in English law, and the lesser protection offered to non-legal communications. If it were not for this limitation the equitable rule of confidentiality would become in part a *de facto* privilege.

Article 8 will affect both English privilege law and the scope of relief which English courts grant for breach of confidence, as can be seen from cases such as

[61] See pp. 94–6 below; also see pp. 74–5 below.

[62] There are of course other important limits to the doctrine, such as the requirement of a relationship of confidence, the rules that protection is lost once the information is made public, that there is no confidence in an iniquity and that a real public need for disclosure may displace the doctrine.

MS v. *Sweden*, discussed below at p. 54. However one difficulty here is that the relationship between these two rules of English common law and equity are by no means clear.[63] In particular, there appears to be a lacuna in the jurisdiction English courts purport to exercise when granting relief under the equitable breach of confidence doctrine in order to prevent the use of inadvertently disclosed documents in legal proceedings.[64] As stated above, the breach of confidence doctrine cannot be a bar to compelled disclosure. So, for example, the fact that confidential marital communications which would not be privileged or otherwise exempted from executive or curial compulsion have been disclosed in breach of confidence does not give those communications any greater protection from compulsion than they would otherwise have had. Yet English courts frequently apply the breach of confidence doctrine to evidence sought to be adduced in court, in reliance on the equitable doctrine rather than the privilege.

If Article 8 is thrust into this lacuna as an attempted remedy for it, this may cause more problems for the law than it solves. First, the relationship between the substantive limitations and derogations in Article 8 will have to be reconciled with the relief sought on inadvertent disclosure. Some of these issues are addressed below. Another, perhaps trickier, set of problems is that the conditions governing equitable relief will have to be reconciled with Article 8 itself, as well as possibly Article 6(1). While the conditions governing equitable relief are the subject of some dispute, two factors in particular may need to be re-examined: the knowledge of the recipient of the disclosed communication,[65] and the temporal limit courts have sought to place on equitable relief, barring relief either at the point where the material is actually adduced to the court,[66] or at some earlier point in time.[67] It is not immediately apparent why either of these factors should necessarily be taken into account. It may be possible to argue that the denial of relief for inadvertant disclosure on the ground that the recipient had no actual or constructive knowledge of the inadvertent nature of the disclosure, or because inspection has taken place, is a disproportionate infringement of the Article 8 right to private correspondence. Specifically, English courts have never properly articulated what detriment, if any, is caused to the person receiving the inadvertently disclosed communication by not being able to make use of it despite the fact that the above two factors may be in his favour. Put another way, just because the recipient is entirely innocent and had no

[63] See pp. 244–9 below.

[64] Note that r.31.20 of the Civil Procedure Rules 1998 provides for this eventuality, but only by leaving it to the unguided discretion of the judge. Previous drafts of the Rules contained guiding factors which attempted to reflect the existing law. See pp. 231–2 below

[65] See pp. 253–5 below . E.g. *Guiness Peat Ltd.* v. *Fitzroy Robinson Partnership* [1987] 2 All ER 716 at 731; *Derby* v. *Weldon (No. 8)* [1991] 1 WLR 73; *Hayes* v. *Dowding* [1996] PNLR 578 at 597–8 (overruled on another ground by *R.* v. *Bowden* [1999] 1 WLR 823).

[66] See pp. 255–8 below. *Goddard* v. *Nationwide Building Society* [1986] 3 All ER 264 at 271g; *Def American Inc* v. *Phonogram Ltd*, LEXIS 29 July 1994, *The Times*, 16 Aug. 1994.

[67] *Pizzey* v. *Ford Motor Co*, LEXIS 26 Mar. 1993, *The Times*, 8 Mar. 1993, *Independent*, 10 Mar. 1993 (once inspection had taken place); *Black & Decker* v. *Flymo*, *The Times* [1991] 1 WLR 753 at 755 (as soon as disclosed in an exchange of witness statements).

knowledge of the mistake, what unfairness would be occassioned to him by still giving force to the confidentiality of those documents? It may be that the only justifications for these conditions circumscribing relief are instrumental ones relating to the need for litigating parties and their representatives to be able to rely on each others' actions with certainty. However it remains to be seen whether such justifications are a sufficient basis for the derogation from Article 8 rights.

Justified Interferences and Proportionality

Article 8(2) provides that any interference with an Article 8(1) right must be "in accordance with the law". The English text of Article 8 could be read as requiring only that the interference does not contravene any domestic law. However the Court has read it as requiring positive authorisation in domestic law.[68] Therefore it is necessary to point to some specific legal rule which justifies interference. Privilege rules in civil litigation are mainly found in a combination of the Civil Procedure Rules 1998 and the common law. Both of these may provide a sufficiently certain basis for interferences.[69]

One area for concern in relation to the rule of law criterion is the amount of discretion given to judges to override the privilege, and the attendant uncertainty of the law as a result. The general test is that the law must be " formulated with sufficient precision to enable the citizen to regulate his conduct" and to foresee the consequences of his actions.[70] Where the law confers a discretion, it must also indicate with sufficient clarity the limits of that discretion.[71] In *Kruslin* v. *France*[72] a very broad provision in the Code of Criminal Procedure empowering an investigating judge to "take all investigative measures which he deems useful for establishing the truth" did not satisfy this criterion. The broad discretion conferred by the Civil Procedure Rules should not contravene the rule of law criterion. The discretion is exercised openly and judicially, rather than administratively; there is supervision of its exercise by means of judicial appeal; and the circumstances of intervention are so varied that a broad discretion is necessary.[73] *Kruslin* v. *France* is distinguishable on the basis, inter alia, that

[68] *Sunday Times* v. *United Kingdom* (1989–80) 2 EHRR 245 at paras. 46–49.

[69] On delegated legislation, see *Barthold* v. *Germany*, A 90 at paras. 45–46 (1985) (rules of professional conduct). On the English common law, see *Sunday Times* v. *United Kingdom* A 30 at paras. 50–53 (1979); also see *Kruslin* v. *France* (1990) 12 EHRR 547 at para. 29. But note the criticism based on the lack of democratic legitimacy of the common law made by D.J. Harris, M. O'Boyle and C. Warbick, *Law of the European Convention on Human Rights* (Butterworths, London, 1995) at 286.

[70] *Sunday Times case*, n. 68 above, at para. 49.

[71] *Silver* v. *United Kingdom* (1983) 5 EHRR 347 at para. 88.

[72] n. 69 above at para. 29.

[73] Compare *Olsson* v. *Sweden (No 1)* (1989) 11 EHRR 259, where a statute giving social workers a very broad discretion to intervene in child care matters was upheld on the grounds that the varied circumstances of intervention required a broad discretion and there were procedural safeguards in

under French law there is no formal doctrine of precedent, and so the administrative guidance and judicial decisions regarding telephone tapping were not sufficiently certain.

However it is worth noting that the instrumental goal of private legal communications, discussed both above and below, should have the effect that a higher degree of certainty than usual is required. The right may be an empty one if you do not know beforehand whether you will have it or not; knowledge of the application of the right may be just as important as actually having that right in theory. Some cautious comparisons may perhaps be drawn with sexuality cases such as *Dudgeon* v. *United Kingdom*[74] and *Norris* v. *Ireland*.[75] In both cases the state argued that the lack of prosecutions meant that the right was not being interfered with, and in *Norris* the state also said this meant the complainant was not a "victim" for the purposes of Article 25. Both arguments were rejected by the ECtHR on the basis that the existence of penalties was an effective interference with a person's private life.[76] Attacks on defamation laws operate in a similar way. That is, it is not just that individual defamation claims prevent the particular exercise of free expression in the instant case, but that the existence of defamation laws as a whole constitutes a threat which inhibits the free exercise of the right.

The next requirement for a valid interference with an Article 8 right is that the interference must be justified by a purpose in Article 8(2). These are "national security, public safety or the economic well-being of the country, or for the prevention of disorder or crime, for the protection of health or morals, or for the protection of the rights and freedoms of others". Where one party is seeking access to privileged materials the last of these justifications can be used. Most importantly, Article 8(2) states that the interference must be "necessary in a democratic society". The Court's case-law giving effect to this term is explained at length in the numerous texts on the Convention, and in learned academic articles. To those unfamiliar with the interpretation of the Convention, it may very briefly be noted that the Court has developed two concepts to explain this requirement: "proportionality" and the "margin of appreciation". The margin of appreciation is only part of the European Court's supervision of the Convention, and may not be applicable in a domestic legal context.[77] The principle of proportionality holds that the interference must be "proportionate to

place, including judicial supervision: see para. 62. Also see *Christie* v. *United Kingdom*, 78-a DR 119 at 133–5 where the Commission held that new safeguards introduced in response to *Malone* v. *United Kingdom* (1984) 7 EHRR 14 (i.e. the Interception of Communications Act 1995) were sufficient. These included the warrant of the Home Secretary, a complaints mechanism to an independent tribunal and overall supervision by an independent commissioner reporting to Parliament.

[74] (1981) 3 EHRR 40.

[75] A 142 (1988).

[76] Also see *Modinos* v. *Cyprus* (1993) 16 EHRR 485 at paras. 17–24; but compare *Seven Individuals* v. *Sweden*, (1982) 29 DR 104 at 113.

[77] See R. Singh, M. Hunt and M. Demetriou, "Is there a Role for the 'Margin of Appreciation' in National Law after the Human Rights Act?" [1999] *EHRLR* 15; for a different view see H. Fenwick, "The Right to Protest, the Human Rights Act and the Margin of Appreciation" (1999) 62 *MLR* 491 at 497–505.

the legitimate objective pursued".[78] This principle clearly applies in relation to Article 8(2)[79] and is also used as an implied limitation on Article 6.[80] A leading text describes it thus:

> (Proportionality) enables the Court to balance all the relevant interests and factual circumstances, and also to take into account the intensity of the infringement as well as the question whether the essence of the right invoked has been infringed. The scale the Court utilises seems to imply that the more far-reaching the infringement or the more essential the aspect of the right that has been interfered with, the more substantial or compelling the legitimate aims pursued must be.[81]

The ECtHR clearly values the right to private legal communications very highly. In *Campbell* v. *United Kingdom*[82] the Court confirmed a line of authorities establishing the importance of unimpeded legal communications, and in particular the correspondence of prisoners with their legal advisers. Note also that Article 6 supports the Article 8 interest. In *Niemitz* v. *Germany*[83] the Court noted that: "[w]here a lawyer is involved, an encroachment on professional secrecy may have repercussions on the proper administration of justice and hence on the rights guaranteed by Article 6 of the Convention".

It is also important to assess the interest in the interference and whether there is, in the terminology of the ECtHR, a "pressing social need" for it. Some accommodation must be made between the competing rights. When in Strasbourg the state's assessment of how that accommodation should be made has carried great weight. It is unlikely that English courts will take a deferential approach, particularly in the field of procedural law, an area in which judges are perfectly experienced to form their own views on the necessities of particular justifications. The interest advanced by an attempted derogation from the privilege will no doubt vary greatly, as will be shown below.

There are a number of areas in which the Commission and Court of Human Rights have sought to protect the privacy of legal communications under Article 8. The first relates to challenges to the opening of prisoners' correspondence by prison authorities. It was this line of cases that was used by Toulson J in *General Mediterranean Holdings SA* v. *Patel*. At first the Commission regarded such interferences as inherent in the detention of prisoners. However in *Silver* v. *United Kingdom*[84] the Commission rejected its doctrine of implied restrictions and conducted a more independent inquiry into the reasonableness of the interference, holding that such restrictions can be justified only on one of the grounds

[78] There are many such statements: e.g. *Olsson* v. *Sweden*, n. 73 above, at para. 67.

[79] E.g. *Ibid.*

[80] *Ashingdane* v. *United Kingdom*, (1985) 7 EHRR 528 at paras. 57–59; *Lithgow* v. *United Kingdom*, (1986) 8 EHRR 329.

[81] P. van Dijk and G.J.H. van Hoof, *Theory and Practice of the European Convention on Human Rights* (3rd edn., Kluwer, The Hague) 537.

[82] n. 16 above at para. 46.

[83] n. 60 above at para. 37.

[84] (1983) 5 EHRR 347.

in Article 8(2), which was not the case here. In *Campbell* v. *United Kingdom*[85] the interference was with correspondence to and from a lawyer and the Commission itself. It was held that such interferences were not necessary in a democratic society, as there was no compelling reason why letters from the Commission should be opened, and there were various alternatives available to the prison authorities which would have involved far less interference with prisoners' Article 8 rights. In *Schönenberger and Durmaz* v. *Switzerland*[86] it was similarly held not to be necessary to stop a letter from a lawyer to a remand prisoner advising the prisoner to exercise his lawful right to remain silent. These principles have already been applied in English domestic law in cases such as *R.* v. *Secretary of State for the Home Department, ex parte Leech*[87] and *R.* v. *Secretary of State for the Home Department, ex parte Simms.*[88]

However, this line of cases must be used carefully. There was no conflict with any right to disclosure of evidence; that is, with a right recognised by the Convention. In each case the state asserted a justification for the restriction, but there was no conflict between the Convention rights of the parties.[89] In addition, the right of correspondence may be of greater importance to prisoners than to others because letters and visits are prisoners' only methods of communication with the outside world, and they are living in dangerous surroundings where their rights and freedoms are heavily curtailed already.

A second group of cases concerns police surveillance and searches.[90] In *Halford* v. *United Kingdom*[91] the tapping of a police officer's telephone to gain information to use against her in a sex discrimination case against the police force was held to be a violation of Article 8 and not justified by law as it was outside the domestic United Kingdom legislation authorising such practices. In *Kopp* v. *Switzerland*[92] the tapping of a lawyer's telephone violated Article 8. There was a distinction in Swiss law between matters arising specifically out of the lawyer–client relationship and other matters, and the impugned order had stated that conversations relating to the lawyer's work should be disregarded. However the Court held that the distinction in domestic law was not sufficiently clear as it did not adequately indicate how the authorities' discretion was to be exercised. In *Niemitz* v. *Germany*[93] a police search of a lawyer's office for information about the whereabouts of a criminal suspect violated Article 8 on the

[85] n. 16 above.
[86] (1989) 11 EHRR 202 at para. 28.
[87] [1993] 4 All ER 539 at 554–5.
[88] n. 6 above, though this related more to Art. 10 than Art. 8.
[89] This point was made in *General Mediterranean Holdings SA* v. *Patel* [1999] 3 All ER at 691.
[90] In the civil realm, note *Chappell* v. *United Kingdom*, (1990) 12 EHRR 1 where it was held that an Anton Piller order was an interference with the other party's private life, but was justified by the need to protect the plaintiff's copyright. Further, the issue and execution of the order were not disproportionate to this end.
[91] (1997) 24 EHRR 523.
[92] (1999) 27 EHRR 91.
[93] (1993) 16 EHRR 97.

ground that professional relationships are within a person's private life.[94] However, as with the prison correspondence cases, these cases involved no conflict with any competing right to the disclosure of evidence.

There are a limited number of cases involving such a conflict with another individual's interest in the disclosure of confidential information. In *MS* v. *Sweden*[95] the Social Insurance Office, in dealing with a claim for compensation made to it, gained access to the claimant's medical records. The claimant argued that her rights under Article 8 had been breached, and that she was protected from disclosing this material, even though she had launched the compensation claim herself. The Court found that disclosure of the medical records had infringed Article 8, but that the interference served the legitimate aim of protecting the economic wellbeing of the country, as it was decisive for the allocation of public funds. Further, considering the scope and safeguards in the relevant Swedish law governing disclosure, the measure was not disproportionate. In *Z* v. *Finland*[96] a man was charged with rape and manslaughter for knowingly infecting people with HIV. The accused's wife attempted to prevent disclosure of her medical records to the court on privacy grounds and failed. Disclosure was a legitimate pursuit of the intersts in preventing crime or disorder, as well as protecting health and morals. The measures adopted were not disproportionate, although the domestic court's decision to publish details of the medical data was impugned on the ground that the court had not considered its discretion not to publish.

It is impossible to distil from these cases any strict rules. Much will depend on the weight which the court attaches to the comparative interests affected, and to the perceived proportionality of the interference to the aim pursued. In relation to this last aspect, there appears to be little proportionality in the existing English common law. An inadvertent disclosure can lead to loss of the privilege forever, even though the party seeking to set the privilege aside has little discernible need or justification for doing so other than good fortune. Conversely, the interest of a criminal accused in gaining access to exculpatory evidence will not justify overturning the privilege, even where the party seeking to restrict disclosure can claim no remaining interest to protect in doing so.[97]

There are two main points to bear in mind in relation to the proportionality of measures which impinge on the privilege. The first is that the general opposition that the English common law has taken to considering the recognition of new privilege derogations, or of extending existing ones, must now be called into question. This issue has been addressed above in the context of Article 6. The second point is that the issue should not be viewed as a choice between either upholding or overriding the privilege. A court faced with such a conflict

[94] Importantly in that case, the aplicant owned his office premises personally. On this issue now see *Halford* v. *United Kingdom*, n. 91 above.

[95] (1997) 3 BHRC 248.

[96] (1998) 25 EHRR 371.

[97] This is the effect of overruling *R.* v.*Ataou* [1988] 1 QB 898; see pp. 184–5 and 189–90 below.

of Convention rights could reconcile them by ordering disclosure to the court only, perhaps combined with examination in the first instance by counsel, or disclosure subject to other strict undertakings concerning the use of the material.[98] In the United States *in camera* review and use immunities have been proposed for similar purposes.[99] The protection for documents disclosed on discovery may prove to be important in justifying the interference with Article 8 rights in the Civil Procedure Rules. The ECtHR in *Kruslin* v. *France*[100] stressed the need to provide adequate safeguards against the abuse of disclosure. Alternatively, these lesser interferences could be used to support an argument that a total ban on the reception of such evidence is a disproportionate response to the problem. The ECtHR's approach in *Campbell* may be a useful comparison.[101] Where the privilege is asserted in criminal cases, with the effect of denying the accused access to potentially exculpatory evidence, the defence may seek a permanent stay of the criminal proceedings on the basis that it is not possible for the accused to have a fair trial. This has been suggested by a number of judges and has become an acceptable course of action following the denial of exculpatory evidence in many Commonwealth jurisdictions.[102] Alternatively, the prosecuting authority may decide that it either should not or cannot use the evidence, and hence have no alternative but to abandon the prosecution. In relation to forms of executive compulsion such as search warrants, the experience of countries such as Australia in developing agreed guidelines for the search of lawyers' premises may be a useful source of ideas about the proportionality or otherwise of English practices.[103]

CONCLUSION

The status and structure of English privilege law have been in a problematic state for some time, and courts never quite managed to reconcile the rule's extended application beyond the courtroom with what many perceive to be the

[98] Note there are already restrictions on the use which may be made of material disclosed on discovery. On the court's inherent power to impose restrictions on the use to be made of such material see S.B. McNicol, *The Law of Privilege* (Law Book Co, Sydney, 1992) at 40–2.

[99] F.D. Heather, "Attorney–Client Confidentiality: A New Approach" (1976) 4 *Hofstra LR* 685 at 691–7. On *in camera* disclosure see *United Jersey Bank* v. *Wolosoff* 483 A.2d 821 at 826 (NJ Super.AD) and references cited therein.

[100] n. 69 above at para. 34.

[101] (1993) 15 EHRR 137 at para. 48, considering less severe alternatives such as opening but not reading a prisoner's correspondence and opening it in the presence of the prisoner.

[102] See p. 96 below.

[103] E.g. see Law Council of Australia, "General Guidelines between the Australian Federal Police and the Law Council of Australia as to the Execution of Search Warrants on Lawyers' Premises", the text of which are printed in: (1986) 21(11) Australian Law News 21–4; as well as being set out in *Propend Finance Pty Ltd* v. *Commissioner, Australian Federal Police* (1995) 58 FCR 224 at 245–8; 128 ALR 657; also see K. Tronc, C. Crawford and D. Smith, Search and Seizure in Australia and New Zealand (Law Book Co., Sydney, 1996) chapter 10 and *Commissioner, Australian Federal Police* v. *Propend Finance Pty Ltd* (1997) 141 ALR 545 at 571, 581.

more modest doctrinal beginnings of the rule. The growing pains experienced by the English rule were also felt by its counterparts across the Commonwealth. The incorporation of the Convention into domestic law offers an opportunity to breathe new life into a rule that has ossified somewhat over the last decade. However the rule spans at least two Articles of the Convention, and supports competing interests in at least one of those Articles. The balancing of these different interests within the context of Convention rights will not be a simple task.

4

Confidentiality

INTRODUCTION

The following two chapters will attempt to set out the issues which determine the balance struck by the privilege. This chapter will focus on the demands of professional confidentiality. The next chapter will then deal with the countervailing demands: the importance of disclosure and the values underlying it. It will be argued that the rules of legal privilege do not play as crucial a role as traditionally thought in achieving the candid nature of legal communications, and that other factors, such as professional ethics rules, may be more important in practice in determining client attitudes and behaviour. Before turning to the practical relationship between confidentiality and legal communications it may be useful first to examine the theoretical importance of confidentiality, both apart from and within the privilege.

SECTION I: THEORETICAL IMPORTANCE OF CONFIDENTIALITY

Confidentiality of Itself

The confidentiality of legal communications is affected by at least four different doctrines, as follows:

(i) the competence of lawyers to testify[1];
(ii) the ethical duty of lawyers to respect the confidences of their clients;
(iii) the equitable breach of confidence doctrine, which protects communications made in circumstances of confidentiality;[2] and
(iv) legal professional privilege.

The last three of these rules all serve a similar purpose. The extent to which they differ and to which they overlap will be the central issue in this section.

[1] Judges and jurors are generally not competent to testify to the circumstances surrounding previous actions, but lawyers generally are.

[2] Generally see F. Gurry, *Breach of Confidence* (Clarendon Press, Oxford, 1984); R.G. Toulson and C.M. Phipps, *Confidentiality* (Sweet & Maxwell, London, 1996).

Confidentiality has been recognised as an implied term in certain professional contracts.[3] Equity also provides a duty of confidence.[4] This duty may be enforced by remedies such as an injunction, destruction or delivery up of documents, an account of profits or damages.[5] This equitable rule covers all confidential communications, not just those between lawyers and clients. An injunction may also be obtained to prevent the use of documents disclosed on discovery from being used for other purposes.[6] In this latter case, the public interest in the proper administration of justice and the encouragement of candour before the courts happens to coincide with the confider's own interest in the continued confidentiality of the information.[7]

The equitable rule is based on the public interest that confidences should be preserved, rather than the individual's private interest in confidentiality.[8] As such it can be "outweighed by some countervailing public interest which favours disclosure".[9] For example, in *W* v. *Egdell*[10] a psychiatric patient's interest in the confidentiality of a psychiatric report concerning him was overridden by the public interest in ensuring that mentally ill criminals who are still a danger to the community are not released prematurely. This allowed the patient's own private doctor to breach confidentiality by passing on his report to certain authorities, against the wishes of the patient. Where similar material is subject to legal professional privilege, its disclosure can be justified only by the recognition of a new exception to the privilege. The Canadian Supreme Court did exactly this in the case of *Smith* v. *Jones*,[11] a case which was not dissimilar on its facts to *W* v. *Egdell*.

[3] *Tournier* v. *National Provincial and Union Bank of England* [1924] 1 KB 461 (CA); *Parry-Jones* v. *Law Society* [1969] Ch. 7; *Cohen* v. *Cowles Media* 501 US 663, 111 S Ct 2513 (SC 1991); but see *Ott* v. *Fleishman* [1983] 5 WWR 721 at 728 (SC BC), where the confidentiality of legal communications was wrongly held to rest on an implied contractual term.

[4] *Attorney-General* v. *Guardian Newspapers (No 2)* [1988] 3 WLR 776 at 781 (HL); *Smith Kline & French Laboratories* v. *Department of Community Services* (1991) 99 ALR 679 (Fed. Ct.). This applies to barristers as well: *Carter* v. *Palmer* (1841) 1 D & Wal. 722 at 743, aff'd. 8 Cl & Fin 657, 8 ER 256 (HL).

[5] See R.G. Toulson and C.M. Phipps, n. 2 above, chap. 10.

[6] *Distillers Co (Biochemicals) Ltd* v. *Times Newspapers Ltd* [1975] QB 613 (QB); *Riddick* v. *Thames Board Mills* [1977] QB 881 (CA); *Sony Corporation* v. *Time Electronics* [1981] 1 WLR 1293 (Ch.); *Harman* v. *Home Office* [1983] 1 AC 280 (HL); *Crest Homes plc* v. *Marks* [1987] AC 829 (HL); P. Prescott, "Improper Uses of Discovery" (1978) 94 *LQR* 488; I. Eagles, "Disclosure of Material Obtained on Discovery" (1984) 47 *MLR* 284; A.A.S. Zuckerman, "Privilege and Public Interest" in C. Tapper, (ed.), *Crime, Proof and Punishment: Essays in Memory of Sir Rupert Cross* (Butterworths, London, 1984) 248 at 257; F. Gurry, n. 2 above, 169–70, 350; S.L. Phipson, M.N. Haward, P. Crane and D.A. Hochberg, *Phipson on Evidence* (14th edn., Sweet & Maxwell, London, 1990) 541–7.

[7] F. Gurry, n. 2 above, 350.

[8] Compare this with the way such a rule may operate within the context of human rights legislation, as discussed in the previous chapter.

[9] *Attorney-General* v. *Guardian Newspapers (the 'Spycatcher' case)* [1990] 1 AC 109 at 282 (HL).

[10] [1990] Ch. 359 (CA), noted in (1989) 52 *MLR* 715.

[11] (1999) 132 CCC (3d) 225.

At common law it is clearly established that confidentiality alone, in the absence of a relationship which the law values, is not a sufficient reason to justify non-disclosure to the court.[12] This principle is firmly entrenched in Commonwealth common law. However, confidentiality may still be a "very material consideration to bear in mind" in determining the application of public interest immunity.[13] As was seen in the previous chapter, Articles 6 and 8 of the European Convention on Human Rights provide some protection for confidential communications where such communications would not necessarily be protected by the English common law. And in the United Kingdom a statutory provision has extended the privilege to non-lawyers who provide advocacy, conveyancing or probate services as an authorised practitioner.[14]

The United States Supreme Court has shown a willingness to countenance common law privileges for other professions.[15] However this is rarely done in other common law jurisdictions.[16] The common law privileges for priests in Ireland[17] and Scotland[18] are notable exceptions. This is despite[19] the willingness of legislatures around the world to create statutory privileges for doctors,[20]

[12] *Alfred Crompton Amusement Machines Ltd* v. *Commissioners of Customs and Excise (No. 2)* [1974] AC at 433; *D* v. *NSPCC* [1978] AC 218, at 230, 238–9; *McGuiness* v. *Attorney-General (Vic.)* (1940) 63 CLR 73 at 102–3 (HCA); D. Unterhalter, "Notes and Comments: Professional Privilege and the Proof of Innocence" (1988) 105 *SALJ* 291 at 296–7; New Zealand Law Commission, *Evidence Law: Privilege*, Preliminary Paper No. 23 (New Zealand Law Commission, 1994) para. 9; also see S.B. McNicol, *Law of Privilege* (Law Book Company, Sydney, 1992) 3–4 and the cases cited therein.

[13] *Alfred Crompton Amusement Machines Ltd* v. *Commissioners of Customs and Excise (No. 2)* [1974] AC at 433 per Lord Cross; *D* v. *NSPCC* [1978] AC at 239.

[14] S. 63 of the Courts and Legal Services Act 1990 (UK).

[15] E.g. *Jaffee* v. *Redmond* 116 S Ct 1923 (SC 1996) (psychiatrists); also see T.J. Molony, "Is the Supreme Court Ready to Recognize Another Privilege?" (1998) 55 *Wash and Lee LR* 247 (discussion of possible accountant's privilege).

[16] For cases on the common law's denial of privilege to other professional relationships see C. Tapper, *Cross and Tapper on Evidence* (8th edn., Butterworths, London, 1995) 494–8, Phipson (1990), n. 6 above, para. 20–13; S.B. McNicol, n. 12 above, 3–7 and Zeffertt, *The South African Law of Evidence* (4th edn., Butterworths, Durban, 1988) 266–7. Also see *D* v. *NSPCC* [1978] AC at 245. It is arguable that the priests' privilege was recognised in England before the Reformation: see *Cook* v. *Carroll* [1945] IR 515 at 517 (HC). However *R* v. *Hay* (1860) 2 F & F 4, 175 ER 933, does not support such a privilege, as the issue there was that the priest was asked about a fact rather than a communication. The Canadian Supreme Court seems to be moving towards the recognition of privileges for other professions, based on the Wigmore criteria: see the dissenting judgment of L'Heureux-Dubé J in *A. (L.L.)* v. *B. (A.)* [1995] 4 SCR 536 at 569–85.

[17] *Cook* v. *Carroll* [1945] IR at 519. Though query whether it would apply in criminal cases, as current authority appears limited to civil litigation.

[18] This is a contentious issue in Scotland and there are a large number of cases. An early case is *HM Advocate* v. *David Ross* (1859) 3 Irvine 434 and a modern one is *HM Advocate* v. *Daniels*. The latter case is unreported, but an interesting description of the issue and proceedings can be found in J. Beltrami, The Defender (W & R Chambers Ltd, 1980) 186–91. The debate is set out in I.D. Macphail, *Evidence 1987* (Law Society of Scotland, Edinburgh, 1987) 18.38–18.40 and in D. Field, *The Law of Evidence in Scotland* (W. Green, Edinburgh, 1988) 265.

[19] In *Gruenke* v. *R.* [1991] 3 SCR 263 (SC) the Canadian Supreme Court, in refusing to recognise a common law privilege for priests, rejected an argument that the wide statutory recognition of the privilege around the world suggested the common law should take a similar approach. The US Supreme Court took the opposite approach in *Jaffe* v. *Redmond* 116 S Ct. at 1930.

[20] E.g. Rule 503(b) of the *Uniform Rules of Evidence* (USA); s. 32 of the Evidence Amendment Act (No 2) 1980 (NZ); s. 127 of the Evidence Act 1995 (Aust.); s. 28(2) of the Evidence Act 1958 (Vic.).

clergy,[21] journalists[22] and a host of other professions,[23] although it should be noted that many of these statutory provisions are limited to civil litigation only. In general though, outside North America courts do not seek to protect the confidences of professionals.

This is subject to one qualification, which is that there may be a general judicial discretion not to require answers that may betray confidences, even though the evidence is otherwise relevant and admissible. Such a discretion probably exists in England[24] and Scotland,[25] though not Australia,[26] and possibly not in South Africa.[27] New South Wales now has legislation providing for a "professional confidential relationship privilege".[28] This permits the withholding of evidence arising from a confidential communication made in the course of a relationship in which the confidant was acting in a professional capacity and gave an express or implied obligation that he would not disclose the contents of the communication.[29] This statutory privilege also applies to legal communications and is in some ways wider than legal professional privilege.[30]

[21] Every US jurisdiction has some statutory recognition for this privilege. For a useful list see either M.H. Mitchell, "Must Clergy Tell?" (1987) 71 *Minn LR* 723 at 734, n. 56 or *Jaffe* v. *Redmond* 116 S Ct. at 1929 n.11; s. 6 of the Evidence Act 1970 (Newfoundland) (RSN 1970 C.115); art. 9 para. 2; Charter of Rights and Freedoms 1990 (Quebec) (RSQ 1990 C–12); s. 31 of the Evidence Amendment Act (No 2) 1980 (NZ); s. 127 of the Evidence Act 1995 (Aust.); s. 3 of the Evidence (Religious Confessions) Amendment Act 1989 (NSW).

[22] Over half the states of the USA have such a statutory privilege, which may also have a constitutional basis depending on one's interpretation of *Branzburg* v. *Hayes* 408 US 665; also see s. 10 of the Contempt of Court Act 1981 (UK).

[23] E.g. accountants (Idaho, Nevada); patent attorneys (UK, New Zealand, Japan); social workers (most American states); marriage counsellors (New Zealand); counsellors or doctors treating victims of sexual assault (Victoria, New South Wales); nurses (Oregon); school teachers (Oregon); dentists (Japan, Quebec); pharmacists (Japan, Quebec); veterinary surgeons (Quebec). Further, constitutional privacy rights are sometimes interpreted as conferring professional privileges: e.g. see *Frenette* v. *Metropolitan Life Insurance* [1992] 1 SCR 647 (SC), creating a doctor–patient privilege from the privacy right in the Quebec *Charter*.

[24] *Attorney-General* v. *Clough* [1963] 1 QB 773 at 792 (CA) (in a special case the court may find that a journalist is immune from testifying on the grounds of public policy); *Attorney-General* v. *Mulholland* [1963] 2 QB 477 at 489–90, 492 (CA) (the question must be whether the evidence is both relevant and necessary, and there may be other requirements); *British Steel Corp.* v. *Granada Television Ltd* [1981] AC 1096 at 1174–5, 1184 and 1203 (as the remedy is equitable it is therefore discretionary, so it may be that on other occasions the public interest militates against disclosure); *D* v. *NSPCC* [1978] AC at 227.

[25] *HM Advocate* v. *Airs* [1975] JC 64 at 70, SLT 177 at 180 (Ct. of Justiciary) (requirements of relevance and necessity).

[26] *McGuiness* v. *Attorney-General of Victoria* (1940) 63 CLR at 102–3; *Re Buchanan* (1964) 65 SR (NSW) 9 at 11 (NSW SC); *McAuliffe* v. *McAuliffe* (1973) 4 ACTR 9 at 10–11 (ACT SC), though only *Re Buchanan* was decided in light of *Clough* and *Mulholland* and expressly dealt with the issue of discretion.

[27] R. v. *Parker* 1965 (4) SA 47 (Southern Rhodesia App. Div.); D. Zeffertt, *The South African Law of Evidence* (2nd ed., Butterworths, Durban, 1988) 267 ("dubious doctrine").

[28] Evidence Amendment (Confidential Communications) Act 1997 (NSW), inserting a new Division 1A into the Evidence Act 1995 (NSW).

[29] See R.J. Desiatnik, *Legal Professional Privilege in Australia* (Prospect Media, Sydney, 1999) chap. 11.

[30] *Ibid.*, at 175.

Importance of Legal Communications

The lawyer–client relationship is the "pivotal or central nerve of the legal system itself".[31] It helps to bring relevant information before the court, ensures clients know and remain within the bounds of the law and is the instrument through which substantive rights are satisfied.[32] Even if such benefits are difficult to quantify, there is no reason to assume that they are small.[33]

In contrast, the New Zealand Law Commission has criticised the sacred nature of lawyer–client communications, saying that this is "no longer a satisfactory answer to current social and ethical issues".[34] The assumed "weightiness" of legal communications, central to Wigmore's thesis,[35] has been denounced as arbitrary and simply a function of lawyers' self-interest.[36]

Communications between other professionals and their clients have very strong claims to confidentiality.[37] The profession which may perhaps be most deserving of the support of a privilege rule is that of the psychiatrist, where the communications are of a highly personal character and are essential to the effective performance of the professional skill.[38]

One argument raised in favour of the special place of legal communications and advice is that lawyers play a unique role, serving as the means by which individuals relate to and assert their rights against other individuals and the state. Other fiduciary or confidential relationships are not exclusively concerned with

[31] S.B. McNicol, n. 12 above, 6. Unfortunately there is not the room in this book to explore Bentham's strong criticisms of the supposed importance of legal advice. On this see M. Freedman, "Judge Frankel's Search for Truth" (1975) 123 *U. Pa. LR* 1060 and F.C. Zacharias, "Rethinking Confidentiality" (1989) 74 *Iowa LR* 351 at 366–7. For a defence of Bentham, see J. Thomas-Fishburn, "Attorney–Client Confidences: Punishing the Innocent" (1990) 61 *U Col LR* 185 at 195. This discussion will not examine the far more contentious issue of the value of the contribution made by the profession as a whole. For competing views on this latter issue compare L. Kaplow and S. Shavell, "Legal Advice about Information to Present in Litigation" (1989) 102 *Harv. LR* 1685 at 600 (the social value of lawyers is ambiguous and debateable) with S. Bundy and E. Elhauge, "Do Lawyers Improve the Adversary System?" (1991) 79 *Calif. LR* 313 at 408.

[32] C. Fried, "The Lawyer as Friend: The Moral Foundation of the Lawyer–Client Relation" (1976) 85 *Yale LJ* 1060; Note, "Attorney–Client Privileve for Corporate Clients: The Control Group Test" (1970) 84 *Harv. LR* 424 at 425.

[33] Comment, "Developments in Law-Privileged Communications" (1985) 98 *Harv. LR* 1450 at 1474.

[34] New Zealand Law Commission, n. 12 above, para. 132.

[35] Wigmore justified the lawyer's privilege while denying the doctor's privilege largely by asserting the importance of legal communications: J.H. Wigmore and J.T. McNaughton, *Evidence in Trials at Common Law* (Little, Brown & Co., Boston, 1961) viii at para. 2285.

[36] E.M. Morgan, "The Evolving Concept of Professional Responsibility" (1977) 90 Harv LR 702 at 738, M. Frankel, "The Search for Truth Continued: More Disclosure, Less Privilege" (1982) 44 *U Col LR* 51 at 55, 62. For the same reasoning applied across the spectrum of professional privileges in the USA, see M. Reutlinger, "Policy, Privacy and Prerogatives" (1973) 61 *Calif LR* 1353 at 1379.

[37] E.g. see J.T. Noonan, "The Purposes of Advocacy and the Limits of Confidentiality" (1966) 64 Mich. LR 1485.

[38] See *Jaffee* v. *Redmond* 116 S Ct 1923. Also see R. Slovenko, "Psychiatry and a Second Look at the Medical Privilege" (1960) 6 *Wayne LR* 175; D.W. Louisell, and K. Sinclair, "Reflections on the Law of Privileged Communications" (1971) 59 *Calif LR* 30.

rights enforceable in law.[39] Further, lawyers play a dual role. They are not just private advisers. They also have a public function, as officers of the court with duties to it as well.

However the work of other professionals may have an important public as well as private role.[40] Further, the public function of other professionals has been used as a reason for denying them a privilege. For example the doctor in the breach of confidence case of *W* v. *Egdell*[41] was held to have a duty to the public which necessitated disclosure, as well as a duty to his patient.[42] Similar public duties are also shown by cases such as *Tarasoff* v. *Regents of the University of California*.[43] It is difficult to see why the doctor–patient communications of a doctor preparing a report for a lawyer are protected by the powerful privilege rule, but the same communications prepared solely for the purposes of treatment are not protected in a similar manner.[44] The public function argument is an insufficient reason for granting lawyers a special rule which is denied to other professionals with equally important public functions.

Another reason why the confidentiality of legal communications should be given special protection may be that the work of lawyers occurs in environments that are usually more proximate to sources of judicial or executive compulsion, and so inevitably carries with it a more immediate danger of compulsion at some later stage.[45] That is, when people go to lawyers they will have the fear of court or executive compulsion foremost in their minds, whereas when people go to other professional advisers they may have a fear of other forms of disclosure in their minds, but will rarely be thinking of potential compulsion as their main concern. One text has explained the argument thus:

> It is in the nature of a lawyer's work that those who come for his advice may well be involved ultimately in litigation, and the more likely that is, the more the client will be aware of the possibility. The frankness with which a client discloses his case to a lawyer is intimately associated with the legal process. This is simply untrue of medical advice. A medical adviser will equally require openness from his patients; but it will only be in highly exceptional cases that either doctor or patient would give any thought to the possibility of disclosure of what passed between them under compulsory process of law.[46]

[39] G.L. Peiris, "Legal Professional Privilege in Commonwealth Law" (1982) 31 *ICLQ* 609 at 610. This was one of the main bases for the denial of a common law privilege to priests in Canada in *Gruenke* v. *R.* [1991] 3 SCR 263.

[40] E.M. Morgan, "Suggested Remedy for Obstructions to expert Testimony by Rules of Evidence" (1943) 10 *Uni Chicago LR* 285 at 290–1, discussing the important role doctors play in promoting public health; also see D.W. Louisell and K. Sinclair, n. 38 above, 51–5.

[41] [1990] Ch 359.

[42] *Ibid.*, at 392.

[43] 551 P.2d 334 (Calif. SC 1976). Also see nn. 94–6 below.

[44] Compare *Smith* v. *Jones* (1999) 132 CCC (3d) 225.

[45] E.g. S. Bundy and E. Elhauge, n. 31 above.

[46] Phipson, n. 6 above, 502.

However the proximity of court proceedings varies within each professional relationship. Some legal communications occur in an environment that is far less proximate to potential future litigation than others. Conversely, the work of other professions may often be extremely proximate to litigation. In *Baker* v. *Campbell* Mason J queried why communications made for the purposes of seeking legal advice but when litigation is not contemplated should be privileged, when communications with other professionals made when litigation is contemplated are not so privileged.[47]

For example, medical care following a crime, workplace injury, road accident or any accident which involves the mere possibility of liability of another person will be so proximate. Similarly, much of the work of an investigative journalist is extremely proximate to potential court proceedings or other investigative compulsion. An important role of investigative journalism is to perform a non-governmental investigative function in relation to issues that are deemed worthy of investigation. By nature such work is likely to cover matters that are also the subject of judicial or administrative investigation. Finally, the work of psychiatrists will frequently be done against a backdrop of possible litigation or administrative compulsion.[48] In these cases "it is obvious that the patient is likely to have the possibility of litigation in mind".[49]

With these considerations in mind, it is illuminating to see the way this issue is dealt with by the courts. In *W* v. *Egdell* counsel seeking to enforce confidentiality over a psychiatrist's report argued that this was necessary, given the fact that such communications are made against the backdrop of tribunal review of the patient's case.[50] However Scott J rejected this argument, stating that:

> I do not think that this answer has much weight. The possibility of a lack of frankness must always be present when a psychiatric examination takes place. An experienced psychiatrist would, I think, expect to be able to detect it. And the lack of frankness itself would constitute material of interest to the psychiatrist.[51]

It would be interesting to see the reaction of the legal community if a judge dismissed a claim to privilege on the basis that "the possibility of a lack of frankness must always be present" and that an experienced lawyer should be able to detect this. Such arguments have no place in determining the need to protect the confidentiality of communications.

[47] (1983) 153 CLR at 75.

[48] M. Guttmacher and H. Weihofen, "Privileged Communications Between Psychiatrist and Patient" (1952) 28 *Indiana LR* 32 at 33–4; e.g. will contests in which the testator's mental competence is in issue; cases of individuals seeking treatment for "perverse sexual behaviour" (*ibid.*, at 34).

[49] *Ibid.*; also see Slovenko, n. 38 above, 187.

[50] [1990] 1 Ch. 359 at 393 (upheld on appeal to the Court of Appeal, see *ibid.* at 405). Evidence showed that independent psychiatric reports were used in about 80% of the cases reviewed by mental health tribunals.

[51] *Ibid.*

Place of Confidentiality in Privilege

"Confidence lies at the very heart of legal professional privilege".[52] There is no doubt that confidentiality is both an essential value the privilege seeks to protect and, from the very start, fundamental to the practical operation of the rule.[53] As will be shown below in Chapter 10, confidentiality plays a role in determining the application of the privilege in three ways: the substantive requirement of confidentiality; waiver by loss of confidentiality; and effective derogations from the waiver rule such as selective disclosure and limited waiver.

However the strength of the privilege may not seem to reflect the importance of the doctrine, as so often espoused by Commonwealth courts. The privilege gives only limited protection to client confidences. It is a bar only to compulsory process.[54] The rule does not protect confidentiality completely, as a rule of inadmissibility would do. This is shown most clearly in the issue of inadvertently disclosed privileged documents, dealt with in Chapters 10 and 12. There it will be shown that, although judges greatly value the continued confidentiality of legal communications, the privilege itself may be insufficient to ensure such protection.

The apparent inconsistency between the value of confidentiality as a goal and the court's ability to protect it may in small part be explained by distinguishing between confidentiality as a goal to be achieved and confidentiality as a requirement in the recognition of the privilege. The privilege exists to foster candid legal communications. The best way to do this is to protect the confidentiality of the relationship as it currently exists, in the hope that this will influence the future behaviour of clients. However there is no automatic reason why we must demand that confidentiality exists or continues to exist in the present communications at issue in order to protect the goal of confidentiality in all future legal communications in general.

This argument also raises the issue of the importance of confidentiality in the practical maintenance of the rule and the achievement of its goals; an issue that will now be addressed in the second part of this chapter.

[52] C. Tapper, *Cross and Tapper on Evidence* (8th edn., Butterworths, London, 1995) 474, citing *Ventouris* v. *Mountain* [1991] 3 All ER 472 at 475 (CA).

[53] E.g. it is a requirement in the most frequently cited formulation of the rule: see J.H. Wigmore, n. 35 above, para. 2285.

[54] T.R.S. Allan, "Legal Privilege and the Principle of Fairness in the Criminal Trial" (1987) *Crim LR* 449 at 456; *Wilson* v. *Rastall* (1792) 4 TR 753, 100 ER 1283; *Sandford* v. *Remington* (1793) 2 Ves. Jun. 189, 30 ER 587.

SECTION II: PRACTICAL IMPORTANCE OF CONFIDENTIALITY; THEORIES OF PRACTICE

Speculative Nature of Confidentiality Benefits

The remainder of this chapter will focus on an assessment of the role and effectiveness of confidentiality in maintaining good lawyer–client relations. The practical operation of the privilege can tentatively be summed up in two possibly contradictory points. First, the benefits of the privilege in terms of candid legal communications are not susceptible to reliable measurement, and so we can never properly know what benefit the privilege brings. Secondly, most practising lawyers will defend the privilege to the hilt and are usually opposed to any attempt to weaken it in favour of competing interests. These two propositions may seem inconsistent.

To express this first point in another way, the confidentiality side of the privilege equation will usually be a benefit that is speculative in nature. This may be in contrast to a detriment, in the form of evidence denied, that is real and immediate. To quote from a well known passage from Wigmore's treatise: "[i]ts benefits are all indirect and speculative; its obstruction is plain and concrete".[55] The problem here is one of trying to conduct a balancing of interests at the same level of abstraction. The danger and error that result from not doing this are analysed in Chapter 6.

The rule of privilege, like many evidential rules, is essentially built on the notion of systemic harm. That is, we must safeguard confidentiality in order to prevent harm to the system of legal communications at large. It may often be difficult for laymen to accept the validity of such an approach; foregoing known and reliable evidence for the benefit of an abstract principle. Such scepticism may be present whenever evidential rules bar the use of clear and uncontroverted evidence for the sake of a broader principle that may not even have any application in the case at hand. Indeed, such scepticism may be present whenever it appears that an unjust or unduly harsh result has been achieved in the case at hand for the sake of the maintenance of a broader rule.

Equally, there may be a tendency among lawyers to dismiss any attacks on the privilege which are framed in this fashion. Lawyers are confident that their experience in dealing with clients shows that the abstract principle behind the privilege holds true in practice. Thus it may be partly *because* the privilege is, on one level, counter-intuitive, and so demands justification from those who use it, that it has drawn such stern defence from the legal profession.

However there may be more to the layman's intuition than practising lawyers give credit for. If the benefits to confidentiality resulting from the privilege are

[55] J.H. Wigmore, n. 35 above, 542; also see Note, "The Lawyer–Client Privilege" (1961) 56 *Nw ULR* 235 at 257: "all of the policy arguments in favor of the privilege are tenuous, and they all rest upon the dubious assumption that enough clients actually know of the privilege so that it has more than a negligible effect in encouraging full disclosure".

unknown, there is no reason to assume they are slight. At the same time, there is no reason to assume that such benefits would be completely destroyed by further incursions into the over-stated sanctity of the privilege.

An example of this may be seen in a recent case on the privilege heard by the United States Supreme Court: *Swidler & Berlin* v. *United States*.[56] This was an appeal arising from the Independent Counsel's inquiry into, among other matters, the sacking of members of the White House travel office and the death of Vincent Foster. The Independent Counsel sought disclosure of documents previously owned by Foster while he was alive, and argued before the Supreme Court that the privilege should cease on the death of the client where the material was required for a criminal investigation. The Independent Counsel argued that such an exception would not materially affect the confidence of clients in their lawyers. However the Supreme Court rejected this argument, stating that:

> [w]hile the arguments against the survival of the privilege are by no means frivolous, they are based in large part on speculation—thoughtful speculation, but speculation nonetheless—as to whether posthumous termination of the privilege would diminish a client's willingness to confide in an attorney.[57]

As Ho points out, it was equally speculative of the Supreme Court to assume that disclosure in such circumstances *would* have a detrimental effect on client candour.[58]

It should be noted that the following discussion will necessarily be restricted to legal advice privilege and not litigation privilege. There are no recorded empirical studies on the effectiveness of litigation privilege,[59] and few academic attempts at evaluation of the effect of the rule.[60]

Chilling Effect Theory

The argument often raised for absolute confidentiality is that without it people would be reluctant to speak openly and honestly with their lawyers ("the chilling effect"). For example Knight-Bruce V-C in *Pearse* v. *Pearse* referred to the "general evil of infusing reserve and dissimulation, uneasiness, and suspicion and fear, into those communications which must take place".[61] In the *Carter* case Deane J said that:

> Ultimately much depends upon one's assessment of the extent of the detriment to the efficacy of legal professional privilege which would be likely to result from the pro-

[56] 118 S Ct 2081.

[57] *Ibid.*, at 2087.

[58] H.L. Ho, "Legal Professional Privilege After Death of Client" (1999) 115 *LQR* 27 at 29.

[59] Note, "Attorney–Client and Work Product Protection in a Utilitarian World: An Argument for Recomparison" (1995) 108 *Harv. LR* 1697, 1701 n.32.

[60] For one such discussion, see D.C. Wells, "The Attorney Work Product Doctrine and Carry-Over Immunity: An Assessment of Their Justifications" (1986) 47 *U. Pitt LR* 675 at 683.

[61] (1846) 1 De G. & Sm at 28–9, 63 ER at 957.

posed curtailment of the protection which it affords. In my view, that detriment could well be significant.[62]

In the *Derby Magistrates* case *amicus curiae* argued for a non-absolute rule with balancing in exceptional circumstances. Lord Taylor CJ rejected this on the ground that "once any exception to the rule is allowed, the client's confidence is necessarily lost".[63] Lawyers may also be duty-bound to recite the court's powers on disclosure,[64] and this may worsen the chilling effect.[65] This form of argument is used in other areas of law, such as the rule protecting journalists' sources[66] and the restrictive defamation rule for public figures.[67]

Critique of the Chilling Effect Theory: The Chicken Little View

In argument in the *Carter* case the chilling effect theory was described as the "sky is falling approach".[68] There are many reasons to doubt whether the sky would fall and the administration of justice be severely damaged if further exceptions to the privilege were recognised.[69] First, the privilege has existed for centuries. Its scope and operation have changed over this time, yet there is nothing to suggest that this has had any effect on lawyer-client relations. There are already many exceptions to the privilege. As Lindsay J noted (unusually for recent English judges) in *Saunders* v. *Punch Ltd*:

> it is possible to exaggerate the force of the argument that once *any* exception to the general rule is allowed the client's confidence is necessarily lost . . . no one suggests that on . . . account [of *R.* v. *Cox and Railton*] clients have been inhibited in their dealings with legal advisers.[70]

Another example is the possible exception for criminal exculpatory evidence, discussed in Chapter 9 below. The decision in *R.* v. *Barton* was accepted by

[62] *Carter* v. *The Managing Partner, Northmore Hale Davy & Leake* (1995) 183 CLR at 139. Also see Brennan J at 129; McHugh J at 164.

[63] *R* v. *Derby Magistrates' Court, ex p. B* [1996] 1 AC at 508.

[64] *Carter* v. *The Managing Partner, Northmore Hale Davy & Leake* (1995) 183 CLR at 139; New Zealand Law Commission, n. 12 above, at para. 153.

[65] However J. Thomas-Fishburn, "Attorney–Client Confidences: Punishing the Innocent" (1990) 61 *U Col LR* 185, sees no problem with a lawyer advising his clients as to the limits of confidentiality.

[66] E.g. see *Goodwin* v. *United Kingdom* (1996) 22 EHRR 123 at para. 39; compare the attitude of the House of Lords in the same litigation: *X Ltd* v. *Morgan Grampian (Publishers) Ltd* [1991] AC 1; especially see Lord Bridge at 48–9.

[67] E.g. *New York Times Co* v. *Sullivan* 376 US 282 (1964); *Theophanous* v. *Herald & Weekly Times Ltd* (1994) 182 CLR 104.

[68] Mr Barker QC, High Court of Australia, transcript, 15 Nov. 1994 at 21.

[69] Compare R.A. Sedler and J.J.Simeone, "The Realities of Attorney–Client Confidences" (1963) 24 *Ohio St LJ* 1 at 3: "[c]ontrary to the implied assertions of the evidence authorities, the heavens will not fall if all relevant and competent evidence cannot be admitted."

[70] [1988] 1 WLR at 996.

texts, largely without doubt or qualification,[71] as representing the law for many Commonwealth countries for over 20 years. If this was thought to be the law then legal advisers should have been acting on this and the lawyer–client relationship should have been affected accordingly. There is no reason to believe that the candid nature of legal communications in Commonwealth countries was adversely affected by the pre-1995 state of authorities. Nor does it seem to have been affected in Australia by the adoption of a *Barton*-type exception in section 123 of the Australian Evidence Act 1995. The views of judges such as McHugh J, who warned that such an exception "could have serious consequences for the general administration of justice",[72] and commentators such as Dr Desiatnik, who described section 123 as "a devastating blow to the concept of privilege",[73] must now be viewed with some scepticism. The fact that the entire prrivilege has not collapsed as soon as section 123 came into force shows that lawyer–client communications are a more robust phenomenon that previously thought.

It is worth noting that similar arguments were raised when modern civil discovery procedures were contemplated. Then it was argued that wide disclosure requirements would undermine the adversary system.[74] Such arguments have been used in the United States to defend the psychotherapy patient's privilege,[75] which is firmly entrenched there in all states.[76] One American commentator has pointed to English and Canadian law to show that the psychiatric profession can survive without such a privilege.[77] English judges have had no problems with quickly rejecting these arguments when raised for professionals such as psychiatrists[78] or journalists.[79] Finally, it may be worth noting American concerns about the proposed abolition of the privilege for marital communications. At the time such proposals were being considered one commentator warned that:

[71] The closest any text came to suggesting this was the use of the word "may" in the fourth Australian edition of Cross on Evidence: see D. Byrne and J.D. Heydon, *Cross on Evidence: Fourth Australian Edition* (Butterworths, Sydney, 1991) at 25,118. In the *Carter* case it was argued that this showed that *Barton* was not accepted as authoritative. However this reading of the fourth Australian edition does not sit well with the description of *Barton* as "the rule".

[72] *Carter* v. *The Managing Partner, Northmore Hale Davy & Leake* (1995) 183 CLR at 164.

[73] R.J. Desiatnik, n. 29 above, at 156; also predicting that the message of s.123 that the privilege is not too well established to be altered "will reverberate in many portals of the law" (*ibid.*).

[74] For a long list of arguments against pre-trial discovery, see W.A. Glaser, *Pretrial Discovery and the Adversary System* (Russell Sage Foundation, New York, 1968) 12.

[75] M. Guttmacher and H. Weihofen, n. 48 above 33–5, but note the qualification for criminal cases at 36; Slovenko, n. 38 above, at 187–8.

[76] Applying by statute in all states: see *Jaffee* v. *Redmond* 116 S Ct. at 1929 n.11.

[77] See D.W. Shuman and M.S. Weiner, "The Privilege Study: An Empirical Examination of the Psychotherapist–Patient Privilege" (1982) 60 *North Carolina LR* 893 at 894–5.

[78] E.g. Scott J. in *W* v. *Egdell* [1990] 1 Ch. at 393.

[79] *British Steel Corp.* v. *Granada Television* [1981] AC at 1184, *per* Viscount Dilhorne: "we were told . . . of the dire consequences . . . likely to follow if disclosure were ordered . . . I find it difficult to accept that those consequences will follow".

> if the communications privilege were now to be abolished, publicity about the change might reach large segments of the population of a state. One might then expect a decrease in communication between spouses.[80]

Many other academic views to the same effect can be found.[81]

SECTION III: PRACTICAL IMPORTANCE OF CONFIDENTIALITY; EMPIRICAL EVIDENCE

Overview of the Empirical Studies

The effects of disclosure on the privilege are notoriously difficult to determine.[82] Toohey J has said that while the chilling effect must be taken into account, it is not capable of assessment.[83] It is often said that the evidence is unclear and the issue is impractical to research.[84] The United States Supreme Court has recently commented that empirical evidence on the privilege is limited and inconclusive.[85]

The most often cited study is the one conducted by the *Yale Law Journal* in 1962 ("the Yale Study").[86] This study surveyed lay-people and a number of different types of professionals, including psychologists, psychiatrists, social workers, marriage counsellors and accountants. Another study[87] (the "Cornell study") was conducted in 1989 by surveying attorneys and lay-people in Tompkins County, New York, by means of a posted questionnaire. One Australian attempt at quantitative research[88] purports to be a survey, but is a very different form of survey from that usually undertaken in this area.[89] This research addresses a different issue,[90] and in any case does so in such a manner

[80] Comment, "Marital Privileges and the Right to Testify" (1966) 34 *U Chi LR* 196 at 200 n. 25.

[81] E.g. M. Reutlinger, "Policy, Privacy and Prerogatives" (1973) 61 *Calif LR* 1353 at 1378. See the discussion at n. 118 below.

[82] For an extreme example of the problems faced in studying the lawyer–client relationship, see the entertaining article by B. Danet, K.B. Hoffman and N.C. Kermish, "Obstacles to the Study of the Lawyer–Client Interaction: The Biography of a Failure" (1980) 14 *Law & Society Rev.* 905. Rosenthal's rejoinder at the end is perhaps even more illuminating.

[83] *Carter* v. *The Managing Partner, Northmore Hale Davy & Leake* (1995) 183 CLR at 157. Also see McHugh J. at 164.

[84] New Zealand Law Commission, n. 12 above, para. 12. Also see Danet *et al.*, n. 82 above, 912–13; H.I. Subin, "The Lawyer as Superego: Disclosure of Client Confidences to Prevent Harm" (1985) 70 *Iowa LR* 1091 at 1163.

[85] *Swidler & Berlin* and *James Hamilton* v. *United States* 118 S. Ct. 2081 at 2087 n. 4 (1998).

[86] Note, "Functional Overlap Between the Lawyer and Other Professionals: Its Implications for the Privileged Communications Doctrine" (1962) 71 *Yale LJ* 1226.

[87] F.C.Zacharias, "Rethinking Confidentiality" (1989) 74 *Iowa LR* 351.

[88] R.J. Desiatnik, "The Contracting Concept of Legal Professional Privilege in Australia", unpublished SJD thesis, University of Sydney (1997), ch. 5: Surveys.

[89] It is actually a list of the number of times the privilege has been upheld or denied in reported appellate court decisions in Australia over a 21 year period.

[90] The research attempts to assess the degree to which Australian appellate courts have upheld or weakened the privilege. Desiatnik's thesis was that courts have been weakening the privilege, and asserts that this survey supports that conclusion.

that the findings it makes are of little use and may be misleading.[91] There have been two studies of the effectiveness of the privilege for corporate clients,[92] however these are of limited use for the purposes of this book. There have been a number of studies into the issue of whether privilege assists communications between psychiatrists and their patients. A Texas study[93] surveyed psychiatrists, patients, lay-people and judges to determine their views on the effects of the introduction of a statutory privilege for psychotherapists in Texas. Another study ("the Stanford study")[94] was conducted in response to a decision of the Supreme Court of California in 1976[95] which held that therapists owe a duty of care to protect people threatened by their patients.[96] A year after the decision the *Stanford Law Review* surveyed Californian psychiatrists to determine the effects of the decision. Finally, reference will be made where appropriate to studies of the importance of confidentiality in other relationships, such as a 1971 study of journalists.[97]

There are a number of problems with these studies, including the small sample size used in some of them,[98] poor selection of the pool of laymen[99] and

[91] The restriction of the study to reported appellate court decisions gives sufficient cause for concern. However even if the author had considered every appellate court decision on the privilege over the relevant period (which he did not do) the fundamental problem with his approach is that it is not possible to make any quantitative assessment of what is a complex qualitative issue. The important issue is not the number of times an apellate court is refusing to recognise the privilege, but the importance of the new derogations or extensions recognised in the appellate decisions individually and as a whole. One massive extension of the privilege (e.g. the recognition of privilege beyond the courtroom in *Baker* v. *Campbell*) can have far greater impact on the rule and its application than 10 decisions all involving small derogations from the rule (e.g. refinements to particular waiver rules). However under Desiatnik's analysis we are asked to believe that courts have been significantly curtailing the privilege, when in fact the opposite may be true. Despite this fundamental flaw the author asserts that the results are meaningful: "mere indulgence the surveys were not . . . Given the size of the canvas, it is firmly contended that broad brush-strokes, if they exist, comprised of like findings, were discernible, and are meaningful" (n. 88 above, at 131); "[w]ith such coverage in terms of time, geography and publications, the surveys do not lack depth. Within their stated limitations, it is submitted they can be, and should be, relied upon" (*ibid.*, at 132).

[92] E.P. Sloter, and A.M. Sorenson, "Corporate Legal Ethics—An Empirical Study" (1983) 8 *J Corp. L* 601; V.A. Alexander, "The Corporate Attorney–Client Privilege: A Study Of Participants" (1989) 63 *St John's* LR 191.

[93] D.W. Shuman and M.S. Weiner, n. 77 above.

[94] T.P. Wise, "Where the Public Peril Begins: A Survey of Psychotherapists to Determine the Effects of *Tarasoff*" (1978) 31 *Stan LR* 165.

[95] *Tarasoff* v. *Regents of the University of California* 551 P.2d 334 (Cal. SC). There have been an enormous number of law review articles criticising the decision. Just a few may be found in (1975) 24 *Cleveland State LR* 375 (1975); (1976) 90 *Harv. LR* 358; (1975) 12 *San Diego* 932; (1977) 48 *U. Colo. LR* 283; (1977) 22 *NY Law School LR* 1011.

[96] Many people believed that this case would greatly damage the conduct of therapy in California, e.g. see A.A. Stone, "The Tarasoff Decisions: Suing Psychotherapists to Safeguard Society" (1977) 90 *Harv. LR* 358.

[97] V. Blasi, "The Newsman's Privilege: An Empirical Study" (1971) 70 *Mich LR* 229.

[98] The Yale study surveyed 108 lay-people and 125 lawyers. The Cornell study surveyed 73 laymen and 63 lawyers, only one of which dealt with criminal law. The Stanford study did not share this problem, surveying over 1,000 psychiatrists.

[99] The Yale subjects were not chosen sufficiently randomly (see Note n. 86 above, at 1227 n. 6) and the Cornell study's laymen surveyed were self-selected from a group of people who had already shown an interest in legal issues.

a failure properly to isolate privilege and ethical confidentiality rules.[100] However these studies are the only empirical evidence available and provide useful information with which to assess the importance of confidentiality.[101]

Awareness of Existence of Confidentiality

The relevance of the chilling effect has been challenged on the basis that the public probably do not appreciate the different position with regard to confidentiality between lawyers and other professionals.[102] For instance, they may expect financial or medical advice to be more secure.[103] This was an important argument in the American debate to have the marital privilege abolished.[104]

This issue is open to debate. The Yale study found that most people were either unaware of the attorney–client privilege or believed it extended to other professional relationships as well.[105] The Cornell study found that clients specifically warned about the limits to confidentiality were as ready to provide information as those not told about such limits.[106] The Texas study found that 74 per cent of people surveyed were unaware of a professional privilege there.[107]

Yet at the same time the Yale study found that a far greater proportion of people correctly believed a particular communication would be privileged than incorrectly believed the privilege would exist in a communication.[108] Thus it has been argued, with reference to this element of the study, that even if privileges do not affect the behaviour of most people, the effects on this marginal group[109] may provide sufficient justification for the privilege.[110]

[100] E.g. F.C. Zacharias, n. 87 above, 384. Also see L. Kaplow and S. Shavell, "Legal Advice about Information to Present in Litigation: Its Effects and Social Desirability" (1989) 102 *Harv. LR* 565 at 610.

[101] For further criticism of the relevance of the studies, see H.I. Subin, n. 84 above, 1163 n. 349.

[102] For a discussion of this issue in the context of corporate clients, see V.A. Alexander, n. 92 above, 234–41.

[103] C. Tapper, "Prosecution and Privilege" (1996) 1 *Evidence and Proof* 5, 13.

[104] See R. Hutchins and D. Slesinger, "Some Observations on the Law of Evidence: Family Relations" (1929) 13 *Minn LR* 675. This formed the basis for the recommendation of the Advisery Committee on the Proposed Federal Rules of Evidence that the privilege be abolished: see 34 L Ed 2d iv (1973).

[105] Note, n. 86 above, 1232.

[106] F.C. Zacharias, n. 87 above, 386. Apart from the very small survey pool the Cornell study is unhelpful on this point as the distinction centred on awareness of the limits to *confidentiality*. The study failed to distinguish properly between the sources of confidentiality (ethical and legal) and so does not help us determine the extent to which the privilege encourages disclosure over and above ethical confidentiality rules. The same fault greatly limits the usefulness of a survey conducted by the Law Foundation of New South Wales, which for this reason has not been included in the present discussion. For details of the survey see R. Tomasic, *Law, Lawyers and the Community* (Law Foundation of New South Wales, Sydney, 1976) 81.

[107] D.W. Shuman and M.S. Weiner, n. 77 above, 925. Further, insurance statistics showed no increase in the use of psychotherapists following the enactment of the statutory privilege: *ibid*.

[108] Note, n. 86 above, 1262.

[109] i.e. the greater number of people who correctly identified the privilege's application, as opposed to those who were wrong; the Yale study puts this group at around 25–30% of people surveyed.

[110] Comment, n. 33 above, at n. 23.

An American study of journalists found that 44 per cent thought that a legal privilege would "make sources more willing to believe my current promises of confidentiality".[111] However only 28 per cent thought that such protection would "make sources more willing to talk in situations in which I do not make explicit promises of confidentiality".[112] The gap would seem to be due to the presumed lack of awareness of the hypothetical legal rule. With this in mind, it is worrying to note that only 35 per cent of journalists in states which have shield laws for their profession were aware of this privilege.[113]

It is likely that litigants generally,[114] and in particular criminal defendants,[115] will be better informed about the privilege than the rest of the population.[116] Further, Krattenmaker argues that even if a person is unaware that his communications are privileged, the privilege may at least provide a "subconscious backdrop"[117] to his discussions.

However, even if people know of the existence of confidentiality, what is it that they know? It will be suggested below that most people equate confidentiality with non-legally binding professional conduct rules, rather than a legally binding privilege.

Absence of Confidentiality

The degree of awareness of the existence of the privilege should not be the crucial consideration. The issue is not whether confidentiality is an incentive to candid discussion, but whether the lack of confidentiality would be a deterrent. This point has been made in relation to the American debate over abolition of the marital privilege.[118] Whether the lack of confidentiality would be a deterrent depends on two factors, namely whether clients would (a) become aware of, and (b) act on, an absence of confidentiality.[119]

111 V. Blasi, n. 97 above, at 275.

112 *Ibid.*

113 *Ibid.* at 275–6.

114 M. Reutlinger, n. 81 above, 1377.

115 See Note, n. 99 above 1236.

116 The authors of the Yale study acknowledge this: *ibid.*

117 T.G. Krattenmaker, "Testimonial Privileges in Federal Courts: An Alternative to the Proposed Federal Rules of Evidence" (1973) 62 *Geo LJ* 61 at 92, discussing marital communications and clergy–penitent privilege.

118 The Advisory Committee on the Federal Rules proposed the abolition of the privilege. M. Reutlinger, n. 81 above, 1377–8 argued against this, under the heading "If We Didn't Know It Existed, We Will Surely Know It's Gone". He said at 1378: "[i]n the future, as the negative privilege to be silent becomes the positive compulsion to testify, the public will doubtless begin to learn of defendants who are condemned by revelation in open court of their private marital acts and communications. . . . And it may well be that even persons who, in ignorance of the marital privilege, did not formerly hesitate to confide in their spouses because they took confidentiality for granted, will choose their words more carefully in the new-found knowledge that the privilege and its protection do not exist."

119 This issue is analysed extensively by M. Reutlinger, n. 81 above, 1371–81; also see E. Cleary *et al.* (ed.) *McCormick on Evidence* (3rd edn., West Publishing, St Paul, Minn., 1984) 201. Note that both of these discussions concern the American marital privilege.

On the latter issue of whether clients would act on a known absence of confidentiality the Yale study found that 51 per cent of laymen said they would be deterred from consulting their lawyer if they knew they had no privilege.[120] Similarly, 52 per cent of respondents in the Cornell study predicted they would withhold information from lawyers if no firm obligation of confidentiality existed.[121] The Texas study[122] found that while people were not more willing to disclose information when they knew they had a privilege, they were far less willing to reveal sensitive information when told they had no privilege.[123]

The Stanford study found that when psychotherapists warned their patients that their discussions may not be kept confidential, nearly one quarter of patients were reluctant to discuss some matters and approximately the same proportion of therapists reported losing patients due to fears regarding confidentiality.[124] When psychotherapists were asked if telling their patients that information may be discussed with others would affect their relationship with their patients, 79 per cent of psychotherapists said they thought patients would be less likely to divulge information.[125]

These results may be compared to studies done on the effects of the *Miranda* warning in the United States.[126] These studies show that suspects hardly ever reacted to the warning given to them. They usually still talked to police and did not call for the assistance of lawyers. This was despite the known lack of confidentiality, brought about by the warnings. Some commentators have even argued that the use of a warning about the limits of confidentiality may even increase client disclosure.[127]

On the first issue of whether clients would be aware of the lack of confidentiality in the first place, it has been suggested that it may take just one sensational and publicised case effectively to destroy confidence in a professional adviser.[128] If lawyers were duty-bound to recite to their clients the courts'

[120] Note, n. 86 above, n. 59.

[121] F.C. Zacharias, n. 87 above, n. 141.

[122] D.W. Shuman and M.S. Weiner, n. 77 above.

[123] *Ibid.*, at 929.

[124] T.P. Wise, n. 94 above, at 177 n. 67, although note that this was in relation to the discussion of violent tendencies.

[125] *Ibid.*, at 176 n. 63.

[126] Most of the studies are conveniently summarised in Y. Kamisar, W. La Fave and J. Israel, *Modern Criminal Procedure* (4th edn., West Publishing, St Paul, Minn., 1974) 592–6.

[127] Burt, "Conflict and Trust Between Attorney and Client" (1981) 69 *Geo LJ* 1015 at 1019 (lawyers being honest with their clients about the limits of the relationship may lead to a more trusting relationship); S. Bundy and E. Elhauge, n. 45 above, 410–11. For views on the obligation to give such a warning, see n. 129 below.

[128] M. Guttmacher and H. Weihofen, n. 48 above, 36; M. Reutlinger, n. 81 above, 1377–8. However there were two such cases, one in England and one in America, during the course of the writing of this chapter: Anon., "Psychiatrist Tipped Off Police About Daniel's Murderer", *The Times*, 9 May 1996 at 6; Anon., "Vatican Anger over Bugged Confession", *Daily Telegraph*, 25 May 1996 at 15.

powers of disclosure, this might have a similar effect.[129] Absent such a duty, we have little reason to believe that most litigants[130] would have such an awareness.

The Cornell study found that 72 per cent of lawyers surveyed admitted they told their clients only generally that all communications are confidential, and only 28 per cent of lawyers routinely told their clients that exceptions to confidentiality exist.[131] The Yale study found that most people wrongly assumed that many types of professionals had such a privilege[132] and 60 per cent said that the removal of their accountant–client privilege (which they wrongly believed they had) would seriously hamper their relations with that professional. The Stanford study found that 86 per cent of psychotherapists were of the opinion that their patients believed that the psychotherapist–patient communications were absolutely protected from disclosure.[133]

It seems we have a situation where, if the privilege were weakened, this might affect client behaviour if it were known to the client, but that it is possible that clients would not gain such knowledge and that lawyer–client relations would remain largely unaffected. Further, most people probably believe lawyer–client communications are protected to a greater extent than they in fact are.[134] For example, one may doubt whether most clients are aware of the rules of implied waiver, and the possibility it creates for inadvertent loss of the privilege. To take another example, clients probably assume that any confidentiality protection that they have covers the entirety of their communications with their lawyer, and are unaware of the requirement that the communication must be made for the purpose of obtaining legal advice.[135] An awareness of the crime-fraud exception may significantly affect the use of legal advice in criminal cases, particularly where clients wrongly believe they are breaking the law. In short, clients confide freely in their lawyers because they may be aware of the privilege and also because they are usually unaware of the exceptions.[136]

[129] Compare though the view cited in n. 127 above. It is a matter of debate whether such an obligation exists in many jurisdictions. One American proposed ethical rule did place such a responsibility on lawyers: see Rule 1.4(b) of the American Bar Association Commission on Evaluation of Professional Standards, Model Rules of Professional Conduct (Discussion Draft of 30 Jan. 1980) reprinted in 48 USLW 1 (19 Feb. 1980); also see M. Frankel, n. 36 above, 57; New Zealand Law Commission, n. 12 above, para. 153; A. Alschuler, "The Preservation of a Client's Confidences: One Value Among Many or a Categorical Imperative?" (1981) 52 *U Col LR* 349, 353; L.A. Pizzimenti, "The Lawyer's Duty to Warn Clients About Limits on Confidentiality" (1990) 39 *Catholic ULR* 441 at 471–89; H.I. Subin, n. 84 above, 1166, especially n. 354.

[130] Civil litigants at the least.

[131] F.C. Zacharias, n. 87 above, 386.

[132] 70% of laymen believed that privileges existed for psychiatrists, psychologists, marriage counsellors and social workers: Note, n. 86 above, 1255.

[133] T.P. Wise, n. 94 above, 176 n.64. In California the psychotherapist–patient communications are confidential, but, like legal professional privilege, there are a number of exceptions to confidentiality.

[134] To similar effect, see H.I. Subin, n. 84 above, 1165.

[135] See R. Black, "A Question of Confidence" (1982) *J Law Soc Scotland* 229, discussing various hypothetical situations.

[136] D.J. Fried, "Too High a Price for Truth: The Exception to the Attorney–Client Privilege for Contemplated Crimes and Frauds" (1986) 64 *North Carolina LR* 443, n. 270.

This may explain the seemingly contradictory results obtained in some of the studies. For example the Stanford study is typical. On the one hand, it found that 79 per cent of psychotherapists felt that a known absence of confidentiality would deter effective communications.[137] On the other hand 70 per cent of the same group of psychotherapists felt that confidentiality was "important, but may be breached under certain circumstances".[138]

It is hard to resist the conclusion that the law of privilege is built on active deceit. Lawyers either do not discuss this issue with clients and foster an assumption of absolute confidentiality, or actively assert that this is the case. They never tell their clients about the limits to confidentiality.[139] The instrumental benefits of the privilege are partly due to the result of this deceit.

Need and Competing Motives

There is much support for the view that even without confidentiality clients would not damage their own prospects by leaving their lawyer ill-informed.[140] They will still seek advice as they have no alternative.[141] In some types of cases, such as ongoing commercial transactions, clients may need legal services if they wish to function at all.[142] In other cases, the need to communicate outweighs the low risk of disclosure.[143] This may apply equally where litigation is not involved, with the inability to understand or deal with a legal matter being the catalyst.[144] In all of these situations, it may be that the added inducement of confidentiality is unnecessary to encourage candour. As one writer summarised:

> people base decisions to reveal what they would rather keep secret on an assessment of self-interest that extends well beyond the question whether the revelation will be disclosed, and, quite possibly, despite a known risk that it will be . . . there obviously exist forces that operate regardless of a confidentiality rule.[145]

137 See n. 125 above.

138 T.P. Wise, n. 94 above, 176 n. 65.

139 On the possible duty to warn clients of the limits to confidentiality, see the references cited in n. 129 above.

140 W.H. Simon, "Ethical Discretion in Lawyering" (1988) 101 *Harv LR* 1083 at 1142; New Zealand Law Commission, n. 12 above, para. 13; H.I. Subin, n. 84 above, 1163.

141 J. Gardner, "A Re-Evaluation of the Attorney–Client Privilege" (1963) 8 *Vill LR* 279 at 318; Note, "The Attorney–Client Privilege: Fixed Rules, Balancing and Constitutional Entitlement" (1977) 91 *Harv LR* 464 at 470.

142 H.I. Subin, n. 84 above, 1164.

143 M.L. Schwartz, "The Professional Accountability of Lawyers" (1978) 66 Calif LR 669 at 683–4; S. Bundy and E. Elhauge, n. 31 above, 404; Comment, n. 33 above, 476; Note, "Immunized Witnesses and the Attorney–Client Privilege" (1954) 6 *Stan LR* 363 at 366 ("The danger of deterring disclosure is speculative at best, and whatever danger does exist is offset by the desire to have the full benefit of legal advice.")

144 M.L. Schwartz, n. 143 above, 683–4; F.C. Zacharias, n. 87 above, 364.

145 H.I. Subin, n. 84 above, 1164.

Conversely, there are many other reasons why clients may withhold information despite guarantees of confidentiality.[146] For example, they may have their own views about what their legal adviser needs to know. Personal embarrassment may cause more inhibition than the possibility of disclosing legally punishable actions.[147] Clients may be concerned that if their lawyer knows the awful truth the lawyer will not continue to represent them enthusiastically.[148] Most importantly, the criminal defendant may not trust his lawyer.[149] It has even been suggested that in criminal defence work express guarantees of confidentiality may be counter-productive[150] and that if a lawyer representing a criminal defendant tells the client at the outset that she may be compelled to disclose information in certain circumstances, then "[t]he client may more readily accept her as an ally *within the defined boundaries*, both because the lawyer has exhibited integrity and because the limitations on the alliance make the total package more believable".[151]

Type and Source of Confidentiality

Most of the above discussion about the relationship between confidentiality and disclosure assumes that we are dealing with the possibility of disclosure compelled by a court process. However the concept of confidentiality may also refer to the ethical rules which require a lawyer not to reveal client confidences outside the courtroom.[152]

The Yale study found that 66% of people thought that lawyers would not disclose a confidence,[153] but when asked whether a lawyer would have an obligation to disclose if questioned in court half of those questioned either did not know or thought the lawyer must disclose. The Texas study found that while most people were unaware of the existence of a statutory psychotherapist–

[146] See K. Mann, *Defending White Collar Crime* (Yale University Press, New Haven, 1985) 40–52; J. Gardner, n. 141 above, 318; W.H. Simon, n. 140 above, 1142.

[147] D.W. Shuman and M.S. Weiner, n. 77 above, 926. The Texas study found that far more people withheld from their psychiatrists information concerning sexual thoughts than thoughts of violence: *ibid.*

[148] M.L. Schwartz, n. 143 above, 684; H.I. Subin, n. 84 above, 1164–5.

[149] In particular, criminal defendants tend to distrust public defenders: see J.D. Casper, *American Criminal Justice: The Defendant's Perspective* (Prentice Hall, New Jersey, 1972) 105–15 (an empirical study reaching this conclusion); R.B. Flemming, "Client Games: Defense Attorney Perspectives on Their Relations with Criminal Clients" [1986] *Am B Found. Res J* 253 at 258–60. Such distrust renders a promise of confidentiality otiose: Burt, n. 127 above, 1032; E.M. Morgan, "The Evolving Concept of Professional Responsibility" (1977) 90 *Harv LR* 702 at 738.

[150] "[C]ounterintuitive claims by attorneys that they will never act against the client can only serve to put the client on guard even further": F.C. Zacharias, n. 87 above, n. 76.

[151] *Ibid.*, 368 (emphasis in original). For one of the best short refutations of the need for confidentiality, see H.I. Subin, n. 84 above, 1163–5.

[152] One study into the corporate attorney privilege found numerous other factors important in influencing candour, such as "trust" and "faith in the lawyer's ethical responsibility": V.A. Alexander, n. 92 above, 247. These are consistent with the lawyer's ethical obligations.

[153] Note, n. 86 above, 1239.

patient privilege, 96 per cent of patients considered that the therapist's ethics provided a satisfactory assurance of confidentiality.[154] Similarly, the Yale study also shows that other professions have operated successfully because lay people overestimate the safety of confiding in them.[155] Zacharias claims that the Cornell study supports this view, although the significance of its data on this issue is questionable.[156] He suggests that most clients disclose information because they view lawyers as professionals from whom they expect discretion.[157] He concludes that, if this is the case, allowing lawyers to disclose information to protect superior third party interests may not affect client trust greatly.[158]

Thus while confidentiality may be important in maintaining good lawyer–client communications, it appears that the layman's belief in confidentiality owes more to rules of professional ethics than to the privilege rule and that most people may be relying on a professional's ethical duties, rather than the law, to protect their disclosures.

CONCLUSIONS

In *Swidler & Berlin* v. *United States* the United States Supreme Court said that the empirical studies, while not conclusive "suggest that a substantial number of clients . . . think the privilege encourages candor".[159] This is not the case. The empirical data suggest that the privilege is in fact not as important as usually assumed. However such data are notoriously difficult to interpret. The fact that confidentiality encourages disclosure only in a small number of cases may be used both to support and to oppose a strict privilege rule.

While we will never know with any certainty what effect further exceptions to the privilege would have on the administration of justice, we also will not know the extent to which the privilege itself advances the administration of justice. This is not to suggest that there is no merit in the current rationale for the privilege. Rather, it suggests two things: first, that the privilege is more robust than often suggested. It can accommodate changes and exceptions, and still fulfil its main purpose. The rule is not, and need not be, absolute. Its robustness

[154] D.W. Shuman and M.S. Weiner, n. 77 above, 925, 926. Confidentiality here referred to court-ordered disclosure as well disclosure to an insurance carrier, a state agency or a potential employer.

[155] A view shared by D.L. Rhode, "Ethical Perspectives on Legal Practice" (1985) 37 *Stan LR* 589 at 614. The other explanation is that the layman's opinion is correct and not an overestimate. In other words, some professionals, such as journalists and priests, may provide more security through a greater readiness to defy the law in order to maintain confidentiality. For example, see J. Beltrami, *The Defender* (W & R Chambers Ltd, 1980) 189, describing a case in which no less an authority that Pope John XXIII ordered a Scottish priest not to break the seal of the confessional in a murder trial.

[156] The questions designed to elucidate this point did not adequately distinguish between privilege and ethical rules.

[157] F.C. Zacharias, n. 87 above 381.

[158] *Ibid*.

[159] 118 S Ct. at 2087 n. 4.

may come from the fact that the privilege, through its rationale in maintaining client confidence in the secrecy of legal communications, to some extent depends less on what the law actually is than on what the public assume the law to be. Such assumptions and expectations can survive changes in the scope and operation of the legal rule itself.[160] Secondly, if the evidence is ambiguous it may be that the decision whether or not to compel disclosure is a normative question depending on the particular context.[161] In resolving this issue courts should be very careful in subordinating other important interests, the effects of which are known and easily quantifiable, to the pursuit of an interest the value of which is difficult to assess and may well have been overrated by lawyers.

Following on from this last point, it may be fitting to conclude this evaluation of the importance of confidentiality with one final statistic drawn from the empirical studies. This is that the studies show that professionals have a much greater belief in the utility of the privilege than laymen. The Yale study found that while 72 per cent of lawyers surveyed thought that their privilege encourages free disclosure,[162] 51 per cent of laymen surveyed said they would not make free disclosure without the privilege.[163] Similarly the Texas study found that while 79 per cent of psychotherapists thought that a lack of confidentiality would inhibit the communicative behaviour of their patients,[164] only a quarter of therapists actually reported this effect in their practice.[165] The authors of the Yale study commented that this may explain why there is such a privilege in the first place.[166] At the very least such statistics should lead us to demand more from proponents of the privilege who simply cite "the experience of the profession" to support their factual contentions.[167]

[160] This is not to say that we should consider fashioning disclosure laws to take advantage of expectations of confidentiality. Comment, n. 33 above, 1475 n. 23 points out the unfairness of disappointing justifiably held expectations. Clearly laws should strive to reflect social values and intuitive notions of fairness. However the issue here is one of balancing competing and irreconcilable notions of fairness, both of which may appeal to intuition.

[161] D.W. Shuman and M.S. Weiner, n. 77 above, 928; F.C. Zacharias, n. 87 above, 377.

[162] Note, n. 86 above, n. 38; 10% thought that it did not and the remaining 18% did not know.

[163] *Ibid.*; 34% said they still would and 15% said they did not know.

[164] D.W. Shuman and M.W. Weiner , n. 77 above, 176 n. 63.

[165] *Ibid.*, at 177.

[166] Note, n. 86 above, 1232.

[167] R.A. Sedler and J.J. Simeone, n. 69 above, 4; C. Wright and K. Graham, *Federal Practice and Procedure* (West Publishing, St Paul, Minn., 1986) xxiv, 84 n. 100.

5

Disclosure

INTRODUCTION

There are two sides to any analysis of the role and place of the privilege: (a) the need for confidentiality; and (b) the need for disclosure. While Chapter 4 examined the reasons we attempt to withhold privileged information from courts and other bodies, this chapter effectively looks at the status of the countervailing value: the value of disclosure within the judicial system. It is this countervailing value which promotes both restrictions in the scope of the privilege and the derogations from the privilege. The need for disclosure forms part of the rationale for derogations from the privilege as a whole. It should be noted that the following discussion will assume a rationalist view of truth as an objective reality.[1] It will not address philosophical, jurisprudential[2] or political theories[3] questioning the notion of objective truth.

The first part of this chapter will look at the role of truth in the theoretical goals of the litigation process. This will be followed by an examination of the practical value placed on disclosure and compulsion. The final section of this chapter will attempt to assess the detriment to truth determination resulting from the privilege.

SECTION I: THEORY; GOAL OF TRUTH IN LITIGATION

Civil Litigation is Not Aimed at Physical or Scientific Truth

There appears to be ready acceptance of the place of broad exclusionary rules divorced from concerns for the accuracy of fact-finding. "Every discussion of the merits or demerits of our rules of evidence should begin with a reminder that a lawsuit is not a scientific investigation or primarily a proceeding for the

[1] E.g. see W.L. Twining, "The Rationalist Tradition of Evidence Scholarship" in L. Waller and E. Campbell (eds.), *Well and Truly Tried* (Law Book Co., Sydney, 1982) 211, especially at 242–9.

[2] E.g. see B. Jackson, *Law, Fact and Narrative Coherence* (Deborah Charles Publications, 1988) 7–12; P. Haldar, "The Evidencer's Eye: Representations of Truth in the Laws of Evidence" (1991) 2 *Law and Critique* 171; Z. Bankowski, "The Value of Truth: Fact Scepticism Revisited" (1981) 1 *Legal Studies* 257.

[3] For a sample of the literature, see the articles listed in D. Nicolson, "Truth Reason and Justice: Epistemology and Politics in Evidence Discourse" (1994) 57 *MLR* 726 at nn. 17, 21–23, 29 and especially n. 101.

discovery of truth."[4] To put the matter another way, forensic inquiries do not attempt to determine physical truth.[5]

To arrive at scientific or physical truth, it may be essential to examine everything which relates to the problem and to explore every approach which may lead to a solution.[6] Clearly this is not practical in the judicial process:

> if we lived for a thousand years instead of about sixty or seventy, and every case were of sufficient importance, it might be possible, and perhaps proper . . . to raise every possible inquiry as to the truth of the statements made . . . In fact, mankind finds it to be impossible.[7]

The very concept of an onus of proof is a recognition of this.[8] The compromise reached is that litigation should strive for a particular form of truth: "the search is not in the hope of absolute truth but for the closest one can come to truth on the evidence presented".[9]

In contrast, litigation may be more important for the legitimacy conferred by the procedure undertaken rather than the outcome. This may accord with what Rawls describes as "pure procedural justice":[10] the outcome is fair or correct provided that the procedure has been properly followed. Newbold even says that this order of priorities is somehow the product of a "democratic society".[11] One of the great evidence writers of this century, Professor Edmund Morgan, has argued from this that litigation is not even primarily aimed at the discovery of truth.[12] Rather it is essentially a procedure for the orderly settlement of disputes between litigants to attain desired political and social, rather than scientific, objectives. Morgan later states that the object of the lawsuit is the adjustment of legal relations between the parties and as decisions regarding factual issues affect the parties only, it is reasonable to have the parties defining the area of dispute.[13]

There are other streams of evidence scholarship which either downplay the need for litigation to determine truth, or emphasise and condone the degree to which litigation does not advance the search for truth. Twining identifies one stream as the "complacent rationalists",[14] who believe that the aim of trials should be the rectitude of decisions, but are complacent about the extent to

[4] E.M. Morgan, "Suggested Remedy for Obstructions to Expert Testimony by Rules of Evidence" (1943) 10 *Uni Chicago LR* 285.

[5] Royal Commission Inquiry into Civil Rights (Queen's Printer, 1968) 814.

[6] *Ibid.*

[7] *Attorney-General* v. *Hitchcock* (1847) 1 Exch. 91 at 105, 154 ER 38 at 44.

[8] R.W. Fox, "Expediency and Truth-Finding in the Modern Law of Evidence" in L. Waller and E. Campbell (eds.), n. 1 above, at 152.

[9] *Hurd* v. *Hewitt* (1994) 120 DLR (4th) 105 at 112, *per* Carthy JA (Ont. CA).

[10] J. Rawls, *A Theory of Justice* (Harvard Uni. Press, Cambridge, Mass., 1971) 85–6.

[11] A.L.E. Newbold, Legal Professional Privilege (Unpublished PhD thesis, University of London, 1990) 7.

[12] E.M. Morgan, n. 4 above, 285.

[13] *Ibid.*, at 286. Note that it is clear from his following discussion of criminal cases that Morgan does not restrict his view to civil litigation.

[14] W.L. Twining, n. 1 above, 247.

which trial procedure actually achieves this. Another strand of evidence thinking has been described as "complacent fact positivism"[15] and is characterised by the:

> hard-nosed, practical and unreflective practitioner whose overwhelming concern is the winning of cases, rather than the search for . . . truth or anything as prosaic as justice . . . questions of truth are not questions for lawyers, but for head-in-the-cloud philosophers, endlessly debating whether or not unobserved trees 'really' fall in the Black Forest.[16]

Similar attitudes may also be seen in the works of extreme pro-client ethics writers such as Freedman,[17] and also in the rather different views of those who advocate a swap of accuracy for speed and cost in civil litigation. Indeed, Lord Woolf's Report, *Access to Justice*, reflected the view that while procedural fairness required just and fair results, it did not necessarily require perfectly accurate results: "a more proportionate but workable system, not one which is theoretically impeccable but unaffordable".[18]

These views clearly have an impact on the acceptability of the derogation from fact-finding which is the privilege. Professor Louisell boldly justifies attorney–client privilege[19] on the basis that "there are things even more important to human liberty than accurate adjudication. One of them is the right to be left by the state unmolested in certain human relations."[20] This attitude to the role of evidence in the trial process is also reflected in the much-quoted[21] statement of Knight-Bruce VC in *Pearse* v. *Pearse*[22] that the privilege is more important than truth itself.

Truth as a Paramount Objective

The problem with many of the views discussed in the previous section is that they often start from the fact that trials rarely find perfect truth in order to

[15] D. Nicolson, "Truth, Reason and Justice: Epistemology and Politics in Evidence Discourse" (1994) 57 *MLR* 726 at 728.

[16] *Ibid.*

[17] See M. Freedman, "Judge Frankel's Search for Truth" (1975) 123 *U Pa LR* 1060; F.C. Zacharias, "Rethinking Confidentiality" (1989) 74 *Iowa LR* 351 at 366–7.

[18] H. Woolf, *Access to Justice*, Final Report to the Lord Chancellor on the Civil Justice System in England and Wales (HMSO, London, 1996) 106.

[19] Along with marital privilege and priest–penitent privilege.

[20] D.W. Louisell, "Confidentiality, Conformity and Confusion: Privileges in Federal Court Today" (1956) 31 *Tulane LR* 31 at 110; D.W. Louisell and K. Sinclair, "Reflections on the Law of Privileged Communications" (1971) 59 *Calif LR* 30 at 53–54; also see Note, "Attorney–Client and Work Product Protection in a Utilitarian World: An Argument for Recomparison" (1995) 108 *Harv LR* 1697, n. 37.

[21] E.g. see: *Baker* v. *Campbell* (1983) 153 CLR at 115; *Attorney-General (N.T.)* v. *Maurice* (1986) 161 CLR at 490; *Carter* v. *The Managing Partner, Northmore Hale Davy & Leake* (1995) 183 CLR at 133–4; Comment, "Developments in the Law—Privileged Communications" (1985) 98 *Harv LR* 1450.

[22] (1846) 1 De G. & Sm at 28–9, 63 ER at 957. Also see *Reece* v. *Trye* (1846) 9 Beav. 316 at 319, 50 ER 365 at 366.

conclude that this is not their real aim.[23] This is wrong. There are many forms of litigation in which the ultimate remedy is far less relevant than the simple result of establishing a set of facts which it is important for one party to present to the world as the "truth". Obvious examples include libel claims or actions in which a declaration is the primary remedy sought. Even if the aim of trials is solely to provide a legitimate means of dispute resolution, this legitimacy is derived from the fact that the process consists of an attempt to discover truth. The fact that this attempt will not necessarily succeed does not change this conclusion. What is important is the attempt at truth-seeking, as it is this which confers the legitimacy. In contrast many writers take the opposite approach. For example:

> The habit of lawyers in referring to the litigation process as 'a search for truth' seems pretentious. Subject, as it is, from the uncertainties and inaccuracies which flow [from perception errors, perjury etc.] . . . litigation does not aspire to realise truth as an understanding of reality. Rather, it seeks dispute resolution based upon the opinion of an arbitrary portion of those . . . randomly drawn from an arbitrary sample.[24]

This explanation of the role of truth in litigation has some academic support. American evidence writing in the first half of this century was dominated by an ideology known as the Progressive procedural paradigm. The Progressives, who included Professors Wigmore and Chafee,[25] had a significant impact on proposals for procedural reform in North America through the American Law Institute and other bodies.[26] The movement exalts truth-seeking as the ultimate judicial value. The trial is a scientific search for truth, not a political method of resolving disputes.[27]

Apart from the Progressives, there are a number of commentators who argue that truth is the paramount objective of the legal system.[28] For example Judge Frankel argues that lawyers tend to devalue the importance of truth[29] and proposes that counsel be under a duty to disclose all material favourable to the other side without the restriction of professional privilege.[30] There are similar

[23] Such reasoning is very common among American writers, e.g. R.W. Nashtoll, "The Lawyer's Allegiance: Priorities Regarding Confidentiality" (1984) *Wash and Lee LR* 421 at 441 n. 54.

[24] *Ibid.*

[25] Indeed Morgan may also be counted among the Progressives. However he clearly took a very different view of the nature of the trial process, believing that it was designed to produce political, rather than scientific, outcomes.

[26] See the excellent historical account in C. Wright and K. Graham, *Federal Practice and Procedure* (West Publishing, St Paul, Minn., 1986) xxvi 77–92.

[27] E.g. see *Strass* v. *Goldsack* (1975) 58 DLR (3d) 397 at 420–1 (Alberta SC). The headnote summary of Clement JA's judgment is misleading. If Clement JA had actually said this in his judgment it would provide excellent support for this point.

[28] See F.O. Heather, "Attorney–Clienht Confidentiality: A New Approach" (1976) 4 *Holstra LR* 685, 689–691; Noonan (1966) 1487, 1489; M. Frankel, "The Search for Truth: An Umpireal View" (1975) 123 *U Pa. LR* 1031.

[29] M. Frankel, "The Search for Truth Continued: More Disclosure, Less Privilege" (1982) 54 *U Col LR* 51, 52–53.

[30] *Ibid.*, at 51. This proposal must be assessed in the context of Judge Frankel's suggested programme for reform of the adversarial system in general. For analysis of Frankel's argument see

English statements to the effect that the object of litigation is the determination of truth.[31]

Finally, it must of course be noted that there are many contexts outside of the courtroom in which compulsion is used for the sole purpose of getting closer to the truth, and the privilege frequently operates in such contexts. For example, there are two main functions of commissions of inquiry such as Royal Commissions: to discover the truth and to build public confidence by the discovery of the truth. In some such situations there may be very heavy policy reasons for disclosing privileged communications in order to assist the ascertainment of truth, for example, where the privileged communications disclose a risk to public safety, such as in *W* v. *Egdell*.[32] The Canadian Supreme Court has recently recognised an exception to the privilege for such cases.[33]

Different Priorities of Criminal Litigation

There may be good reasons why both the goal of truth-finding and the value attached to the privilege may be different in criminal trials. As decisions made in civil litigation usually affect the parties only[34] it is reasonable to allow the parties themselves to define the area of dispute, and hence it may be easier to accept a broad bar to disclosure, such as the privilege.[35] However decisions made in criminal trials serve a wider purpose; vindicating public goals and interests often in a more immediate manner than civil litigation does. Thus the goal of truth-finding may have a greater weight in criminal litigation.

As discussed in Chapter 9 below, the privilege may operate differently in criminal cases. The criminal law places the accused in a special position, and affords him many extra procedural safeguards. These arise from the public policy recognising the special difficulties the accused faces, and include the effective provision of legal advice as an important part of this system of safeguards.

Adversarial System as a Whole

The choice between use of an adversarial or an inquisitorial approach to litigation may have a profound effect on the value of truth determination as a

W.T. Pizzi, "Judge Frankel and the Adversary System" (1981) 52 *U Col LR* 357; A. Alschuler, "The Search for Truth Continued, The Privilege Retained: A Response to Judge Frankel" (1982) 54 *U Col LR* 67.

[31] E.g. *Jones* v. *National Coal Board* [1957] 2 QB 55 at 63 (CA).

[32] [1990] 1 All ER 835.

[33] *Smith* v. *Jones* (1999) 132 CCC (3d) 225.

[34] E.M. Morgan, n. 4 above, 286.

[35] Cf. Newbold, n. 11 above, 8.

systemic goal.[36] In an inquisitorial procedure there may be no specific allegations and the tribunal is charged with finding the truth.[37] Thus it may be seeking to establish truth as an absolute. In comparison, under an adversarial procedure, one party alleges facts and the other seeks to deny them. Thus the procedure is designed to do justice only between the parties.[38]

Common law procedure has historically been conducted on largely adversarial lines. At one time this included secrecy until the trial, and no general power to order discovery, with only a few isolated common law procedures for gaining information in certain circumstances.[39] This was in comparison to the Chancery procedure, which allowed bills of discovery in the course of common law actions to remedy this common law defect.[40] It should be noted that there are some exceptions either way. Some forms of inquisitorial procedure exist in the common law, child welfare proceedings being one example. Further, some legal doctrines suggest that litigation produces absolute truth rather than relative fact-finding; for example the doctrine of issue estoppel.

The dominant thinking among Anglo-American evidence writers last century was that the adversarial system was the best means of determining the truth. For example, Bentham was committed to rectitude of decision-making as the primary goal of litigation,[41] and at the same time was also committed to the adversarial approach. Wigmore said that the practice of examination and cross-examination is the best means of discovering the truth.[42] These traditional views are still shared by some modern writers, such as Freedman.

The dominant modern view seems to be that the adversarial approach is not necessarily the best method of finding the truth. Rather, it gives effect to "fox-hunter's justice", where the goal is not so much that the truth be discovered as that the parties may have fair play.[43] Frankel said that the adversary system does not necessarily promote truth so much as a believable story.

The principle of party control means that the adversarial procedure is not concerned with the truth of the material facts, but the truth of the facts put in

[36] Compare J.D. Jackson, "Two Methods of Proof in Criminal Procedure" (1988) 51 *MLR* 549, arguing that neither the adversarial nor the non-adversarial method of proof gives sufficient weight to modern conceptions of truth-finding (*ibid.*, at 557–61) and that instead we should look to the "dialectic method of proof" as a better alternative (*ibid.*, at 561–8).

[37] P. Matthews and H.M. Malek, *Discovery* (Sweet & Maxwell, London, 1992) 3.

[38] Also see P. Devlin, *The Judge* (OUP, Oxford, 1979) 54.

[39] See S.D. Simpson, D.L. Bailey and E.K. Evans, *Discovery and Interrogatories* (2nd edn., Butterworths, Sydney, 1990) 13–14.

[40] E.g. see the description in *McLean* v. *Burns Philp Trustee Co Pty Ltd* (1985) 2 NSWLR 623 at 644 (NSW SC, Eq Div); also see N.J. Williams, "Discovery of Civil Litigation Trial Preparation in Canada" (1980) 58 *Can Bar Rev* 1.

[41] See W.L. Twining, *Theories of Evidence: Bentham and Wigmore* (Weidenfeld & Nicolson, London, 1985) 52–66.

[42] J.H. Wigmore and J.H. Chadbourn, *Evidence in Trials at Common Law* (Little, Brown and Co., London, 1974)v, 32 para. 1367.

[43] A. Paizes, "Towards a Broader Balancing of Interests: Exploring the Theoretical Foundations of Legal Professional Privilege" (1989) 106 *SALJ* 109, quoting Bentham.

issue by the parties.[44] Relevant evidence considered harmful by both sides may not be put in evidence, and hence the truth not discovered. This applies in criminal litigation as well as civil. For example, the defence of insanity is usually not pleaded for non-capital offences because of the uncertain nature of the sentence it carries. Thus if an insane person is alleged to have committed a non-capital offence the truth of the matter may be that the person was guilty by reason of insanity. However if the defence is not willing to raise it, then the case will be resolved in another manner and the truth avoided.

Other aspects of the adversarial system may similarly not promote truth-finding. For example, while it has been claimed that cross-examination is aimed at truth-determination, in reality counsel will often use it to attempt to obscure the truth.[45] Large differences between the financial resources of the parties may have an effect on their ability to determine the truth by means of fair competition. Thus it seems that an important qualification on the truth-finding goal of litigation is the acceptance of an adversarial method.

Truth is a vitally important goal of litigation. The search for the truth forms the basis of the legitimacy of this approach as a means of dispute resolution and a justification for state enforcement. The litigious process, and in particular the adversarial procedure, is far from a search for scientific or physical truth. Rather it seeks to achieve as much truth as is possible within certain boundaries, or to determine truth as a relative value between two competing accounts. Courts must often decide which of the parties' cases is closer to the truth, or what the truth is on the basis of the facts presented.[46] However even with all these qualifications in mind, one should not go too far in downplaying the role of truth determination. As a goal it is the central source of legitimacy for the justice system. The search for truth is still the defining element of the process.

SECTION II: PRACTICE; VALUE PLACED ON DISCLOSURE AND COMPULSION

Looking at the emphasis placed on disclosure in practice, it can be seen that there has been a significant change in attitude across the Commonwealth over the last two decades. Over the wide range of areas involving disclosure to fact-finders in trial, pre-trial and non-judicial contexts, the overwhelming trend has been to encourage and facilitate more extensive disclosure in order to present

[44] J.D. Jackson, *Law, Fact and Narrative Coherence* (Deborah Charles Publications, 1988) 560. Note though that some writers seems oblivious to this conflict. For example M. Rosenfeld, "The Transformation of Attorney–Client Privilege" (1982) *Hastings LJ* 495 at 499 praises the adversary system for both aiming at truth discovery as well as maximising individual control over the gathering and presentation of evidence.

[45] R.W. Fox, "Expediency and Truth-finding in the Modern Law of Evidence" in L. Waller and E. Campbell (eds.), n. 1 above, 151.

[46] B. Jackson, n. 2 above, 7 described "legal truth" as "that which a jury believes, after seeing a witness state matters orally on oath, and be subjected publicly to cross-examination".

more material to courts and investigatory bodies. This general trend represents a real change in values within the curial system.

Non-judicial

Powers of search and seizure have been developed largely in the last fifty years. Historically the common law provided only for the issue of a warrant to search a place for stolen goods. There was no general power to search or seize goods, and the common law refused to permit a constable to enter private property without permission.[47] The post-war period has seen a proliferation of investigative bodies with powers to require the production of material or to search for and seize material.[48] In *Inland Revenue Commissioners* v. *Rossminster Ltd* Lord Wilberforce said:

> A formidable number of officials now have powers to enter people's premises, and to take property away, and these powers are frequently exercised, sometimes on a large scale. Many people, as well as the respondents, think that this process has gone too far; that is an issue to be debated in Parliament and in the press.[49]

In the field of police powers, the Police and Criminal Evidence Act 1984 (UK) has clarified and widened police powers in relation to stop and search, arrest and detention. There has also been a rapid growth in the number and power of statutory non-curial tribunals, such as Royal Commissions and other commissions of inquiry, which are often invested with powers similar to those of courts to require the attendance of witnesses, production of documents and the answering of questions.[50]

Trial Disclosure and Rules of Admissibility

The greatest area of change has occurred within trial procedure itself. The general trend over the last two decades has been a reduction or abolition of barriers to the reception of relevant evidence in order to allow in material not previously considered admissible. Kirby, when President of the New South Wales Court of Appeal, commented on what he saw as a "general trend of authority in Australia . . . towards the reduction of the rules of exclusion".[51] For example, the hearsay rule has been greatly cut back. In the UK it has been largely

[47] *Entick* v. *Carrington* (1765) 19 St Tr 1029; also see *George* v. *Rockett* (1990) 170 CLR 104 at 110 (HCA).

[48] E.g. Companies Act 1985 (UK), ss. 434, 443, 444, 446–448; Insolvency Act 1986 (UK), s. 133; Banking Act 1987 (UK), ss. 39–43.

[49] *Inland Revenue Commissioners* v. *Rossminster Ltd* [1980] AC 952 at 997 (HL).

[50] E.g. for a full list of Australian statutory provisions on the powers of Royal Commissions to compel production and attendance, see S.B. McNicol, *Law of Privilege* (Law Book Co., Sydney, 1992) 20 n. 112.

[51] *Polycarpou* v. *Australian Wire Industries Pty Ltd* (1995) 36 NSWLR 49 at 62.

abrogated in civil litigation.[52] In criminal cases statute now allows for the reception of first hand documentary hearsay and business documents that contain hearsay, both subject to certain conditions.[53]

Even where exclusionary evidential rules have not been completely abrogated, they have in many cases been significantly cut down. This frequently amounts to an attack on policies grounding long-established safeguards in favour of the general interest in further disclosure. For example, the rule restricting the use of similar fact or propensity evidence in criminal trials[54] has been weakened by the new test of admissibility laid down in *DPP* v. *P*,[55] a decision possibility reflecting developments across the Commonwealth.[56] The House of Lords has further reduced the protection afforded by the similar facts rule in favour of greater trial disclosure by holding, in *R.* v. *H*,[57] that in cases of possible contamination or collusion, credibility is not to be taken into account in determining the admissibility of the evidence, as this is a matter for the jury.

Other well-known privileges or immunities, apart from legal professional privilege, have been diluted or weakened recently. The right to silence now affords far less protection following legislative changes which give much greater scope than previously existed for the drawing of inferences from an accused's silence.[58] The right has also been abrogated in many pieces of legislation dealing with particular forms of inquiry.[59] In the area of public interest immunity it was thought that there had been a recent watershed in the English approach to the law resulting from the House of Lords decision in *R.* v. *Chief Constable of the West Midlands, ex parte Wiley*,[60] in which Lord Woolf stated that new class-based categories of claims to immunity would not be created, and the inquiry conducted by Sir Richard Scott[61] ("the Scott Report"), which gained

[52] S. 1 Civil Evidence Act 1995 (UK).

[53] Ss. 23 and 24 of the Criminal Justice Act 1988 (UK); also see the Law Commission's recommendations for a complete overhaul of this rule in Law Commission, *Evidence in Criminal Proceedings: Hearsay and Related Topics*, Law Comm Report No. 245, Cm 3670 (HMSO, London, 1997).

[54] This discussion does not relate to the use of such evidence in civil litigation, where the rule has never been as strong: see C. Tapper, *Cross and Tapper on Evidence* (8th edn., Butterworths, London, 1995) 410–13.

[55] [1991] 2 AC 447 at 460 (HL), the test being that such evidence may be admitted where its probative force is so great as to make it just to admit the evidence, notwithstanding the prejudice to the accused in tending to show guilt of another crime.

[56] *R.* v. *B (CR)* [1990] 1 SCR 717 (SC); *R.* v. *McIntosh* (1991) 8 CRNZ 514; compare *Pfennig* v. *R.* (1995) 182 CLR 461 (HCA).

[57] *R.* v. *H* [1995] 2 AC 596 (HL).

[58] See Criminal Justice and Public Order Act 1994 (UK), s. 34 (failure to mention facts), s. 35 (failure to testify; cf. s. 1 of the Criminal Evidence Act 1898 (UK), which prohibited comment by the prosecution, but allowed the judge and co-accused to comment); s. 36 (failure to account for objects or marks).

[59] E.g. s. 1 of the Official Secrets Act 1911 (UK); s. 433 of the Insolvency Act 1986 (UK); s. 2 of the Criminal Justice Act 1987 (UK); s. 98 of the Children Act 1989 (UK); generally see J.D. Heydon, "Statutory Restrictions on the Privilege Against Self-Incrimination" (1971) 87 *LQR* 214; C. Tapper, n. 54 above, 463–467.

[60] [1995] 1 AC 274 (HL).

[61] R. Scott, *Report of the Inquiry into the Export of Defence Equipment and Dual-Use Goods to Iraq and Related Prosecutions* (HMSO, London, 1996).

significant publicity and harshly criticised the existing government practice on the procedure for issuing public interest immunity certificates. The government responded to the Scott Report by announcing a new approach to this procedure which emphasised a commitment to the principle of "maximum disclosure" and under which "immunity should only be claimed for the bare minimum of documents".[62] However despite this apparent watershed the immunity is still an extremely strong obstacle to disclosure in many areas.[63] Even after *Wiley* it seems class claims are not a dead letter.[64] The rule relating to inspection to determine applications for immunity may have become more restrictive.[65] Protection of informers under the immunity is still very strong, and has possibly been recently extended.[66]

There are some exceptions to the general trend towards greater court disclosure. The widest such exception may be the development this century of a general discretion to exclude evidence the prejudicial effect of which exceeds its probative value.[67] Stricter rules governing the questioning of rape complainants have reduced the amount of evidence before the fact-finder.[68] Finally, it should be noted that the use of the voir dire to determine issues such as the competence of children and mentally handicapped witnesses and the admissibility of propensity evidence reduces the level of trial disclosure to the extent that such evidence is not heard by the jury.

In general though it can be seen that in many cases where relevant evidence is traditionally withheld in favour of other goals in the justice system, these rules have, in the last two decades, been pared down. This trend may indicate an increase in the value placed on the disclosure of all relevant evidence and a willingness to put up with some of the problems and dangers arising from such evidence for the sake of having the evidence disclosed and put to the fact-finder. As has been shown, there have been very few exceptions to this general trend.

[62] See HC Debs., 19 Dec. 1996, cols. 949–958; also see HL Debs., 19 Dec. 1996, cols. 1507–1517.

[63] Generally see G. Ganz, "Volte-Face on Public Interest Immunity" (1997) *MLR* 552.

[64] *Taylor* v. *Anderton* [1995] 1 WLR 447, [1995] 2 All ER 420 (CA); also see *Halford* v. *Sharples* [1992] 1 WLR 736, [1992] 3 All ER 624 (CA).

[65] *Balfour* v. *Foreign and Commonwealth Office* [1994] 1 WLR 681, [1994] 2 All ER 588 (CA), holding that where the claim is to national security and is supported by a certificate, the court should not inspect the material.

[66] E.g. see *R.* v. *Adams* [1997] Crim LR 292 (CA); *Swinney* v. *Northumberland Police* [1996] 3 All ER 449 (CA).

[67] *Noor Mohamed* v. *R.* [1949] AC 182 at 192 (PC); for a thorough treatment of this discretion, see R. Pattenden, Judicial Discretion and Criminal Litigation (2nd edn., Clarendon Press Oxford, 1990) 232 ff.

[68] S. 2 of the Sexual Offences (Amendment) Act 1976 (UK).

Criminal Pre-trial Disclosure[69]

Originally the common law and equitable courts had no general powers to order discovery to either the prosecution or defence in criminal cases. The Court of Chancery allowed bills of discovery only for civil cases.[70] The reason probably had more to do with the absence of a precedent for the use of a bill of discovery in a criminal trial than with wider issues of policy.[71] Over time the common law developed and imposed onerous disclosure obligations, though only on the prosecution. It had a duty to disclose all relevant evidence in advance of trial, including prosecution evidence and witness statements.[72] The accused was still exempt from disclosure obligations, and this was seen as an important principle flowing from the privilege against self-incrimination.[73] Slowly, from the 1960s, statutory reforms introduced a few limited obligations on the defendant, such as the obligation to disclose in advance his use of an alibi,[74] experts[75] and certain matters in cases of serious or complex fraud.[76]

This situation in England then dramatically changed with the passing of the Criminal Procedure and Investigations Act 1996 (UK). As well as providing for pre-trial disclosure by the prosecution, the Act requires the defence to give a written statement setting out the general nature of its defence, the areas of dispute and, if an alibi is to be used, the particulars of any witnesses.[77] Failure to comply with these requirements can lead to the drawing of an adverse inference[78] and the denial of access to secondary unused material. These disclosure obligations imposed on the defence are not found in other Commonwealth jurisdictions,[79] and are highly problematic.[80] Perhaps the most far-reaching

[69] Generally see Royal Commission on Criminal Justice, *Report*, Cm 2263 (HMSO, London, 1993) 91–100; R. Leng and R.D. Taylor, *Blackstone's Guide to the Criminal Procedure and Investigations Act 1996* (Blackstone Press, London, 1996); J. Nisbett, *Disclosure in Criminal Proceedings* (Blackstone Press, London, 1997); D. Corker, *Disclosure in Criminal Proceedings* (Sweet & Maxwell, London, 1996).

[70] *Lord Montague* v. *Dudman* (1751) 2 Ves Sen 396, 28 ER 253; also see R. v. *Ambergate etc. Railway Co* (1852) 17 QB 957, 117 ER 1548.

[71] *Sobh* v. *Police Force of Victoria* [1994] 1 VR 41 at 45–6 (Vic SC).

[72] E.g. see *Practice Note* [1982] 1 All ER 734; *Berry* v. *R* [1992] 2 AC at 376–7, 380; ss. 3 and 7 of the Criminal Procedure and Investigations Act 1996 (UK). Note though that American criminal procedure was slower to develop pre-trial disclosure than was Commonwealth law: see R.C. Donnelly, "The Law of Evidence: Privacy and Disclosure" (1954) 14 *Louisiana LR* 361 at 371.

[73] R. v. *Mead* (1703) 2 Ld Raym 927, 92 ER 119; *R* v. *Purnell* (1748) 1 Wils 239, 95 ER 595; R. v. *Adams* [1965] VR 563 at 565 (Vic SC).

[74] S. 11 of the Criminal Law Act 1967 (UK).

[75] S. 81 of the Police and Criminal Evidence Act 1984 (UK); Crown Court (Advance Notice of Expert Evidence) Rules 1987 (SI 1987/716).

[76] S. 9 Criminal Justice Act 1987 (UK).

[77] S. 5 of the Criminal Procedure and Investigations Act 1996 (UK).

[78] *Ibid.*, s. 11; also see R. Leng and R.D. Taylor, n. 69 above, 26–9.

[79] E.g. see *R.* v. *Peruta* (1992) 78 CCC (3d) at 370–1.

[80] For just a few of the many criticisms of this provision, see R. Leng, "Losing Sight of the Defendant" [1995] *Crim LR* 704; D. Corker, n. 69 above, at 95–6.

problem with this reform is that it changes the nature of the criminal trial. The defence's role is to test the prosecution case in the light of the presumption of innocence; it should not be required to put an alternative case.[81] However the House of Lords, in the recent case of *Taylor* v. *Serious Fraud Office*,[82] recognised an implied undertaking at common law that documents disclosed by the prosecution to the defence may be used only for the conduct of the defence.

Civil pre-trial Disclosure

The scope of civil discovery has increased greatly over time. A century ago courts took a very different view of its importance. For example, consider Lord Lindley's attitude to pre-trial disclosure just over 100 years ago:

> In England it is considered contrary to the interests of justice to compel a litigant to disclose to his opponent before trial the evidence to be adduced against him . . . our rules of evidence and of discovery are not based upon the theory that it is advantageous to let each side know what the other can prove, but rather the reverse.[83]

This may be compared to the much greater openness expected today, where litigants are expected to play the game with their "cards face up on the table".[84] In *Arab Monetary Fund* v. *Hashim (No 5)* Hoffman J said:

> The last 20 years have seen a judge-made revolution in English civil procedure. Under pressure from the increase in cases of commercial fraud, the courts have provided plaintiffs with remedies and investigative powers which previously, if they existed at all, were available only to the police.[85]

Discovery is now seen as an important means of determining the truth in civil litigation.[86]

However over the last two decades the focus has shifted from expanding the powers of discovery to a recognition of the cost and delay that heavy discovery obligations may cause. It has often been claimed that much of the excessive cost and delay of modern civil litigation is caused by discovery.[87] This is accepted as a direct trade-off of accuracy for speed and cost:

[81] Justice, *Disclosure: A Consultation Paper* (Justice, 1995) 19; also see page iv, *ibid.*

[82] [1998] 3 WLR 1040 (HL).

[83] *In re Strachan* [1895] 1 Ch 439 at 445–6 (CA).

[84] *Naylor* v. *Preston Area Health Authority* [1987] 1 WLR 958 at 967 (CA).

[85] [1992] 2 All ER 911 at 913 (Ch.).

[86] E.g. "discovery is a vital contributor to achieving a just result. It is not mere anecdote that discovery wins cases": Bar Council submission to H. Woolf, *Access to Justice*, Interim Report to the Lord Chancellor on the Civil Justice System in England and Wales (HMSO, London, 1994) 165.

[87] Submission of the City of London Law Society to Lord Woolf's inquiry, reproduced in *ibid.*, 164 ("[o]ne of the major factors responsible for long delays and significant expense in the current procedural system is discovery of documents. In major commercial litigation in particular, discovery can be a huge task and the resources required to be deployed in carrying it through are often the single most costly item for which the litigant will have to pay in bringing his case to trial"). But compare this with Mackie's survey (cited in n. 103 below), which found that discovery took up to 5–10% of the time spent in small cases, and up to 20% of the time spent in larger cases.

> it makes sense to trade some quality for speed and economy. For the needs of the community may be better served by faster and simpler proceedings, albeit at some cost to accuracy, than by a highly accurate procedure in which delays can rob judgments of their utility and which expense places the protection of the law beyond the reach of the great majority.[88]

Or, as other writers have put it, "buying comparative speed and cheapness (and hence accessibility to the courts) at the price of less perfect justice".[89] However not everyone agrees with this trade-off between accuracy and speed and cost. For example, Andrews warns that:

> If access to [discovery and other procedural tools] is denied or restricted, it follows that the chance of arriving at an accurate decision is reduced. Does this matter? The author thinks it does matter a great deal . . . Lord Woolf might discover that the value attached to accuracy in adjudication is the very kernel of our system of civil justice.[90]

The desire to make civil litigation quicker and cheaper has lead to a change of attitude, and a new, more restrictive approach to discovery. A 1995 Practice Direction[91] indicated greater judicial control over the preparation and conduct of cases with a view to reducing cost and delay, and identified discovery as one area in which courts would actively exercise their discretion to limit. To similar effect, the Woolf Report identified four categories of documents and set out a different treatment for each, generally including greater court control over the process.[92] The Civil Procedure Rules 1998 implemented the main body of Lord Woolf's recommendations. Rule 31.6 provides that "standard disclosure" consists of the documents relied upon, the documents adversely affecting his own or another party's case, documents supporting another party's case and documents required to be disclosed by a practice direction. The "train of inquiry" documents previously required to be disclosed are no longer required. Further, the extent of disclosure is limited by rule 31.7, which gives factors relevant to determining the "reasonableness" of a search, and rule 31.8, which limits the concept of "control" of a document for the purposes of the duty of disclosure. The general mood is one of tighter control over the discovery process and an end to unlimited discovery obligations.

Traditionally at common law all evidence was given orally at trial. However there has been a "revolution in the past two decades"[93] in the form of procedures for the exchange of witness statements. This started in 1981 with a

[88] A.A.S. Zuckerman, "Quality and Economy in Civil Procedure" [1994] *OJLS* 353 at 354.

[89] P. Matthews and H.M. Malek, n. 37 above, at 4.

[90] N. Andrews, "The Adversarial Principle, Fairness and Efficiency: Reflections on the Recommendations of the Woolf Report" in A.A.S. Zuckerman and R. Cranston (eds.), *Reform of Civil Procedure, Essays on "Access to Justice"* (Clarendon Press, Oxford, 1995) at 175–6.

[91] *Practice Direction (Civil Litigation: Case Management)* [1995] 1 WLR 262.

[92] See H. Woolf, *Access to Justice*, Interim Report to the Lord Chancellor on the Civil Justice System in England and Wales (HMSO, London, 1994) at 167–72; *Access to Justice*, Final Report, n. 18 above, at 124–8.

[93] C. Tapper , n. 54 above, 267.

voluntary scheme set up by the Official Referees, and was gradually extended.[94] The procedure was then governed by Order 38 rule 2A of the Rules of the Supreme Court.[95] The early pilot scheme was described by the White Book as "an enormous and notable advance towards the open system of pre-trial procedure" and "an outstanding and far-reaching change in the administration of justice".[96] Now the Civil Procedure Rules 1998 provide that courts will order the exchange of all witness statements which parties propose to rely on,[97] and that if this is not done then "the witness may not be called to give oral evidence unless the court gives permission".[98]

However this change was not prompted by concerns for greater accuracy of fact-finding. The express purpose is the saving of time and cost.[99] The change may even be contrary to the goal of accuracy of fact-finding. Significant time is spent over the production of these statements, and they may go through many drafts. The end-product may bear little relation to the witness's original version of events. This problem is exacerbated by a 1995 Practice Direction which provides that the statement should stand as evidence in chief.[100] The Woolf Report has therefore recommended greater flexibility in allowing witnesses to amplify their statements, as well as a number of recommendations about the content and form of statements,[101] and these have been taken up in the Civil Procedure Rules 1998[102] in an attempt to cure these problems.

In general, the last two decades have seen an increase in powers of investigation, compulsion and admissibility of evidence in a wide variety of forms. The trend seems to be going largely in one direction: towards greater disclosure. The only significant exception to this trend is in the area of civil pre-trial disclosure, where reform has been driven by a strong countervailing policy interest in making civil litigation quicker and cheaper.

[94] In 1986 it was extended to the Chancery Division, Admiralty and Commercial Courts. In 1988 it was extended to the Queen's Bench Division.

[95] S. 5(1)(c) and (2) of the Courts and Legal Services Act 1990 (UK) also provides that if a party refuses to exchange a statement on grounds of privilege, then he will not be able to adduce oral evidence of that statement at trial. This may be compared with the situation in Australia, where it has recently been held that a witness statement exchanged pursuant to court rules requiring pre-trial exchange is nonetheless still privileged as the disclosure was made under "compulsion of law" and so falls under s. 122(2)(c) of the Evidence Act 1995 (Aust.): see *Akins* v. *Abigroup Ltd* (1998) 43 NSWLR 539 (NSW CA), also stating that the position is the same at common law: *ibid*., at 552–3.

[96] J.I.H. Jacobs *et al*., *The Supreme Court Practice 1988* (Sweet & Maxwell, London, 1988) i, 595.

[97] R. 31.4 of the Civil Procedure Rules 1998.

[98] *Ibid*. R. 31.10.

[99] E.g. see Review Body on Civil Justice, *Report*, Cmnd 394 (HMSO, London, 1988) para. 229.

[100] See n. 91 above.

[101] E.g. in the witness's own words, not discuss legal propositions, not comment on documents: *Access to Justice*, Final Report, n. 18 above, at 129–30.

[102] See r. 32.8 and para.18 of the accompanying Practice Direction.

SECTION III: ASSESSING THE DETRIMENT TO TRUTH

This section will examine the likely effect of the privilege on the accuracy of curial decisions. It will not deal with the wider and more difficult question whether discovery itself actually contributes to truth-determination. This latter issue has never been properly tested.[103] It is possible that in many cases discovery has been used to obscure the truth, or to make the finding of the truth more difficult.[104] Maximisation of discovery does not necessarily lead to a maximisation of truth-discovery.[105]

Opportunity Cost

The empirical studies discussed above show that most judges and lawyers believe that the privilege does not harm the administration of justice in any meaningful way.[106] However there is some debate about how to evaluate the evidential cost of the privilege. Judge Frankel, an ardent critic of the privilege,[107] assesses the cost as the value of the evidence not disclosed. Other prominent writers share this view.[108]

However Wigmore regards this loss as comparatively small due to the significant overlap of evidence.[109] Further, Alschuler largely rejects Frankel's assessment of the loss, arguing that the cost of the privilege is not necessarily equal to the value of the evidence which it withholds from a court, as some evidence exists

[103] One survey has shown that in 17 out of 86 cases considered discovery yielded significant documents which would not otherwise have come to light: D. Mackie, "Discovery in Commercial Litigation" in A.A.S. Zuckerman and R. Cranston (eds.), *Reform of Civil Procedure, Essays on "Access to Justice"* (Clarendon Press, Oxford, 1995) 139.

[104] E.g., a study by the American Bar Association highlighted the practice of flooding discovery in order to burden the opposition and increase the likelihood that a significant document will be overlooked: see S.M. Umin, "Discovery Reform: A New Era or Business as Usual?" (1979) 65 *ABAJ* 1050; J.L. Ebersole, "Discovery Problems: Is Help on the Way?" (1980) 66 *ABAJ* 50.

[105] "[A]n overgenerous approach to discovery can be as disadvantageous to the outcome of a trial as a failure to give proper discovery" (submission of the Bar Council to *Access to Justice*, Interim Report, n. 92 above at 165).

[106] E.g. only 5 out of 107 lawyers and none of the 42 judges giving an opinion in the Yale study believed that justice was harmed in any meaningful way by the rule: Note, "Functional Overlap Between the Lawyer and Other Professionals: Its Implications for the Privileged Communications Doctrine" (1962) 71 *Yale LJ* 1226 at 1245.

[107] See M. Frankel, n. 28 above and M. Frankel, n. 29 above.

[108] E.g. this is implicit in the criticisms made by E. Cleary *et al.*, *McCormick on Evidence* (3rd edn., West Publishing, St Paul, Minn., 1984) 171.

[109] J.H. Wigmore and J.T. McNaughton, *Evidence in Trials at Common Law* (Little, Brown & Co., Boston, 1961) viii 553 argues that the real impact of the privilege was only felt at the time when the party's own privilege of silence was in force, as then his admissions to his attorney would have constituted a distinct and substantial addition to the available sources of proof. This is supported by the Yale study, where over half of the lawyers surveyed estimated that privileged information is usually available from another source: Note, n. 106 above, 1238. Though compare this with Wigmore's later statement, *ibid.* at 554, about the obstructions resulting from the privilege.

only because of the privilege in the first place.[110] Frankel's mistake lies in determining the cost of the privilege at the time at which the lawyer has secured the client's confidences so that the issue is merely whether they should be revealed. This view disregards the very stage of the relationship that the privilege aims at influencing.[111] The unavailability of such evidence cannot be deemed a cost of having the privilege.[112] This is a popular justification for the privilege, particularly with the United States Supreme Court,[113] and recently the Canadian Supreme Court.[114] Saltzburg argues from this that any loss of information when the privilege is upheld may be more imagined than real.[115] As one writer puts it: "[i]n the final analysis, compelling the disclosure of the client's communication would make the court no wiser than if the privilege exists".[116] This is a common theme in many academic[117] and judicial rationalisations of the privilege.[118]

However this position is also problematic. Surely there is an important distinction to be drawn between the discovery of "truth" by a legal representative and the adducing or withholding of relevant evidence to a court. When critics such as Judge Frankel complain about the loss of evidence to fact-finders resulting from the privilege, it does not meet this argument to say that the privilege encourages disclosure to a separate body (the client's lawyer). Disclosure to the lawyer does not serve the same truth-seeking function as disclosure to the court. The difference between the two is the primary purpose of the privilege.

Wrongful Inducement

The empirical studies discussed in the previous chapter show that most laymen are willing to reveal confidential information to a variety of professionals due to

110 Comment, n. 21 above, 1477.

111 See A. Alschuler, "The Preservation of a Client's Confidences: One Value Among Many or a Categorical Imperative?" (1981) 52 *U Col LR* 349 at 351. See also D.W. Louisell and K. Sinclair, n. 20 above, 53–4; H.L. Ho, "History and Judicial Theories of Legal Professional Privilege" (1995) *SJLS* 558 at 580 ("the privilege does not affect the quantity of evidence that would ultimately come before the court: with the privilege, the lawyer cannot testify as to what his client has told him, whereas without the privilege, the lawyer can testify but would have little to reveal since the assumption is that his client would be guarded in communicating with him.").

112 *Upjohn Co* v. *United States* at US 395 [S Ct at 685].

113 E.g. *Swidler & Berlin* v. *United States* 118 S Ct at 2086–7; *Jaffee* v. *Redmond* 116 S Ct at 1929; *Fisher* v. *United States* 425 US 391 at 403 (SC).

114 See the partially dissenting judgment of Major J in *Smith* v. *Jones* (1999) 132 CCC (3d) 225, especially at paras. 22–3, 30–1.

115 S. Saltzburg, "Privileges and Professionals: Lawyers and Psychiatrists" (1980) 66 *Virginia LR* 597 at 610; language copied by the Supreme Court in *Swidler & Berlin* v. *United States* 118 S Ct at 2087.

116 H.L. Ho, n. 111 above, 580.

117 J.M. Callan and H. David, "Professional Responsibility and the Duty of Confidentiality" (1976) 29 *Rutgers LR* 332 at 395; S. Bundy and E. Elhauge, "Do Lawyers Improve the Adversary System?" (1991) 79 *Calif LR* 313 at 403.

118 E.g. see *Fisher* v. *United States* 425 US at 403; *Upjohn Co* v. *United States* 449 US at 395 (the "privilege . . . puts the adversary in no worse position than if the communications had never taken place").

a faith in their professional ethical rules. It is most likely that clients are aware of the privilege, but completely unaware of its exceptions. It is usual for lawyers during the first meeting with clients to tell them that everything said is confidential, but not to explain to them the limits of confidentiality.

By offering apparent confidentiality and encouraging communications which are then disclosed the privilege could theoretically make more evidence available than would have existed in its absence.[119] One American writer has developed a broad principle around this idea, calling it "acoustic separation".[120] It is unfair to induce a person to part with information this way, and obtaining information by such a deception cannot be justified on the ground that it is useful.[121] However some think that this disparity may be acceptable simply because it may not have been intentionally created.[122] Other academic writers defend the existing approach and raise but ignore the problem of wrongful inducement.[123]

There has been a deliberate effort on the part of practitioners to resist efforts to require them to advise their clients about the limits to confidentiality. For example, rule 1.4(b) of the American 1980 Discussion Draft of the Model Rules of Professional Conduct required lawyers to advise their clients on the limits to confidentiality, rather than pretend that the privilege is absolute.[124] However this provision was then deleted from the final draft.

The practice of not advising clients about the limits to confidentiality is defended by academic writers on grounds of practical utility:

> if a client's misconceptions will cause a harmful failure to share information, advice that confidentiality is absolute, although technically inaccurate and arguably paternalistic, may be more efficient, more likely to induce helpful sharing of information, and, under present rules, substantively correct for most clients most of the time.[125]

This may be compared with the much more serious view taken by lawyers and judges when other professionals fail to warn their clients about the risks arising from the professional relationship.

The fact is that lawyers continue to take advantage of this disparity between client expectations and reality, and it is considered a legitimate circumstance to be taken into account in evaluating the practical operation of the rule.[126] Taking

[119] Comment, n. 21 above, 1478.

[120] See M. Dan-Cohen, "Decision Rules and Conduct Rules" (1984) 97 *Harv LR* at 630–6.

[121] A. Alschuler, n. 111 above, 351.

[122] Comment, n. 21 above, 1479: "[i]f this disparity between appearance and reality were intentionally created, it would undoubtedly be deceptive and delegitimating, but it seems instead to have resulted from judicial attempts to achieve certainty that simply proved unsuccessful in the face of individual cases. . . . The only benefit of eliminating the disparity would be to fulfil the expectations of those who would not deserve protection".

[123] Cf. A. Alschuler, n. 111 above, 352.

[124] See W. Hodes, "The Code of Professional Responsibility, the Kutak Rules, and the Trial Lawyer's Code: Surprisingly, Three Peas in a Pod" (1981) 35 *U Miami LR* 739 at 786.

[125] S. Bundy and E. Elhauge, n. 117 above, 406 n. 235.

[126] Comment, n. 21 above, 1489: "actual certainty may not be necessary to encourage communication: the *appearance* of certainty may be enough. Rules that are certain in form, yet ambiguous in fact, can both encourage communications and allow judicial fine-tuning to reduce over- and under-inclusion".

into account the reluctance among the profession to warn clients of the limits to confidentiality and privilege, it is not readily apparent why this disparity between client expectations and reality is anything other than wide-scale professional deceit. This is particularly inappropriate given the lawyer's role in the administration of justice.[127]

Prosecutions Foregone

The cost of the privilege has so far been considered in terms of the value of the evidence not adduced. Where the privilege is asserted to prevent a criminal accused gaining access to potentially exculpatory information, this is the measure of the detriment to the accused. However it may be that the proper measure of the cost of the privilege is the detriment to the public interest in prosecutions foregone. This can arise in two ways.[128]

First, the prosecuting authority may decide that it either should not or cannot use the evidence, and hence have no alternative but to abandon the prosecution. Alternatively, a conviction following the exclusion of potentially exculpatory privileged information may be considered unsafe.[129]

Secondly, the defence may seek a permanent stay of the criminal proceedings on the basis that the denial of access to the potentially exculpatory material means that it is not possible for the accused to have a fair trial. This has been suggested by a number of judges[130] and has become an acceptable course of action following the denial of exculpatory evidence in Canada,[131] Australia[132] and New Zealand.[133] Such a stay was actually sought in the *Carter* trial.[134] The application there was rejected on the grounds that the accused had not demonstrated that the documents in question tended to establish his innocence.[135]

[127] See further A. Alschuler , n. 111 above, 351–2.

[128] There is a third way in which this consideration can arise: that is if the privileged material is inculpatory rather than exculpatory. E.g., see M. Guttmacher and H. Weihofen, "Privileged Communications Between Psychiatrist and Patient" (1952) 28 *Indiana LJ* 32 at 36.

[129] Within the meaning of that term in s. 2(1)(a) of the Criminal Appeal Act 1968 (UK).

[130] *Alister v The Queen* (1983) 154 CLR at 431; R. v. *Ward* [1993] 2 All ER 577 at 633 (CA); *Carter v The Managing Partner, Northmore Hale Davy & Leake* (1995) 183 CLR at 137–8.

[131] R. v. *Curragh Inc* [1997] 3 SCR 537 (SC); R. v. *O'Connor* [1995] 4 SCR at 455–63, 465–8; R. v. *Carosella* [1997] 1 SCR 80 (SC), noted 40 *Crim LQ* 28.

[132] E.g. see R. v. *Pearson*, New South Wales Supreme Court (Court of Criminal Appeal), 5 Mar. 1996.

[133] R. v. *B* [1995] 2 NZLR 172 (CA). Here the defence sought to compel a child rape complainant to undergo medical tests. The Court of Appeal on various grounds declined to make such an order, and all judges held that the real issue was whether the prosecution could proceed without such evidence.

[134] R. v. *Connell & Ors*, Supreme Court of Western Australia, 10 July 1995. The stay application was heard only three weeks after the decision in the High Court was handed down. Clearly the application and submissions for a stay were completed in anticipation of the High Court decision.

[135] *Ibid.*, at 7, 26.

CONCLUSIONS

When we speak of litigation as a search for truth, we have in mind a particular form of truth that is something less than scientific or physical truth. This notion of truth is still vitally important as the goal and foundation of our system of adversarial litigation. The general modern trend is to place greater emphasis on the importance of this goal, at the expense of other values in the justice system. However it remains difficult to determine the effect the privilege has on the determination of truth.

6

Structure of the Privilege—General Theory

INTRODUCTION

It has always been recognised that there is a need to confine or place limits on the privilege. The most often quoted statement of this sentiment is that of Wigmore:

> It is worth preserving for the sake of a general policy, but it is nonetheless an obstacle to the investigation of the truth. It ought to be strictly confined within the narrowest possible limits.[1]

Similar statements are frequently made by judges. For example the Australian High Court has said that "there are powerful considerations which suggest that the privilege should be confined within strict limits".[2] One of the most difficult issues in the law of privilege is how such limits should be determined.

In dealing with this issue over the course of this century, judges and academics have viewed the problem in terms of whether the privilege should be "absolute" in nature, and whether any form of "balancing" test has a place in the operation of the rule. It may be useful first to say a few words about these two terms, which have dominated the debate over the structure of the privilege. There are many possible meanings for a statement such as "the privilege is absolute". It could mean that there are no limitations on its scope. Alternatively, it could mean that there are no exceptions to its operation. Another meaning could be that the privilege is mandatory, in that once it is shown to apply a judge cannot decide in his discretion nonetheless to require production of the privileged material.[3] While this issue will be examined in more detail in the next chapter,[4] it may be worth noting here that the interpretation usually intended by judges is the second of these possibilities: that is, that the privilege is absolute in the sense that there can be no exceptions to it. "Balancing" broadly refers to a process of determining an issue by a comparison or weighing of competing interests. In practice it can take any form along the continuum between a pure discretion and a closely directed

[1] J.H. Wigmore and J.T. McNaughton, *Evidence in Trials at Common Law* (Little Brown & Co., Boston, 1961) viii, 554.

[2] *Grant* v. *Downs* (1976) 135 CLR at 685.

[3] These three possibilities are taken from L.B. Frantz, "Is the First Amendment Law?" (1963) 51 *Calif LR* 729 at 750–3.

[4] See Chap. 7 below.

judgment based on hard or inflexible criteria.[5] There are many different types of balancing, such as ad hoc balancing and rule balancing.

The purpose of the next two chapters is to examine the nature of an "absolute" rule in theory and as it applies to the privilege. This chapter will begin with a brief outline of many of the arguments and considerations surrounding balancing and absolutism as general concepts. Then it will be shown how this issue may depend largely on the way the interests are formulated in the first place. Specifically, the level of abstraction of interests to be balanced (the input into the balancing machine) may predetermine the answer given by the balancing process. The following chapter will then apply these general theoretical concepts to the specifics of modern privilege case law. It will be shown that Commonwealth courts have, in the main, regarded the privilege as "absolute" and rejected the use of a "balancing" process. It will then be argued that this approach is misguided to the extent that it assumes that a balancing process is used only at a highly particularised level of abstraction. The decision whether to employ a balancing analysis in determining privilege issues is also intrinsically bound up with the issue of when particular facts grounding the privilege are known to the client seeking its benefit. It will be shown that a rejection of balancing is based on incorrect views about the current operation of the privilege in practice, specifically in relation to the timing of knowledge of these grounding facts.

SECTION I: RATIONALE AND THE BALANCING ISSUE

Issue

Whether the common law privilege rule is an absolute one or not may be determined independently of the rationale. There are other factors which affect the desirability of absolute rules as compared with balanced ones. These include concerns regarding judicial arbitrariness, the rule's under- and over-inclusiveness and the administrative costs of litigating evidentiary questions.[6] However it may be expected that the rationale for the privilege will have a significant effect on the decision whether the rule should be applied in a fixed or flexible manner.

As will be shown later in this chapter, there is significant judicial and academic discussion of the common law rationale for the privilege. It will be seen in the next two chapters that there is also significant debate over whether the common law privilege should be a fixed or balanced rule. However there has been extremely little analysis by either academics or judges of the relationship between a particular common law rationale and the nature of the common law

[5] New Zealand Law Commission, *Evidence Law: Privilege*, Preliminary Paper No. 23 (New Zealand Law Commission, 1994) 146, para. 366.

[6] See Comment, "Developments in the Law—Privileged Communications" (1985) 98 *Harv LR* 1450 at 1487–90.

rule as fixed or balanced. There is a tendency, especially in the case law, to assume that a particular form of the rule follows from a particular rationale. In Commonwealth jurisdictions it is usually assumed that the common law instrumental rationale demands an absolute rule. In American case law it is often assumed that a rights- or privacy-based rationale demands a flexible rule.

It is therefore necessary to examine the relationship between the common law rationales for the rule and the rule's structure, in an attempt to determine whether the chosen rationale dictates a particular structural approach. For convenience the rationales will be simplified to two options: the traditional instrumental or Wigmorean rationale, and a rights- or privacy-based rationale. However, as has been mentioned above and will be discussed further below, these two categories are not necessarily mutually exclusive. These categories are chosen as they are the ones most often used in the academic literature.

Rights

There has been a recent trend in Commonwealth case law to hold that the rights rationale dictates an absolutist approach to the operation of the privilege.[7] For example, in the *Carter* case, McHugh J, while holding that he was adopting a "rights" rationale, rejected an exception to legal professional privilege for the interests of accused on the ground that:

> The argument that any document that might assist a person to defend a criminal charge should be available to that person might seem instinctively to be unanswerable. But to uphold it would be inconsistent with the rationale of the doctrine.[8]

Judges are usually unclear about the logic underlying this link. The reasoning seems to be that the privilege is important because it helps to safeguard important values or rights[9] and important values deserve a high degree of protection; hence an absolute rule.[10]

The interest in having particular evidence adduced to a court may be considered a right in itself and so require balancing against the right to the continued confidentiality of legal communications. This seems to be a common approach in American writing.[11] The United States Supreme Court has not felt

[7] E.g. A. Paizes, "Towards a Broader Balancing of Interests: Exploring the Theoretical Foundations of Legal Professional Privilege" (1989) 106 *SALJ* 109 refers to rights theorists as "absolutists".

[8] *Carter* v. *The Managing Partner, Northmore Hale Davy & Leake* (1995) 183 CLR at 161–2.

[9] This discussion excludes US authorities which may employ rights terminology, though use it not in the sense discussed below, but merely to describe an important value. Such cases are usually quite consistent with a balancing approach and an instrumental rationale. E.g. see *In the Matter of Kozlov* 398 A.2d at 887.

[10] For examples of this implicit reasoning see: *Baker* v. *Campbell* (1983) 153 CLR at 95, 118–20; *Attorney-General (N.T.)* v. *Maurice* (1986) 161 CLR at 490; *A.M. & S. Europe* v. *Commission* [1983] 1 QB at 941, 947.

[11] The editors of the *Harvard Law Review* note that "scholars commonly state . . . that privileges justified by the privacy rationale should be qualified by case-by-case balancing of privacy against the need for evidence" (Comment, n. 6 above, 1487). But also see the different views of an earlier set of

constrained to adopt an inflexible absolutist approach in determining the scope of rights enshrined in the Constitution. Brennan J correctly points out[12] that if legal professional privilege is indeed an individual right,[13] then it must give way to the higher rights of criminal defendants.[14] Unterhalter explains *R.* v. *Barton*[15] this way.[16] This is how issues of privilege are determined under the Canadian Charter.[17] There are concerns that the "constitutionalisation" of evidence law by the Canadian Charter may have led to an inflexibility in the law in that country.[18] It may also be the way the issue is resolved under the new South African Constitution[19] and in England once the European Convention on Human Rights is incorporated into English law by the coming into force of the Human Rights Act 1998, as clearly shown by the recent case of *General Mediterranean Holdings SA* v. *Patel.*[20]

Dworkin pointed out that "rights may . . . be less than absolute; one principle might have to yield to another, or even to an urgent policy".[21] Thus even if the interest in disclosure does not constitute a right it may still act as a limit on the privilege. Rosenfeld argues that even a purely individualist approach to the privilege still demands that there be a balance between individual rights and the common good of society.[22] As Professor Paizes points out, "invoking a language of rights does not per se . . . make out a case for absolutism".[23]

The same result may also be reached simply by saying that, under a rights-based rationale such as privacy, there are limits to the underlying need for privacy, and that this has the effect of making the privilege less than absolute. This is the view taken by Professor Saltzburg. He says that, under a privacy rationale "[a]lthough the presumption in favor of confidentiality should be strong, the privilege need not be absolute".[24] There may be little difference between saying

editors of the same journal: Note, "The Attorney–Client Privilege: Fixed Rules, Balancing, and Constitutional Entitlement" (1977) 91 *Harv LR* 464 at 473.

12 *Carter* v. *The Managing Partner, Northmore Hale Davy & Leake* (1995) 183 CLR at 130.

13 Though Brennan J also discusses the privilege in terms of the instrumental rationale.

14 R. Dworkin, *Taking Rights Seriously* (Duckworth, London, 1977) 92. This would be done on a balancing model: see A. Peczenik, "Weighing Rights" in N. McCormick and Z. Bankowski (eds.), *Enlightenment, Rights and Revolution* (Aberdeen Uni. Press, Aberdeen, 1989) 183.

15 [1972] 2 All ER 1192 (Crown Ct.).

16 D. Unterhalter, "Notes and Comments: Privilege and the Proof of Innocence" (1988) 105 *SALJ* 291 at 325–6 (in a hierarchy of rights the right not to be wrongly convicted overrode the right to a secure lawyer–client relationship).

17 E.g. see D.M. Paciocco, *Charter Principles and Proof in Criminal Cases* (Carswell, Toronto, 1987) generally, and especially 209–12, dealing with privilege.

18 See the discussion in *ibid.*, 7–8.

19 In *Jeeva* v. *Receiver of Revenue, Port Elizabeth* [1995] 2 SALR at 456 Jones J described the privilege as a right which may have to give way to the constitutional right of access to information.

20 [1999] 3 All ER 673 (QB).

21 R. Dworkin, n. 14 above, 92.

22 M. Rosenfeld, "The Transformation of the Attorney–Client Privilege" (1982) 33 *Hastings LJ* 495 at 499.

23 A. Paizes, n. 7 above, 124 n. 76.

24 S. Saltzburg, "Privileges and Professionals: Lawyers and Psychiatrists" (1980) 66 *Virginia LR* 597 at 610 n. 43, giving as examples the crime-fraud exception and the exception for litigation against the solicitor.

as above that privacy, as a right, can be overridden by another right, and saying that there are limits on the scope of the right to privacy. Some of the examples given by Saltzburg to illustrate the latter form of argument may be better explained under the former (for example the crime–fraud exception and the exception for litigation against the solicitor).

There is little discussion about the extent to which a rights-based rationale in the common law privilege exists to further instrumental, as well as purely intrinsic, goals. Professor Cleary seems to think that the American rights-based privacy rationale only exists for intrinsic reasons. He says: "[i]f the object aimed at is not the inducement of conduct in certain relations but the protection of individual privacy . . . the implementation of the privilege is amenable to the finer touch of the specific solution". The reasoning appears to be that because the rights and privacy rationales do not focus on behavioural consequences for their legitimacy,[25] therefore the need for certainty is not paramount, and a more balanced rule is possible. Similarly, Wright and Graham argue that predicability is essential if the purpose is to encourage future communication, but less important if the rationale is the protection of the privacy of past communications.[26] Professor Black expressed this rejection of the need for certainty in the rights or privacy rationales when, in giving evidence to a Congressional Committee examining the Proposed Federal Rules of Evidence, he said:

> Is it so obvious that the effect of *prior* knowledge on conduct is the one and only reason for respecting the privacies of human life? Is it not the intrinsically private character of the relation, and the reciprocal indecency of invading that privacy, rather than the parties' knowledge of the law of evidence, that chiefly justifies confidentiality?[27]

It is probably for this reason that Professor Paizes believes that uncertain rules are not self-defeating on a non-instrumental rationale.[28] Even if privacy serves instrumental functions as well, these are not dependant on the client's confidence in the applicability of the privilege.[29] If certainty and predicability of operation are not of paramount importance, then it follows that the resulting privilege need not be absolute.[30] However the problem with these arguments is that it is quite possible that a rights-based rationale supports both instrumental and non-instrumental goals, and is dependent on the client's expectation of the applicability of the privilege.

[25] E. Cleary *et al.* (eds.), *McCormick on Evidence* (3rd edn., West Publishing, St Paul, Minn., 1984) 172, 187; also see Comment, n. 6 above, 1480, 1487.

[26] C. Wright and K. Graham, *Federal Practice and Procedure* (West Publishing, St Paul, Minn., 1986) xxiv 86 n. 117.

[27] Letter from Prof. Charles Black in *Hearings on Proposed Rules of Evidence Before the Special Subcommittee on Reform of Federal Criminal Evidence* at 232, quoted in T.G. Krattenmaker, "Testimonial Privileges in Federal Courts: An Alternative to the Proposed Federal Rules of Evidence" (1973) 62 *Geo LJ* 61 at 92.

[28] A. Paizes, n. 7 above, 124 n. 82.

[29] Comment, n. 6 above, 1487 n. 104.

[30] E. Cleary, n. 25 above, 187; also see *ibid.* at para. .86, p. 202. Compare the very different view of Krattenmaker (1973) 92. Also see S. Saltzburg, n. 24 above.

As will be discussed below, the United States Supreme Court uses a balancing test to determine the application and scope of constitutionally enshrined rights. This has received significant judicial and academic attention in the United States. One view holds that a balancing test is inappropriate for determining issues of rights. As one writer has put it, courts:

> should not . . . employ balancing as a substitute for an effort to find a rule or principle that can guide a decision. Balancing, in other words, is not acceptable as the principle. It is acceptable (and doubtless inevitable) as the technique for making a purely prudential choice between alternatives that are, in principle, equally permissible.[31]

By this view, where it is a matter of determining the application of protected rights in new situations, the proper approach is first to ascertain the purpose of the grant or prohibition, and then to decide on a principled basis whether the particular new situation falls within this.[32] Further, all such purposive determinations can be stated in terms of balancing because, unless there is a competing interest, there is no occasion to seek a limit or sub-rule relating to the right.[33] However, it is argued that it is not the weight of a competing interest that is determinative. Rather it is that the nature of the opposing consideration (here disclosure) was not such as to compromise the foundations supporting the operation of the rule.

Instrumentalism

Some academic commentators assert or assume that an instrumental rationale necessitates the application of a balancing rule. The editors of the *Harvard Law Review* have perhaps gone farthest down this line, by stating that "the instrumental underpinnings of the attorney–client privilege should compel courts to engage in an *ad hoc* balancing of utilities whenever a claim for privilege is asserted".[34] Desiatnik appears to be of a similar view.[35]

The argument seems to be that the instrumental rationale must take into account the costs incurred by its application, and that the need for certainty is not absolute. Therefore an unwillingness to adopt a balancing approach is inconsistent with the rationale. As the same authors put it:

> This stress on the need for certainty, however, conflicts with the underlying rationale for the privilege. So long as attorney–client privilege is justified instrumentally—as a means to the end of maximum lawyer–client discussion—courts should not neglect the competing costs incurred by its application. Certainty, for instance, may not be absolutely necessary, and even if it is, not all clients have an equal need for its protec-

[31] B. Frantz, "Is the First Amendment Law?" (1963) 51 *Calif LR* 729 at 732.

[32] *Ibid.*, at 734.

[33] *Ibid.*, at 736.

[34] Note, "The Attorney–Client Privilege: Fixed Rules, Balancing, and Constitutional Entitlement" (1977) 91 *Harv LR* 464 at 479.

[35] R.J. Desiatnik, *Legal Professional Privilege in Australia* (Prospect Media, Sydney, 1999) 44.

tions. An instrumental theory of attorney–client privilege thus requires recourse to full-scale balancing.[36]

One practical example of this thinking may be the operation of the privilege where corporate clients are involved. The same author argues that corporations have less need for certainty and possess particular attributes that make an absolutist approach to the privilege even less appropriate to them.[37] Finally, if the purpose of the rule is the "perfect administration of justice",[38] then the rule should be extended only so far as it promotes this purpose.[39] As the central element of this rationale is the fostering of confidence in legal communications, the statement in the previous sentence can be taken to mean that, under an instrumental rationale, the privilege should be protected only to the extent that doing so is required in order to protect the general expectation of confidentiality held by all clients at large. As has been shown above, this does not dictate a condition of absolute confidentiality.[40]

An instrumental rationale can certainly be consistent with a balancing approach. However some academic writers may go too far in proceeding on the basis that the two concepts are inextricably linked. For example, the same author quoted above sees them almost as one issue: "this unswerving demand for certainty ignores the ultimate justification for the attorney–client privilege in utilitarian balancing".[41] The same authors posit that balancing must occur under a "utilitarian" rationale, because utilitarianism is about the balancing of interests to determine a case.[42] This issue will be dealt with in the next chapter, where it will be shown that, although instrumentalism may demand a weighing of interests, this process may occur at the level of determination of a rule, rather than as an ongoing *ad hoc* balancing process.[43]

The contrary view is that the furtherance of the instrumental goal of maximising lawyer–client communications requires absolute certainty:[44] a "bright-line test".[45] Predicability of operation is important in a rule which emphasises the encouragement of action in reliance on it;[46] "certainty is necessary to

36 Note, n. 34 above 464.

37 *Ibid.*, at 473–7.

38 *Bullivant* v. *Attorney-General for Victoria* [1901] AC at 200–1; *Varawa* v. *Howard Smith & Co Ltd* (1910) 10 CLR 382 at 389 (HCA); *Attorney-General (N.T.)* v. *Kearney* (1985) 158 CLR at 532.

39 *Russell* v. *Jackson* (1851) 9 Hare at 391, 68 ER at 560; *R* v. *Bell, ex p. Lees* (1980) 146 CLR at 153; *Re Kearney* (1984) 55 ALR 545 at 555 (Fed. Ct.); *United States* v. *Goldfarb* 328 F.2d 280 at 282 (6th Cir. 1964); *Prichard* v. *United States* 181 F.2d 326 at 328 (6th Cir. 1950).

40 See Chap. 4, above.

41 Note, n. 34 above 486.

42 E.g. see *ibid.*, at 477.

43 See Chap. 7 below.

44 *Pearse* v. *Pearse* (1846) 1 De G. & Sm 12 at 28–9, 63 ER 950 at 957, stipulated that the instrumental rationale required a "condition of absolute security". Also see *Upjohn Co* v. *United States* 449 US at 393; *Baker* v. *Campbell* (1983) 153 CLR at 89; *Waterford* v. *The Commonwealth* (1987) 163 CLR at 368.

45 Note, "Attorney–Client Privilege for Corporate Clients: The Control Group Test" (1970) 84 *Harv LR* 424 at 426.

46 C. Wright and K. Graham, n. 26 above, xxiv, 86.

modify the behaviour of communicators and thereby secure the supposed benefits of privilege law".[47] This view is reflected in Wigmore's formulation of the privilege, and thus has been influential in American case law this century.[48] Additionally, this line of thinking has been significant in Commonwealth case law at least over the last two decades.[49]

However absolute protection is not a necessary result of an instrumental argument.[50] This is not for the reason that Paizes states, namely that candour and its benefits "do not in all cases outweigh the interests of the public . . . in having all relevant information available".[51] A privilege rationalised on an instrumental basis could still insist on absolutism even though there were some instances where assessment of the individual case would suggest disclosure. It has even been argued that applying instrumentalism to support an inflexible rule is inherently contradictory[52] and that:

> Courts faced with a claim of privilege should not be able to resist appeals to balancing so long as the privilege remains grounded—as it currently is—in an instrumentalist concern for lawyer–client relations. Inevitably, there will be instances in which that balance must suggest relaxing an otherwise absolute privilege.[53]

It is by no means clear that either a fixed or absolute approach to the privilege is mandated by a particular rationale. The structure of the privilege may ultimately depend on an analysis of the need for certainty or predictability of operation of the privilege, and the degree of certainty or predictability required. This degree of certainty of operation probably does vary according to the rationale chosen. Under the instrumental rationale the degree of certainty required for the common law privilege has traditionally been placed at a very high level. It will be argued later that this need for certainty has been vastly over-estimated,[54] and for this reason a more flexible approach to derogations from the privilege should be adopted in the future. Under a rights-based rationale, the common law privilege may not depend solely on an analysis of the behavioural consequences of the disclosure of information. Certainty of operation would still have some role, however there are other reasons why the common law privilege should be maintained apart from the behavioural consequences. These other reasons may not necessarily demand absoluteness in the application of the rule. There may well be room for a more flexible approach to the common law privilege under the rights-based rationale as well as under the traditional non-rights-based instrumental one.

[47] Comment, n. 6 above, 1487.

[48] "[S]cholars commonly state that privileges justified by the traditional justification should be cast as absolute rules" (Comment, n. 6 above, 1487); for a recent application of this reasoning see *Swidler & Berlin and James Hamilton* v. *United States* 118 S Ct 2081 at 2087 (1998).

[49] E.g. *Waugh* v. *British Railways Board* [1980] AC at 535, 536; *S* v. *Safatsa* 1988 (1) SA at 886.

[50] A. Paizes, n. 7 above, 118 ("not a logical product").

[51] *Ibid.*

[52] Note, n. 34 above, 470.

[53] *Ibid.*, 473.

[54] See Chap. 4, above.

SECTION II: BASICS OF THE BALANCING DEBATE

The concept of balancing has played a central part in the structure of the modern privilege. Before considering the role of this concept in the overall rule, it may be useful first to set out some of the general arguments that have been made against and for balancing as a means of determining legal issues.

Against Balancing

The most common argument against the balancing process is the certainty argument, as recently stated by the United States Supreme Court:

> Balancing *ex post* the importance of the information against client interests . . . introduces substantial uncertainty into the privilege's application. For just that reason, we have rejected use of a balancing test in defining the contours of the privilege.[55]

The theoretical role of certainty as a value in the application of rules has been examined by Professor Kennedy.[56] Although couched in general terms, his analysis is directly relevant to the place of certainty in legal professional privilege:

> Certainty . . . is valued for its effect on the citizenry: if private actors can know in advance the incidence of official intervention, they will adjust their activities in advance to take account of them. From the point of view of the state, this increases the likelihood that private activity will follow a desired pattern.[57]

It is claimed that a balanced rule would be uncertain in operation and would undermine the client's confidence in obtaining legal advice, thereby threatening the entire system of the administration of justice.[58] This may stem from the nature of balancing as a broad standard that seeks to accommodate numerous conflicting interests and therefore cannot be structured with any specificity without losing its usefulness.[59] The certainty argument will be discussed in detail later, where it will be shown that balanced rules are not necessarily uncertain[60] and that there are strong reasons to doubt that a flexible rule would have a significant chilling effect on the candour of lawyer–client communications.[61]

[55] *Swidler & Berlin* v. *United States* 118 S Ct at 2087; also see A.L.E. Newbold, *Legal Professional Privilege* (Unpublished PhD thesis, University of London, 1990) 9.

[56] D. Kennedy, "Form and Substance in Private Law Adjudication" (1976) 89 *Harv LR* 1685.

[57] *Ibid.*, at 1688.

[58] Alternatively, it could be suggested that such uncertainty may be a beneficial feature: by making disclosure harder to obtain it restricts invasions of privacy to cases of real need.

[59] Comment, n. 6 above, 1600 n. 47. E.g., even though the US rule in *Rovario* v. *United States* 353 US 53 (1957) has been fleshed out with detailed rules, the balancing approach may always make the rule unpredictable in operation.

[60] See Chap. 7 below.

[61] Standards of reasonableness are used throughout the law and people are frequently expected to make decisions dependant on such standards.

There is a long-standing debate about the appropriateness of using a balancing approach in American constitutional jurisprudence.[62] One line of argument is that the constitutional provisions at issue are unequivocal commands with no room for abridgment.[63] Another objection is that balancing usually undermines the right it is supposed to determine.[64] The results of a balancing test will necessarily vary according to the values of the judges deciding the cases.[65]

A more conceptual objection to balancing is that it is a rather meaningless and artificial process. The concept of interests having a particular "weight" is completely subjective and ambiguous.[66] These interests may not be comparable in any relevant sense; "they are not quantitative and therefore they cannot, except in a vague metaphorical sense, be 'weighed' at all . . . they can no more be compared quantitatively than sheep can be subtracted from goats".[67] There is no scale upon which to calibrate these disparate interests. As Professor Tapper has explained:

> It is not at all clear exactly what mental process is involved in [balancing]. . . . in everyday life balancing involves the comparison of two different objects by reference to one common factor, that of weight . . . It commonly includes the use of a precise technique, for example scales . . . It is far from clear how far this model applies to forensic balancing . . . it is far from clear that they possess a common element, or that the forensic process of comparing them is in any way more precise than that which would have been accorded without reference to balancing at all.[68]

The balancing process therefore may not provide any real criterion for choice[69] and may serve only to mask a different and more objectionable process of decision-making. Alternatively, the balancing process may simply give back whatever is fed into it.[70] The result of the balancing process depends largely on the way in which the interests to be weighed are formulated. This issue will be considered in detail below,[71] where means of reducing this problem will be discussed.

[62] For a very useful discussion of the concept of balancing in the context of the rights jurisprudence of the Supreme Court, see chap. 3 of M. Shapiro, *Freedom of Speech: The Supreme Court and Judicial Review* (Prentice Hall, New Jersey, 1966) 104.

[63] E.g. *Königsberg* v. *State Bar of California* 366 US 36 at 61, 81 S Ct 997 at 1012, (1961) (discussing First Amendment rights).

[64] Note, "Constitutional Privacy" (1977) 90 *Harv LR* 945 at 982–3: "[w]hile it is true that balancing need not invariably lead to results undercutting personal privacy, the history of fourth and fifth amendment protections since the shift to legal relativism demonstrates that there is no reason to assume balancing will reinforce privacy values. Past cases suggest that, while the method is itself indeterminate, the relative premises which underlie a balancing approach actually discourage protective results."

[65] *Königsberg* v. *State Bar of California* 366 US at 74–5, 81 S Ct at 1019–20.

[66] Note, "Specifying the Procedures Required by Due Process: Towards Limits on the Use of Interest Balancing" (1975) 88 *Harv LR* 1510 at 1519–20.

[67] L.B. Frantz, n. 3 above, 748–9.

[68] C. Tapper, "Trends and Techniques in the Law of Evidence" in P. Birks (ed.), *Pressing Problems in the Law* (OUP, Oxford, 1995) i, 28–9.

[69] Note, n. 64 above, 984, arguing that the balancing process can never dictate a factually compelled conclusion.

[70] L.B. Frantz, n. 3 above, 748.

[71] See the section on the "Level of abstraction", below in this chapter.

There is also the fear that vague and unpredictable tests may give to the judiciary[72] a measure of discretion[73] which should inhere only in the legislative domain. Some of these arguments are extremely spurious and unsourced.[74] A related argument is that laws administered in this manner are open to the risk of official arbitrariness.[75]

Further, attention has been drawn to the potential costs of litigating evidentiary questions. There is also the problem that a balancing test may lead to enormous practical difficulty and inconvenience in cases involving a large volume of documents subject to privilege claims.[76] Finally a general argument is often made that the privilege is too well settled to allow a balancing of public interests.[77]

For Balancing

The basic argument used to support a balancing approach is that the privilege must not violate a public policy that is weightier than the protection of client confidences.[78] More generally, by allowing courts to assess the individual merits of cases[79] and their competing public interests,[80] the rule's over-inclusiveness[81] and official arbitrariness can be reduced.[82] The balancing process used to determine the application of public interest immunity[83] is an

[72] Responses of non-lawyers to law reform inquiries are concerned more with the adequacy of the judges who would be administering such rules than with the effect of the rules on the privilege as a whole: e.g. see Law Reform Commission of Western Australia, *Discussion Paper on Professional Privilege for Confidential Communications*, Project No. 90 (Law Reform Commission of Western Australia, 1991) para. 8.35 and New Zealand Law Commission, n. 5 above, para. 369.

[73] Note, n. 34 above, 479.

[74] E.g. A.L.E. Newbold, n. 55 above, 9 ("judges, in general, do not seem to like judicial discretion").

[75] "Official arbitrariness means the sub rosa use of criteria of decision that are inappropriate in view of the underlying purposes of the rule. These range from corruption to political bias. Their use is seen as an evil in itself, quite apart from their impact on private activity." (D. Kennedy, n. 56 above, at 1688).

[76] Note, n. 45 above, at 426–27.

[77] E.g. *R.* v. *Uljee* [1982] 1 NZLR at 576–57; T.R.S. Allan, "Legal Privilege and the Principle of Fairness in the Criminal Trial" [1987] Crim LR 449 at 487; see Chap. 7 below.

[78] *United States* v. *Nixon* 418 US 683 at 710 (1974); *Valente* v. *Pepsico* 68 FRD 361 at 367 (DC Del. 1975).

[79] Law Reform Commission of Western Australia, n. 72 above, 125.

[80] See Cooke J's justification of the wide discretionary power to exclude confidential information conferred by s. 35 of the Evidence Amendment Act (No 2) 1980 (NZ) in *R.* v. *Howse* [1983] NZLR 246 at 251 (CA).

[81] That is, the withholding of relevant information where the particular confidence concerned does not deserve protection. See D.J. Galligan, "More Scepticism About Scepticism" [1988] *OJLS* 249 at 256.

[82] D. Kennedy, n. 56 above, 1689. Kennedy's thesis can also be used to argue for the recasting of general rules in the form of more detailed rules.

[83] Leading examples of this balancing process are *United States* v. *Nixon* 418 US 683; *Conway* v. *Rimmer* [1968] AC 910 at 950–3, 956–7, 972, 986–7, 992 (HL); *Rogers* v. *Secretary of State for the*

example, though the relevance of the comparison is contentious.[84] Finally, individualisation of decision-making through use of balancing may be a valuable result in itself. Gardner writes that "[t]he uniqueness of personality has led to a revulsion from the over-mechanisation of justice in the nineteenth century to the individualisation of justice through judicial discretion in the twentieth century".[85]

However the scope of the arguments supporting balancing should be recognised. The two sides of the balancing equation may not have similar breadth and scope. In particular, the interests in disclosure of information will vary enormously across a very wide variety of situations. Yet the harm to the administration of justice resulting from such a disclosure may be more constant across these various situations.[86] Hence it may be that the interests promoting confidentiality are more susceptible to a fixed rule than the interests promoting disclosure.

The balancing approach is used in numerous common law jurisdictions and does not seem to have destroyed the foundations of the privilege. A rough survey of all American state jurisdictions shows that case-by-case balancing is commonly used in at least 24 United States state jurisdictions;[87] though there are some states which adhere to a fixed rule[88] and some for which the rule is difficult to discern.[89] However in United States federal courts, while a flexible test is used for the work-product privilege, the test for attorney–client privilege does not apply a balancing process,[90] except for certain types of shareholder litiga-

Home Department [1973] AC 388 at 405, 406, 412 (HL); *Air Canada* v. *Secretary of State for Trade (No 2)* [1983] 2 AC 394 at 432, 446 (HL); *Sankey* v. *Whitlam* (1978) 142 CLR 1 at 39, 42, 58–9, 61–2, 95–6 (HCA); *Carey* v. *Ontario* [1986] 2 SCR 637 (SC); *Aboriginal Sacred Sites Protection Authority* v. *Maurice* (1986) 65 ALR 247 at 257 (Fed. Ct.); *Konia* v. *Morley* [1976] 1 NZLR 455 (CA); *Environmental Defence Society Inc* v. *South Pacific Aluminum Ltd (No 2)* [1981] 1 NZLR 153 (CA); *Glasgow Corp.* v. *Central Land Board* [1956] SC (HL) 1 at 12–14, 16, 18–19; *Van der Linde* v. *Calitz* 1967 (2) SA 239 (Appellate Div.) (note the report to this case is in Afrikaans, but there is an English headnote).

[84] All the judges in *Waterford* v. *The Commonwealth* (1987) 163 CLR 54 held this to be the main point of distinction between the two rules: see *ibid.*, at 64–5, 74, 98–9. Taylor LCJ in *R.* v. *Derby Magistrates' Court, ex p. B* [1996] 1 AC at 508 held that the use of a balancing test in this area does nothing to advance the case for its adoption in the determination of legal professional privilege.

[85] J. Gardner, "A Re-Evaluation of the Attorney–Client Privilege" (1963) 8 *Vill LR* 279 at 460.

[86] The relevant harm from disclosure is the harm to the class of professional relations as a whole, rather than the harm to the individual claiming the privilege. However judges sometimes stray from this. E.g. see *In re Dr John Doe* 711 F 2d 1187 at 1193 (2nd Cir. 1983) (harm to the individual psychotherapist–patient relationship); *Carter* v. *The Managing Partner, Northmore Hale Davy & Leake* (1995) 183 CLR at 140 (Deane J referring to individual harm to the privilege claimant).

[87] Alabama, Alaska, Arkansas, Colorado, Delaware, Florida, Georgia, Illinois, Kansas, Louisiana, Massachusetts, Michigan, Montana, Nebraska, Nevada, New Hampshire, New Jersey, New York, Ohio, Pennsylvania, Tennessee, Texas, Virginia and Washington.

[88] California, Connecticut, Idaho, Mississippi, North Carolina and Rhode Island.

[89] Arizona, Hawaii, Indiana, Iowa, Kentucky, Maine, Maryland, Minnesota, Missouri, New Mexico, North Dakota, Oklahoma, Oregon, South Carolina, South Dakota, Utah, Vermont, West Virginia, Wisconsin and Wyoming.

[90] *United States* v. *United Shoe Machinery Corp* 89 F.Supp 357 (DC Mass. 1950); *In re National Mortgage Equity Corp* 120 FRD 687 (DC Calif. 1988). However the District of Columbia does use a balancing test: see *United States* v. *American Tel & Tel Co.* 524 F Supp 1381 (DC Colum. 1981).

tion.[91] Most statutory provisions around the world creating privileges for other professions provide some exception for the general administration of justice.[92]

SECTION III: LEVEL OF ABSTRACTION

The result of the balancing process will depend upon the level of abstraction with which one chooses to define the rights or interests being balanced. For example, the interest in disclosure could be defined as anything from the forensic benefit gained by the particular documents or testimony sought to the generalised benefit of having all relevant evidence adduced. The countervailing interest in confidentiality can similarly be cast at different levels of abstraction. The interests to be considered in determining the application and extent of the privilege rule were analysed in detail in the chapters on confidentiality and disclosure.[93] Here it is necessary briefly to point out some features of the actual question. That is, what is the appropriate level of abstraction of the interests to be weighed?

Professor Fried has analysed the balancing test that the United States Supreme Court uses for determination of constitutional disputes.[94] He reaches a number of conclusions about this balancing process. Two of these conclusions may be of particular relevance to the privilege considered here.

Same Level of Abstraction for Each Interest

The first point drawn from Fried is a relatively simple one: that whatever level of abstraction is chosen, it should be the same for both sides of the balancing equation.[95] If this principle is not adhered to, then the issue will be cast in a form which conceals the true conflict to be resolved.[96] Another American commentator suggests that in such cases it is very difficult to identify the interests to be balanced without predetermining the result:

> The difficulty is emphasized by the ease with which . . . it would produce an opposite result. He (the judge) simply trims the asserted governmental interest to more moderate size, puts a more generalized (and therefore weightier) . . . interest on the other side of the scales, and there you are. Anyone can do it. And anyone can reverse it just as easily by the opposite process.[97]

[91] The much debated rule in *Garner* v. *Wolfinbarger* 430 F.2d 1093 (5th Cir. 1970).

[92] Law Reform Commission of Western Australia, n. 72 above, 39, 53 and 56 gives examples from the UK, Denmark and Japan.

[93] See chapters 4 and 5, both above.

[94] C. Fried, "Two Concepts of Interests: Some Reflections of the Supreme's Court's Balancing Test" (1963) 76 *Harv LR* 755.

[95] *Ibid.*, at 763.

[96] *Ibid.*

[97] L.B. Frantz, n. 3 above, 747–8.

Applying this argument to the privilege, we must ensure that both sides of the balancing equation are cast at the same level. For example, if we are considering the right of a particular individual to privacy in his or her legal communications, then, if a balancing approach were adopted, this right should be weighed against the individual detriment caused by the non-disclosure of that information in the instant case. Alternatively, if we consider the rights of all people to private legal communications, then this should be weighed against the loss of information resulting from the imposition of the privilege as a whole. This latter formulation of the equation, if then applied back to the individual at issue, will not necessarily produce the same result as if an individualised balancing had been conducted in the first place. For example, there may be a difference in our judgement of the value of the information lost on the different approaches.

Judges deciding privilege cases sometimes fall foul of Fried's warning against balancing interests at different levels of abstraction. For example in the *Carter* case, Brennan J, in rejecting *Barton*, held that:

> The view [in *Barton*] would have some validity if legal professional privilege be regarded simply as an individual right. . . . But if the purpose of the privilege is to facilitate the application of the rule of law in the public interest, it is not possible to allow the interest of an individual accused to destroy the privilege which is conferred to advance that public interest.[98]

A similar mistake was made by two American academics, Professors Sedler and Simeone, in analysing the privilege:

> The relationship and the continued existence of the giving of legal advice by persons accurately and effectively trained in the law is of greater societal value, it is submitted, than the admissibility of a given piece of evidence in a particular lawsuit.[99]

Here Sedler and Simeone, like Brennan J, have balanced one individual's interest in disclosure against all people's interest in confidentiality. Faced with such a biased set of scales, the interest in disclosure could never prevail.

Appropriate Level of Abstraction: Rejecting Fried

The second point arising from Fried's writing is perhaps the more important point: choosing the level of abstraction to be employed. Fried argues that a highly particularised level of abstraction is appropriate for the area of law he describes. He argues for this because he says such a level of thinking is more common in the work of governments, is familiar to courts and, crucially, is the most common level of abstraction chosen for individual personal decisions.[100] He says that:

[98] *Carter* v. *The Managing Partner, Northmore Hale Davy & Leake* (1995) 183 CLR at 130.

[99] R.A. Sedler and J.J. Simeone, "The Realities of Attorney–Client Confidences" (1963) 24 *Ohio St LJ* 3.

[100] C. Fried, n. 94 above, 763–4.

> surely the most common decision is a decision taken upon a very particular balance. Those who would suggest that rational[101] decisions can only be made according to fixed rules are focusing on a particular sort of case, and cannot have in mind the more usual situation with which each of us is constantly confronted: should I take the time to write this article, should I have beef or veal for dinner, should I vote for this candidate or the other? . . . only infrequently do we imagine that we are establishing precedents for ourselves, or that there are rules governing our conduct.[102]

The purpose of Fried's analysis here is to criticise the judicial balancing of interests as being carried out on a level of abstraction that is too generalised, or at least more generalised than seems natural when judged by the standards of personal decision-making.[103]

There is little point in addressing Fried's assertions that such a level of conceptualising of problems is more common in the work of governments and is familiar to courts. Both governments and courts frequently engage in decision-making at all levels of abstraction, and so such comparisons are not of much assistance. There is no obvious reason why judicial and legislative decision-making should proceed in a similar fashion to personal and purely self-referential decision-making. Decisions that affect an entire community, as opposed to an individual, may well be made on the basis of community-wide, or generalised, factors. Fried's assertion about the nature of individual decision-making is the most interesting, and seems difficult to maintain. Individuals are continually making rules to live their life by. Fried's examples of typical individualised decision-making could equally be framed on a more general basis. "should I pursue an academic career, eat well (i.e. without red meat) and be an active or apathetic member of the polity?" The fact that rules are important to us for the purpose of individual, personal decision-making is illustrated by the need people have for justifying departures from their self-imposed rules by means of defined exceptions: "I will eat healthily and cut out red meat, except on special occasions, or when it cannot be avoided, such as dinner parties". These are broad-based rules, sub-rules and exceptions which people impose in order to give their conduct greater rationality and predicability.

[101] One immediate difficulty with Fried's formulation of the problem is his use of the word "rational". Surely it is correct that rational decisions can be made only according to fixed rules, because that is the meaning of a "rational decision": that is, it is a decision mediated through the application of a reasoning or rule-based process, as opposed to, for example, a decision made randomly or based on an inexplicable "sixth sense". It seems that Fried's formulation is therefore necessarily question-begging. Either we are to ignore the word "rational", or we must read in some limitation on the words "fixed rules", shortly thereafter. Given that Fried is ultimately attacking judicial decision-making, which at least aspires to rationality, then the latter alternative may be more attractive. Thus the sentence and argument may make more sense if Fried is attacking the notion that rational decisions can be made only according to fixed rules cast in a generalised manner.

[102] C. Fried, n. 94 above, 764.

[103] *Ibid.*, at 766.

All this goes to show that there are good reasons to doubt Fried's view that the particularised formulation of interests is more appropriate, or in some way natural. Fried was looking at the balancing of interests to determine rights under the Constitution of the United States. However the arguments he employs, as seen above, are general and theoretical in nature and the same could be said of the formulation of interests within legal professional privilege in Commonwealth jurisdictions.

Appropriate Level of Abstraction: Influence of Rationale

The appropriate level of abstraction with which to determine the scope of the privilege may be different according to the rationale chosen for the rule. As the Wigmorean instrumental rationale seeks to justify the privilege by reference to the global advantage accruing to the entirety of legal relations, the balancing test should probably be formulated in a more general fashion. If a non-instrumental rights-based rationale is employed then any level of abstraction is potentially available. It should not be assumed that a rights rationale dictates an individualised formulation of the interests to be assessed. For example, writing about the balancing involved in the exclusion evidence seized in contravention of constitutionally guaranteed rights, one American commentator has said that "the focus should not be on the marginal loss of deterrence from refusing to apply the rule, but upon the cumulative decrease in overall deterrence caused by all the incremental exceptions".[104] Although the right to confidential legal relations is regarded as worth protecting because of its inherent value to the individual, it is still equally possible to consider this issue as a matter of balancing generalised interests, such as the right of all people to confidential legal communications. This is especially appropriate where an appellate court must lay down clear guidance to lower courts, litigants and the general public.[105]

CONCLUSIONS

This chapter has surveyed some of the general and conceptual arguments surrounding the concepts of absolutism and balancing and has shown how the way the competing interests are defined will influence, and may even determine, the outcome of any balancing process. It is frequently argued that a balancing process is unnecessary, as this has already been carried out in order to arrive at the privilege. In the next chapter it will be shown how such a refusal to engage in balancing in part stems from a misunderstanding of the level of abstraction at

[104] Note, n. 64 above, 983.

[105] *Ibid.*, at 1026: the Supreme Court "should also provide the maximum possible guidance for lower courts and litigants. An excessively particularized opinion lacks that quality".

which the balancing process may be carried out. Specifically, courts tend to view further balancing on an overly particularised level of abstraction. A more generalised analysis of the balancing process would enable them to further expand on or modify derogations from the privilege in the same way that they do for elements of the substantive privilege rules.

7

Structure of the Privilege—Application

INTRODUCTION

Commonwealth appellate courts through this century have in general sought to expand the scope of legal professional privilege and rarely allowed derogations to the privilege which would cut back its operation. This is frequently expressed in a reluctance even to consider changing the rule, especially at times when it is suggested that the rule be limited in order to take account of competing interests. This is in stark contrast to United States case law on the attorney–client privilege, where judges constantly heed Wigmore's warning that the privilege "ought to be strictly confined within the narrowest possible limits consistent with the logic of its principle".[1]

This judicial conservatism is frequently expressed as a rejection of a "balancing" approach when determining proposed changes to the rule. This is usually intended as a rejection of an *ad hoc* balancing approach, but recently there have been indications that this may also cover any form of decision-making by means of balancing, including rule balancing. This seems to stem from a fundamental fear of creating "exceptions" to the privilege, which is also based on a reasoned but incorrect view that there are no "exceptions" to the privilege already. Underlying the current approach to the privilege is the principle relating to the timing of knowledge: all circumstances determining the validity of a claim to privilege are capable of being known at the time the relevant legal communication is made. This is a central tenet of the privilege as presently formulated and draws directly from the privilege's rationale of encouraging or enabling candid legal communications.

It will be argued in this chapter that the current approach to the formulation of derogations from the privilege is too strict. A refusal to engage in "balancing" is justifiable to the extent that it implies a rejection of *ad hoc* balancing. However a refusal to countenance any new exceptions to the privilege at all requires further justification. It will be argued that the reason given for this refusal, being based on the time at which the facts grounding the derogation are known, involves a distinction which is not observed in other rules within the privilege.

[1] J.H. Wigmore and J. T. McNaughton, *Evidence in Trials at Common Law* (Little, Brown & Co., Boston, 1961) viii, 554. E.g. *Prichard* v. *United States* 181 F.2d at 328; *United States* v. *Goldfarb* 328 F.2d at 282; *Valente* v. *Pepsico* 68 FRD 361 at 367 (D. Del 1974); *United States* v. *White* 970 F.2d 328 at 334 (7th Cir 1992).

SECTION I: CURRENT APPROACH AND EXPLANATION

Commonwealth courts have frequently stated that the settled rule of legal professional privilege is itself the result of a balancing process[2] which was performed once and for all in the sixteenth century,[3] and that such arguments were either presumed[4] or considered and rejected[5] in the course of the development of the common law. Therefore once the rule applies no further balancing process need be carried out.[6]

One of the frequently cited passages setting out this reasoning is in the judgment of Mason and Wilson JJ in *Waterford* v. *The Commonwealth*, where it was held that:

> Legal professional privilege is itself the product of a balancing exercise between competing public interests whereby, subject to the well-recognised crime-fraud exception, the public interest in "the perfect administration of justice" is accorded paramountcy over the public interest that requires, in the interests of a fair trial, the admission in evidence of all relevant documentary evidence. Given its application, no further balancing exercise is required.[7]

In the same case Brennan J also said that "[i]f legal professional privilege applies, the court has no function to perform in deciding whether the privilege otherwise advances or diminishes the public interest".[8]

This point has been emphasised in recent cases. In particular, in the *Derby Magistrates* case, Lord Taylor CJ held that:

> if a balancing exercise was ever required in the case of legal professional privilege, it was performed once and for all in the sixteenth century, and since then has applied across the board in every case.[9]

Similarly, Lord Lloyd held that:

> courts have for very many years regarded legal professional privilege as the predominant public interest. A balancing exercise is not required in individual cases, because the balance must always come down in favour of upholding the privilege.[10]

[2] E.g. *Waterford* v. *The Commonwealth* (1987) 163 CLR at 64–5; *Australian Federal Police* v. *Propend Finance* (1997) 141 ALR at 592, 609.

[3] R. v. *Derby Magistrates' Court, ex p. B* [1996] 1 AC at 508.

[4] R. v. *Uljee* [1982] 1 NZLR at 576–7.

[5] *Carter* v. *The Managing Partner, Northmore Hale Davy & Leake* (1995) 183 CLR at 138.

[6] *Waterford* v. *The Commonwealth* (1987) 163 CLR at 64, 74, 98–9; *Attorney-General (N.T.)* v. *Kearney* (1985) 158 CLR at 532; *Carter* v. *The Managing Partner, Northmore Hale Davy & Leake* (1995) 183 CLR at 128, 134 and 137; *Australian Federal Police* v. *Propend Finance* (1997) 141 ALR at 592, 609.

[7] (1987) 163 CLR at 64–5.

[8] *Ibid.*, at 74.

[9] [1996] AC at 508.

[10] *Ibid.*, at 509.

Finally, in the *Carter* case Brennan J held that:

> there is no occasion for the courts to undertake a balancing of public interests: the balance is already struck by the allowing of the privilege . . . if there can be no public interest which defeats the privilege, there can be no individual interest which does so.[11]

In the same case Deane J held that "[w]here legal professional privilege attaches, there is no question of balancing . . . The privilege itself represents the outcome of such a balancing process".[12] These statements have been picked up and applied in subsequent Australian cases.[13]

Parallels may be drawn between these statements, in particular that of Lord Taylor CJ in the *Derby Magistrates* case, and opponents of a balancing test in American constitutional jurisprudence. For example, note Black J's dissenting opinion in *Königsberg* v. *State Bar of California*:

> I do not subscribe to that doctrine for I believe that the First Amendment's unequivocal command that there shall be no abridgment of the rights of free speech and assembly shows that the men who drafted our Bill of Rights did all the 'balancing' that was to be done in this field.[14]

These statements have generally been made in the context of a rejection of *ad hoc* balancing, that is, balancing the factors for confidentiality and for disclosure as they apply to the individual case. For example the comments of Mason and Wilson JJ in *Waterford* v. *The Commonwealth* formed part of their argument rejecting a link between the application of public interest immunity and legal professional privilege.[15] Similarly, Brennan J's comments quoted above were preceded by the statement that "[t]he public interest which accounts for legal professional privilege explains the existence of the general rule, but it does not fall to be evaluated by the court in every case as must be done when public interest immunity is raised".[16] In *Attorney-General (N.T.)* v. *Kearney*, when Dawson J says of the privilege that "once it is claimed it is conclusive",[17] he says this for the purpose of comparison with public interest immunity. The *Carter* case has now been taken in Australia as authority for a rejection of *ad hoc* balancing in the privilege generally.[18]

We have seen above that many American courts are willing to embrace a case-by-case balancing approach.[19] While there are isolated judgments in

[11] [1995] CLR at 128–9.

[12] *Ibid.*, at 133.

[13] *Australian Federal Police* v. *Propend Finance* (1997) 141 ALR 545; *Somerville* v. *Australian Securities Commission* (1995) 131 ALR at 525.

[14] 366 US 36 at 61, 81 S Ct 997 at 1012 (1961).

[15] It had been suggested that the fact that a document was denied public interest immunity should necessarily mean it cannot benefit from legal professional privilege.

[16] (1987) 163 CLR at 74.

[17] (1985) 158 CLR at 532.

[18] *Somerville* v. *Australian Securities Commission* (1995) 131 ALR at 521.

[19] The Supreme Court in *Swidler & Berlin* v. *United States* 118 S Ct 2081 was split on the issue, with the majority rejecting a balancing approach and a strong dissenting opinion by O'Connor J arguing for a balancing approach. For relevant cases and texts discussing the American approach, see the references cited *ibid.*, at 2090.

Commonwealth courts which seem to proceed on the basis of a case-specific balancing of public interests,[20] in the main Commonwealth courts have rejected this approach. The statements regarding balancing being "already done" should therefore add relatively little to our understanding of the privilege as one which, apart from the anomalous category of child-welfare cases, does not involve an *ad hoc* balancing test.

However the balancing of interests can be undertaken at many different levels of abstraction. In particular, an important distinction should be made between two types of balancing process:[21] the balancing of general factors for and against disclosure of a specified type of information or in a specified situation calling for disclosure; and balancing of the individual circumstances of the party requesting disclosure against the circumstances of the party asserting the privilege.[22] This is not so much a question of the content of the balancing test[23] as the stage at which it is carried out.

Perhaps the best example of this distinction can be seen in the cases dealing with the proposed exception to the privilege for exculpatory material in criminal trials.[24] In the *Carter* case Deane J said that if such an exception were to be implemented one important issue that would need to be addressed would be:

> whether the privilege should be overridden whenever disclosure of the protected material would materially assist in the defence of any person charged with a criminal offence, however minor, or only pursuant to some new balancing process in which account could be taken of matters such as the seriousness of the alleged offence, the amount of material assistance to the defence which is likely to be derived from disclosure and the damage which disclosure might cause to the person entitled to the benefit of the privilege.[25]

[20] R. v. *Bell, ex p. Lees* (1980) 146 CLR at 146, 155; *Re Kearney* (1984) 55 ALR 545 at 555 (Fed. Ct.) (expressly overruled on this point by Dawson J in the High Court: see *Attorney-General (N.T.)* v. *Kearney* (1985) 158 CLR at 532). Query whether Richardson J in *R* v. *Uljee* [1982] 1 NZLR 561 was proceeding on this basis: see T.R.S. Allan, "Legal Privilege and the Principle of Fairness in the Criminal Trial" (1987) Crim LR 449, n. 50. Canadian courts seem to be moving towards a case-by-case approach for some communications: see *A. (L.L.)* v. *B. (A.)* [1995] 4 SCR at 562–3 (SC).

[21] Really the stage at which the balancing process is carried out, which also impacts on the nature of the considerations taken into account. The Canadian Supreme Court is the only court cognisant of this distinction: see *A. (L.L.)* v. *B. (A.)* [1995] 4 SCR at 562.

[22] However a decision reached by a balancing of the facts peculiar to the individual case may nonetheless set a useful precedent for the disposition of similar fact situations and so may harden into a relatively fixed rule. For example consider the status of privileged information concerning grounds for suspected juror bias in New Jersey. While New Jersey uses an *ad hoc* balancing test (*In re Richardson* 157 A.2d 695 at 701 (NJ SC 1960)) the practical effect of the decision in *In the Matter of Kozlov* 398 A.2d at 887–8 is that after that case it would be highly probable that such information would be privileged.

[23] In *Attorney-General (N.T.)* v. *Kearney* (1985) 158 CLR 500 the majority held that not to have recognised the proposed extension to the crime-fraud rule would have been contrary to the better administration of justice on which the privilege is based. However by formulating the balancing test this way the majority included the need for disclosure within the public interest in the "administration of justice". This effectively considers both sides of the balancing under the factor "administration of justice". In doing so, these judges open themselves up to the very balancing they claim not to be doing.

[24] This is dealt with in detail in chapter 9.

[25] (1995) 183 CLR at 140.

The latter type of balancing may be equated with case-by-case balancing and raises the familiar dangers of uncertainty. However the former type of balancing may simply be part of the proper common law process in which laws develop by the creation of exceptions or the addition of new rules.[26]

In the *Carter* case Deane J uses the "balancing already done" reasoning to reject both types of balancing process. After describing the need for certainty in the operation of the privilege, he says:

> if the privilege could be overridden by the courts by reason of the outcome of some subsequent balancing process or whenever particular circumstances arise in subsequent litigation, an assurance of confidentiality could never be given.[27]

Deane J is clearly warning against two types of danger: "subsequent balancing process" refers to *ad hoc* balancing, and "whenever particular circumstances arise" encompasses rule balancing. Both types are rejected, for reasons that will be described below.

Deane J's rejection of both types of balancing is intrinsically bound up with the "balancing already done" reasoning:

> The compelling answer to the argument in this Court is . . . that the argument was considered and firmly rejected in the course of the development of the common law when it was established . . . The fundamental principle is now so well entrenched in the common law of this country that it should not be overturned or significantly curtailed by the courts.[28]

And in the preceding paragraph he says:

> *R.* v. *Barton* . . . addressed but one side of the argument in that it failed to advert to the fact that, as has been seen, legal professional privilege . . . itself evolved from a balancing process.[29]

This use of the familiar "balancing already done" reasoning to reject rule balancing may have stemmed from the court below, or at least can also be seen in that court. Rowland J, delivering the main judgment for the majority, held that:

> Legal professional privilege is itself a product of a balancing exercise between competing public interests (therefore) any argument that it cannot apply where it is in competition with some other rule based on public interest cannot be sustained. The balancing exercise has already occurred in the enunciation of the doctrine itself.[30]

[26] A. Paizes, "Towards a Broader Balancing of Interests: Exploring the Theoretical Foundations of Legal Professional Privilege" (1989) 106 *SALJ* 109 at 135: "[w]hen this happens, the mechanical application of rules of thumb is not possible, and a court is forced to readdress the balancing process and, if necessary, to shift the fulcrum".

[27] (1995) 183 CLR at 135.

[28] *Ibid*., at 138.

[29] *Ibid*., at 137.

[30] *Carter* v. *The Managing Partner, Northmore Hale Davy & Leake*, Supreme Court of Western Australia (Full Court), 15 July 1993, *per* Rowland J at 21.

Later Rowland J also says: "while the privilege remains, there can be no balancing of that policy against other policies".[31] Malcolm CJ agreed, holding, in familiar terminology, that:

> The recognition of legal professional privilege is itself the product of a balancing exercise between competing public interests. Once it is established, it will only yield in limited and exceptional circumstances of fraud or illegality and, as Rowland J suggests, either within the latter category or as a separate exception, to the absolute duty of the Court in relation to wardship. Apart from that the privilege may only be limited by legislation.[32]

These passages from the judgments in the state Supreme Court are clearly dealing with rule balancing as opposed to *ad hoc* balancing. While there was some confusion in the High Court over the precise nature of the submissions, the state Supreme Court was much clearer on this issue. The passages quoted above occur only after *ad hoc* balancing is considered and rejected. Before these quoted passages Rowland J (delivering the first judgment in the Court) says:

> I have set out all that is necessary, in my view, to identify the law in Australia and the basis for it. The doctrine cannot sustain a balancing exercise for its existence. The only question which remains is whether there is another exception known to the common law of this country which is at once capable of being an exception and does not destroy the public interest which sustains the rule, or is there some other way that the privilege may be destroyed?[33]

This form of "absolutism" can also be seen in academic writings. For example, Newbold's stern defence of the traditional absolutist view of the privilege often goes beyond a rejection of ad hoc balancing to encompass a rejection of rule balancing as well.[34]

It has been necessary to set out at some length the "balancing already done" reasoning and the passages in the *Carter* case which appear to extend this reasoning to the rule balancing process. This is because such an extension poses a novel and important issue for the nature of the privilege. Looking to the statements relating to the balancing being "already done", it may be defensible for judges to say that the privilege is itself the result of a balancing process, and therefore that it is inappropriate to use another form of balancing in determining individual claims for privilege. However to say that the balancing exercise has been performed once and for all in the formation of the rule, and no further balancing can ever be carried out when considering proposed amendments to the rule is tantamount to declaring that the law can never change. What then is the basis for this latter insistence on judicial conservatism?

[31] *Ibid.*, at 30.
[32] *Ibid.*, per Malcolm CJ at 8–9.
[33] *Ibid.*, *per* Rowland J at 23.
[34] See A.L.E. Newbold, *Legal Professional Privilege* (Unpublished PhD thesis, University of London, 1990) 3–6, 9–10.

One possible explanation may be that there is a general fear among courts of creating "exceptions" to the privilege. Many Commonwealth appellate courts adhere to the view that strictly speaking there are actually no exceptions to the privilege: that is, all the circumstances in which the privilege does not apply that are traditionally listed as "exceptions" are in truth limits to the substantive scope of the privilege, rather than exceptions proper (taking an "exception proper" to be where the privilege arises and is then overridden by an exception). For example, in the *Carter* case, Deane J held:

> a critical characteristic of those 'exceptions' is that they are exclusions from the reach of legal professional privilege rather than exceptions to the scope of the protection which it affords. They are directed to circumstances in which the privilege does not attach with the result that the particular communication or document is not protected by legal professional privilege at all. They are not directed to circumstances in which, notwithstanding that legal professional privilege does attach, the courts will overrride the privilege and order that the privileged document be produced for inspection or that the privileged communication be disclosed.[35]

In the same case McHugh J held that:

> The so-called exceptions to the doctrine are in truth not exceptions at all. Rather they identify circumstances where the doctrine does not apply to communications between lawyer and client . . . Thus, communications that come within the exceptions never attract the grant of legal professional privilege. The rule formulated in Barton, however, qualifies the operation of the privilege. It seeks to divest of protection communications that have become the subject of privilege.[36]

Similar comments were made in *Australian Federal Police* v. *Propend Finance*[37] and in *Hing* v. *National Crime Authority*.[38]

This distinction is much more than mere semantics. First, it will alter the requirements for proof of the "exception". To establish a true exception it will usually be necessary positively to prove the relevant criterion. However if the various rules usually termed "exceptions" to the privilege are not actually exceptions proper, then it may not be necessary fully to prove the relevant criterion as a matter of evidence.[39] The second difference relates to the timing of when relevant facts are known in each circumstance (the privilege not arising and arising but being overridden), which may have a significant effect on the principles underlying the entire basis of the privilege. This will be discussed in the next section.

The importance of the distinction between the privilege not arising and arising but being overridden is that it in the former case it is at least arguable that the relevant circumstances may be identified in advance and the client appropriately warned in regard to the effect of his disclosing information. This may

[35] (1995) 183 CLR at 134–5.
[36] *Ibid.*, at 163.
[37] (1997) 141 ALR at 578, 587.
[38] (1995) 39 ALD 298 at 301.
[39] *Australian Federal Police* v. *Propend Finance* (1997) 141 ALR at 579.

be compared with the situation where the privilege arises but is overridden, where it may be impossible for the lawyer and client to know at the time of giving advice whether the information may be disclosed.

These two situations are presumed to have a vastly different effect on the certainty of the rule and the resultant chilling effect. For this reason there is a very strong priority within the doctrine of legal professional privilege to have the criteria grounding the privilege's application assessed from the perspective of the client's state of knowledge at the time the relevant information is imparted. For example, communications made to a person whom the client subjectively but wrongly believes to be his lawyer or lawyer's agent may still be protected, even though no lawyer–client relationship exists between these people.[40]

This reasoning, from the view that in current "exceptions" the privilege never arises in the first place and therefore rests on facts known to the client at the time of the communication, underlies much of the modern Commonwealth judicial thinking on the privilege. It was best expressed by Deane J in the *Carter* case, where he held that:

> The achievement of that 'necessity' [of providing an environment of complete confidentiality] is not frustrated by the established exclusions in the form of particular identified circumstances in which legal professional privilege will not attach. Those circumstances can be identified in advance and the client can be advised that, provided they do not exist at the time when the relevant communication or document is made or comes into existence, legal professional privilege will attach to it and will . . . provide conclusive protection in the future.[41]

Deane J goes on later to refer to:

> the recognised exclusions which preclude communications or documents made or brought into existence in certain circumstances from ever coming within the ambit of legal professional privilege. As has been said, those recognised exclusions do not defeat the rationale of legal professional privilege or undermine the protection of the confidentiality of communications or documents to which the privilege attaches. They operate only if the relevant circumstances exist at the time the relevant communication or document is made or comes into existence. If those circumstances exist at that time, there will simply be no privilege. If they do not exist at that time, the relevant exclusion is spent.[42]

Deane J uses this distinction as the ground for rejecting the proposed *Barton*-type exception. This is because the effect of the *Barton*-type situation is:

> not that legal professional privilege does not attach at all to the relevant communications or documents but that, notwithstanding that it has attached, it will be unavailing if and wherever the designated circumstances might subsequently arise.[43]

[40] See section "Consistency with other privilege rules" in Chap. 8, below.
[41] (1995) 183 CLR at 135.
[42] *Ibid.*, at 137.
[43] *Ibid.*

The result of this is stark. It would:

> undermine the efficacy of legal professional privilege by creating a necessarily unpredictable gap in the general protection which it accords to documents to which it has attached. It would convert an unqualified and conclusive privilege into a qualified and provisional one.[44]

Clearly it is assumed that other "exceptions" do not do this.

On this theory of the meaning of "exceptions" to the privilege, when judges say that the "balancing is already done" what they mean is: that the basic priority of confidentiality over disclosure of legal communications was established in the sixteenth century and cannot be challenged; that there are no common law exceptions to this principle:[45] that all[46] current rules classified as "exceptions" are simply limitations on the scope of the privilege and arise from circumstances that can be known at the time the legal communication is effected; that consequently such "exceptions" do not affect the rationale underlying the rule, being the maintenance of client confidence; and that true "exceptions", being circumstances where the privilege arises and is then overridden by a competing interest, do not exist and will not be recognised.

An example of the application of this reasoning can be seen in the post-*Carter* Australian case of *McLachlan* v. *August*.[47] There it was argued that an exception to the privilege should be recognised where this was necessary to negate a criminal defence. Unsurprisingly (particularly in light of the *Carter* litigation), that submission was sternly rejected. In doing so, Malcolm CJ[48] observed that "[a]s was made clear in *Carter* . . . this balancing of public interests takes place at a point where the question is whether or not legal professional privilege attaches to the documents".[49] Malcolm CJ was clearly troubled by the fact that one of the leading Australian privilege cases, *R* v. *Bell, ex parte Lees*,[50] clearly defies this pattern. Thus the judge went to great pains to cast doubt upon and distinguish this authority, in a rather strained fashion.[51]

The following chapters will look in detail at the main exceptions to the privilege: waiver, crime-fraud and the possible exceptions for exculpatory criminal

[44] *Ibid.*

[45] Note that there is great variety in the formulation of this limb of the argument. Some judges or writers say that there are no exceptions apart from waiver (e.g. Wigmore) some say no exceptions apart from the crime-fraud exception (the most popular formulation among judges); some say no exceptions apart from the child-welfare exception (e.g. Deane and McHugh JJ). If one were to accept the rationalisation of the "exceptions" to the privilege discussed above, the best formulation (though one not seen) may be that there are no common law exceptions at all; child-welfare being a statutory exception by virtue of the statute-imposed paramountcy of the welfare of the child, though waiver may be the most difficult to defend as not being an "exception".

[46] Or "most", subject to the previous footnote.

[47] (1996) 16 WAR 75 (SC).

[48] Who had delivered a judgment in *Carter* v. *The Managing Partner, Northmore Hale Davy & Leake* in the Western Australian Supreme Court.

[49] (1996) 16 WAR at 85.

[50] (1980) 146 CLR 141 (HCA).

[51] (1996) 16 WAR at 85.

evidence and secondary evidence. These chapters will analyse the nature and extent to which these rules can be considered to be "exceptions", and the extent to which they are determined by a balancing process. Before undertaking this task, the final section of this chapter will examine the third proposition listed above, namely that all current "exceptions" are simply limitations on the scope of the privilege and arise from circumstances that can be known at the time the legal communication is effected. This theory is also expressed by saying that the privilege is never "overridden" by a competing interest; it merely does not arise in some circumstances. It will also be useful to compare these traditional "exceptions" with rules usually categorised as substantive components of the rule, from the same point of view of when the constituent facts grounding the relevant rule are known, if at all. The next section therefore will analyse these rules in terms of: (a) whether the relevant circumstance grounding the exception arises during or before any legal communication is imparted, thereby having the effect that no relevant lawyer–client relation arises, or whether the circumstance arises after a legal communication is validly imparted and overrides the effect of that communication; and (b) whether, and if so when, the facts determining the existence or non-existence of the privilege are known to the client.

SECTION II: CONSISTENCY WITH PRIVILEGE DEROGATIONS

Crime-fraud

As regards the crime-fraud exception, the dominant modern judicial thinking holds that this is not an "exception". This is because the criminal or fraudulent intent vitiates the lawyer–client relationship, with the effect that the advice is outside the scope of the professional relationship between the lawyer and the client, and so no protection is afforded.[52] In Chapter 8, on the crime-fraud exception, it will be shown that this modern rationale for the rule is misleading and inconsistent with other principles, and that the exception is in fact based on a balancing of costs and benefits.

The decision in *R* v. *Cox and Railton*[53] can be adequately explained on the basis that the privilege arose and was later overridden. In that case the advice at issue was a request by the clients (two partners) for information about how they could lawfully defeat a damages claim. At that stage there was lawful advice sought in the course of a valid professional relationship. It was only after this advice was received that the clients proceeded to attempt to do illegally what they previously may have thought they would be able to do legally.[54] The case

[52] See Chapter 8, below.

[53] *R.* v. *Cox and Railton* (1884) 14 QBD 153 (Ct. for Crown Cases Reserved).

[54] Note, "The Future Crime or Tort Exception to Communications Privileges" (1964) 77 *Harv LR* 730 at 731 states that the crime-fraud exception covers cases involving the subsequent formation of criminal intent. If this is the case then this part of the exception (at least) cannot rest on the "scope of the relationship" justification.

of *R.* v. *Cox and Railton* will also be explained in more detail in Chapter 8, which deals with the crime-fraud rule.

Looking at the matter from first principles, it should be obvious that the privilege is in reality being overridden and not simply failing to arise. Again, this issue will be examined in greater detail in Chapter 8, relating to the crime-fraud rule, where it will be shown that, in reality, at the time of imparting information the client and usually also the lawyer will expect that their discussions will benefit from confidentiality and would not have thought that there was no legal relationship between them at that particular time. The reality of what the client is aware of at each point in time firmly suggests that a valid lawyer–client relationship exists at the time the communication is made, and that the effect of this is overridden later on.

Criminal Exculpatory Evidence

It is unclear whether a *Barton*-type exception necessarily involves the overriding of the privilege. In Caulfield J's classic statement of the rule in *Barton* he held that if documents help a criminal defence, then "no privilege attaches".[55] On its natural construction this seems to indicate, not that the privilege is overridden at a later time, but that it never arose in the first place. However Deane J in the *Carter* case argued that Caulfield J did not actually mean this and that he really meant that notwithstanding that the privilege attaches, it will be unavailing in certain circumstances.[56] McHugh J was of a similar view.[57] Toohey J argued that the distinction was largely irrelevant.[58] To the extent that Deane and McHugh JJ are seeking to distil Caulfield J's intent, their construction is a strained one. In the *Derby Magistrates* case Lord Taylor CJ rejected the proposed exception partly as it conflicted with the "long established rule that . . . once privileged, always privileged".[59] However the defendant had argued for a recognised interest exception determined on a case by case basis. The cases have not determined the issue. It is equally open to argue that in a *Barton*-type exception the privilege does not arise in the first place as the exculpatory nature of the information will generally be known at the outset.

Such a view would accord well with the nature of the information at issue. The most common situation in which privilege may be claimed over exculpatory information will be where the communication was made by another party involved in the transaction. If a particular piece of information is at any point likely to have the effect of exculpating another person from a serious criminal charge, it is most probably likely already to have that flavour from the outset,

[55] *R.* v. *Barton* [1972] 2 All ER at 1194.
[56] *Carter* v. *The Managing Partner, Northmore Hale Davy & Leake* (1995) 183 CLR at 137.
[57] *Ibid.*, at 163.
[58] *Ibid.*, at 154.
[59] R v. *Derby Magistrates' Court, ex p. B* [1996] 1 AC at 503.

rather than be a benign or irrelevant piece of information which then has an added significance once further events occur in the future.

A simplified version of the facts in the *Derby Magistrates* case may serve to illustrate this. In this case two men were suspected of a murder, in circumstances where it was clear that both had been present at the time of killing, though each claimed the other was responsible. At the time that each of the two men went to his lawyer for advice, any information imparted at that time that later turned out to be exculpatory must have been clearly recognisable as exculpatory at the time it was initially imparted. Or, to use another example, if an accused person says to his lawyer "we all helped with the crime, except for X, who tried to stop us", then the exculpatory effect of this information for X should be obvious at the outset. This is not to say that the client will also know of the legal rule that provides an exception to the privilege for exculpatory material (assuming such a rule to be in operation). However the entire rationale and many of the fundamental principles of the rule rest on the assumption of client knowledge of the privilege and its bounds. Thus we may make the same assumption here.

It is of course possible to imagine situations in which the privileged material takes on an exculpatory nature only some time after it was originally imparted to the lawyer. This may be the case where it was inconceivable at the time that the relevant legal communications were made that the person whom the information exculpates would ever be charged with an offence. To take the last example used above, the exculpatory nature of this statement with respect to X may not have been recognised at the time the statement was made if it was inconceivable that X would ever be charged. On one level any inculpatory information may help to exculpate everyone else in the world. However this problem will not be present where the privileged information is not inculpatory of the client, but rather provides some fact which serves to exculpate particular people without specifically inculpating others, for example a fact which establishes the inability of the accused to commit the crime. In any case, the proposed *Barton*-type exception is only an exception to a privilege. It does not make the evidence admissible if there is some other reason for excluding it. Any evidence which is inculpatory of the speaker and exculpatory of some third party would perhaps not be protected by legal professional privilege (if a *Barton*-type exception were in operation), but may still be eligible for protection by the privilege against self-incrimination.

A better answer is that, even in the example of X given above, the exculpatory nature is still immediately apparent. All that is not apparent is the possibility that the person eventually charged would ever be so charged, and therefore have need for access to the information. An example may help to illustrate the effect of this. Imagine you go to a large family dinner one night, and the next morning hear that your sister-in-law was murdered across town that night and that your brother (the deceased's estranged husband) is arrested for the murder. The conversation with your lawyer later that same day in which you recount the people present at the dinner may exculpate your brother from the charge. However the information also exculpates the others present, even though you had not thought that any of them might be charged. If it later turns out that, as a complete surprise to everyone, your grandmother is charged with the murder and not your brother, then the same communication will prove equally exculpatory with respect to her. And, crucially, it will always have been exculpatory, even though you never turned your mind to the possibility of your grandmother being charged.

Moreover, there is possibly a greater chance that the exculpatory nature of a piece of information will be realised at the outset than, say, the nature of some information in inculpating its speaker in a crime or fraud. There is a blurred line between seeking advice about the implementation of a plan of uncertain legality, and seeking advice on the implementation of a plan of certain illegality. Therefore it is likely that the full significance of the sort of legal communications which would form the criteria of a *Barton*-type exception would be known at the time the information is imparted.

Waiver

The many different rules classified under the term "implied waiver" will be considered in detail in Chapters 10 and 11 below. Due to the disparate nature of this rule[60] it is impractical and of little use to survey the authorities on implied waiver to determine whether the privilege here is considered "never to arise" or to be "overridden". It is necessary here to consider only the practical operation of the rule, in order to see whether the facts grounding the criteria for the rule are capable of being known at the time the legal communication is imparted.

Many of the possible circumstances which may give rise to implied waiver cannot be known or defined in advance. A ready example may be found in a recent leading case on waiver, *Goldberg* v. *Ng*,[61] also discussed in Chapter 10 below. In that case the client[62] objected to disclosing documents to an inquiry as he was keen to retain confidentiality in them. He agreed to submit the documents on the basis that confidentiality and the privilege would be retained. Privilege was later found to have been waived by the disclosure of the documents to the inquiry. The result meant that a clear expectation of confidentiality had been disappointed, despite the fact that the disclosure was only made in reliance on that expectation. Many similar examples can be given.

It should however be possible to predict the application of the waiver rules discussed below in some of these situations. Parties may be able to see in advance when they are putting privileged communications in issue in a proceeding, or that their partial disclosure of some material may threaten the continued secrecy of other related information. These rules are sometimes triggered

[60] Or, as will be explained below, this category of exceptions.
[61] (1996) 185 CLR 83.
[62] Actually a lawyer being sued by his own client.

by an active decision of a party. One immediate problem of advance prediction of the operation of these rules is that some exceptions may turn on inherent or systemic unfairness in the litigation. This issue will be discussed in greater detail in Chapter 11 below. A wider and more serious problem is that, even though many of these exceptions must be triggered by specific voluntary acts of parties, people other than the parties may have authority to perform the acts which lead to loss of the privilege. First, lawyers have wide powers to perform acts which deprive their clients of the privilege. Lawyers have ostensible authority to bind their clients in any matter arising in or incidental to the litigation, and this may lead to loss of the privilege even though the express wishes of the client are that privilege be maintained.[63] Courts seem keen to uphold the principle of ostensible authority, and place great importance on the need for parties to litigation to be able to rely on representations made by their opponents' solicitors.

As well as loss of privilege caused by a party's lawyer, there are other circumstances in which the safe operation of the privilege is beyond the control or even knowledge of the privilege-holding party. For example, in some cases representatives such as the trustee in bankruptcy,[64] liquidator[65] or personal representative of an estate[66] may cause the party they are representing to lose its privilege. Such possibilities must diminish the expectation a client holds of the confidentiality of his communications. Finally, with the danger of a largely *ad hoc* and improperly articulated fairness test, there is a risk that courts may simply order disclosure because the material is important.[67] An example of this may be the tendency of some courts to find waiver due to partial disclosure without insisting on actual detriment,[68] as discussed in Chapter 11 below.

The current rule of implied waiver seriously undermines the absoluteness and predicability of the privilege as it is extremely difficult and in many cases impossible for the client to know in advance whether he will lose the benefit of the privilege as a result of this rule.

Child Welfare

The Court of Appeal in *Oxfordshire County Council* v. *M*[69] held that the paramount interests of the child, as enshrined in section 1 of the Children Act 1989

[63] E.g. as in *Causton* v. *Mann Egerton (Johnsons) Ltd* [1974] 1 All ER 453 at 457 (CA) and *Great Atlantic Insurance Co* v. *Home Insurance Co* [1981] 2 All ER 485 at 492 (CA).

[64] *Re Königsberg (a bankrupt)* [1989] 3 All ER 289 (Ch D).

[65] *Re Stanhill Consolidated Ltd* [1967] VR 749 (SC) (this case is discussed in detail in Chap. 11 below); *Commissioner for Corporate Affairs (WA)* v. *Eastoe* (1989) 15 ACLR 694 (WA SC).

[66] *Chant* v. *Brown* (1849) 7 Hare 79, 68 ER 32; *Doe d. Marriott* v. *Hertford* (1849) 19 LJQB 526 (QB).

[67] R.L- Marcus, "The Perils of the Privilege: Waiver and the Litigator" (1986) 84 *Mich LR* 1605 at 1649.

[68] E.g. *Nye* v. *Sage Products Inc* 98 FRD 452 at 453 (DC Ill. 1982); *R.J. Hereley & Son Co* v. *Stotler & Co* 87 FRD 358 (DC Ill. 1980); *Harbour Inn Seafoods Ltd* v. *Switzerland General Insurance* [1990] 2 NZLR 381 at 383.45 (HC).

[69] [1994] Fam 151 (CA).

(UK), may lead to the overriding of legal professional privilege[70] over experts' reports. In *Re L*[71] the House of Lords approved *Oxfordshire County Council* v. *M* and went further, holding that litigation privilege had no operation in Children Act proceedings.

This rule clearly turns on an element external to the communication and so calls for a straight balancing exercise to be carried out at the time when the exception is being considered. There is not even a hope of the sort of fictional theory used to reconcile the crime-fraud exception with the traditional rationale for the privilege. When the exception operates it does so by overriding an already existing privilege. At the time the legal communication is made the client has no significant method of being able to determine the operation of the exception. Even the most ardent supporters of the view that in all exceptions the privilege is not overridden but rather never arises accept that this statutory exception is anomalous and inconsistent with the general policy and rule of the privilege.[72] This has caused more than a little discomfort for those wishing to uphold the purity of the traditional explanation for the privilege, as was shown above in relation to *McLachlan* v. *August*.[73]

SECTION III: CONSISTENCY WITH SUBSTANTIVE RULES OF PRIVILEGE

As stated above, the theory of the structure of the privilege articulated by, amongst others, Deane and McHugh JJ holds that there can be no "exception" to the privilege which rests on criteria determinable after the legal communication is made.[74] It has just been shown how this view of the privilege does not accord with the reality of the current exceptions to the privilege. Now it will be shown how some of the substantive rules that make up the privilege likewise may depend on criteria which cannot be determined at the time the legal communication is made.

Definition of Client: Common Interest

Communications between co-parties are not privileged merely by virtue of having been made between co-parties. However there is an exception to this rule where the parties have a "common interest" in the litigation. In *Buttes Oil &*

70 All the judges in *Oxfordshire County Council* v. *M* discussed the issue in terms of "legal professional privilege" rather than "litigation privilege".

71 [1997] AC 1 (HL).

72 E.g. Deane J in *Carter* v. *The Managing Partner, Northmore Hale Davy & Leake* (1995) 183 CLR at 135.

73 (1996) 16 WAR 75; see p. 125 above.

74 Apart from waiver, and perhaps the child welfare exception.

Gas Co v. *Hammer (No. 3)*[75] this exception was extended to cover information exchanged between a party to litigation and third persons with a common interest and legal advisers in common, where this information related to pending litigation. This was taken even further in *Guiness Peat Ltd.* v. *Fitzroy Robinson Partnership*,[76] where communications between an insurance company and its lawyers were privileged in the hands of the insured, in litigation in which neither the insurance company nor its lawyers were involved.[77] It now seems clear that, in some jurisdictions at least, the retention of a common solicitor is not necessary for such a common interest to arise.[78] However, as Donaldson LJ correctly pointed out in *Buttes Oil & Gas*,[79] some of the documents protected by this application of privilege were made before the parties in that case had a joint solicitor.[80] Therefore, at the time the communication was made, they could not have been aware of the existence of the privilege over their communications. The party asserting the privilege in *Guiness Peat* would have had even less of a chance of knowing the privileged nature of their communications at the time the communications were actually made. This seems to make a nonsense of the argument that clients will always know of the privilege at the time it arises.

Even if a party is aware of the possibility of benefiting from the common interest rule, it will be impossible for it to know with certainty whether it actually can take advantage of the rule. In *Network Ten Ltd* v. *Capital Television Holdings Ltd* Giles J held that "the concept is not rigidly defined and it is a question of fact in each case".[81] Further, the privilege arising from a clear and established common interest can be threatened at a later point in time if the parties turn out to have a conflict of interest.[82] Similarly, parties will be unable to know at the time of making the communication that the communication may stop being privileged against a joining party. Thus a legitimately held belief in the operation of the privilege may be frustrated at a later date. Thus this element of

[75] [1981] 1 QB 223 (CA); Brightman LJ at 267: "if two parties with a common interest and a common solicitor exchange information for the dominant purpose of informing each other . . . or of obtaining legal advice in respect of contemplated or pending litigation, the documents or copies containing that information are privileged from production in the hands of each"; also see Lord Denning MR, *ibid.*, at 243 ("I would sweep away all those distinctions"). Note though that this was an unusual case, in that two of the groups with the greatest commercial interest in the litigation, the rulers of the emirates claiming title over the oilfield, could not be parties to the action. However the judges, particularly Lord Denning, thought that this was a principle with wide application.

[76] [1987] 2 All ER 716 at 725d (CA).

[77] *Buttes Oil & Gas* was cited as direct authority; also see *Somerville* v. *Australian Securities Commission* (1995) 131 ALR 517.

[78] *Bulk Materials Pty Ltd* v. *Coal and Allied Operations Pty Ltd* (1988) 13 NSWLR 689 at 695 (NSW SC); *Network Ten Ltd* v. *Capital Television Holdings* (1995) 16 ACSR 138 at 142 (NSW SC).

[79] [1981] 1 QB at 252, reserving the point for "another case in which the facts are less unusual and point essential to the decision"; although he did say that "some such proposition must be correct".

[80] *Ibid.*, at 251–2.

[81] (1995) 16 ACSR at 142.

[82] E.g. *State Government Insurance Commission* v. *Paneros* (1988) 48 SASR 349 (SA SC); also see *Leif Hoegh A/S* v. *Petrolsea Inc (The "World Era")* [1993] 1 Lloyd's Rep 363 at 367 (QB).

the substantive rules that make up the privilege suffers from some of the same problems that judges warn against when they reject the creation of "exceptions".

Definition of Lawyer: Accountants and Multi-disciplinary Practices

English law has not yet resolved difficult questions regarding whether the privilege should exist in areas of legal advice conducted by both lawyers and non-lawyers, and if the privilege exists who should be entitled to benefit from it. This in turn raises the issue whether, at the time legal communications are made, the client has all the information he needs to determine whether his communications may benefit from the privilege.

One place where this may particularly be a problem is in the emerging area of multi-disciplinary practices ("MDPs").[83] This trend started with the creation or acquisition of small law firms by the "Big Six" international accounting firms. Some of these accounting firms are now able to offer combined legal and commercial advice. Legislation to cover MDPs exists or is being considered in many common law jurisdictions,[84] including England and Wales.[85]

An International Bar Association ("IBA") report on MDPs said that IBA Councillors surveyed did not consider loss of lawyer–client privilege as a threat posed by MDPs; however the IBA itself felt that this was a significant problem.[86] The danger is not hard to see. If the legal communication is also disclosed to non-lawyers in the same firm, this can lead to loss of confidentiality and loss of the privilege. It may be difficult to bring such non-lawyers under the extension to the privilege given to agents of the lawyer, where such non-lawyers are partners in the same firm and are instrumental in giving advice. It is also virtually impossible in such combined accounting and law firms as the Garretts-Arthur Anderson office to shield legal work in a way that would ensure the maintenance of the privilege, as well as being against the *raison d'être* of such offices.[87]

[83] I am indebted to Mr Patrick Wilkins, editor of *Commercial Lawyer* magazine, for supplying me with much of the background information relating to MDPs.

[84] E.g. New South Wales and Victoria: see Anon., "Australian State Gives Green Light to MDPs", *The Lawyer*, 3 Nov. 1998. The Law Society of Upper Canada voted in Oct. 1998 to lift its ban on MDPs: see Anon., "MDPs Get Cautious Approval from Law Society in Canada", *The Lawyer*, 13 Oct. 1998. Inquiries into the issue are currently being conducted by the American Bar Association, the Law Council of Australia and the New Zealand Law Society: see N. Rose, "Americans Launch MDP Probe", *LS Gaz.*, 12 Aug. 1998.

[85] S. 39 of the Solicitors Act 1974 (UK) has been repealed by ss. 66(1), 125(7) of and Sch. 20 of the Courts and Legal Services Act 1990 (UK) in order to enable MDPs to practise in this country. Also see s. 89 of and Sch.14 to of the same Act. The Law Society of England and Wales is currently investigating the subject.

[86] See Bower, n. 86 above, 158–9.

[87] "Garretts' managing partner, Julia Chain, said Garretts was 'very mindful of Law Society rules and is assiduous in compliance with them.' In practice, at the joint Garretts-Arthur Andersen headquarters off London's Strand, this means that employees of both entities are now allowed to enter each other's working areas without first ringing a bell": ("Arthur Andersen Associate Firms Prosper within Referral Rules", *LS Gaz.*, 3 Sept. 1997 at 10).

If a client goes to an MDP for legal advice, or combined legal-commercial advice, then under current English law that client could perhaps benefit from the privilege only if advised by lawyers only, and perhaps not even then. Crucially for the present issue, the client seeking legal advice from an MDP has no real way of knowing, at the time when the legal communication is made, whether that communication will benefit from the privilege, as this depends largely on who within the firm contributes to that particular piece of advice. The application of the privilege cannot be known in advance in such firms.

Confidentiality and Eavesdropping

The complex role of confidentiality in the operation of the privilege will be analysed in Chapter 10 below. This will examine the interrelationship between the substantive requirement of confidentiality the rule of waiver by virtue of lack of confidentiality, and the separate rules of selective disclosure and limited waiver. This section will briefly look at the substantive requirement of confidentiality. It will seek to determine whether this substantive requirement operates in a manner consistent with that demanded of all rules of legal professional privilege, being that the facts grounding the existence of the criterion are capable of being known at the time the communication is made. It will be argued that the substantive requirement of confidentiality contravenes this important principle.

The confidentiality requirement is largely a matter of the intention of the communicating party, determined on both a subjective and objective basis. That is, courts will look to the subjective intent of the party, but will also take into account the surrounding circumstances in which the communication was made and assess whether the belief in the party's ability to maintain confidentiality was reasonably held.[88] This can best be seen in the cases in which a third party was present during the conversation between lawyer and client.

In *R.* v. *Braham and Mason*[89] the accused telephoned his solicitor from the police station in the presence of a police officer for the purpose of obtaining legal advice. During the course of this conversation the accused confessed to the crime. The prosecution did not attempt to adduce this confessional evidence in cross-examination, but counsel for the co-accused did.[90] Lush J held that there was no privilege because at the relevant time the accused had no intention of keeping the communication confidential. He held that:

[88] An example of the mix of subjective and objective analyses can be seen in *R.* v. *Uljee* [1982] 1 NZLR 561: "[i]f the true inference is that the communication was not intended to be confidential, there is, of course, no problem. When outsiders were known to be within earshot it may be right to draw that inference, *R.* v. *Braham and Mason* is such a case. But, in my view, once it is found that confidentiality was intended that should be enough."

[89] [1976] VR 547 (Vic. SC); also see *R.* v. *Atkinson* [1990] 2 NZLR 513 (NZ CA).

[90] As Tapper points out, it is not clear why this was necessary since the privilege does not normally exclude secondary evidence.

> In my opinion, each case must be examined to see whether the communication was one which should be classed as confidential. The fact of the presence of a third party should be examined to see whether that presence indicates that the communication was not intended to be confidential, or whether the presence of the third party was caused by some necessity or some circumstances which did not affect the primary nature of the communication as confidential.[91]

Thus there are numerous factors which all go towards determining whether the substantive requirement of confidentiality is satisfied. These cannot be fixed in advance with much specificity, and the requirement is not amenable to effective rule balancing. Lush J in R. v. *Braham and Mason*[92] expressly rejected the possibility of resolving the issue before him once and for all on a rule balancing basis. Some of the factors may be known, or the significance appreciated, only after the communication is made. Therefore the substantive requirement of confidentiality presents a hole in the theory that all the circumstances which determine the operation of the privilege are capable of being known at the time the communication is made.

SECTION IV: RULE BALANCING AS A JUDICIAL FUNCTION

One remaining issue is whether it is appropriate for judges to consider new exceptions to the privilege rule at all, or whether the privilege has reached the stage that any further rule balancing should now only be undertaken by Parliament, as has been suggested in some of the cases considered above. This is a complex issue, and could occupy an entire book of its own. The treatment of the issue below will be brief, and limited to a consideration of the main arguments often used. Select comparisons will be made with other areas of evidence law, and other areas of the common law, where similar issues have arisen. It should be noted, though, that such examples are intended to be merely illustrative, and not a comprehensive treatment of this issue in the common law as a whole.

Some Arguments Against Judicial Intervention

There are two main arguments most frequently advanced when judges seek to divest themselves of the ability to reform the common law: first, that the law is so settled that reform is now the sole responsibility of the legislature; secondly, that the matter is, for a variety of possible reasons, so complex that judicial intervention would be undesirable or ineffective.

[91] R. v. *Braham and Mason* [1976] VR at 549.

[92] *Ibid.*: "I have been concerned by Mr Duckett's argument that this kind of evidence may, if it came to be tendered regularly, raise a question of importance, but I think that the situation in any case in which any party to proceedings seeks to lead evidence of this kind will have to be examined individually as I have endeavoured to examine the facts in this case."

In relation to the privilege, Australian judges in particular have stated on numerous occasions that the law of privilege can be significantly abrogated only by the legislature, and not the judiciary, partly because the law is now so settled.[93] In the *Carter* case McHugh J said that past formulations of the privilege doctrine contain no hint of the exception presently proposed and so implicitly accepted that any reform of the doctrine was a matter for the legislature.[94] Similar arguments have been used to justify the refusal to recognise new common law exceptions to the hearsay rule, as will be considered below in a separate section. Moving away from evidence law, the argument has been employed in other fields, such as restitution. In *Woolwich Equitable Building Society* v. *IRC* Lord Keith, in a dissenting speech, said of the long-established mistake of law rule that "though heavily criticised in academic writings and elsewhere, [it] is in my opinion too deeply embedded in English jurisprudence to be uprooted judicially".[95] However in that case all of the Law Lords in the majority effectively took the opposite view, and suggested that it may now be time to reconsider the mistake of law rule.[96] This latter view proved to be correct. In *Kleinwort Benson Ltd* v. *Lincoln City Council*,[97] the House of Lords overturned the mistake of law rule, which had previously stood for two centuries, and in doing so also dismissed the argument put forward by the respondents that any change in the law is best left to Parliament.[98] Lord Goff, in the majority, said that the present appellate committee holds a "more robust view of judicial development of the law" than that exhibited by Lord Keith in *Woolwich*.[99]

The second main strand of argument often advanced in support of judicial non-intervention in established common law doctrine is that the area of law has become so complex that reform is best left for detailed consideration by Parliament, perhaps with the aid of a law reform body. It may be possible to break this argument down into three sub-arguments. The first is that where a proposed reform involves issues of social policy, complex economic issues or questions of moral judgement, these are more appropriately determined by elected representatives, both because they have a better machinery in place to consider such issues, and because it may be considered to be more appropriate in a representative democracy that standards of morality and issues of social policy are set by the elected representatives. One example of this type of logic can be found in the judicial debate over the level of damages awards for personal

[93] *Grant* v. *Downs* (1976) 135 CLR at 685; *O'Reilly* v. *State Bank of Victoria Commissioners* (1983) 153 CLR at 23–4, 34–5; *Baker* v. *Campbell* (1983) 153 CLR at 96, 114; *Carter* v. *The Managing Partner, Northmore Hale Davy & Leake* (1995) 183 CLR at 138, 140–2, 167.

[94] *Carter* v. *The Managing Partner, Northmore Hale Davy & Leake* (1995) 183 CLR at 162.

[95] [1993] AC 70 at 154.

[96] *Ibid.*, at 177, 192, 199.

[97] [1998] 3 WLR 1095.

[98] Also see *David Securities Pty Ltd* v. *Commonwealth Bank of Australia* (1992) 175 CLR 353; *Air Canada* v. *British Columbia* [1989] 1 SCR 1161.

[99] *Kleinwort Benson Ltd* v. *Lincoln City Council* [1998] 3 WLR at 1116.

injuries. In what are commonly referred to as the "trilogy cases",[100] the Supreme Court of Canada reacted to press-induced fears of escalating personal injury awards and imposed an arbitrary cap on damages for non-pecuniary loss of Can$100,000. Dickson J expressed the view that periodic payments would be the best solution to the problem, but that this reform could be achieved only by Parliament, and that until such a comprehensive reform were put in place, the judicially imposed cap was the next best option. Less than six months after the trilogy cases were handed down, and without reference to them, Lord Denning MR in *Lim Poo Choo* v. *Camden Health Authority*[101] suggested that judges could treat damages awards as "interim awards" and, if the need arose, award further sums later in the victim's life. On appeal Lord Scarman strongly rejected this proposal on the bases that:

> so radical a reform can be made neither by judges nor by modification of the rules of court. It raises issues of social, economic and financial policy not amenable to judicial reform, which will almost certainly prove to be controversial and can be resolved by the legislature only after full consideration of factors which cannot be brought into clear focus, or be weighed and assessed, in the course of the forensic process. The judge—however wise, creative and imaginative he may be—is 'cabin'd, cribb'd, confin'd, bound in' not, as Macbeth was, to his 'saucy doubts and fears' but by the evidence and arguments of the litigants. It is this limitation, inherent in the forensic process, which sets bounds on the scope of judicial law reform.[102]

The second aspect of this argument relating to the complexity of the area of law is that any reform of the relevant rule would give rise to significant further problems within the legal doctrine, and that all of these issues are best considered as a whole at the same time. In *Carter* v. *The Managing Partner, Northmore Hale Davy & Leake* Deane J said:[103]

> there are some practical reasons why any such curtailment should be by legislative enactment rather than judicial decision. Such a legislative alteration of the common law would, one would expect, be made only after proper inquiry and informed advice about a variety of questions which would arise for essentially pragmatic decision.

Deane J then went on to consider some of the complexities which would arise for consideration in relation to the proposed reform. McHugh J also examined the complexities of the proposed change to the law in some detail, and reached a similar conclusion that the fact that the proposed reform would create such a myriad of further issues for resolution militated in favour of leaving any possible change to Parliament.[104] This argument features significantly in the decisions of the House of Lords following *Myers* v. *DPP*, which have sought to justify the continued adherence to that decision. These cases will be discussed below.

[100] *Andrews* v. *Grand and Toy Alberta* (1978) 83 DLR (3d) 452; *Thornton* v. *Board of School Trustees of School District No 57* (1978) 83 DLR (3d) 480; *Arnold* v. *Teno* (1978) 83 DLR (3d) 609.

[101] [1979] QB 196 at 220 (CA).

[102] *Lim Poo Choo* v. *Camden Health Authority* [1980] AC 174 at 183.

[103] (1995) 183 CLR at 140.

[104] *Ibid.*, at 164–7.

The third aspect of the argument from complexity is closely related to the second; it is that the proposed reform draws in issues from other areas of law altogether, and that this complexity is best resolved as a whole by a law reform body. The Law Commission recommended that the mistake of law rule be altered by Parliament, rather than being left to the judiciary to change, partly because any reform must also consider what related reforms need to be made in the field of public law.[105] Similarly, Lord Browne-Wilkinson, in his dissenting speech in *Kleinwort Benson Ltd* v. *Lincoln City Council*, held that abrogation of the mistake of law rule was best left to Parliament, as such a change would have significant broad ramifications and must be considered along with the issue of limitation periods.

However the argument from complexity can work both ways. The complexity of an issue may be such that it would be extremely difficult to draft an appropriate statutory provision.[106] Further, because of the difficulty in foreseeing the variety of future problems that will arise, it may be best to reform the law case by case as new problems arise. The legislative process is often not well suited to such an incremental method of reform.

Finally, it is interesting to note that one reason sometimes advanced by law reform bodies for recommending that a particular proposed reform be undertaken by Parliament rather than being left to the judiciary is that it may take a long time, if ever, for an appropriate case to reach the appellate courts.[107] However this is obviously not a relevant consideration when an appellate court is already seised of the issue in a case to which it has granted leave to appeal.[108]

The *Myers* Debate

In *Myers* v. *DPP*[109] the prosecution sought to adduce evidence of the chassis numbers of allegedly stolen cars by producing the microfilm of cards on which workers had written the chassis, engine and engine block number of each car as it was built. This was conclusive evidence of the guilt of the accused, and the

[105] Law Commission, *Restitution: Mistakes of Law and Ultra Vires Public Authority Receipts and Payments*, Law Comm No. 227, Cm 2731 (HMSO, London, 1994) at paras. 3.11, 3.12, 5.4–5.7.

[106] *Ibid.*, at para 5.4: "there was some support on consultation for leaving the question to the common law, because of the complexity of the issues and the difficulty of drafting a suitable statutory provision"; however the Law Commission stated that the fact that legislative solutions to the problem in Commonwealth jurisdictions did not appear to have caused significant problems to be a factor in favour of legislative (rather than judicial) reform of the law in England and Wales: see *ibid.*, at para 5.5, but compare para. 5.6.

[107] *Ibid.*, at paras. 3.8 and 3.10.

[108] *Kleinwort Benson* [1998] 3 WLR at 1116. Compare the position where, on leave to appeal, an appellate court considers that an important issue of law reform is before the court, however the instant case is, for whatever reason, not an appropriate vehicle for the airing of that issue. The denial of leave to appeal on this basis is common. For an example relevant to the issue in this book see *Locsam Ltd* v. *Brambles Holdings Ltd* (unreported, High Court of Australia, 18 June 1993).

[109] [1965] AC 1001 (HL).

dangers often associated with hearsay evidence were not present.[110] However a majority of the House of Lords held that it was no longer possible for judges to create new exceptions to the hearsay rule and, as this evidence could not be brought within any of the previously established exceptions to the rule, it was inadmissible.[111] The creation of new exceptions was, the majority held, a matter solely for the legislature. Perhaps the most important majority speech on this issue was delivered by Lord Reid. His treatment of the issue presently under consideration is often quoted in summary form, but it is worth setting out in full. Lord Reid said:

> I have never taken a narrow view of the functions of this House as an appellate tribunal. The common law must be developed to meet changing economic conditions and habits of thought, and I would not be deterred by expressions of opinion in this House in old cases. But there are limits to what we can or should do. If we are to extend the law it must be by the development and application of fundamental principles. We cannot introduce arbitrary conditions or limitations: that must be left to legislation. And if we do in effect change the law, we ought in my opinion only to do that in cases where our decision will produce some finality or certainty. If we disregard technicalities in this case and seek to apply principle and common sense, there are a number of other parts of the existing law of hearsay susceptible of similar treatment, and we shall probably have a series of appeals in cases where the existing technical limitations produce an unjust result. If we are to give a wide interpretation to our judicial functions questions of policy cannot be wholly excluded, and it seems to me to be against public policy to produce uncertainty. The only satisfactory solution is by legislation following on a wide survey of the whole field, and I think that such a survey is overdue. A policy of make do and mend is no longer adequate. The most powerful argument of those who support the strict doctrine of precedent is that if it is relaxed judges will be tempted to encroach on the proper field of the legislature, and this case offers to my mind a strong temptation to do that which ought to be resisted.[112]

Lord Hodson, also in the majority, put the matter briefly:

> Hedge the extension about with safeguards as you will, this surely would be judicial legislation with a vengeance in an attempt to introduce reform of the law of evidence which if needed can properly be dealt with only by the legislature.[113]

There were two strong dissenting speeches. Lord Pearce held that changing the law here would not pose any problems in relation to the certainty of the law for those who order their affairs upon a settled interpretation of it.[114] He also

[110] See *ibid.*, at 1008, 1019, 1036: the evidence was cogent; there was no risk of distortion; given the practical impossibility of workers ever having direct recollection of such details, this was in reality the best evidence available; direct evidence from the workers would not have been more reliable in any case and in all likelihood little would have been gained from observing the workers giving direct evidence or from cross-examining them; evidence of the accuracy of the recording system as a whole was available.

[111] Note that all the Law Lords rejected the appeal on the basis that there had been no substantial miscarriage of justice.

[112] *Ibid.*, at 1021–2.

[113] *Ibid.*, at 1034; also see Lord Morris at 1028.

[114] *Ibid.*, at 1037.

pointed out that there has never been a rule for the total exclusion of hearsay evidence without exception.[115] After tracing the general development of the rule over the centuries, he concluded that:

> The courts were gradually working out their own compromises to obtain satisfactory machinery for handling evidence and ascertaining the truth. They were adopting the hearsay rule in general with such adaptations and exceptions as would make it work and conduce to just decisions.
>
> The process of improvement and evolution was carried out by the inherent power of the courts to conduct its process so as to prevent abuse and secure justice. I see no reason why at some stage the courts should decide that evolution was now complete and that thereafter no further change must occur, however great the absurdity or injustice.
>
> . . . That the court should be slow to introduce or adapt exceptions is reasonable. That the court should debar itself forever from introducing further exceptions or adapting them under any circumstances, however unforeseen or unforeseeable, would be unreasonable.[116]

Lord Donovan said:

> The common law is moulded by the judges and it is still their province to adapt it from time to time so as to make it serve the interests of those it binds. Particularly is this so in the field of procedural law.

Unfortunately the comprehensive review of this area of law, which Lord Reid had to some extent pinned his hopes on, did not materialise for thirty years. Legislative reform of the hearsay rule in criminal trials was limited.[117] *Myers* received significant academic criticism in England and overseas.[118] However the House of Lords re-asserted their formal *Myers* position in later cases, such as *R.* v. *Blastland*[119] and *R.* v. *Kearley*.[120] In these subsequent cases their Lordships justified their stance primarily on the basis of the complexity of the law, an argument considered in other contexts above. For example Lord Bridge in *Kearley* said:

> However strong the temptation to legislate judicially in favour of what is seen as a 'common sense' result and however tardy Parliament may appear to be in reforming

[115] [1965] AC at 1037.

[116] *Ibid*., at 1038.

[117] For a history of the law reform proposals and legislative reforms since *Myers* see C. Tapper, *Cross and Tapper on Evidence* (8th ed., Butterworths, London, 1995) 597–9. The Criminal Evidence Act 1965 (UK) introduced a limited exception for "trade and business" records, and further reforms were introduced by the Criminal Justice Act 1967 (UK), ss. 68–70 of the Police and Evidence Act 1984 (UK) and ss. 23–28 of the Criminal Justice Act 1988 (UK). Compare the reforms of the Civil Evidence Acts 1968 and 1972 (UK).

[118] As well as other articles and texts cited in this section of the book, also see the following: R. Cross, "What Should be Done About the Rule Against Hearsay?" [1965] Crim LR 68 at 70–1, 73–4; R.E. Megarry, "Exceptions to the Hearsay Rule" (1964) 80 *LQR* 457; J.A. Andrews, "The Shackles of Rigidity and Formalism" (1964) 27 *MLR* 606; E.G. Moore, Casenote on *Myers* v. *DPP* [1965] *CLJ* 14; P.B. Carter, "Hearsay: Whether and Whither?" (1993) 109 *LQR* 573.

[119] [1986] 1 AC 41 at 52.

[120] [1992] 2 AC 228.

an area of law which is seen to be in need of radical reform, the uncertainty and confusion to which well-intentioned attempts at judicial legislation can lead have been clearly demonstrated by recent decisions of your Lordships' House. The operation of the hearsay rule in modern conditions is in many respects unsatisfactory. . . . However long overdue we may feel an overhaul of the hearsay rule in criminal cases to be, we should not be deluded into thinking that we can achieve it piecemeal.[121]

However this may be compared with the dissenting speech of Lord Griffiths:

> Over a quarter of a century has passed since that decision [in *Myers*] but no overall legislative review of hearsay evidence in criminal law has been attempted. The hearsay rule was created by our judicial predecessors and if we find that it no longer serves to do justice in certain conditions then the judges of today should accept the responsibility of reviewing and adapting the rules of evidence to serve present society.[122]

While the House of Lords maintains formal opposition to new common law exceptions, the reality of the actual development of the law may be somewhat different. Ashworth and Pattenden[123] examined many of the existing exceptions to the hearsay rule as it was developed in relation to criminal trials after 1964, and found that courts have in fact managed to relax the hearsay rule despite the strictures imposed by *Myers*. In doing so the authors noted that courts rarely mention the 1964 authority, much less attempt to distinguish it. Choo's analysis of English hearsay cases since *Myers* is similar.[124]

In other Commonwealth jurisdictions the courts have, despite *Myers*, continued to develop new common law exceptions to the hearsay rule.[125] In a New Zealand case shortly after *Myers, Smith* v. *Police*,[126] a new hearsay exception was recognised and the *Myers* approach rejected, on the basis that:

> The hearsay rule is judge-made, and when a particular application is no longer helpful but obstructive, it should be cleared away. This is adjectival law, and ought always to be under the hands of judges.[127]

The strongest opposition to *Myers* has been in the Canadian Supreme Court. In *Ares* v. *Venner*[128] the Court rejected the restrictive approach of the majority in *Myers*, created a wide new exception and expressly preferred the dissenting speeches in *Myers*.[129] The Supreme Court has since been active in creating exceptions to the rule, affirming their rejection of the majority view in *Myers*

121 *Ibid.*, at 251.

122 *Ibid.*, at 237; also see Lord Oliver, *ibid.*, at 276–8.

123 A. Ashworth and R. Pattenden, "Reliability, Hearsay Evidence and the English Criminal Trial" (1986) 102 LQR 292 at 296–326.

124 A.L.-T. Choo, *Hearsay and Confrontation in Criminal Trials* (Clarendon Press, Oxford, 1996) chap. 3.

125 E.g. see the cases cited in C. Tapper, n. 117 above, 596.

126 *Smith* v. *Police* [1969] NZLR 856.

127 *Ibid.*, at 860; also see Haslam J in *Transport Ministry* v. *Garry* [1973] 1 NZLR 120 at 123, advocating a liberal approach to common law exceptions.

128 (1970) 14 DLR (3d) 4 at 16.

129 For extensive commentary on the Canadian position following *Ares* v. *Venner* see J. Sopinka *et al.*, *The Law of Evidence in Canada* (Butterworths, Toronto, 1992) 192–8.

and advocating a more flexible approach.[130] Some of the reasons for this opposition to the *Myers* approach are discussed below.

Arguments for Judicial Intervention

The main argument in support of not leaving further reform solely to the legislature is that, as a general principle, the common law should continue evolving in accordance with its established method of development of the law through the determination of novel fact situations, unless and until Parliament expressly restricts such development. In the *Carter* case Toohey J said:

> While acknowledging the force of the argument that legislative action is the appropriate way to deal with any change to the scope of legal professional privilege, this Court is required to answer the question posed by the ground of appeal. It must do so in a contest where there is a tension between two important strands in the development of the common law. It is inconsistent with the function of this Court in the development of that law to answer the question in the way indicated.[131]

The fact that a particular rule has not been recognised in the past should be no reason for holding that it should not now be considered; and the past non-recognition of a rule does not, despite the opposite view taken by McHugh J and referred to above, imply that judges deciding past cases accepted or assumed that any reform of the doctrine is a matter for the legislature. There may have been no apparent need for the particular exception in the past. Social conditions or the surrounding law may have changed, or modern conditions may dictate that the law develop faster in order to keep pace with rapidly changing technologies and modes of communication.

These claims to judicial modesty may sometimes be motivated at least in part by the fact that a law reform body is presently considering the matter in issue. Where this parallel system of review is present, judges seldom make explicit reference to it. This has been advanced as an explanation for the *Myers* case, considered above. It may also have been an unarticulated factor in the *Carter* case, as the very reform which the High Court decided in that case was more appropriately left to Parliament was in fact before the federal Parliament at the time the case was being heard.[132] However even when a law reform body is presently seised of a matter this should not hinder the development of the common law. The legislature and the judiciary are jointly responsible for the development of the law. There is no reason why these different systems of decision-making cannot operate at the same time. English constitutional law has developed mecha-

[130] E.g. see *R.* v. *Khan* [1990] 2 SCR 531 at 540, *per* McLachlin J; *R.* v. *B. (K.G.)* [1993] 1 SCR 740 at 774–6, *per* Lamer CJC. While the *Myers* approach has been repeatedly rejected by the Supreme Court, it occasionally surfaces in lower courts: see J.D. Ewart, *Documentary Evidence in Canada* (Carswell, 1994) 48–9, 51.

[131] (1995) 183 CLR at 157–8.

[132] Cl. 123 of the federal Evidence Bill.

nisms for regulating the relationship between these two law-makers. Even if a law reform body is seised of an issue, this is no guarantee that Parliament will act, or will act in a comprehensive manner, as the state of hearsay evidence in the criminal law post-*Myers* illustrates. In *Kleinwort Benson Ltd* v. *Lincoln City Council*[133] Lord Goff said "I can see no good reason for postponing the matter for legislation, especially when we do not know whether or, if so, when Parliament may legislate". This was in the context of the Law Commission having recently recommended that Parliament legislate rather than wait for judicial reform.

The second main form of argument against judicial intervention outlined above relates to the subject-matter of the proposed reform: its complexity; interaction with other areas of law and rules within the same doctrine; and the inability of the judiciary adequately to address issues of social or economic policy or general moral standards. In the Law Commission's Report, *Damages for Personal Injury: Non-Pecuniary Loss*[134] the Commission concluded that personal injury awards for non-pecuniary loss were too low and recommended that they be raised by a factor of between 1.5 and 2.[135] Further, the Law Commission recommended that such a change should not be undertaken by Parliament, but should be effected by means of judicial reform. It had been submitted to the Law Commission that the level of such awards is really a matter for what society regards as fair compensation, having regard to current social, economic and industrial conditions in England and Wales, and that the only body competent to give effect to society's views on such matters was Parliament, which had the machinery in place to consult thoroughly with appropriate organisations such as trade unions, employers, medical experts and professional bodies.[136] However, perhaps surprisingly, the Law Commission rejected this argument on the ground that the decision was one of "legal policy" which the courts had experience in dealing with and, perhaps implicitly, were sufficiently equipped to deal with. At the time of writing the Court of Appeal is hearing a group of test cases in an attempt to deal with this issue.

Issues of legal professional privilege may be important to society in general and to particular vulnerable groups such as people in detention. However this area of law does not present difficult issues of social policy, complex economic questions or finely balanced issues of moral judgement which are more appropriately determined by our elected representatives. Lord Devlin, writing extra-judicially, argued that the rules of evidence and procedure should be treated as a special case and that "the public is entitled to know how the judges would order their affairs—for the administration of justice is their affair—before the legislature lays down the law".[137] The result of this, according to Lord Devlin,

[133] [1998] 3 WLR at 1116.

[134] No. 257, HC 344 (HMSO, London, 1999).

[135] *Ibid.*, at para. 3.110.

[136] See the submission recorded *ibid.*, at 82 n. 198; compare the views of an earlier Law Commission in Report No. 56, *Report on Personal Injury Litigation—Assessment of Damages* (HMSO, London, 1973) at paras. 32–33.

[137] Lord Devlin, "Judges and Lawmakers" (1976) 39 *MLR* 1 at 13.

is that judges should see themselves as having particular responsibilities for developing the common law in these areas. While one may question Lord Devlin's characterisation of the rules of evidence and procedure as simply a matter of the judge's "order[ing] their affairs", the fact is that evidence and procedure are certainly areas within the knowledge and competence of judges to determine. This factor may also have played a part in the growth of judicial activism in the far more contentious field of public interest immunity.[138]

Despite the strongly held views of Deane and McHugh JJ[139] to the contrary, this is not an area that necessarily requires a law reform body's report before consideration of any changes. In contrast to many areas of the law, here it is possible to look at one small aspect of the rule in relative isolation. Courts would not be greatly hampered by a failure to consider all aspects of the rule as a whole. Further refinement of a new common law exception could be determined as the need arose, in accordance with long-established common law methods. For example, if the courts in the *Derby Magistrates* and *Carter* cases had recognised new exceptions for criminal exculpatory evidence, then the application or otherwise of such a rule to co-accused could simply have been determined on another occasion. Deane and McHugh JJ thought that the more complex problem of exculpatory evidence in criminal trials involving multiple accused was one complexity that rendered the issue inappropriate for judicial resolution. However it is difficult to see why this is so. It is interesting to note that when the Australian Federal Parliament introduced an exception for exculpatory evidence in criminal trials, they also simply exempted co-accused from this rule. There is no reason why the same result could not have been achieved by the common law over the course of more than one decision.

Another factor which may bear on the appropriateness of judicial intervention in the development of the common law is whether the surrounding law is predominantly judge made. The Law Commission, in the above-mentioned report, Damages for Personal Injury: Non-Pecuniary Loss, relied on the fact that such awards are "inextricably intertwined with the rest of the law of tort in personal injury cases, which has to date largely been developed by the judges".[140] In *R.* v. *B. (K.G.)* Lamer CJC said:

> The *duty* of the courts to review common law rules has a pragmatic basis: courts are best situated to assess the operation and possible deficiencies of common law rules in practical situations[141] (emphasis added).

To similar effect another Chief Justice of Canada wrote extra-judicially that:

> When everything considered relevant has been weighed and an overruling decision commends itself to a judge, he ought not at that stage to stay his opinion and call upon the legislature to implement it. This is particularly true in respect of those areas of law

138 See J. Bell, *Policy Arguments in Judicial Decisions* (Clarendon Press, Oxford, 1983) 127–9.

139 In the *Carter* case.

140 N. 134 above, at para.3.159.

141 [1993] 1 SCR at 775.

> which are judge-made . . . A final court must accept a superintending responsibility for what it or its predecessors have wrought, especially when it knows how little time legislatures have (and also, perhaps, little inclination) to intrude into fields of law fashioned by the courts alone.[142]

Many areas of evidence law have been greatly altered by legislative intervention, often with the aim of clearing away what are often regarded as arcane and overly complex common law rules. However in England the bulk of the rules of legal professional privilege remain predominantly judge-made. Even the statutorily based privilege in section 10 of the Police and Criminal Evidence Act 1984 may be taken to reflect the common law.[143] Further, important decisions on the scope of existing exceptions, which the judges have less reluctance to determine,[144] may have just as significant an impact on the privilege as a decision on the existence of what are formally described as new exceptions, particularly when the exception is as broad and ill-defined as the waiver doctrine. In a similar vein, a change in a substantive rule of the privilege may have just as great an effect as the recognition of a new exception.

The final reason appellate courts should not refrain from developing the common law is that they have a duty to determine the merits of the individual case before them, and this duty may sometimes necessitate the recognition of new principles. For example, in *Kleinwort Benson Ltd* v. *Lincoln City Council*[145] the argument for judicial non-intervention was rejected partly because it would have been "unjust to deprive the appellant bank of the benefit of the decision of the House on this point". And in *Andrews* v. *Grand and Toy Alberta*, one of the "trilogy cases" referred to above, Dickson J held that "[u]ntil such time as the legislature acts, the Courts must proceed on established principles to award damages which compensate accident victims for the losses they suffer".[146]

CONCLUSIONS

Commonwealth courts have been too strict in their treatment of derogations from the privilege. The view that the rules and exceptions grounding the privilege, with the possible exceptions of waiver and the child welfare rule, can always be known at the time the legal communication is made does not accord

142 B. Laskin, "The Role and Functions of Final Appellate Courts: The Supreme Court of Canada" (1975) 53 *Can Bar Rev* 469 at 478–9.

143 See *Francis & Francis (a firm)* v. *Central Criminal Court* [1988] 3 All ER 775 at 789, 791b, *per* Lords Griffiths, and at 797c, *per* Lord Goff; but for the opposite view see Lord Bridge (dissenting), *ibid.*, at 781b–d, and the note in [1989] Crim LR 444 at 447.

144 Compare Lord Bingham CJ's decision in *Paragon Finance Plc & Ors* v. *Freshfields (a firm)* [1999] 1 WLR 1170, where he was reluctant to extend an existing waiver rule partly because of what he regarded as the strictures on further development imposed by the *Derby Magistrates* case.

145 [1998] 3 WLR at 1116.

146 (1978) 83 DLR (3d) at 458–9.

with the practical operation of the exceptions to the privilege. It is even inconsistent with some of its substantive rules. The simple reality is that it is often not possible for a client to know at the time of requesting legal advice whether his legal communications will definitely be privileged. There is an element of uncertainty in the operation of the rule that currently exists and may well be unavoidable.

There seems to be a disparity between the appearance and the reality of the level of certainty in the privilege. Assuming that this situation has not been created intentionally, some writers argue that such a disparity may be beneficial in that it both encourages communications and allows for judicial fine-tuning to reduce over- and under-inclusion.[147] However, as shown above, one problem created by this disparity is that it can lead to a flawed view of the structure of the privilege. In this case it has led courts to feel unduly constrained in their treatment of existing and proposed derogations from the privilege.

[147] Comment, "Developments in Law-Privileged Communications" (1985) 98 *Harv LR* 1450 at 1489; on the possible benefits of vagueness in the construction of legal rules. Also see M. Dan-Cohen, "Decision Rules and Conduct Rules" (1984) 97 *Harv LR* 625.

PART B

PRACTICAL APPLICATIONS

8

Crime-fraud Exception

INTRODUCTION

It has been seen in previous chapters that the concept of *ad hoc* balancing is used by judges determining points of privilege law as a kind of folk devil; a scapegoat for their concerns over flexible privilege standards. Such fears mask the true nature of the privilege as inherently dependent on a balancing of issues or competing policy concerns. It has also been argued in previous chapters that the refusal of judges to embark upon a balancing process to determine whether to recognise new exceptions to the privilege is erroneous, especially where this refusal is based upon a belief that the nature of the privilege does not permit such a process, and that any form of balancing would lead to uncertainty and the defeating of the purpose of the rule.

This chapter will focus on one of the most significant[1] exceptions to the privilege, the crime-fraud exception. It will be shown that this rule is in fact the result of a balancing of interests on a category-wide level. That is, the crime-fraud rule has arisen as the result of a basic assessment of the competing policy interests relating to confidentiality in such circumstances. This explanation for the rule conflicts with the rationale traditionally given for it, which is that the privilege never arises over such communications because they are outside the scope of the professional relationship. It will be shown that this explanation is insufficient and misleading. It masks the true nature of the rule which is, like the rest of the privilege, determined by a balancing of competing public policy concerns.

It is not within the aims of this chapter to embark on a general analysis of the workings of the crime-fraud exception.[2] The only purpose in discussing it here is to show that the modern justification offered for it is misleading and that the exception is in fact based on an assessment of generalised policy concerns. This

[1] Assuming the volume of law review articles written on a subject to be an appropriate measure of the area's importance. The best American articles on the rule are, in addition to articles cited elsewhere in this chapter, D.J. Fried, "Too High a Price for Truth: The Exception to the Attorney–Client Privilege for Contemplated Crimes and Frauds" (1986) 64 *North Carolina LR* 443; E.J. Silbert, "The Crime-Fraud Exception to the Attorney–Client Privilege and Work-Product Doctrine, The Lawyer's Obligations of Disclosure, and the Lawyer's Response to Accusation of Wrongful Conduct" (1986) 23 *Am Crim LR* 351.

[2] See generally C. Tapper, *Cross and Tapper on Evidence* (8th ed., Butterworths, London, 1995), 490; C. Passmore, *Privilege* (CLT, Sutton Coldfield, 1998) chap. 8.

chapter will also not discuss the possible final step in cases of client misconduct: the duty of lawyers to report voluntarily certain client misconduct.[3]

Throughout this chapter I will apply the distinction between the privilege "overriding" and "never arising" at length. This distinction may at first appear to have little real consequence. However the central issue is what clients know of the application of the privilege at the time they impart their confidential information. The importance of this issue will be explained below. The overriding/never arising distinction stems from the difference between what judges claim is happening and what is in reality happening. When judges state that the privilege "never arises" they are implicitly positing that there is no expectation of confidentiality in such situations, or at least no overlap between the expectations of confidentiality of those that retain the privilege and those that do not, and so there is no danger of the purpose and operation of the privilege being frustrated. If the rule is examined in terms of the "overriding" of the privilege, then one may be forced to acknowledge that a client's expectations of the operation of the privilege have been frustrated in a manner beyond that client's control, and also acknowledge the fact that this appears to occur without any weakening of the lawyer–client relationship. Such an acknowledgment would raise serious questions about the current justification for the privilege.

There are conceptual alternatives that may seem to accommodate both views, such as regarding the privilege as solid at inception, but with internal holes in it; with exceptions that arise only when triggered. Such an alternative formulation may sufficiently explain the results obtained by the case law in this area. This explanation may have the same result as saying that the privilege has been overridden. In any case it would probably be equally unacceptable to judges taking the "never arising" views explained in the chapter, as this alternative formulation also acknowledges the timing problem discussed in this chapter. That is, at the time the client imparts confidential information, he does not know whether his privilege, which at this time he believes he has, will ultimately be upheld or not. If this is the case, then it becomes difficult to justify the strict approach to derogations which is attacked in this book.

Finally, the debate considered in this chapter is completely independent of the underlying normative question involved in the crime-fraud rule. Both approaches advocate the same ultimate legal result. The issue relates to the structural question of how this result is rationalised in theory. It is argued below that while the exception may be driven by normative concerns, it is justified on the basis of a conceptual distinction that is independent of those concerns.

[3] For a comprehensive discussion of the American position on this issue, see H.I. Subin, "The Lawyer as Superego: Disclosure of Client Confidences to Prevent Harm" (1985) 70 *Iowa LR* 1091, 1112–44.

BRIEF HISTORY

The crime-fraud exception seems to have been recognised at an early stage in the development of the privilege as a whole. In 1671, when the privilege was still very much in its formative stage, ir was held in the case of *Cutts* v. *Pickering* that the privilege did not apply, partly on the ground that "no secrecy (is) due to the client in crimes".[4] Shortly after, in *Rothwell* v. *King*, it was held that "the trust of a counsel does not extend to suppression of deeds or wills".[5] However the rule was not well-established in the seventeenth century.[6] It has sometimes been said that the rule first developed in the controversial case of *Annesley* v. *Anglesea*.[7] Some of the arguments of counsel in that case certainly support such a rule,[8] and there can be no doubt that these arguments themselves were used in subsequent cases as the reasoned basis for those later decisions.[9] However the decision in *Annesley* v. *Anglesea* on this issue was made on the basis that the communication was not for the purpose of legal advice.[10] The focus was on the objective content of the communication, not on the subjective intent of the client.[11] Evidence texts in the period following the case do not mention anything like a crime-fraud rule.[12] This case did nothing to establish any exception for criminal or fraudulent communications,[13] and the state of the rule was still in considerable doubt through much of the eighteenth and nineteenth centuries.

[4] Lord Nottingham, *Prolegomena of Chancery and Equity* (D.E.C. Yale ed., CUP, 1965) 317, para. 29.9. Neither the report of the case in (1671) 3 Ch. Rep. 66, 21 ER 730, nor Nelson 81, 21 ER 795, is helpful in determining the basis for the decision. *Quaere* though the interpretation of *Cutts* v. *Pickering* in *Annesley* v. *Anglesea* (1743) 17 How St Tr 1139, both in the argument of Mr Harward (*ibid.*, at 1232) and in the judgment of the Lord Chief Baron (*ibid.*, at 1240), which seem to base the decision solely on the ground that the communication was made before the retainer.

[5] Ch. 1673 (cited in *Parkhurst* v. *Lowten* (1819) 2 Swanst 194 at 221 n. 9, 36 ER 589 at 599 n. 9).

[6] E.g. *Anonymus* [*sic.*] (1693) Skinner 404, 90 ER 179; *Anonymous* (1699) 1 Ll Raym 733, 91 ER 1390; also see D.J. Fried, n. 1 above, n. 32.

[7] 17 How St. Trials 1139 (1743). For a detailed analysis of this case, see D.J. Fried, n. 1 above, 446–50.

[8] It was only Annesley's attorneys who argued that certain statements disclosed an intention to have Annesley hanged and that this could not be privileged: see *ibid.*, at 1229–30, *per* Serjeant Tisdall and at 1231–2 per Mr Haward.

[9] E.g. *Gartside* v. *Outram* (1857) 26 LJ (Ch) 113 at 115 (Ch.) ("Mr Taylor refers to a case, not of the same authority, but one in which the same point is put so ably and clearly by the counsel in argument, that I adopt that argument as the best expression of my own opinion"); R. v. *Cox and Railton* (1884) 14 QBD at 173.

[10] The defendant just said he wished he could have Annesley hanged because he wanted the estate. Wishing that a person were hanged is not in itself criminal or fraudulent. Similarly, the defendant's expressed desire to retain control of his estate was not a communication for the purpose of any legal advice: see D.J. Fried, n. 1 above, 449–50. This was probably the basis for the judgment (see 17 How St Tr at 1240).

[11] D.J. Fried, n. 1 above, 450.

[12] E.g., see the texts of Gilbert, Greenleaf and Starkie (surveyed in *ibid.*, nn. 16–17).

[13] D.J. Fried, n. 1 above, 450 ("Strictly speaking, the *Annesley* court did not create any exception to the attorney–client privilege . . . Rather, it held that communications were confidential only if they were made in the pursuit of legal advice").

While there was strong authority in support of a crime-fraud exception,[14] there was also good authority against such a rule.[15]

The matter was conclusively settled by the great case of *R.* v. *Cox and Railton*.[16] The composition of the bench hearing the appeal in this case was increased from five to ten for this purpose.[17] This case and its precise meaning and effect will be discussed in detail below. The modern statement of the rule, arising from this case, has been accepted in Canada,[18] Australia,[19] New Zealand[20] and South Africa.[21] The rule was applied almost immediately in the United States.[22] However it may have been modified there.[23] There have been vastly more reported cases on the rule in the United States than in the Commonwealth.[24] The American cases present an enormous breadth of novel fact situations, including some bizarre and disturbing uses of legal advice.[25] The rule has, not surprisingly, achieved a greater level of complexity and sophistication in that jurisdiction.

[14] E.g. *Follett* v. *Jefferyes* (1850) 1 Sim. (NS) 3, 61 ER 1; *Russell* v. *Jackson* (1851) 9 Hare 387, 68 ER 558; *Gartside* v. *Outram* (1857) 26 LJ (Ch) 113.

[15] E.g. *Cromack* v. *Heathcote* (1820) 2 Bro. & Bing 4, 129 ER 857 (however the only grounds for seeking disclosure were that the client did not consult his solicitor in connection with any cause and the solicitor refused the employment. Contrary to the view of this case taken in R. v. *Cox and Railton* (1884) 14 QBD at 173–4 this case did not expressly raise the issue presently considered); *Doe* v. *Harris* (1833) 5 C&P 592, 172 ER 1113 (interestingly, the main reason for Parke J's decision was that, as it would be impossible to know whether the communication was for a lawful or unlawful purpose without breaching the privilege, the question could not be asked); *Greenough* v. *Gaskell* (1833) 1 My & K 98, 39 ER 628 (privileged documents were sought as indicative of a fraud committed by the very solicitor who was arguing that they should not be revealed; this is brushed over by Brougham LC, who significantly omits fraud as one of the things which prevents privilege from being claimed); *R.* v. *Tuffs* (1848) 1 Den 319, 169 ER 263; *Charlton* v. *Coombes* (1863) 4 Giff 377, 66 ER 751; *Robson* v. *Kemp* (1881) 5 Esp. 52, 170 ER 735.

[16] (1884) 14 QBD 153.

[17] See *ibid.*, at 158.

[18] *Re United States of America* v. *Mammoth Oil* [1925] 2 DLR 966 (Ont. SC); *Solosky* v. *Canada* [1980] 1 SCR 821; *Descôteaux* v. *Mierzwinski* [1982] 1 SCR 860.

[19] E.g. *Plumb* v. *Monck* [1974] 4 ALR 405 (NT SC).

[20] *Keep Brothers* v. *Birch and Bradshaw* [1928] NZLR 360 (SC).

[21] *Botes* v. *Daly* 1976 (2) SA 215 at 222 (NPD).

[22] *Clark* v. *United States* 289 US 1 (1933). *Cox and Railton* was applied almost immediately: see *Orman* v. *State* 3 SW 468 at 471–2 (Texas CA 1886) and *Matthews* v. *Hoagland* 21 A 1054 at 1059–60 (NJ Ct of Chancery, 1891). However there appear to have been many doubtful moments in the development of the exception in the United States: see J.H. Wigmore and J.T. McNaughton, *Evidence in Trials at Common Law* (Little, Brown & Co., Boston,1961) viii 573–5.

[23] The first Supreme Court case of *Alexander* v. *United States* 138 US 353 (1891) seems to have added a requirement that the rule applies only where the communication was made in furtherance of the same crime the witness is being tried for (*ibid.*, at 360). Federal courts have not applied this limitation, but neither has it been overruled: see D.J. Fried, n. 1 above, 460.

[24] D.J. Fried, n. 1 above, 460–1 says that "[t]he paucity of cases in great Britain after *Reg* v. *Cox* is notable, even considering the small number of reporting courts and the smaller volume of litigation. . . . The contrast with the sophisticated elaboration of the exception in the United States is astonishing. .. One can only speculate that the division between solicitors and barristers, the small size and social cohesiveness of the trial bar, and the fact that the criminal bar as a whole both prosecutes and defends leads to an unwillingness to make one's case out of the mouth of opponent's counsel".

[25] E.g. *Orman* v. *State* 3 SW 468 (client murders man who had insulted his family, after receiving advice from his lawyer about a law reducing the penalty from murder to manslaughter in such cases) compare D. Zeffertt, *The South African Law of Evidence* (4th ed. Butterworths, Durban, 1988) 253:

SECTION I: THE TWO RATIONALES

Traditional Rationale

The rationale usually given this century for the crime-fraud rule is that communications for a criminal or fraudulent purpose are outside the scope of the lawyer–client relationship, and therefore no privilege arises. This was stated clearly in *R.* v. *Cox and Railton*:

> In order that the rule may apply there must be both professional confidence and professional employment, but if the client has a criminal object in view in his communications with his solicitor one of these elements must necessarily be absent. The client must either conspire with his solicitor or deceive him. If his criminal object is avowed, the client does not consult his adviser professionally, because it cannot be the solicitor's business to further any criminal object. If the client does not avow his object he reposes no confidence, for the state of facts, which is the foundation of the supposed confidence, does not exist.[26]

The rule in *Cox and Railton* was set out after having extensively considered previous authority. As stated above, this authority was divided on the issue at hand.[27] The pre-*Cox and Railton* cases that ordered disclosure of otherwise privileged communications did so on the basis of the limits of the professional relationship. The judicial reasoning was simply that the communications were not part of the professional relationship. For example, in *Reynell* v. *Sprye*[28] a client wrote to his lawyer ordering the lawyer to write a letter back to him (the client) giving advice as set out by the client in the letter sent by the client. This was done in order to deceive a third party as to the nature of a legal case at issue. The letter written by the client was held to be admissible. The Master of the Rolls held that:

> this is not a letter written in professional confidence for the purpose of obtaining the advantage of professional assistance; for Sprye [the client], having a particular purpose in view, makes this gentleman his tool, and not his adviser. I think that that letter is not entitled to any protection whatsoever.[29]

Thus the rationale for the rule there set out was that the client was in no way seeking legal advice; he was simply telling his lawyer what to write back to him. While the rationale turns on the scope of the professional relationship, as in *Cox and Railton* and later cases, the reasoning did not rely on the presence of any

"[i]t is not easy to imagine anyone committing treason or murder with impunity on the strength of legal advice"); *Commonwealth* v. *O'Brien* 388 NE.2d 658 (Mass. SC 1979) (during divorce negotiations involving spouses and lawyer, husband fatally shoots wife, then asks lawyer to represent him). An even stranger fact situation is presented by *Cummings* v. *Commonwealth* 298 SW 943 (Kentucky CA 1927).

26 (1884) 14 QBD at 168.

27 See nn. 14–15 above.

28 (1846) 10 Beav 51, 50 ER 501.

29 *Ibid.*, at 10 Beav at 56–7, 50 ER at 503.

fraud. The same result would have been reached if the letter the client requested his lawyer to write back to him was for a wholly innocent purpose.

Perhaps the most frequently cited pre-*Cox and Railton* case is *Russell* v. *Jackson*.[30] In that case the client wanted to establish a testamentary trust in order to build a socialist school. His lawyer advised him that this was an illegal object. The client then bequeathed part of his estate to his executors, in confidence that they would carry out his intention. The next of kin challenged the bequest as a secret trust and sought disclosure of the legal advice. The court held that no privilege arises:

> because the contriving of a fraud is no part of his duty as solicitor; and I think it can as little be said that it is part of the duty of a solicitor to advise his client as to the means of evading the law.[31]

The clearest judicial statement of the pre-*Cox and Railton* rationale for the crime-fraud rule is in *Follett* v. *Jefferyes*.[32] In that case it was actually decided that there was no fraud and so the advice was still privileged. However Lord Cranworth did go on, in a passage partly quoted in *R.* v. *Cox and Railton*,[33] to describe the basis of the rule:

> The transaction . . . is one as to which it was perfectly lawful for the client to ask, and for the solicitor to give professional advice. And this seems to me to be the true test . . . as to whether what has passed is or is not privileged.
>
> It may not be unfit that I should repeat an observation I made in the course of the argument, namely, that it is not accurate to speak of cases of fraud contrived by the client and solicitor in concert together, as cases of *exception* to the general rule. These are not cases coming within the rule itself; for the rule does not apply to all which passes between a client and his solicitor, but only to what passes between them in professional confidence; and no Court can permit it to be said that the contriving of a fraud can form part of the professional occupation of an attorney or solicitor.[34]

It is from these and other cases that Wigmore set out the rationale for the crime-fraud rule, stating that it exists "for the logically sufficient reason that no such enterprise falls within the just scope of the relationship between legal adviser and client".[35] Subsequent American writers have followed this rationale. For example, one law review summarised the rationale as follows:

> the exception rests primarily on a finding that certain communications are outside the class which a particular privilege is designed to protect . . . The rationale for the exception in these cases is . . . [that] the type of professional relationship that the privilege was designed to protect is absent.[36]

30 (1851) 9 Hare 387, 68 ER 558.

31 *Ibid.*, at 9 Hare at 392–393, 68 ER at 560.

32 (1850) 1 Sim. (NS) 3, 61 ER 1.

33 (1884) 14 QBD at 168.

34 *Follett* v. *Jefferyes* (1850) 1 Sim. (NS) at 16–17, 61 ER at 6.

35 J.H. Wigmore and J.T. McNaughton, n. 22 above, 572.

36 Note, "The Future Crime or Tort Exception to Communications Privileges" (1964) 77 *Harv LR* 730, 730–1.

This is also reflected in American case law. For example, in *Kneale* v. *Williams*:

> perpetration of a fraud is outside the scope of the professional duty of an attorney and no privilege attaches to a communication and transaction between an attorney and client with respect to transactions constituting the making of a false claim or the perpetration of a fraud.[37]

Similarly, in *Coveney* v. *Tannahill*:

> there can be no such relation as that of attorney and client, either in the commission of a crime, or the doing of a wrong by force of fraud to an individual. The privileged relation of attorney and client can only exist for lawful and honest purposes.[38]

Many other American cases follow the same reasoning.[39] Commonwealth courts after *Cox and Railton* have also justified the crime-fraud rule on the basis of the scope of the professional relationship. For example in *O'Rourke* v. *Darbishire*[40] Lord Parmoor held that:

> it is no part of the professional duty of a solicitor either to take part in the concoction of fraud, or to advise his client how to carry through a fraud. Transactions and communications for such purposes cannot be said to pass in professional confidence in the course of professional employment.[41]

Similarly, in *Crescent Farm (Sidcup) Sports Ltd* v. *Sterling Offices Ltd* Goff J held that "the principle of the exception is that the communication in such circumstances is not in truth within the scope of professional privilege at all".[42] Most writers of leading Commonwealth evidence texts have adopted this rationale.[43]

Alternative Rationale: Public Policy

An alternative explanation for the crime-fraud rule would be simply to say that as a matter of public policy the law will not shield communications used for the purpose of evading the law. To uphold the privilege in such circumstances would, as Stephen J of the High Court of Australia said in relation to the slightly different rule relating to the whereabouts of a ward, "be to allow that privilege to be used for a purpose alien to its whole purpose and history".[44] This

37 30 So.2d 284 at 287 (Florida SC 1947).

38 1 Hill 33 at 35 (NY SC 1841), quoted in J.H. Wigmore and J.T. McNaughton, n. 22 above, 577.

39 E.g. *SEC* v. *Harrison* 80 F. Supp 226 at 230 (DC Colum. 1948) ("not consulting that attorney for the legitimate purposes which are protected by the privilege").

40 [1920] AC 581 (HL); this was not a Privy Council case (compare *United States* v. *Zolin* 491 US 554 at 563, 109 S.Ct. 2619 at 2626 (1989)).

41 [1920] AC at 621.

42 [1972] Ch 553 at 564 (Ch.).

43 E.g. S.L. Phipson, M.N. Howard, P. Crane and D.A. Hochberg, *Phipson on Evidence* (14th edn., Sweet & Maxwell, London, 1990) 514; D. Zeffertt, n. 25 above, 253.

44 *R.* v. *Bell, ex p. Lees* (1980) 146 CLR at 154.

approach may even be traced back to *Annesley* v. *Anglesea*,[45] discussed briefly above. In that case Serjeant Tisdall submitted in argument that if an attorney is employed in an unlawful act, then his duty to the public obliges him to disclose this and that the obligation to the public must override the obligation to the client.[46] In his judgment Baron Mounteney was unclear which of these views he would subscribe to. However the judgment is more consistent with an acceptance of Serjeant Tisdall's argument.[47]

Whatever the historical origins, this approach to the crime-fraud rule is certainly present in some of the modern case law. In *Barclays Bank* v. *Eustice* Schiemann LJ seems to have used a straight public policy rationale for the rule, observing that:

> to me the most important consideration is that we are here engaged not in some semantic exercise to see what adjective most appropriately covers the debtor's course of conduct but in deciding whether public policy requires that the documents in question are left uninspected.[48]

Later in his judgment Schiemann LJ holds that:

> I regard this purpose [defrauding creditors] as being sufficiently iniquitous for public policy to require that communications between him and his solicitor in relation to the setting up of those transactions be discoverable.[49]

The Australian editors of *Cross on Evidence*[50] go the furthest in resting the exception explicitly on public policy grounds, saying that:

> [t]he privilege is rooted in public policy. It is for this reason that the judges have created the exception for communications to facilitate crime or fraud. Public policy cannot be invoked to protect activities which are themselves inimical to public policy.[51]

This may reflect the extent to which some Australian courts have gone to rest decisions in this area on the basis of express public policy. For example, in *Re Moage* Mansfield J explained the rule as follows: "[t]he balancing of public policy considerations which is reflected in the law's recognition of legal professional privilege does not arise in such circumstances".[52] The Federal Court majority in *Attorney-General (N.T.)* v. *Kearney* went a step further, not even resting their decision on the crime-fraud rule itself, but on a first-principles analysis of public policy.[53] This judgment has been criticised as "a short but

[45] (1743) 17 How St Tr 1129.

[46] *Ibid.*, at 1241.

[47] E.g. *ibid.*

[48] [1995] 4 All ER 511 at 523 (CA).

[49] *Ibid.*, at 524.

[50] D. Byrne and J.D. Heydon, *Cross on Evidence: Fourth Australian Edition* (4th edn., Butterworths, Sydney, 1991).

[51] *Ibid.*, at para 25300.

[52] (1998) 26 ACSR 726 at 731 (Fed. Ct.).

[53] "The community's respect for and observance of the law will not be enhanced by the law itself casting a shroud of secrecy around the subordinate law-making process, and to do so would be to subvert the principles upon which the privilege is founded." ((1984) 55 ALR 545 at 556, *per* Woodward and Neaves JJ).

jarring ride upon the horse of public policy, with all the usual dangers that such a ride involves".[54]

Occasionally the two rationales are both used at the same time. This may be what was originally intended in *R.* v. *Cox and Railton,* where Stephen J held that:[55]

> The reason on which the [privilege] rule is said to rest cannot include the case of communications, criminal in themselves, or intended to further any criminal purpose, for the protection of such communications cannot possibly be otherwise than injurious to the interests of justice, and to those of the administration of justice. Nor do such communications fall within the terms of the rule. A communication in furtherance of a criminal purpose does not 'come into the ordinary scope of professional employment'[56] (emphasis added).

There are numerous other examples of the use of both rationales at the same time.[57]

As stated at the start of this chapter, there is no inconsistency between these two rationales in terms of the normative judgments underlying them; both hold that it is wrongful or repugnant to the justice of the situation to allow the privilege to be recognised in such circumstances. The only difference is in the structural rationalisation of this process.

If the crime-fraud rule was seen as resting on a directly overriding public policy interest, rather than the limits of the scope of the professional relationship, then there are a number of ways in which this public policy interest could be framed. One formulation could be that nothing can override the need to investigate wrongdoing. For example, one writer has described the rule as a reflection of the "paramount duty of the courts to investigate and deal with criminal conduct".[58] However, given that the privilege (as well as other privileges) operates in the criminal law in the first place, it is difficult to see how such an explanation could be tenable. A better formulation may be that the law will not allow itself to be used to aid the breaking of the law. This may be what was intended by the statement quoted above that "[p]ublic policy cannot be invoked to protect activities which are themselves inimical to public policy".[59] This formulation also sits well with the recognition of crime-fraud exceptions in statutory privileges for other confidential relationships.[60] This may be the sentiment behind some of

[54] C.A. Sweeney, Casenote on *Attorney-General (N.T.)* v. *Kearney* (1985) 59 *ALJ* 175 at 176.

[55] (1884) 14 QBD at 167.

[56] This passage was approved by Lord Goff in *Francis & Francis (a firm)* v. *Central Criminal Court* [1988] 3 All ER at 799h.

[57] E.g. *Attorney-General (N.T.)* v. *Kearney* (1985) 158 CLR at 524 (quoted below); *Francis & Francis (a firm)* v. *Central Criminal Court* [1988] 3 All ER at 799j–800a; *Banque Keyser Ullmann SA* v. *Skandia (UK) Insurance Co Ltd* [1986] 1 Lloyd's Rep. 336 at 338 (CA).

[58] New Zealand Law Commission, *Evidence Law: Privilege*, Preliminary Paper No. 23 (New Zealand Law Commission, 1994), para. 184.

[59] D. Byrne and J.D. Heydon, *Cross on Evidence: Fourth Australian Edition* (Butterworths, Sydney, 1991) para. 25300.

[60] For example the privilege for communications with clergy in New South Wales, Tasmania and the Northern Territory (see Law Reform Commission of Western Australia, Discussion Paper on

the strong and simple explanations for the rule, such as the reasoning that to allow the privilege here "would be to turn the policy upon which the rule is based upside down",[61] or that such a proposition "is self-evidently absurd".[62] Similar principles are also found in other areas of law. For example there is a general rule of contract law that prevents a contract being enforced for a purpose inimical to public policy, including a contract to commit a crime, fraud or tort on a third party.[63] This principle is based on "the absolute rule that the courts will not recognise a benefit accruing to a criminal from his crime".[64]

Difference in Rationales and Overriding the Privilege

It can be seen from the cases quoted above that the traditional rationale assumes the non-existence of the privilege in circumstances of crime or fraud. Such a position could have been reached by saying that the legal relationship already applying[65] in respect of particular communications has been vitiated by the presence of crime or fraud and therefore the effects of that pre-existing legal relationship no longer exist. However the crime-fraud rule has never been explained in this manner. The cases and articles referred to above in the context of the traditional rationale explain the lack of privilege in terms of the absence of a condition precedent to the recognition of the privilege (i.e. a legal relationship).[66] If this is the case then it must be that under this rationale no privilege ever existed with respect to these communications. For example, in *Russell* v. *Jackson* it was held that:

> the existence of the illegal purpose would prevent any privilege attaching to the communication. Where a solicitor is party to a fraud no privilege attaches to the communications with him upon the subject because the contriving of a fraud is no part of his duty as solicitor.[67]

Professional Privilege for Confidential Communications, Project No. 90 (Law Reform Commission of Western Australia, 1991) para. 3.24). For a discussion of the crime-fraud rule in the United States in relation to statutory privileges for doctors and clergy, see Note, "The Future Crime or Tort Exception to Communications Privilege" (1964) *Harv LR* 730 at 733.

[61] *Day* v. *Dalton* [1981] WAR 316 at 318, *per* Burt CJ (SC).

[62] *Ibid.*, at 319–20, *per* Jones J.

[63] See G.H. Treitel, *The Law of Contract* (9th edn., Sweet & Maxwell, London, 1995) chap. 11; M.P. Furmston, "The Analysis of Illegal Contracts" (1965) 16 *Uni Toronto LJ* 266 at 269–72; M.P. Furmston, *Cheshire, Fifoot and Furmston's Law of Contract* (13th edn., Butterworths, London, 1996) 370–84; A.G. Guest *et al.*, *Chittty on Contracts* (27th edn., Sweet & Maxwell, London, 1994) chap. 16.

[64] *Beresford* v. *Royal Insurance Co Ltd* [1938] AC 586 at 599 (HL).

[65] In some cases there is no pre-existing relationship and the first communication was itself concerned wholly with the commission of a crime or perpetration of fraud. The explanation offered by the traditional rationale may be sustainable in such cases. The discussion in this chapter applies to other instances of the recognition of the crime-fraud rule.

[66] The usual terminology employed by judges is that "no privilege attaches". For example, see *Seamar Holdings Ltd* v. *Kupe Group Ltd* [1995] 2 NZLR 274 at 277.39 (CA).

[67] (1851) 9 Hare at 392, 68 ER at 560.

It is for this reason that it is sometimes said the crime-fraud rule is not an exception to the privilege at all.[68]

Adoption of the public policy rationale leads to a different result in this respect. Under this rationale the privilege could exist at the time the relevant communication was made, but then be overridden by a later decision to vitiate the previously valid privilege. One commentator has observed that the crime-fraud exception reflects a recognition that some values outweigh the values advanced by protecting confidential relations and so a balancing process must be involved.[69] For example, in the leading American statement of the exception, Cardozo J said that: "[t]he privilege takes flight if the relation is abused".[70] In *Francis and Francis* Lord Goff, in construing the statutory crime-fraud exception in section 10(2) of the Police and Criminal Evidence Act 1984, which he regarded as equivalent to and reflecting the common law, said that "[s]ubsection (2) is concerned to negative the legal privilege which would otherwise be conferred." In *R.* v. *Cox and Railton* itself Stephen J quotes a passage from *R.* v. *Orton* (a case he describes as "directly in point"[71]) which holds that in such cases "the fraudulent character of the communication takes away the privilege . . . it deprives the communication of the privilege".[72] Other cases have taken a similar view.[73] If a client believes his communications to be confidential at the time they are made, then has that expectation frustrated by the operation of a rule such as the crime-fraud rule, this may have an effect on the expectation of confidentiality held by other clients in the future. This issue will be returned to shortly. Such a result may damage the basis on which the non-rights-based instrumental rationale for the privilege as a whole operates. Thus there may be an important difference between the two rationales for the crime-fraud rule, in terms of the perceived impact on the privilege as a whole.

SECTION II: CHOOSING BETWEEN THE TWO RATIONALES

Assuming, then, that both rationales cannot apply at the same time, the issue then becomes one of choosing which rationale is more appropriate. This must be done because, as has been shown above, the two rationales have different effects in terms of the structure of the crime-fraud rule. The claims of the two rationales will be analysed initially as a matter of first principles, then by examining the consistency with other privilege rules and other elements within the

[68] E.g. *Carter* v. *The Managing Partner, Northmore Hale Davy & Leake* (1995) 183 CLR at 163, *per* McHugh J; *Re Moage* (1998) 26 ACSR 726 at 733 (Fed. Ct.).

[69] Note, "The Attorney–Client Privilege: Fixed Rules, Balancing, and Constitutional Entitlement" (1977) 91 *Harv LR* 464 at 467.

[70] *Clark* v. *United States* 289 US at 15–16. Although the case concerned juror contempt, Cardozo J's passage is widely cited as the authoritative statement on the law regarding the crime-fraud exception.

[71] *R.* v. *Cox and Railton* (1884) 14 QBD at 170.

[72] See *ibid.*, at 171.

[73] E.g. *In re Postlethwaite* (1886) 35 Ch D 722 at 726, *per* North J (Ch.).

crime-fraud rule, as well as looking at the general nature of the crime-fraud rule as a whole.

First Principles Analysis and *R.* v *Cox and Railton*

Moving away from past authority and looking at the matter from first principles, it should be obvious that the argument that in such circumstances the privilege never arises, rather than arising and being overridden, places technical niceties above the clear and simple reality of the situation. If a client goes to his lawyer with a criminal or fraudulent plan and the lawyer discusses the matter with the client, then advises the client that everything they have said will not benefit from confidentiality, certainly at that point there may be no privilege and the client will be aware of this. However this is not normally the case. What will normally happen is that at the time of the discussion the client is not aware of his lack of privilege, either because he is not aware of the illegal or fraudulent nature of the planned action or because he is not told the effect this will have on his privilege. In this more typical situation the client, and presumably also the lawyer, expect that their discussion will be kept confidential. For example, the crime-fraud rule would probably apply where the client has initially obtained legal advice for a proper purpose, but then subsequently appropriated it to an illegal purpose.[74] In these circumstances it is difficult to see how either the lawyer or the client could have known at the time of the relevant communication that no legal relationship arose and therefore there was no privilege over the communications.

To frustrate an existing expectation of confidentiality is to commit the very sin that judges warn against when they argue for an absolute privilege without exceptions. It is no answer to say that in such cases the client deserved to have his expectation of confidentiality frustrated, as this is almost the same argument as Bentham used against the privilege as a whole last century, an argument that has been compellingly refuted by Wigmore and others since then. The reality of what the client is aware of at each point in time firmly suggests that a valid lawyer–client relationship exists at the time the communication is made, and that the effect of this is overridden later on.

As discussed above, the foundation case of *R.* v. *Cox and Railton* employed both rationales at the same time,[75] though probably gave emphasis to the traditional rationale.[76] However the actual decision in the case can be explained on the basis that the privilege arose and was later overridden. The advice at issue was a request by the clients (two partners) for information on how they could lawfully defeat a damages claim. There was no evidence before the court that

[74] E.g. *Fidelity-Phenix Fire Insurance Co* v. *Hamilton* 340 SW.2d 218 (Kentucky CA 1960); *Cox and Railton* may be an example of this, as discussed below.

[75] See text to n. 56 above.

[76] See text to n. 26 above.

the clients had any intention of fraudulently conveying the property at the time they consulted their solicitor.[77] At that stage there was lawful advice sought in the course of a valid professional relationship. As mentioned briefly in the previous chapter, it was only after this advice was received that the clients proceeded to attempt to do illegally what they previously might have thought they would be able to do legally.[78] This may be compared with the view expressed in *Butler* v. *Board of Trade,* where the Court said that in *R.* v. *Cox and Railton* a fraudulent intent existed before the clients went to their solicitor.[79]

It seems clear that the relevant intention was one to do the act they had planned. This did not necessarily involve an intention to commit an illegal result. The clients wanted to achieve a particular result and wanted advice on how to do this. The distinction between these two states was well expressed in an earlier Irish case:

> If any man should confide to a professional person, that he had a treasonable or felonious intention, and wished to know how he might execute it so as to escape punishment, it would be too much to say that such communication, which might make the man consulted guilty of misprison, was privileged; but if a man mediates an act which, exceeding certain limits, would become criminal, and confined within certain bounds would be perfectly justifiable, the person asking the advice must be considered as seeking how he may avoid and not how he may *commit* a crime, and it is impossible that an attorney should be obliged to disclose such communication.[80]

The problem arising from *R.* v. *Cox and Railton* relates more to the effect of events occurring after legal advice is given. It is difficult to see how later fraudulent events could retrospectively negate a prior lawyer–client relationship which has been validly formed. The facts and result of the case cannot be justified by the traditional rationale.

Consistency with Elements of Crime-fraud Rule

The strict interpretation of the scope of the legal relationship for the purposes of the traditional rationale does not fit well with the loose interpretation of the requirement that the relevant communications be made 'in furtherance' of a crime or fraud. There are many cases where this requirement does not operate

[77] D.J. Fried, n. 1 above, 458. The same point was made by the defendants' counsel: *R.* v. *Cox and Railton* (1884) 14 QBD at 162.

[78] Stephen J says (*ibid.*, at 165) that: "[w]e must take it, after the verdict of the jury, that so far as the two defendants, Railton and Cox, were concerned, their communications with Mr Goodman (the solicitor) were a step preparatory to the commission of a criminal offence, namely, a conspiracy to defraud". However it is equally possible that the jury reached this verdict on the basis that the conspiracy to defraud arose after the partners discovered that they could not achieve their purpose by legal means. The only evidence against this conclusion discernible from the report of the case is the record of Goodman's testimony that Railton asked him whether anyone else knew of the existence of the partnership.

[79] *Butler* v. *Board of Trade* [1971] 1 Ch 680 at 684 (Ch.).

[80] R. v. *Haydn* (1825) 2 Fox & Smith Ire. 379 at 381, *per* Bushe CJ (Ire. KB).

literally.[81] A good example of this may be found in the 'two lawyer cases'.[82] This is where a client goes to one lawyer and discloses facts inconsistent with recovery, then goes to a second lawyer and discloses facts consistent with recovery.[83] In truth it may be only the second piece of legal advice which is really "in furtherance" of the fraudulent transaction, however it is the first piece of legal advice which is usually in issue.[84] For example, in *Fidelity-Phenix Fire Insurance Co.* v. *Hamilton*[85] the insured had a policy which protected their tobacco barn except for the time when tobacco was being fired. The insured sought advice on their claim from one set of lawyers, who told them their claim would fail, partly because the fire occurred during the time the tobacco was being fired. The insured then pursued their claim through a second set of lawyers. The communications with the first set of lawyers were held not to be privileged. While it was the first communication that was vital to prove the defence in this case, there can be little doubt that at the time this communication was made, it was made in the course of a valid legal relationship, and quite probably with an intention on the part of the client to make an honest claim. This may be compared to *R.* v. *Craig*, where the defendant was charged with giving perjured evidence while a witness in an earlier civil trial. It was submitted that communications between the witness and the lawyer for the relevant party in the earlier civil trial were within the crime-fraud rule. Cooke J held that the rule did not apply to the witness' communications with the lawyer as, on the applicant's case, the witness was telling the truth on this occasion. It was his later evidence which, it was claimed, was false.[86]

The recognition of some types of conduct within the crime-fraud rule may be difficult to explain under the traditional rationale for the rule. This area of law is in some doubt. Assertions of mere breaches of contract or tortious conduct are insufficient of themselves.[87] The conduct must be "dishonest, and not merely disreputable".[88] In *Keep Brothers* v. *Birch and Bradshaw Ltd*[89] advice was given

[81] D.J. Fried, n. 1 above, 480.

[82] For a useful critique of the temporal distinction, see H.I. Subin, n. 3 above, 1116–17.

[83] E.g. *State* v. *Phelps* 545 P.2d 901 (Oregon CA 1976).

[84] Compare J. Gardner, "A Re-Evaluation of the Attorney–Client Privilege" (1963) 8 *Vill LR* 279 at 320; Gardner seems not to have been aware that there is a body of case law which renders much of his discussion of this issue of questionable relevance or importance.

[85] 340 SW.2d 218 (Kentucky CA 1960).

[86] *R.* v. *Craig* [1975] 1 NZLR at 599.

[87] *Crescent Farm (Sidcup) Sports Ltd* v. *Sterling Offices Ltd* [1972] Ch 553; also see *Skuse Television Ltd* [1994] 1 WLR 1156 at 1166 (QB) (dicta considering alleged maintenance); *Barclays Bank* v. *Eustice* [1995] 4 All ER 511 (advice used to structure transactions at an undervalue in order to defeat creditors was "sufficiently iniquitous").

[88] *Gamlen Chemical Co (UK) Ltd* v. *Rochem Ltd* (1979) 124 So Jo 276 (CA). The Australian High Court has stated that more than a mere hearsay allegation is required to establish a claim to override the privilege on this basis: see *Australian Federal Police* v. *Propend Finance* (1997) 141 ALR 545. Also see *Royscott Spa Leasing* v. *Lovett*, *Independent*, 23 Jan. 1995 (CA); *Birmingham Midshires MSL Ltd* v. *Ansell* [1998] 2 CL 40 (Ch.) (deception as to use to be made of loan is not sufficiently fraudulent to displace the privilege); *Nationwide Building Society* v. *Various Solicitors*, *NLJ*, 20 Feb. 1998 (Ch.) ("deliberate misrepresentation made by a borrower to a building society for the purpose of procuring an advance is within the scope of the exception").

[89] [1928] NZLR 360 (SC).

relating to the issue of a debenture by a company in financial difficulty. The issue was *prima facie* a "fraudulent preference" within the meaning of the relevant insolvency legislation, and on this basis the communications relating to the securing of the debenture by its recipient were held not to be privileged. However surely this advice possessed all the other incidents of a legal relationship. For example, one would imagine that the lawyer giving the advice would have had no problem in charging for his work and suing on the bill if necessary. And presumably the client would have been able to sue for negligent advice if that had been the case. Thus it could not be said that in this case a legal relationship never arose. The status of *Keep Brothers* v. *Birch and Bradshaw Ltd* in other countries, and possibly even in New Zealand, cannot be stated with certainty.[90] However it does serve to illustrate an important problem with the traditional rationale for the crime-fraud rule. This is that the rationale is simply not realistic. It is not right to say that in such circumstances no professional relationship arises, because it seems quite clear that in many of the circumstances covered by the rule other incidents of the professional relationship are still valid and effective.

If neither the client nor the lawyer are aware, nor suspect, that the client's planned actions may be illegal, then it is difficult to see the basis for impugning the professional quality of that relationship at the time the communication is made. In *R.* v. *Campbell and Shirose*[91] the Ontario Court of Appeal held that advice given by the Crown law office to a police officer about the legality of a planned reverse sting operation was not privileged as the police operation "was illegal and it therefore follows that what was being discussed was a future crime, *whether they knew it or not*" (emphasis added).[92]

In *Francis & Francis (a firm)* v. *Central Criminal Court*[93] the House of Lords had to rule on a certified point of law concerning the construction of the statutory crime-fraud exception in section 10(2) of the Police and Criminal Evidence Act 1984,[94] which provides that "[i]tems held with the intention of furthering a criminal purpose are not items subject to legal privilege".[95] The question for

[90] The case has been cited without comment by the leading evidence text in that jurisdiction: see D.L. Mathieson, *Cross on Evidence—New Zealand Edn.* (Butterworths, Wellington, 1998) 10.31.

[91] (1997) 115 CCC (3d) 310 (Ont. CA).

[92] *Ibid.*, at 331. The Court declined to decide the issue whether the relationship between the police and the Crown law office should be treated as a "lawyer–client" relationship for the purpose of the privilege.

[93] [1988] 3 All ER 755. For further commentary on this issue, see also A.L.E. Newbold, "The Crime/Fraud Exception to Legal Professional Privilege" (1990) 53 *MLR* 472 at 476–84; P. Stevenson, "Privilege: *Francis and Francis* and other recent cases", *Law Society Gazette*, 1 Feb. 1989, 26; also see the various comments in [1987] *Crim LR* 824; [1988] *Crim LR* 305 at 306–7; [1988] *Crim LR* 498 at 504–6; [1989] *Crim LR* 444 at 446–7.

[94] The actual facts giving rise to the case stated concerned an application under s. 27 of the Drug Trafficking Offences Act 1986 (UK) for production of certain material. S. 10 of the Police and Criminal Evidence Act 1984 (UK) was incorporated by reference in s. 29 of the of the Drug Trafficking Offences Act 1986.

[95] The case turned primarily on the differing views of the grammatical interpretation of s. 10(2): see Lord Bridge at 780b–781h, Lord Brandon at 787d–791c, Lord Oliver at 792g–794h, Lord Goff at

determination was whether the relevant intention is only that of the solicitor, or whether a criminal intention of the client or third party is sufficient. The majority[96] held that the intent may be that of the client or, most importantly, of the third party only. It is important to note the basis for Lord Goff's application of the exception to the situation where the criminal intent is held by a third party and not by the client. Lord Goff quoted and endorsed both the balancing terminology and the "scope of the relationship" reasoning as rationales for the exception. In the following paragraph[97] Lord Goff, in rejecting the argument that the innocent and unknowing client should be entitled to rely on the privilege, held that "most important of all, it seems to me that the disclosure of the third party's iniquity must, in the interests of justice, prevail over the privilege of the client, innocent though he may be". Such reasoning is completely independent of the "scope of the relationship" justification, and much closer to a first principles balancing analysis. The result of this case was that the crime-fraud rule operated even though neither the client nor the solicitor was participating in, or even aware of, any illegal purpose. Further, it appears that the client may have also been unaware of the actual proceedings.[98]

While this result has been strongly criticised,[99] there may arguably be support for this position in the Australian case of *Capar* v. *Commissioner of Police*.[100] In that case a man was charged with murdering his wife. One of the accused's children put pressure on the other children to fabricate their statements. They did so and these new statements found their way to the solicitor representing the accused. Donovan A-J held that these statements could not be privileged, *inter alia* because they were tainted by the illegality of a third party, namely the son of the accused who had pressured his siblings to make false statements. He held that:

> the plaintiff, has argued . . . that all the cases of illegality which have been put forward are cases which taint the client, in that in some way or another the client is involved in the fraud or illegality. He argues that the present case is no such situation, the plaintiff is not tainted by the illegal acts of Canan. It seems to be that it may be, and I put it no higher, that Canan, in attempting to assist his father by obtaining the allegedly false statements, does, for the present purposes, taint the client. I do not need to decide that issue. Rather, it seems to me that although there are no authorities where illegal-

796d. As the crime-fraud exception here was derived from statute, there was no need to find a justification for the rule. Lord Bridge (dissenting) thought that the provision was not reflective of the common law: *ibid.*, at 781b–d. However both Lords Griffiths (*ibid.*, at 789, 791b) and Goff (*ibid.*, at 797c) held that s. 10(2) corresponds to the common law and thought that their decisions were relevant to general principles of legal professional privilege. Lord Goff also held that the majority result reflects the common law: *ibid.*, at 798. For the contrary view see [1989] Crim LR 444 at 447.

[96] Lords Brandon, Griffiths and Goff; Lords Bridge and Oliver dissenting.

[97] [1988] 3 All ER at 800d.

[98] See Lord Bridge, *ibid.*, at 778c.

[99] E.g. see the articles cited in n. 93 above and in commentaries such as D. Feldman, *Civil Liberties and Human Rights in England and Wales* (Clarendon Press, Oxford, 1993) 448–50.

[100] (1994) 34 NSWLR 715 (SC).

ity has been held to arise where the illegality was that of a third party rather than that of the client or the solicitor,[101] nevertheless the principle of illegality still applies.[102]

There was no suggestion that either the client (the accused father) or his solicitor, who received the fabricated statements, had any knowledge of or involvement in their procuring or production. As far as the evidence before the court suggested, they were the innocent recipients of these communications.

These cases must surely call the rationale for the exception into question. The common law generally takes a liberal view of the elements of the lawyer–client relationship when determining the existence of the privilege. As discussed elsewhere, the privilege may exist before the relationship itself has come into existence, or where a potential client mistakenly believes he is in discussions with his lawyer. This general approach accords with the instrumental rationale for the privilege. Given this broad approach, it is remarkable that in another element of the same rule the law should regard the lawyer–client relationship as completely vitiated by the intention of a third party or by the existence of some other fact which neither the lawyer nor the client is aware of.

In *R.* v. *Guildhall Magistrates' Court, ex parte Primlaks Holdings Co*[103] the Divisional Court quashed the issue of search warrants on the basis that the justice could not have been satisfied either that the material sought did not include privileged material within section 10 of the Police and Criminal Evidence Act 1984 (UK) or that the conditions for an issue set out in section 8 of the same Act were satisfied. The Divisional Court made two findings: first, that there might have been privileged material within section 10(1) of the Act; secondly, that even if all the material sought was within the crime-fraud provision in section 10(2), the material held by legal advisers could still be within section 14(2) as "material . . . in the possession of a person who—. . . (b) holds it subject—(i) to an express or implied undertaking to hold it in confidence". Parker LJ stated that even if privilege is lost by virtue of the crime-fraud provision in section 10(2), "I cannot accept that no express or implied undertaking to hold in confidence can exist".[104] The importance of this finding was that the material did not simply fall into the basic category of unprivileged material, but that, being within section 14 as material communicated to a professional adviser in confidence, was subject to a different and tougher statutory procedure.[105] This decision would be difficult to reconcile with the traditional rationale for the crime-fraud rule. Even taking into account the statutory nature of the rules being considered, the fact is that the Divisional Court clearly held that the professional relationship

[101] The judge's statement that there are no cases in point was of course incorrect. *Francis & Francis*, decided six years earlier, was not cited to the court.

[102] *Ibid.*, at 722.

[103] (1988) 89 Cr. App. Rep. 215 (QB); for further commentary also see [1989] *Crim LR* 448 at 449–50.

[104] *Ibid.*, at 223.

[105] I.e. s. 9 of the Police and Criminal Evidence Act 1984 (UK), requiring application to a judge, rather than to a magistrate.

can still subsist even where the (statutory) crime-fraud rule has been activated. Thus the scope of the crime-fraud rule under section 10(2) of the Act is apparently not contiguous with the scope of the professional relationship.[106]

Consistency with Other Privilege Rules

The traditional rationale for the crime-fraud rule is inconsistent with the view of the scope of the professional relationship taken elsewhere in the privilege. The general approach elsewhere is to focus on the main instrumental goal of maintaining a high expectation of confidentiality, and to minimise the number of occasions where this expectation will be frustrated. To achieve this a very expansive view of the scope of the professional relationship is adopted. This includes giving recognition to the privilege even in cases where it is clear that no professional relationship exists. One such example is the principle that communications made between a solicitor and a client before their relationship has been formally consummated may still benefit from the privilege.[107] Note though that in such cases the relevant communication may not be sufficiently referable to the provision of legal advice.[108]

Another example of a rule that may be inconsistent with the traditional rationale for the crime-fraud rule is the principle that the privilege will usually apply where a person imparts information to a person whom he wrongly believes to be a lawyer[109] or to a lawyer who he wrongly believes has consented to act.[110] This is based on a desire to uphold the reasonable expectations of people seek-

[106] Finally note that the underlying reasoning in R. v. *Guildhall Magistrates' Court, ex parte Primlaks Holdings Co* may be inconsistent with the later Court of Appeal decision in *Finers* v. *Miro*, *NLJ*, 5 Oct. 1990 1387–8. This was a civil case in which a solicitor came to believe that he was holding funds which a client had obtained by fraud. The solicitor froze the client's account and sought directions from the court on how he should proceed, and in particular whether he should notify the possible victim of the fraud. The Court of Appeal held that, as the relevant information *prima facie* fell within the crime-fraud exception, the solicitor was not bound to uphold the privilege and could reveal the information to the possible victim. In doing so Balcombe LJ held that "fraud unravels all obligations of confidence": *ibid.*, at 1388, third column. The other judge giving a judgment, Dillon J, held only that the criminal or fraudulent purpose vitiated the privilege: *ibid.*, at 1388, first column. However his decision is also consistent with the abrogation of other remaining obligations of confidentiality.

[107] *Minter* v. *Priest* [1930] AC 558 (HL); *Descôteaux* v. *Mierzwinski* [1982] 1 SCR at 876–7; but compare R. v. *Medina* (1990) 46 ACR 132 at 141 (WA SC).

[108] As in both *Minter* v. *Priest* and R. v. *Medina*, both n. 107 above.

[109] *Calley* v. *Richards* (1854) 19 Beav 401, 52 ER 406 (lawyer had ceased to practice at time of advice); R. v. *Choney* (1908) 17 Man. LR 467 at 470, 474 (Man. CA); *Feuerheerd* v. *London General Omnibus Co.* [1918] 2 KB 560 (CA); *State* v. *Russell* 53 NW 441 (Wis. SC 1893); but compare *Tobakin* v. *Dublin Southern D.T. Co* [1905] 2 IR 58 (Ire. KB). But see C. Passmore, *Privilege* (CLT, Sutton Coldfield, 1998) 73: "[t]he case law is clear that a professional relationship must exist between a lawyer and his client to which the relevant communication between them must be referable before a legitimate claim to privilege can be made".

[110] For a thorough discussion of some of the case law see *Global Funds (NSW)* v. *Rooney* (1994) 36 NSWLR 122 (NSW SC (Eq. Div)).

ing legal advice.[111] However there is a danger that this rule may be used in the criminal realm to fill gaps in the law relating to improperly obtained confessions, and in a manner that is quite inconsistent with the precepts of the privilege rule.[112] Further, it should be noted that the rule has been applied against the person imparting information. In *Feuerheerd* v. *London General Omnibus Co*[113] the Court of Appeal held that a communication made by the plaintiff to an agent of the defendant, under the mistaken belief that the person taking down the statement was an agent of her own solicitor, was still privileged, with the effect that the plaintiff who made the statement in the first place could not have her own statement adduced. The *Feuerheerd* case surely represents an objectionable principle which, if taken seriously, would throw the entire privilege into chaos.[114] It has been strongly criticised in Australia.[115] Nevertheless, it is clear that this rule proceeds on a different understanding of the scope of the professional relationship for the purposes of the privilege from the traditional rationale. In general the rule of legal professional privilege adopts a very expansive view of the scope of the professional relationship.[116] The emphasis is on what the individual imparting information believes to be the case. The traditional rationale for the crime-fraud rule stands as an odd exception to this

[111] "[T]he result [of disclosure] would be to defeat the operation of the rule, the object of which is to allow the fullest and most unreserved communication between the client and his solicitor" (*Calley* v. *Richards* (1854) 19 Beav at 404, 52 ER at 407 per Romilly MR).

[112] The best example of this is *R.* v. *Choney* (1908) 17 Man. LR 467. In that case a police officer had asked a prisoner who had previously acted as the defendant's interpreter to get the defendant to talk about his case. The defendant wrongly assumed the interpreter was still acting as his solicitor's agent. The police officer also arranged for other police officers to be present near the cell to overhear the conversation. The court held that all the evidence was privileged. The exclusion of the interpreter's evidence accords with other cases, and is quite similar to *Calley* v. *Richards* in many respects. However the exclusion of the eavesdropper's evidence is difficult to justify in terms of the privilege. Phippen JA (with Richards JA concurring on this point) held that "we must treat the whole as an interview with several persons who had fraudulently adopted the character of solicitor's representatives . . . [and] apply the cloak of privilege to what was heard by the listeners without, as well as within, the cell" (17 Man. LR at 474). However this is a strained construction. The conversation was in no way directed to the people outside the cell. They were nothing other than eavesdroppers. The court here invoked concepts of fault and punishment of wrongful police techniques which are alien to the privilege.

[113] [1918] 2 KB 560.

[114] The decision in *Feuerheerd* turns on its head the fundamental principle that the privilege is that of the client, not the lawyer. The result of the case was that the recipient of the communication asserted the privilege *against* the client. *Feuerheerd* would also wreak havoc in the rules of waiver of the privilege. Further, the logic of the decision is largely based on the view that "the privilege is quite independent of the intention of the person making the statement" (*ibid.*, at 568, *per* Pickford LJ). This runs against the fundamental basis of the privilege that, in order to foster effective and unreserved lawyer–client communications, the legitimate expectations of clients in imparting confidential matters should not be frustrated. *Feuerheerd* must be wrong.

[115] *Aydin* v. *Australia Iron & Steel Pty Ltd* [1984] 3 NSWLR 684 at 689–90 (NSW SC); *Feuerheerd* was followed in *Nickmar Pty Ltd* v. *Preservatrice Skandia Insurance Ltd* (1985) 3 NSWLR 44 at 62–3 (NSW SC), though with reservations about its correctness, as also happened in *Vardas* v. *South British Insurance Co Ltd* (1984) 2 NSWLR 652 at 659 (NSW SC).

[116] Though of course there are exceptions to this general statement, such as the strict approach taken by some courts to advice by foreign lawyers: see *Re United States of America* v. *Mammoth Oil* [1925] 2 DLR at 975–8, *per* Ferguson JA; compare the dissenting judgment of Hodgins JA at 966.

approach. This may well suggest that the traditional rationale is used as an excuse to mask the real reason for the rule.

Past–Present Distinction and Ongoing Conduct

It has been shown that the traditional explanation for the crime-fraud rule is that in such circumstances no professional relationship arises in the first place. It has also been explained that this argument is important to the structure and justification of the rule as a whole, as it renders it possible to continue to hold that the non-existence of the privilege is determined by a factor taking place at the start of the relevant communication, that is when the client chooses to impart the information, and therefore should not affect the maintenance of a client's confidence in the confidentiality of his communications. Because of this it can be said that the crime-fraud rule does not even represent a derogation from the privilege, but rather is another circumstance in which the necessary elements of the privilege are not present.

This reasoning is reliant on another associated principle; that the privilege exists only to protect admissions of past wrongdoing, and that discussions of future wrongdoing are caught by the crime-fraud rule and so are outside the cover of the privilege. Thus the distinction between advice given for past and future acts is not only central to the crime-fraud rule, within which the distinction immediately operates, but also has important ramifications for the privilege as a whole. McNicol said that the distinction is "critical" and "lies at the heart of the rule".[117] Wigmore expressed complete faith that the distinction effectively solved the problem of the privilege existing for the culpable.[118] However the reality of the past–present distinction and the phenomenon of ongoing conduct significantly blur the application of the theory described above. The effect is to cast doubt on the rationale for the crime-fraud rule and the view that this rule is in some sense not a derogation from the privilege.

The distinction may not always be adhered to in practice.[119] It is easy to imagine circumstances in which past and future wrongdoing are difficult to separate. Fried gives the example of a client informing his lawyer after the close of testimony but before the close of his case that he has committed perjury.[120] The wrongful action is in the past, but the client is implicitly inviting the lawyer to rely on the false evidence in the lawyer's closing address.[121]

[117] S.B. McNicol, *Law of Privilege* (Law Book Co., Sydney, 1992) 107.

[118] "[T]hese reasons all cease to operate . . . where the desired advice refers not to prior, but to future wrongdoing" (J.H. Wigmore and J.T. McNaughton, n. 22 above, 573).

[119] S.B. McNicol, n. 117 above, 107; an example is *R.* v. *Schmidt* (1893) 11 NZLR 703 (SC), where a clear case of advice on past wrongdoing was held to be within the crime-fraud rule.

[120] D.J. Fried, n. 1 above, 444–5.

[121] For a discussion of whether client perjury should be considered a completed or ongoing crime, see W.D. Brazil, "Unanticipated Client Perjury and the Collission of Rules of Ethics, Evidence, and Constitutional Law" (1979) 44 *Missouri LR* 601 at 618–19 and numerous American cases cited therein.

In the Australian High Court case of *Tuckiar* v. *The King*[122] a person accused of murdering a policeman alleged that he had found the victim in a highly compromising position. The accused was convicted. After conviction but before sentencing the accused admitted to his counsel that his version of events had been a fabrication. The accused's counsel felt obliged to tell the court of this prior to sentencing. The High Court allowed the accused's appeal, holding that it was wrong for counsel to have divulged the privileged communications. The case is similar to Fried's borderline example. On the one hand Tuckiar's admission was of past wrongdoing. On the other hand his counsel had yet to make submissions about sentencing.[123] If the traditional rationale for the crime-fraud rule is applied, then Tuckiar's admission would seem to be outside the scope of the privilege.

This difficulty of distinction is most apparent where the client engages in a course of criminal conduct that continues into the present.[124] Under the strict theory described above, communications relating to the conduct may be protected by the privilege only if the criminal conduct is wholly terminated. However the termination itself may be the subject of legal advice.[125] One example may be a continuing breach of competition laws, such as an abuse of a dominant position in the market.[126] The initial abuse may be a past act. However the failure to remedy the situation, and possibly continue with the same market strategy, may be a continuing breach of the law. It is difficult to say whether advice relating to such actions would be privileged.[127] Another example may be legal advice sought during a kidnapping.[128]

A much more common problem is the status of advice given for the purpose of minimising taxation by evasion or avoidance. In *Bullivant* v. *Attorney-General for Victoria* it was held that the word "evade" was ambiguous, and that a solicitor could advise a client on how to arrange his affairs in order to fall outside the relevant taxation legislation.[129] However the difference between legal and illegal minimisation of tax can be slight, and consequently the application of the privilege here is fraught with uncertainty.[130]

[122] (1934) 52 CLR 335 (HCA).

[123] Determining the status of the admission would require much further analysis. It is difficult to see how Tuckiar's post-conviction statement was made "in furtherance" of his purpose of committing perjury, as disclosure to his lawyer would be likely only to hinder that. At the same time, while made in the course of ongoing legal communications, this particular statement was clearly not made with the intention of seeking legal advice.

[124] G.C. Hazard, "An Historical Perspective on the Attorney–Client Privilege" (1978) 66 *Calif LR* 1061 n. 4; e.g. see *In re Selser* 105 A.2d 395 (NJ SC 1954), concerning the continual bribing of public officials, which the client's lawyer knew had happened in the past and strongly suspected was still occurring in the present.

[125] *Ibid.*

[126] Art. 86 of the EEC Treaty (now Art. 82 of the EC Treaty).

[127] This is of course on the assumption that advice in furtherance of a breach of competition law is within the ambit of the crime-fraud rule. This matter has not been determined by the courts.

[128] H.I. Subin, n. 3 above, 1101–5.

[129] [1901] AC 196 at 201–2, 207 (PC).

[130] See e.g. E.P.G., "Professional Privilege in Relation to Enquiries by Commissioner of Taxation" (1950) 23 *ALJ* 640 at 644; J.A. Speed, "Privilege of Communications Between a Solicitor and his Client" (1965) 28 *MLR* 18 at 25.

Another problem may be where the client makes false statements relating to past actions. Advice concerning past illegal acts may be protected by the privilege, but false statements by the client relating to these past actions may be considered to be part of an ongoing fraud.[131] In such a circumstance the false statement may possibly not be privileged, even though the substance of the advice concerned a completed crime.[132]

Activating the crime-fraud rule by reference to ongoing conduct may be extremely problematic. It may be unclear whether the act has terminated, and, if it has terminated, whether subsequent acts and statements are made in furtherance of this act. Further, it is not at all clear that the crime-fraud rule should be concerned with impugning legal communications made after an essentially completed event (which may be criminal) has been effected. This must be what Ferguson JA had in mind in *Re United States of America* v. *Mammoth Oil* when he said:

> Let us stop to consider the now too common automobile accident in which someone is killed by an unknown person, after which the unknown driver goes to counsel, and, after communicating the facts for advice, directs the counsel to attend the inquest, watch the proceedings, and keep him advised. What would become of the principle [of legal professional privilege] if the counsel attending such inquest may be put in the witness box and questioned as to why and for whom he is attending and watching the proceedings? I am clearly of opinion that counsel so employed could and should refuse to answer such questions.[133]

An analysis which would lead to the displacement of the privilege in such circumstances strays dangerously close to conflict with one of the underlying assumptions of the privilege; that it is for the use of the guilty as well as of the innocent. If the goal of the privilege is the encouragement of candid legal communications, then surely it would be injurious to this goal to impugn all communications where there is *prima facie* evidence that the individual concerned was in fact guilty of a past act and had therefore sought advice for the purpose of evading punishment.[134]

However some of the cases have come close to this. For example, in *Plumb* v. *Monck and Bohm*[135] the accused was first charged with driving an uninsured car, for which he produced an insurance certificate as his defence to the charge. The certificate was dated four weeks prior to the date of the alleged offence. The

[131] Comment, "Developments in the Law-Privileged Communications" (1985) 98 *Harv LR* 1450 at 1510.

[132] E.g. see *United States* v. *Calvert* 523 F.2d 895 (8th Cir. 1975) (lies relating to the past act of murder and previous murders and frauds, but also made in pursuance of a future insurance fraud).

[133] *Re United States of America* v. *Mammoth Oil* [1925] 2 DLR at 974.

[134] This is different from the situation where there is a deliberate plan to evade punishment by means of commission of further offences, such as fleeing the jurisdiction or committing perjury: see *United States* v. *Gordon-Nikkar* 518 F.2d 972 (5th Cir. 1975); *In re Sealed Case (Synanon Church)* 754 F.2d 395 at 402 (DC Cir. 1985) ("To the limited extent that past acts of misconduct were the *subject* of the cover-up that occurred during the period of representation, however, then past violations properly may be a subject of grand jury inquiry.").

[135] *Plumb* v. *Monck* (1974) 4 ALR 405.

same accused was then charged, along with another person, with conspiracy to defeat the enforcement of laws by the procuring of a fraudulently ante-dated insurance certificate. Privilege was claimed over the ante-dated insurance certificate, but this document was held to be within the crime-fraud rule and so not privileged.

However the problem here is that the crime of conspiracy was complete at the time of the agreement to conspire. The relevant legal communication was therefore made in the secret furtherance of a past crime. The issue was resolved by Forster J by describing the act as a "continuing crime and the working-out of the conspiracy".[136] However all communications occurring after the agreement to conspire, while referable to the conspiracy and possibly evidence of the earlier agreement, did not further the substantive element of the crime.

An even stronger example is the New Zealand case of *Re Golightly*.[137] In that case the members of a harbour board were charged with misappropriation and misapplication of the board's funds. The board's solicitor asserted legal professional privilege in challenging a witness summons issued against him. Without conclusively deciding the point, Mahon J indicated that the relevant communications probably would have been within the crime-fraud exception, possibly being in furtherance of an attempt to suppress the evidence of the board's auditor, who initially discovered the fraud.[138] However the events being investigated were, if committed, complete at the time the relevant legal communications were made. The communications therefore essentially related to past acts.

The result of the preceding discussion is that it has been seen that it is very difficult to distinguish clearly between advice which relates to future acts, which should be within the crime-fraud rule and so not privileged, and advice which relates to past and completed acts, which should be privileged. Because of this it cannot be said that the crime-fraud rule is concerned with a condition precedent to the activation of the privilege (or rather the absence of such a condition). The truth is that there are some occasions in which the privileged status of a communication can only be known well after the communication has taken place.

CONCLUSIONS

The traditional rationale for the crime-fraud rule masks the detrimental effect the rule has on the privilege as a whole. By stating that such communications are outside the scope of the legal relationship, it is possible then to discount any chilling effect the rule may have, as it can be said that the crime-fraud rule is somehow outside the area covered by the privilege and that it does not override the privilege.

136 *Ibid.*, at 410–11.
137 [1974] 2 NZLR 297 (HC).
138 *Ibid.*, at 304–5.

This analysis comes very close to conflict with an underlying assumption of the privilege that it is for the use of the guilty as well as the innocent. Judges do not seem to be particularly concerned by this danger. For example, Scheimann LJ in *Barclays Bank* v. *Eustice* held that:

> In so far as those wishing to engage in sharp practice are concerned, the effect of the present decision may well be to discourage them from going to their lawyers. This has the arguable public disadvantage that the lawyers might have dissuaded them from the sharp practice. However, it has the undoubted public advantage that the absence of lawyers will make it more difficult for them to carry out their sharp practice.[139]

This seems to be the basis of what is now a general rule of public policy supporting the crime-fraud rule:

> the attorney–client privilege protects only those attorney–client exchanges that serve the privilege's purpose of allowing a client to secure information about laws he must follow and to pursue freely his right to effective legal representation. If the client seeks legal advice in order to further illegal activities, this policy is not promoted and the privilege should be pierced.[140]

The problem with these sentiments is that they proceed on too narrow a view of the instrumental rationale. In order to work, such logic requires that there be a very specific link between the reality of confidentiality and a client's expectation and subsequent action. That is, that the client will know that advice for a non-fraudulent purpose is protected and so be completely candid in such situations; also that any reduction in his expectation of confidentiality is confined to the situation of communications in furtherance of a crime or fraud, and that the client fully understands that the derogation is confined in this way. However we know that the non-rights-based instrumental rationale operates on a much more general basis than this. The concern should be for candour as a whole. The effect on candour in relation to one type of situation or one type of legal communication is, from this point of view, inseparable from the effect on candour as a whole.

To hold, retrospectively and on a technical ground, that the privilege did not exist at a time when both the client and the lawyer thought that it did undermines the privilege's rationale as much as it does to say that the privilege may validly exist at one point in time, but then later be vitiated by the discovery that the communications were made for an illegal or fraudulent purpose. The simple answer is that it is a fantasy to think that the crime-fraud rule can be completely reconciled with the rationale for the substantive rule. The two rules (or rather, rule and exception to it) do not promote the same interest. The crime-fraud rule represents a concession to the need for absolute confidentiality which is made in the interests of another competing public interest. The crime-fraud exception rests not on some immutable view of the scope of the professional relationship, but rather on a flexible balancing of interests.

139 [1995] 4 All ER at 525b.
140 Comment, n. 131 above, 1510.

9

Criminal Exculpatory Evidence

INTRODUCTION

This chapter will examine the situation where a witness has evidence which may exculpate a criminal accused, but where that witness claims legal professional privilege over the evidence. The general policy favouring disclosure takes on a further dimension in the criminal context when it is the accused that is seeking access to privileged information. In such a case the policy becomes that of not convicting accused where their innocence may be proven.

The only issue dealt with in this chapter is whether in a situation such as that described above the privilege should not yield to the interests of the accused. Other possible solutions to the problem, such as staying the prosecution, restricting the use made of communications compulsorily disclosed or creating a limited recognised interest exception,[1] are outside the scope of this chapter and will be considered only in passing.

It will be argued that the interest of a criminal accused in having access to all exculpatory evidence is a powerful one. It is recognised and has supremacy over many other exclusionary evidential rules. However the interest has expressly not been given effect to in some Commonwealth jurisdictions, which have rejected a proposed exception to legal professional privilege for criminal exculpatory evidence. It will be argued that this position is misguided as it is based on mistaken assumptions about the nature and operation of such an exception, which in turn reflects a mistaken view of the structure of the privilege.

SECTION I: PRINCIPLE OF *IN FAVOREM INNOCENTIAE*

Concept of Criminal Exculpatory Evidence

The regime of the criminal law places the accused in a special position. This is evidenced by such rules as the higher criminal standard of proof.[2] Many

[1] Such a rule may provide that the privilege operates only if the justification for it continues to exist, and this may not be so when the claimants no longer have any recognisable interest in maintaining the privilege. See *R.* v. *Craig* [1975] 1 NZLR at 599; *R.* v. *Ataou* [1988] 1 QB at 807, overruled by *R.* v. *Derby Magistrates' Court, ex p. B* [1996] 1 AC at 529 and 542, but cf. 546; *R.* v. *Dunbar and Logan* (1982) 138 DLR (3d) 221 at 252 (Ont. CA); *Carter* v. *The Managing Partner, Northmore Hale Davy & Leake*, unreported, Supreme Court of Western Australia (Full Court), 15 July 1993, *per* Rowland J at 30–1.

[2] *Woolmington* v. *DPP* [1935] AC 462 (HL).

different foundational legal documents, such as the Canadian[3] and United States[4] Constitutions, the International Covenant on Civil and Political Rights[5] and the European Convention for the Protection of Human Rights and Fundamental Freedoms[6] provide basic minimum rights for accused. Such rights have a long history[7] and are firmly entrenched. These rules operate specifically to benefit the accused out of a general rule of public policy[8] which recognises the special difficulties criminal accused face.[9] Adequate legal advice is seen as an important aspect of these procedural safeguards[10] and is implemented by a variety of rules from the basic right to have a lawyer present to consult with to more complex procedural rights ensuring adequate representation for indigent accused.[11]

Rules relating to the reception of evidence in criminal trials form an essential part of the law's protection of a criminal accused. In criminal trials there are extensive rules relating to disclosure by the prosecution. Most common law jurisdictions, for example, oblige the prosecution to disclose its witness statements[12] and all relevant evidence.[13] However the extent to which these obliga-

[3] S. 11 of the Canadian Charter of Rights and Freedoms (Part 1 of the Constitution Act 1982, enacted by the Canada Act 1982 (UK)).

[4] The "due process" clause of the Fifth Amendment.

[5] See Art. 14.

[6] See Art. 6, which gives the right to have adequate time and facilities for the preparation of a defence and the right to the free assistance of an interpreter when required. This has now been implemented as part of UK law in the Human Rights Act 1998 (UK).

[7] E.g. see 42 Edw. III c.3, providing for a right of due process in 1368.

[8] *Carter* v. *The Managing Partner, Northmore Hale Davy & Leake*, unreported, Supreme Court of Western Australia (Full Court), 15 July 1993, *per* Rowland J at 29. This may be compared with the approach of Brennan J in the High Court: see *Carter* v. *The Managing Partner, Northmore Hale Davy & Leake* (1995) 183 CLR at 129. Brennan J reasoned that as there is no public interest which defeats the privilege then there can be no individual interest which does so.

[9] These difficulties are well articulated by Deane J in *Jago v District Court (NSW)* (1989) 168 CLR 23 at 55 (HCA) and in *Dietrich v The Queen* (1992) 177 CLR 292 at 334–5 (HCA). This factor answers the challenge that the Crown should also have the benefit of any relaxation of the privilege: *Carter* v. *The Managing Partner, Northmore Hale Davy & Leake* (1995) 183 CLR at 154–5; compare *ibid.*, at 131, 166–7 and *R.* v. *Derby Magistrates' Court, ex p. B* [1996] 1 AC at 512.

[10] For a thorough analysis of the theoretical benefits of legal advice to individuals, see L. Kaplow and S. Shavell, "Legal Advice about Information to Present in Litigation: Its Effects and Social Desirability" (1989) 102 *Harv LR* 565 at 580.

[11] E.g. see G. Chowdharay-Best, "The History of Right to Counsel" (1976) 40 *J Crim. L* 275 (survey of Commonwealth law); B.A. MacFarlane, "The Right to Counsel at Trial and on Appeal" (1990) 32 *Crim. LQ* 440 (survey of US and Canadian law).

[12] USA—18 USC §3500 (the "Jencks Act", 1970); Federal Rules of Criminal Procedure (US), rule 26.2; also see *Jencks* v. *United States* 353 US 667 (1957); UK—Attorney-General's Guidelines (1981), especially paras. 2 and 6; *Berry* v. R. [1992] 3 All ER 881 (HL), surveying the law at 886–9; Australia—*Maddison* v. *Goldrick* [1976] 1 NSWLR 651 (NSW CA); South Africa—*S* v. *Smith* 1994 (3) SA 887 (SE Cape Div.); *Khala* v. *Minister of Safety and Security* 1994 (4) SA 218 at 251 (Witwatersrand Div.); however *S* v. *Smith* has not gained universal acceptance in all Provincial Divisions, particularly in the Transvaal.

[13] USA—*Brady* v. *Maryland* 373 US 83 at 87 (1983), cut back by *United States* v. *Agurs* 427 US 97 at 104 (1976). Academic writing on the Brady rule is voluminous and unfortunately cannot be dealt with here. UK—ss. 3 and 7 of the Criminal Procedure and Investigations Act 1996 (UK). For the position in the rest of the Commonwealth see C. Tapper, *Cross and Tapper on Evidence* (8th ed., Butterworths, London, 1995) 271–2. The most stringent disclosure requirements are imposed in Canada: see *Stinchcombe* v. R. [1991] 3 SCR 326 (SC) and cases discussed therein.

tions are followed is questionable,[14] as shown by Sir Richard Scott's Report on the Matrix Churchill prosecution.[15] The rules governing discovery by the prosecution can be contrasted with the limited disclosure obligations placed on the accused.[16] The main reason for imposing wide disclosure obligations on the prosecution is out of a concern for the special position of the accused,[17] rather than because prosecutors are public officials with no clients whose confidences they must respect.[18]

The privilege appears to have been applied to criminal cases, at least since 1765,[19] and certainly by the early part of the nineteenth century.[20] While there may have been some uncertainty in its application around the middle of the nineteenth century,[21] the use of the privilege as a means of resisting a subpœna *duces tecum* has not been seriously challenged. There has been debate surrounding the application of the privilege to defeat search warrants.[22] However the controversy has in the main surrounded the extra-curial nature of such warrants, rather than any considerations arising from the separate demands of criminal procedure. The full application of the privilege in criminal procedure now seems to be beyond argument in most common law jurisdictions.[23]

However, it is possible that the privilege may operate differently in criminal proceedings,[24] in order to recognise the different priorities of criminal as opposed to civil litigation. The acceptance of a near absolute privilege and the

14 See B.A. Babcock, "Fair Play: Evidence Favourable to an Accused and Effective Assistance of Counsel" (1982) 34 *Stan. LR* 1133 at 1143–4. This may be compared with high-minded pronouncements of the broad reach of the Brady obligations, such as that in V. Bass, "*Brady* v. *Maryland* and the Prosecutor's Duty to Disclose" (1972) 40 *U Chicago LR* 112 at 135–40.

15 R. Scott, *Report of the Inquiry into the Export of Defence Equipment and Dual-Use Goods to Iraq and Related Prosecutions* (HMSO, London, 1996) iii at paras. G18.37, G18.41.

16 E.g. see ss. 5 and 6 of the Criminal Procedure and Investigations Act 1996 (UK). For the position in the USA see R.P. Mosteller, "Discovery Against the Defense" (1986) 74 *Calif. LR* 1567 at 1579–81, especially at 1676–80. Also see *R.* v. *Peruta* (1992) 78 CCC (3d) at 356–7 (rejecting the argument of Crown counsel, which the trial judge had surprisingly accepted, that the duty of disclosure should be reciprocal).

17 *Berry* v. *R.* [1992] 3 All ER at 887: "the key is fairness to the accused"; also see M. Frankel, "The Search for Truth Continued: More Disclosure, Less Privilege" (1982) 54 *U Col LR* 51 at 54.

18 As suggested in *Stinchcombe* v. *R.* [1991] 3 SCR at 333 and by A. Alschuler, "The Preservation of a Client's Confidences: One Value Among Many or a Categorical Imperative?" (1981) 52 *U Colorado LR* 349 at 354.

19 *R.* v. *Dixon* (1765) 3 Burrow 1687, 97 ER 1047. While the privilege was not expressly mentioned in the report, it appears to be the principle relied upon.

20 In 1828 Best CJ in *Broad* v. *Pitt* (1828) M & M 233 at 234, 173 ER 1142 at 1143 was in no doubt that the privilege extended to criminal proceedings. Note though that these comments were obiter and the case was a civil one.

21 Compare *R.* v. *Hankins* (1849) 2 Car. & Kir. 823, 175 ER 346, with *R.* v. *Brown* (1862) 9 Cox CC 281.

22 See Chap. 2 above.

23 E.g see *R.* v. *Cahill, ex p. McGregor* (1985) 61 ACTR 7 (ACT SC); *Adams* v. *Anthony Bryant* (1986) 67 ALR 616 (Fed. Ct.); *Grofam* v. *ANZ Banking Group* (1993) 117 ALR 669 (Fed. Ct.); *Truman (Frank) Export Ltd* v. *Metropolitan Police Commissioner* [1977] QB 952. In England the matter is now governed by ss. 10–14 of the Police and Criminal Evidence Act 1984 (UK).

24 P. Byrne and J.D. Heydon, *Cross on Evidence: Fourth Australian Edition.* (Butterworths, Sydney, 1991) para. 27130; *Brown* (1988) 87 Cr App R 52 at 57 (CA) (public interest immunity). Compare *R.* v. *Robertson* (1983) 21 NTR 11 at 19 (NT SC).

concomitant downgrading of the importance of truth seem to be dependent on a regime of litigation which determines factual issues to an acceptable degree or on an acceptable amount of information. Such an approach may be appropriate for civil litigation, but is inappropriate for criminal cases, and particularly when applied to exculpatory information. It may be equally inappropriate to the extent that it conflicts with the strong public interest in the investigation of crimes and apprehension of offenders.[25] So, for example, some statutory privileges for other professions do not apply to criminal trials at all.[26] And when the first Police and Criminal Evidence Bills were drafted in the United Kingdom, the government was committed to a much narrower privilege in criminal cases than that operating in civil litigation.[27]

General Rule?

In *R.* v. *Steyn*[28] Greenburg JA said that the phrase *in favorem innocentiae* describes "a power in the court to relax a rule of privilege if the court is of opinion that such relaxation may tend to show the innocence of the accused". Thus beyond individual rules designed to adduce all the prosecution's evidence, it may be possible to fashion a general rule requiring the disclosure of exculpatory privileged evidence, or the displacement of exclusionary evidential rules which prevent such disclosure.

In *Marks* v. *Beyfus* Lord Esher MR referred to the "public policy . . . that an innocent man is not to be condemned when his innocence can be proved".[29] The Canadian Supreme Court has repeatedly held that section 7 of the Canadian Charter of Rights and Freedoms, which provides for a right to make full answer and defence, includes within it a right to exculpatory evidence which overrides exclusionary rules.[30] This policy interest also may operate to subordinate other well-established rules of inadmissibility, as will be discussed shortly.[31]

[25] D. Feldman, *Civil Liberties and Human Rights in England and Wales* (Clarendon Press, Oxford, 1993) 447, though note that Feldman also balances this against the positive role the privilege may play in criminal investigations.

[26] E.g. the accountant's privilege in US Federal law (*Himmelfarb* v. *United States* 175 F.2d 924 (9th Cir. 1949); *Gariepy* v. *United States* 189 F.2d 459 at 463–4 (6th Cir. 1951)) or the doctor–patient privilege in Victoria, Tasmania and the Northern Territory: s. 28(2) of the Evidence Act 1958 (Vic.); s. 96(2) of the Evidence Act 1910 (Tas.); s. 12(2) of the Northern Territory Evidence Act 1939 (Aust.). Alternatively a statute may impose different conditions of disclosure for criminal and civil cases. A good example of this is the doctors' privilege in New Zealand: see ss. 32 and 33 of the Evidence Amendment Act (No. 2) 1980 (NZ) and *Pallin* v. *Department of Social Welfare* [1983] NZLR 266 at 275 (CA).

[27] M. Zander, *The Police and Criminal Evidence Act 1984* (3rd edn., Sweet & Maxwell, London, 1995) 30; D.J. Feldman, n. 25 above, at 447.

[28] *R.* v. *Steyn* 1954 (1) SA 324 at 335 (AD).

[29] *Marks* v. *Beyfus* (1890) 25 QBD 494 at 498 (CA).

[30] *Dersch* v. *Canada* [1990] 2 SCR 1505 at 1514 (SC); *R. v Stinchcombe* [1991] 3 SCR at 336, 340; *R.* v. *Seaboyer* [1991] 2 SCR 577 at 607 (SC); *R.* v. *O'Connor* [1995] 4 SCR 411 (SC); *A. (L.L.)* v. *B. (A.)* [1995] 4 SCR at 561.

[31] See pp. 127–80 below; also see C. Tapper, "Prosecution and Privilege" (1996) 1 *E&P* 5 at 20.

The next section below will consider the application of an exception for criminal exculpatory evidence in different exclusionary evidential rules. It will be shown that, while such a principle operates in similar ways in relation to some of exclusionary rules, it does not apply to every such rule, and there is no generalised principle supporting the special consideration of criminal exculpatory evidence. However it can still be said that a similar principle, sometimes described as the *in favorem innocentiae* rule, is recognised in some of the main exclusionary rules of evidence.

While discussed in the context of the informer rule the policy articulated in *Marks* v. *Beyfus* was cast in general terms. It is not just a broad rule of inclusion, for as such it would lead simply to the basic rule that all relevant evidence is prima facie admissible. Rather the policy may be seen as specifically directed at exclusionary rules of evidence.[32]

Nor is the policy simply an aspect of the "public interest in facilitating the availability of all relevant materials for production in litigious disputes".[33] The policy is not that there should be ensured the revelation of truth in criminal cases, but that there is a public interest in ensuring that an accused person can adequately defend himself.[34] Viewed in this way, the policy is more accurately placed within the framework of the rules relating to the fairness of criminal trials.[35] This was the approach taken by Brennan J in *Alister* v. *The Queen*, holding that this right "is so basic and important an aspect of our criminal procedure that a trial in which the right is denied cannot be, in my opinion, a trial according to law".[36] A similar analysis was conducted in the New Zealand case of *R.* v. *B.*[37]

Public Interest Immunity and the Informer Rule

It has long been recognised that the public interest immunity may have to give way where the evidence that it seeks to shield is required to establish the innocence of a criminal defendant.[38] The analogy between this rule and legal

[32] Also see *D* v. *NSPCC* [1978] AC 171 at 232 (HL), casting the policy in terms of a general public interest.

[33] *Baker* v. *Campbell* (1983) 153 CLR at 74–5. Also see *ibid.* at 66 and *Waugh v British Railways Board* [1980] AC at 535–6.

[34] *Carter* v. *The Managing Partner, Northmore Hale Davy & Leake*, transcript of High Court hearing, at 66 (argument of Mr Barker QC); also see *ibid.* at 3–4.

[35] See *Jago* v. *District Court (NSW)* (1989) 168 CLR at 57, where Deane J discusses the adequacy of disclosure by the prosecution within the context of the fairness of criminal trials.

[36] *Alister v The Queen* (1983) 154 CLR 404 at 451 (HCA).

[37] [1995] 2 NZLR 172 (CA). In this case the accused was charged with rape and incest in relation to his daughter. He sought an order that the complainant undergo a medical examination. This order was resisted on the basis that it violated the complainant's constitutional rights not to be subject to such procedures. The matter was ultimately resolved, not on the basis of a clash of rights, but on the basis of the requirements of a fair trial.

[38] E.g. *D* v. *NSPCC* [1978] AC at 232; *Neilson* v. *Laugherne* [1981] QB 736 at 753 (CA).

professional privilege may be closer than is usually recognised.[39] While the use of candour reasoning in the immunity may be "fashionable to decry" and has "received an excessive dose of cold water",[40] it is still an influential rationale, particularly in relation to higher levels of government.[41] At least some aspects of the immunity are based upon similar principles to that which grounds the privilege.

The innocence exception to the informer's privilege has developed into almost a free-standing rule. This is a principle with origins in the eighteenth century.[42] It provides that the need for an accused adequately to defend himself may be sufficient to displace the otherwise paramount public interest in not disclosing sources of police information.[43] The principle is found in most common law jurisdictions,[44] with Ireland perhaps being the only exception.[45]

The policy supporting the exception is the need for accused adequately to defend themselves. This was first given form in the landmark informer case of *Marks* v. *Beyfus*,[46] mentioned previously. Subsequent cases have developed the informer rule in line with this policy.[47] This is so despite the fact that the substantive immunity protecting informers is clearly based on concerns regarding candour.[48]

The rule may be seen as a direct application of the principle of *in favorem innocentiae* to the informer's immunity. The public interest in maintaining the confidentiality of police informers must be at least as important to the adminis-

[39] For the contrary view, that the two rules are so different that a *Barton*-type rule should not be applied to the immunity, see D.M. Paciocco, *Charter Principles and Proof in Criminal Cases* (Carswell, Toronto, 1987) 211.

[40] *Burmah Oil Co* v. *Bank of England* [1980] AC 1090 at 1112 (HL).

[41] S.L. Phipson, M.N. Howard, P. Crane and D.A. Hochberg, *Phipson on Evidence* (Sweet & Maxwell, London, 1990) 484.

[42] *R.* v. *Hardy* (1794) 24 St Tr 199 at 808. Also see *R.* v. *Watson* (1817) 32 St Tr 1 at 101.

[43] *Marks* v. *Beyfus* (1890) 25 QBD at 498; Generally see C. Tapper, n. 13 above, 527; Comment, "Developments in the Law—Privileged Communications" (1985) 98 *Harv LR* 1450, 1596–1600; S.B. McNicol, *Law of Privilege* (Law Book Co., Sydney, 1992) 10; J.H. Wigmore and J.T. McNaughton, *Evidence in Trials at Common Law* (Little, Brown & Co., Boston, 1961) viii para. 2374 n. 8; *Cain* v. *Glass (No 2)* (1985) 3 NSWLR 230 at 246–53 (NSW CA).

[44] As well as cases cited in the previous note, see *Rovario* v. *United States* 353 US at 60–1; *R.* v. *Leipert* [1997] 1 SCR 281 at 295–6; *R.* v. *Scott* [1990] 3 SCR 979 at 996; *Solicitor-General* v. *Royal Commission* [1981] 2 SCR 494. South African authorities are collected in *S* v. *Mpetha* 1982 (2) SA 253 at 259 (Cape Div.).

[45] See *Attorney-General* v. *Simpson* [1959] IR 105 at 141 (HC), where Dixon J (Teevan J concurring) doubts the applicability of the rule in Ireland. Davitt P (dissenting) at 133 states that disclosure will be allowed only where "the needs of justice so require". However, given his earlier reluctance to follow English authority (see *ibid.*, at 129) this is an unhelpful formulation. Subsequent Irish cases have not shed light on the status of any innocence exception. However C. Fennell and H.J. O'Flaherty, *The Law of Evidence in Ireland* (Butterworths, 1992) believe that Irish law would safeguard such concerns.

[46] (1890) 25 QBD at 498, quoted above. While this was a civil case for malicious prosecution, its application to criminal proceedings has never been doubted.

[47] E.g. *Rogers* v. *Secretary of State for the Home Department* [1973] AC at 407; *D* v. *NSPCC* [1978] AC at 218, 232–3.

[48] E.g. see *Rovario* v. *United States* 353 US at 59.

tration of justice as the confidentiality of lawyer–client relationships.[49] Hence if secrecy can be overridden in the case of informers, then it should also be in the case of professional confidences.[50]

Hearsay

While there have been some indications in Australian[51] and Scottish[52] case law that the *in favorem innocentiae* principle may operate as a general exception to the hearsay rule, English courts have regarded themselves bound by the spirit of *Myers* v. *DPP*[53] to reject such a possibility. In *R.* v. *Turner (Bryan)*[54] the defendant to a charge of robbery sought to produce evidence of a statement by another person not called as a witness that that person, rather than the defendant, was involved in the robbery. The Court of Appeal held that such evidence could not be admitted, saying:

> The idea, which may be gaining prevalence in some quarters, that in a criminal trial the defence is entitled to adduce hearsay evidence to establish facts, which if proved would be relevant and would assist the defence, is wholly erroneous.[55]

In *R.* v. *Blastland*[56] the correctness of this decision by the Court of Appeal was directly raised in a point of law certified for the House of Lords.[57] The House of Lords refused leave to appeal on this point, but granted leave on a second point. In the later substantive appeal, Lord Bridge noted that the decision in *Turner* was based on the principle in *Myers* v. *DPP*, and the correctness of the latter case could not be doubted. He further said that:

> To admit in criminal trials statements confessing to the crime for which the defendant is being tried made by third parties not called as witnesses would be to create a very significant and, many might think, a dangerous new exception.[58]

[49] Compare *S* v. *Safatsa* 1988 (1) SA at 885E. Note that the fact that the informer rule rests on a different basis from the privilege was recognised very early on in the case of *Home* v. *Bentinck* (1820) 2 Brod & Bing 130 at 162, 129 ER 907 at 920. Compare the cases cited by J.A. Andrews, "Public Interest and Criminal Proceedings" (1988) 104 *LQR* 410 at 415 n. 27.

[50] Compare Franklyn J in *Carter* v. *The Managing Partner, Northmore Hale Davy & Leake*, unreported, Supreme Court of Western Australia (Full Court), 15 July 1993, at 6, who did not regard the informer cases as persuasive.

[51] C. Tapper, n. 31 above, cites *R.* v. *Daylight* (1989) 41 A Crim R 354 at 356 (Qld SC) ("To deprive the accused of the right to present this piece of evidence . . . defies any notion of fair play"); *R.* v. *Astill* (1992) 63 A Crim R 148 at 159, 160 and 165 (NSW CCA); *R.* v. *Radford* (1993) 66 A Crim R 210 at 234 (Vic. CCA).

[52] *Perrie* v. *Lord Advocate* 1991 JC 27 at 31 (High Ct. of Justiciary). But now see *McLay* v. *Lord Advocate* 1994 JC 159 at 166 (High Ct. of Justiciary).

[53] [1965] AC 1001 (HL), holding that any new exceptions to hearsay are a matter for Parliament, not the courts. For a detailed discussion of this issue see pp. 135–45 above.

[54] (1975) 61 Cr App R 67 (CA).

[55] *Ibid.*, at 87–8.

[56] [1986] AC 41 (HL).

[57] *Ibid.*, at 41.

[58] *Ibid.*, at 53.

The treatment of hearsay evidence in English law does not support the view that there is a move towards the development of a general *in favorem innocentiae* exception.

American Constitutional Due Process Clause

In the United States the Sixth and Fourteenth Amendments to the Constitution[59] may guarantee a broad right to override evidential rules when seeking exculpatory evidence. The provisions will operate only when there has been an exclusion of a "fundamental" part of the accused's defence.[60] In *Washington* v. *Texas* evidence from another person that that person, and not the accused, committed the crime was rendered inadmissible pursuant to a Texas statute prohibiting favourable co-participant testimony. The Supreme Court held that this statute was unconstitutional as the right to present the defendant's case and compel witnesses to do this where necessary is "a fundamental element of the due process of law".[61] However Warren CJ, in a footnote at the end of his judgment, expressly stated that this "should [not] be construed as disapproving testimonial privileges".[62] Arguably, this case does not express an opinion either way on the issue of the consistency of privileges with the Sixth Amendment.[63]

In *Chambers* v. *Mississippi*[64] evidence from a number of witnesses that another person had confessed to the crime was rendered inadmissible on hearsay grounds. The Supreme Court found that this decision, which was a correct application of Mississippi law,[65] violated the due process clause.[66] The Court emphasised the fact that this evidence was critical to the accused's defence.[67] It has been suggested that *Chambers* could similarly apply to override legal professional privilege.[68] The case of *Valdez* v. *Winans* may possibly go against this proposition. In that case the defendant claimed that another person had confessed guilt of the crime to his lawyer. This other person invoked the

[59] The Sixth Amendment reads: "[i]n all criminal prosecutions, the accused shall enjoy the right to a speedy and public trial, by an impartial jury of the State . . . and to be informed of the nature and cause of the accusation; to be confronted with the witnesses against him; to have compulsory process for obtaining witnesses in his favor, and to have the assistance of Counsel for his defence." These rules apply to the States by virtue of the 14th Amendment.

[60] *United States* v. *Scheffer*, US Supreme Court, 31 Mar. 1998, holding that the exclusion of polygraph evidence tendered by the defence did not breach the 6th Amendment as it was not crucial to his case and was only to be used to bolster credibility.

[61] *Washington* v. *Texas* 388 US 14 at 19 (1967).

[62] *Ibid*., at 23 n. 21.

[63] Alternatively, it expresses both opinions.

[64] 410 US 284 at 289–93 (1973).

[65] *Ibid*., at 292–4 and 299.

[66] *Ibid*., at 298–303.

[67] *Ibid*., at 302.

[68] J. Thomas-Fishburn, "Attorney–Client Confidences: Punishing the Innocent" (1990) 61 *U Col LR* 185; R. Bartels, "Admissibility of Exculpatory Attorney–Client Communications in Criminal Cases" (1970) 22 *Ariz. St. LJ* 895 at 909.

privilege against self-incrimination and the Federal Appeals Court upheld his lawyer's claim of professional privilege, rejecting a claim by the defendant of breach of Sixth Amendment rights.[69] However there were very unusual circumstances in this case which cast doubt on its weight as an authority on this issue.[70]

Finally, it is worth noting that in the recent Supreme Court case of *Swidler & Berlin and James Hamilton* v. *United States* the minority judges would have created an exception to the rule that the privilege continues beyond the death of the client for "exculpatory evidence or compelling law enforcement need".[71] The majority held that "exceptional circumstances implicating a criminal defendant's rights might warrant breaching the privilege. We do not, however, need to reach this issue, since such exceptional circumstances clearly are not presented here".[72]

State of *In Favorem Innocentiae* Principle

It has been shown above that the *in favorem innocentiae* principle, or a rule with similar effect, operates to override a number of exclusionary evidential rules. However the principle is far from a general rule of evidential inclusion. Where the principle has been recognised, it has displaced interests of great weight, such as the interest in maintaining the confidence of police informers.[73] Some of these displaced interests are strongly reliant on an expectation of confidentiality for their operation, just as legal professional privilege is.[74]

The rest of this chapter will examine the clash between the *in favorem innocentiae* principle and legal professional privilege. The next main section will look at the case law authority on this issue, and the final section will assess this authority in light of the ideas developed in this book.

[69] *Valdez* v. *Winans* 738 F.2d 1087 at 1089 (10th Cir. 1984).

[70] The lawyer called to testify worked for the public defender's office and was actually representing the accused, not the confessing witness. It was the latter's lawyer who asserted privilege over the evidence of the defendant's lawyer. The accused had the information as well, as the confessing witness had confessed to him first. The accused chose not to raise this in his own testimony for reasons not contained in the judgment, nor in the judgment of the state appellate court: see *State* v. *Valdez* 618 P.2d 1234 at 1236 (New Mexico SC 1980). Finally, the exculpatory information was the confession of a person not yet indicted for the offence and that person claimed the privilege against self-incrimination. Surely the court must have been loathe to override professional privilege where this would effectively be overriding the privilege against self-incrimination as well.

[71] 118 S. Ct. at 2088.

[72] *Ibid.*, at 2087 n. 3.

[73] See p. 178 above.

[74] Under the non-rights based instrumental rationale at least.

SECTION II: PLACE IN THE PRIVILEGE

Authority for Privilege Exception

The first case[75] to address the issue was *R. v. Barton*,[76] where Caulfield J held that "[i]f there are documents in the possession or control of a solicitor which, on production, help to further the defence of an accused man, then in my judgment no privilege attaches".[77] While this judgment was given *ex tempore* on circuit without reference to authorities, the case was nonetheless stated to represent the law in England,[78] Ireland,[79] Australia,[80] Canada[81] and New Zealand.[82]

Until 1995 none of the ultimate appellate courts in the Commonwealth jurisdictions had resolved this issue.[83] The closest each of the respective countries' highest courts had come was isolated dicta supporting the exception.[84] During this time decisions of intermediate appellate courts in England,[85] Canada[86] and

[75] The first reported appeal concerning an assertion of privilege over exculpatory evidence was in the 1811 case of *R. v. Withers* 2 Camp 578, 170 ER 1258. In that case the communications were clearly important and strongly exculpatory. However the privilege was upheld without any argument or discussion of the competing rights or interests involved.

[76] [1973] 1 WLR 115 (Crown Ct.).

[77] *Ibid.*, at 118.

[78] E.g. R. Cross, *Cross on Evidence* (5th edn., Butterworths, London, 1979) 290; S.L. Phipson, n. 41 above, 511–12; F. Lawton *et al.*, "Criminal Law" in *Halsbury's Laws of England* (4th edn. Reissue, Butterworths, London) xi(2), para. 1163 and J.R.V. McAulay, G.C.W. Harris and R. Inglis, "Evidence" in Halsbury's Laws of England (4th edn., Butterworths, London) xvii, para. 252 n. 3; J.A. Andrews and D.M. Hirst, *Criminal Evidence* (Sweet & Maxwell, London, 1987) para 12.25; A.A.S. Zuckerman, *The Principles of Criminal Evidence* (Clarendon Press Oxford, 1989) 300; P.J. Richardson, D.A. Thomas and H. Malcolm, *Archbold's Pleading, Evidence and Practice in Criminal Cases* (1993 edn., Sweet & Maxwell, London) i, 1573 para. 12–12; C. Tapper , n. 13 above 492.

[78] C. Fennell and H.G. O'Flaherty, n. 45 above, at 170.

[80] D. Byrne and J.D. Heydon, n. 24 above, paras. 25280–300; S.B. McNicol, n. 43 above, 101–4; Law Reform Commission of Western Australia, *Discussion Paper on Professional Privilege for Confidential Communications*, Project no. 90 (Law Reform Commission of Western Australia, 1991) 61, para. 4.6.

[81] J. Sopinka *et al.*, *The Law of Evidence in Canada* (Butterworths, Toronto, 1992) 660; R.J. Delisle, Evidence: Principles and Problems (3rd edn., Carswell, 1993) 635.

[82] New Zealand Law Commission, *Evidence Law: Privilege*, Preliminary Paper No. 23 (New Zealand Law Commission, 1994) 67 para. 170.

[83] For the position in Scotland see the cases cited in I.D. Macphail, *Evidence* (Law Society of Scotland, Edinburgh, 1987) para. 18.20 n. 65.

[84] England—*D* v. *NSPCC* (1978) AC at 190, also see *Waugh* v. *British Railways Board* [1980] AC at 536, *per* Lord Simon, balancing the competing interests; Australia—*Baker* v. *Campbell* (1983) 153 CLR 68, *per* Gibbs CJ, also see *ibid.*, at 74, *per* Mason J expressing an attitude to the ultimate balancing question favourable to the accused; Canada—*Solicitor-General* v. *Royal Commission* [1981] 2 SCR at 516: "[t]he prosecution has a duty to ensure that innocent persons are not convicted, a duty to see that justice is done, and hence should not seek to withhold from disclosure on the ground of privilege or on the ground of public interest anything that would be material to the defence": *R.* v. *Seaboyer* [1991] 2 SCR 577 at 607.

[85] *R.* v. *Ataou* [1988] QB at 804–8; *R.* v. *Saunders*, unreported, Central Criminal Court, Henry J, 10 Jan. 1990 at 10–13.

[86] *R.* v. *Dunbar and Logan* (1982) 138 DLR (3d) at 251–3.

New Zealand[87] all seemed to resolve the issue by resort to an *ad hoc* balancing approach, as discussed immediately below. These cases also discussed *Barton* with apparent approval. Australia was the only country to have intermediate appellate court authority against *Barton*,[88] and a High Court decision on point, but of little if any weight.[89]

There were very few cases in which the precise issue was raised outside the context of co-accused and the recognised interest exception. The most significant of these cases were *R.* v. *Gray*[90] in Canada and *S* v. *Safatsa*[91] in South Africa. However the manner in which the issue arose in *R.* v. *Gray* diminishes its value as a useful precedent,[92] and Botha JA in *S* v. *Safatsa* expressly cast doubt on *Barton*.[93] In the later South African case of *S* v. *Jija*[94] Erasmus J held

[87] Cooke J in *R.* v. *Craig* [1975] 1 NZLR 597 cited but did not specifically discuss *Barton*. Compare Rowland J in *Carter* v. *The Managing Partner, Northmore Hale Davy & Leake*, unreported, Supreme Court of Western Australia (Full Court) 15 July 1993, stating at 25 that Cooke J "refused to follow" *Barton*. This is wrong.

[88] There were a number of cases in which the privilege was upheld over statements by prosecution witnesses in criminal proceedings: see *Cain* v. *Glass* (1985) 3 NSWLR 39 at 42–3 (NSW SC); *R.* v. *Cahill, ex p. McGregor* (1985) 61 ACTR at 13; *Adams* v. *Anthony Bryant* (1986) 67 ALR at 620–3. In *Cain* v. *Glass* Lusher J declined to follow *Barton*; however the judgment turned on whether legal professional privilege applied at all in criminal proceedings, which *Baker* v. *Campbell* had recently shown to be the case. In both *Cahill* and *Adams, Barton* was neither argued nor cited and the issue was not dealt with at all.

[89] *Locsam Ltd* v. *Brambles Holdings Ltd* (unreported, High Court of Australia, 18 June 1993). This was an application for special leave to appeal to the Court. Leave was refused because the appeal did not have sufficient prospects of ultimate success, having regard to factual conclusions made in the court below.

[90] (1992) 74 CCC (3d) 267 (BC SC) The police had sought advice from Crown counsel regarding the legality of police operations. Oppal J held that any privilege held by the police officers was overridden by the accused's need for exculpatory evidence. In doing so he recognised an "exception to the rule of confidentiality of solicitor–client communications . . . where the adherence to the . . . privilege will prevent an accused person from making full answer and defence" (*ibid.*, at 273h; also see 274f). This was cast as a general rule: "I am guided by the right of a person to make a full answer and defence. That right must take precedence in a judicial system which has as its cornerstone the presumption of innocence"(*ibid.*, at 275).

[91] 1988 (1) SA 868 (AD). 6 people (the "Sharpeville 6") were convicted of murder and sentenced to death, largely on the basis of the testimony of 3 witnesses. One of these witnesses had previously seen the solicitor representing the accused and had made statements suggesting that the police had told him what to say. Defence counsel sought leave to cross-examine the witness on the basis of this information. The trial judge asked the witness if he wanted to claim legal professional privilege, which he did. The judge ruled that he had no discretion to override the privilege. Botha JA for the Appellate Division held that it was unnecessary to decide whether the privilege rule could be relaxed, but on the assumption that it could, then such a relaxation would be a matter of discretion for the trial judge. In the present case there was insufficient information before the trial judge to enable him to exercise such a discretion.

[92] *R.* v. *Gray* was an entrapment case and the information was sought to show the illegality of police operations, rather than to show that the accused did not do the acts alleged. Thus the case concerned a particular type of exculpatory information. The matter was also clouded by doubt as to whether the privilege exists for the police as "clients": *ibid.*, at 270–2 (Oppal J seems to say no), 275e (unnecessary to decide) and 276a (assumes the answer is yes).

[93] Having dispensed with the issue on another basis, Botha JA stated that *Barton* was distinguishable, but that "insofar as Caulfield J purported to lay down a general principle which could be thought to apply to the present case, I respectfully do not agree with it" (*ibid.*, at 887).

[94] 1991 (2) SA 52 (Eastern Cape Div.).

that the place of a *Barton*-type exception in South African law "has not been authoritatively decided but the indications are against such recognition".[95] However he also went on to say that:

> in the absence of direct authority in our law, it is permissible to consider the position in other legal systems. The principle of English law that the rule of privilege is not irrefrangible, but can in appropriate circumstances either fall away or be relaxed, appears to be sound and in accordance with the objectives of doing justice.[96]

During the 1970s and 1980s there were a number of Commonwealth decisions holding that the privilege may be displaced where the claimant no longer has any legitimate interest in asserting the privilege. Where this is the case, the judge should balance the interest of the accused in seeking to displace the privilege with that of the privilege-claimant in seeking to maintain it.[97] These cases include *R.* v. *Ataou*[98] and *R.* v. *Saunders*[99] in England; *R.* v. *Dunbar and Logan*[100] in Canada; and *R.* v. *Craig*[101] in New Zealand. The rule is often described as the "recognised interest exception".

This rule was rejected by all but one of the judges in the *Derby Magistrates* case.[102] However it is clear that the Canadian Supreme Court will look upon this rule favourably, as will be discussed below. Its position in other Commonwealth jurisdictions is yet to be finally determined. Despite its initial popularity, it would be surprising if the rule became established law across the Commonwealth (apart from in Canada that is). This is because the rule probably utilises an *ad hoc* balancing process. As has been discussed previously, such a process may be particularly destructive to confidence in the secrecy of legal communications on which the privilege depends.

The specific problem discussed in these cases was largely resolved in both Australia and England in 1995. In the *Carter* case a three to two majority of the High Court of Australia held that there was no exception which allowed a criminal accused access to privileged information held by a third party, even where this evidence may assist the accused to prove his innocence. The dissenting judges, Toohey and Gaudron JJ, would have ordered production of privileged information where such material was necessary for the defence (*per* Toohey J) or where the withholding of such documents would impede the defence (*per*

95 1991 (2) SA 52 (Eastern Cape Div.) at 65.

96 *Ibid.*, at 66.

97 This formulation comes from *R.* v. *Ataou* [1988] QB at 807.

98 [1988] QB 798.

99 Unreported, Central Criminal Court, 10 Jan. 1990, Henry J, who considered himself bound by *R.* v. *Ataou* (see *R.* v. *Saunders* at 17).

100 (1982) 138 DLR (3d) 221.

101 [1975] 1 NZLR 597. However the remarks of Cooke J are obiter dicta as the privilege was upheld.

102 Lord Nicholls agreed with the rationale of the recognised interest exception. He held that it was not necessary to decide the validity of the exception as the claimant had a legitimate interest in keeping the information confidential in this case (interest in not disclosing information indicating guilt of a horrific murder of which he had been acquitted) and thus he was entitled to claim the privilege.

Gaudron J). In the *Derby Magistrates* case[103] the House of Lords unanimously rejected the creation of any new exception to the privilege. These decisions are not quite as clear-cut as this paragraph, and indeed the headnotes in both cases, suggests. Precisely what was rejected in these judgments will be analysed in detail in the next section below. There it will be shown that there is some ambiguity in these decisions, and that in Australia, at least, only the recognised interest exception is definitely rejected.

Judgment in the *Carter* case was delivered on one of the days on which argument in the *Derby Magistrates* case was being heard, and the decision in the *Derby Magistrates* case was delivered four months after that. The House of Lords made no reference to the High Court decision, nor to the decisions in the Australian courts below, which had been decided the previous year. In the High Court only Deane J made passing reference to the *Derby Magistrates* case in the Divisional Court.[104] There is not space here to discuss in detail the background to the legal issue in these two leading cases. It is worth briefly mentioning though that the criminal prosecutions underlying the two appeals were very different in nature. The appeal in the *Derby Magistrates* case arose in the context of a murder trial, while the *Carter* case concerned the prosecution of the auditor of a merchant bank for concurring in the publication of false financial reports.[105]

Canadian courts seem to take a much more favourable approach to the innocence exception. In *Dunbar and Logan* Martin JA of the Ontario Court of Appeal said:

> No rule of policy requires the continued existence of the privilege in criminal cases when the person claiming the privilege no longer has any interest to protect, and when maintaining the privilege might screen from the jury information which would assist an accused.[106]

[103] For comments see C. Tapper, n. 31 above; C. Passmore, "Privilege in the Lords" [1996] *NLJ Practitioner* 921.

[104] See *Carter* v. *The Managing Partner, Northmore Hale Davy & Leake* (1995) 183 CLR at 141, *per* Deane J; this reference was to the one-page report in the Times Law Reports: [1994] TLR 538.

[105] However the two cases do have one aspect in common: in both cases there was little public sympathy for the accused. In the *Derby Magistrates* case, even on the defence's version of events, the accused had played a significant role in the killing. The *Carter* prosecution was a comparatively small part of a saga that was one of the greatest financial and governmental scandals in Australian history, involving corruption and mismanagement at the highest level. The wider scandal led to the near ruining of a state's finances and the downfall of its government. After a massive Royal Commission and a decade of litigation (e.g. see *Connell* v. *The Queen* (No. 6) (1992) 12 WAR 133 (WA SC)) many related matters were still to be resolved by the courts. The substantive criminal trial of Louis Carter was massive, taking over a year, almost 200 sitting days, 176 witnesses, 15,000 separate exhibits and a transcript running to over 12,500 pages: R. Gibson, "Ex-Rothwells Auditor Fails in Appeal Bid" *The West Australian*, 27 Sept. 1997. The trial also gave rise to an extraordinary number of procedural appeals. This context cannot be divorced from the narrow evidential question presently discussed.

[106] (1982) 138 DLR (3d) at 252.

In *A. (L.L.)* v. *B. (A.)* L'Heureux-Dubé J said:

> When the enforcement of a privilege means that the accused will be limited as to his or her right to make full answer and defence to criminal accusations, this Court has strongly tended to favour disclosure . . . Even the solicitor–client privilege . . . will be overridden to allow the accused to make full answer and defence to criminal charges.[107]

In the most recent case of *Smith* v. *Jones*[108] the Supreme Court expressly disapproved of the decision in the *Derby Magistrates* case and stated its preference for the view of Martin JA in *Dunbar and Logan.* It is now abundantly clear, although there is no direct Supreme Court ratio on point, that the innocence exception will apply in Canada.

The final point which may be made in relation to the Commonwealth case law on this point is in relation to the legislative activity in this field. Only four months before McHugh J warned that "the exception could have serious consequences for the general administration of justice",[109] the Australian Federal Parliament wrote such an exception into its new federal evidence statute. Section 123 of the Australian Evidence Act 1995 provides that "[i]n a criminal proceeding, this Division[110] does not prevent a defendant from adducing evidence". The section goes on to provide an exception for co-accused. In 1999 the New Zealand Law Commission published a draft Evidence Code, section 71(2) of which provides that the judge may disallow a claim to privilege where the evidence is "necessary to enable the defendant in a criminal proceeding to present an effective defence".[111] The explanatory note states that this is an express departure from the *Derby Magistrates* and *Carter* cases.[112]

Leaving the Commonwealth jurisprudence and looking to the position in the United States, there is one case which seems to be directly in point. In *United States* v. *Fair*[113] three soldiers were suspected of murder. One of these soldiers, X, was granted immunity from prosecution and testified that one of the other two had fired the fatal shot. Defence counsel asked X whether he had previously told his lawyer that he himself had fired the shot. X refused to answer this question, claiming attorney–client privilege. The military court upheld his claim to privilege, holding that it was no complete answer to say that the client is protected from prosecution by virtue of the immunity, as he still may fear other consequences, such as social disgrace and humiliation.[114] This case has been

[107] [1995] 4 SCR at 577.

[108] (1999) 132 CCC (3d) 225 at 242–3.

[109] *Carter* v. *The Managing Partner, Northmore Hale Davy & Leake* (1995) 183 CLR at 164.

[110] I.e. Division 1 of the Act, titled "Client legal privilege".

[111] New Zealand Law Commission, *Evidence—Evidence Code and Commentary*, Report 55 (New Zealand Law Commission, 1999) ii, 184.

[112] *Ibid.*, at 185, para. C290.

[113] 2 USCMA 521, 10 CMR 19 (1953).

[114] *Ibid.*, at 2 USCMA at 528, 10 CMR at 26.

criticised on a number of grounds,[115] which will be dealt with in subsequent chapters.

Apart from this one case, which was decided by a military court, analysis of the position in the United States is difficult. There does not appear to be any consistent principle used to reslove the issue across the many jurisdictions. The greatest problem in using United States authority is that many states apply an *ad hoc* balancing test for the privilege. A proper review of these authorities is beyond the scope of this work. All that can be said at present is that it appears that if the precise issue in *R.* v. *Barton* were raised in an American state court, it would probably be resolved in favour of the accused in the following nine states: Colorado,[116] Delaware,[117] Florida,[118] Nevada,[119] New Hampshire,[120] New Jersey,[121] New York,[122] Pennsylvania[123] and Washington.[124] The situation is less clear in other states.

In more general terms, a cursory examination of leading American privilege cases from all jurisdictions shows that greater weight is attached to the importance of the goal of truth-finding and an emphasis on the need to restrict the privilege to situations which identifiably promote its underlying purpose. This can be seen in the jurisprudence of the Supreme Court,[125] federal courts[126] and

[115] See Note, "Immunized Witnesses and the Attorney–Client Privilege" (1954) *Stan LR* 363 at 365–7.

[116] *Law Offices of Bernard D. Morley* v. *Macfarlane* (1982) 647 P.2d 1215 (Colo. SC).

[117] *Hollingsworth* v. *Essence Communications Inc* (1977) WL 2585 (Del. Ch.).

[118] *Sepler* v. *State* (1966) 191 So.2d 588 (Fla. DCA).

[119] *Haynes* v. *State* (1987) 739 P.2d 497 (Nevada SC).

[120] *McGranahan* v. *Dahar* 408 A.2d 121 (New Hamp. SC 1979); *State* v. *Eason* (1990) 577 A.2d 1203 (SC New Hamp.).

[121] *In the Matter of Kozlov* 398 A.2d 882 (NJ SC 1979).

[122] *Hoopes* v. *Carota* (1988) NYS 2d 407 (NY CA).

[123] *Cohen* v. *Jenkintown Cab Co.* (1976) 357 A.2d 689 (Penn. SC).

[124] *In the Matter of the Welfare of Henderson* (1981) 630 P.2d 944 (Wash. CA).

[125] E.g. *United States* v. *Bryan* 339 US 323 at 331 (classic American statement of the public's "right to every man's evidence"); *Herbert* v. *Lando* 441 US 153 at 175 (1979) (citing Bentham and observing that evidentiary privileges are not favoured in federal law); *Elkins* v. *United States* 364 US 206 at 234 (1960) ("normally predominant principle of utilizing all rational means for ascertaining truth" is only curtailed to a very limited extent); *United States v Nixon* 418 US 683 at 710 (1974) (privileges are "not lightly created nor expansively construed, for they are in derogation of the search for truth").

[126] E.g. 6th Circuit—*Prichard* v. *United States* 181 F.2d at 328 (the privilege here would "invite frustration of the administration of the courts . . . seem inimical to the public interest and a perversion of the purpose and spirit of the rule") and *United States* v. *Goldfarb* 328 F.2d at 282 ("privilege is an exception carved from the rule requiring full disclosure, and as an exception should not be extended to accomplish more than its purpose"); 7th Circuit—*Radiant Burners Inc* v. *American Gas Association* 320 F.2d 314 at 323 (1963), *In the Matter of Walsh* 623 F.2d 489 at 493 (1980) (cert. denied 449 US 994) (serious effect of the privilege in derogation of truth), *United States* v. *Weger* 709 F.2d 1151 at 1154 (1983) (need to strictly confine the privilege), *United States* v. *Lawless* 709 F.2d 485 at 487 (1983) (need to strictly confine the privilege), *United States* v. *White* 970 F.2d 328 at 334 (1992); 8th Circuit—*Diversified Minerals Inc.* v. *Meredith* 572 F.2d 596 at 602 (1978); 9th Circuit—*Weil* v. *Investment/Indicators, Research & Management Inc* 647 F.2d 18 at 24 (1981); District Courts—*Valente* v. *Pepsico* 68 FRD at 367 (confine privilege within narrow limits), *Underwater Storage Inc* v. *United States Rubber Co* 314 F.Supp. 546 at 547 (DC Sth Dakota 1970) ("narrowly construed").

many state appeals courts.[127] There are also some very close analagous situations, such as the rule that an accomplice gives up his attorney–client privilege when testifying for the state against his companions.[128]

Rejection of Exception and Balancing

The main ground on which an exception for criminal exculpatory evidence has been rejected in England and Australia is that these courts will not undertake a balancing exercise to determine the content of the rule. This was discussed briefly in Chapter 7 above. That chapter also analysed the use of this argument in previous appellate privilege decisions, and pointed out that the argument that balancing has "already been done" has, until the *Carter* and *Derby Magistrates* cases, been used only when considering claims for *ad hoc* balancing. That is, the argument used to reject an exception for criminal exculpatory evidence is the same as that used to deny any further derogations from the privilege; and it is an argument based on an assumption that it is *ad hoc* balancing that is being proposed.

However, again as alluded to in Chapter 7 above, there is an important difference between balancing that occurs on a case-by-case basis, and balancing that occurs at the level of determination of a rule. It therefore becomes important to determine which type of balancing the proposed exception for criminal exculpatory evidence would involve: *ad hoc* or rule balancing. The matter is somewhat complicated by the many different formulations of this possible exception.

The test originally suggested by Caulfield J in *Barton* was cast as follows: "[i]f there are documents . . . which . . . help to further the defence of an accused man, then . . . no privilege attaches".[129] Caulfield J regarded this conclusion as a rule of general though unprecedented application, rather than a decision flowing from the facts of the particular case, stating later that "I think that is the principle that should be followed".[130] So *Barton* did not involve an issue of case-by-case balancing. Rather, it was the statement of a fixed rule, which is dependent for its operation on facts not all of which may be known at the time the relevant communication is made.

This interpretation is supported by the South African case of *S* v. *Safatsa*, discussed above. There counsel at trial sought leave to cross-examine a witness on

[127] To consider one state as an example, see the extensive jurisprudence of the Supreme Court of New Jersey on this issue: *United Jersey Bank v Wolosoff* 483 A.2d 821 at 825 (1984) ("privilege . . . is at war with truth"); *In re Selser* 105 A.2d 395 (1954); *Longo* v. *American Policyholders' Ins Co* 436 A.2d 577 (1981); *Blitz* v. *970 Realty Associates* 557 A.2d 1386 at 1389 (1989); *Eversun* v. *Bank of New York* 239 A.2d 10 (1968); *In the Matter of Kozlov* 398 A.2d at 890 (1979); *State* v. *Jamison* 316 A.2d 439 (1974).

[128] *Jones* v. *State* 3 So. 379 (Miss. SC 1887).

[129] R. v. *Barton* [1972] 2 All ER at 1194.

[130] *Ibid.*

the basis of privileged information, relying on *Barton* and texts approving that case.[131] The trial judge held he had "no power" to order the witness to be cross-examined in this way. Counsel on appeal argued that the trial judge had refused to exercise his discretion on the issue of whether to allow the cross-examination. The Appellate Division held that the trial judge had not been asked to exercise a discretion as *Barton*'s case involves a fixed rule and not a discretion.

The fixed rule drawn from *Barton* may be compared with the recognised interest exception cases, briefly touched upon above. This latter exception is almost always described as turning on a balancing of factors in each individual case.[132] For example, in *R.* v. *Ataou* French J formulated the test as: "[t]he judge must then balance whether the legitimate interest of the defendant in seeking to breach the privilege outweighs that of the client in seeking to maintain it".[133] However in the *Derby Magistrates* case Lord Nicholls said that this rule:

> would not depend upon carrying out any form of balancing exercise, weighing one interest against the other. It would depend on proof that no rational person would regard himself as having any continuing interest in protecting the privilege.[134]

This is in contrast to the rest of their Lordships deciding that case, who all rejected the recognised interest exception cases on the basis that *ad hoc* balancing was inappropriate for a rule operating within the framework of legal professional privilege.

Some of the judges called upon to determine the status and desirability of a *Barton*-type fixed rule have wrongly grouped it with the recognised interest exception cases and thereby failed to distinguish between the different forms of balancing used in each. The use of a balancing approach to create an exception to the privilege to enable criminal defendants to obtain access to potentially exculpatory information (which for convenience will be termed the "*Barton* exception") is entirely consistent with the framework of current privilege law and the way that it has developed, as long as the resulting rule is fixed and not discretionary. Use of this type of balancing is simply part of the proper common law process in which laws develop by the amendment of existing rules or the addition of new rules.

In the *Derby Magistrates* case counsel seeking disclosure argued for a case-by-case balancing approach,[135] apparently on the basis of both *Barton* and *Ataou*.[136] McGowan LJ in the Divisional Court had considered himself bound by *Ataou*, and also expressed agreement with it. On appeal, Lord Taylor CJ held that both *Barton* and *Ataou* were wrongly decided and overruled them.[137]

131 *S* v. *Safatsa* 1988 (1) SA at 882.

132 *R.* v. *Craig* [1975] 1 NZLR at 598; *R.* v. *Dunbar and Logan* (1982) 138 DLR (3d) at 252; *R.* v. *Ataou* [1988] QB at 807b.

133 *R.* v. *Ataou* [1988] QB at 807.

134 [1996] 1 AC at 513.

135 See *ibid.*, at 511.

136 *Ibid.*, at 492F.

137 *Ibid.*, at 509.

However the only other judge in the majority to give a reasoned judgment,[138] Lord Lloyd, while agreeing with Lord Taylor, held only that *Ataou* was wrongly decided[139] and did not mention *Barton* at all.

This may seem like an overly fine distinction to draw. However there is a relevant difference between the two. Overruling both *Barton* and *Ataou* involves a refusal to consider any new exceptions to the absolute nature of the privilege.[140] Overruling *Ataou* involves a rejection of only the recognised interest exception and its case-by-case balancing approach. This latter approach is still consistent with the development of new fixed rules which narrow the scope of the privilege.[141]

In the *Carter* case the trial judge considered argument on *Barton* and the recognised interest exception cases and held simply that the privilege still applied.[142] On appeal to the Supreme Court of Western Australia all three judges rejected the *Barton* case, although the court was divided on the status of the recognised interest exception.[143] The High Court dismissed a further appeal by a three to two majority. Of the majority judges, Brennan and McHugh JJ rejected both *Barton* and the recognised interest exception cases. Deane J rejected *Barton* but found it unnecessary to decide the validity of *Ataou*.[144]

Therefore once again it is not completely clear what has been rejected: a fixed exception or a balancing approach, though the *Carter* and *Derby Magistrates* cases leave open opposite possibilities. In England it may still be possible to argue that while case-by-case balancing has been rejected, it is still open to a court to conduct a balancing exercise in order to determine whether there should be a fixed rule allowing disclosure. In contrast, in Australia only two out of five judges rejected the recognised interest exception, and so this may still be open to argument. The English position described above may be a tenable situation, whereas the Australian one probably is not. A rejection of *ad hoc* balancing does not necessarily imply a rejection of rule balancing. However a rejection of rule balancing may, in light of the reasons for this rejection, be taken to carry with it a rejection of the even more offensive *ad hoc* balancing process. However, taking into account the wider attitude to the privilege which these appellate courts have displayed over the last two decades, it is extremely

[138] Lords Keith and Mustill agreed with Lord Taylor: see *ibid.* at 495. Lord Nicholls agreed with Lord Taylor on the issue regarding the construction of s. 97 of the Magistrates Court Act 1980, but held that it was unnecessary to decide the validity of the recognised interest exception: see *ibid.* at 513.

[139] *Ibid.*

[140] Paraphrasing Lord Taylor, *ibid.* at 508–9.

[141] Note though that Lord Lloyd still referred to the almost absolute nature of the privilege: see *ibid.* at 509.

[142] R. v. *Connell (No 2)* (1992) 8 WAR 148 at 168 (WA SC).

[143] Rowland J approved the exception; Franklyn J rejected it; Malcolm CJ was undecided.

[144] Note that R.J. Desiatnik, *Legal Professional Privilege in Australia* (Prospect Media, Sydney, 1999) 31 appears to read these judgments differently, stating that Brennan J remained neutral on the lapsing of the privilege and Deane J rejected the concept.

unlikely that either of them will countenance such arguments, which would be perceived as a weakening of the privilege.[145]

The uncertainty resulting from the *Carter* case is exacerbated by (or possibly partly due to) counsel's own ambiguity during the hearing about what he was arguing for. At one point counsel for the appellant (seeking disclosure) appeared to be proposing a case by case balancing process,[146] but probably rested his submissions on the basis of a fixed exception.[147]

Joint Trials

There is one final issue which should be addressed, which is that the recognition of an *in favorem innocentiae* exception to legal privilege could lead to difficult problems in joint trials. This was discussed by each of the majority judges in the *Carter* case. Brennan J said that it would lead to absurd anomalies, such as where two co-accused each seek to override each other's privilege in order to inculpate the other and exculpate themselves.[148] Deane J warned that such a principle could negate the privilege in criminal trials.[149] McHugh J adopted a more practice-minded approach and said that the case where privileged information points unmistakably to the guilt of one co-accused and exculpates the other is likely to be the very unusual situation,[150] and that it is much more likely that the evidence will inculpate one co-accused without positively proving the innocence of the other.[151]

One solution to this problem would be to engage in an *ad hoc* balancing process to determine where the greatest harm and the greatest benefit will lie in the instant case. This was done in some of the recognised interest cases discussed

[145] Compare the views of some Australian writers that because *Carter* was decided by a 3:2 majority "the reasoning of the dissenting judges may be picked up by other justices of the High Court in the years to come, especially in the light of the newly enacted Evidence Acts": R.J. Desiatnik, n. 144 above, 74; L. Holland, "Legal Professional Privilege Still Unqualified—But for How Long?" (1995) 7 *Australian Construction Law Bulletin* 61 at 64. However the High Court would be extremely reluctant to hear argument on an issue covered by a considered decision of a previous bench, notwithstanding that it was by a bare 3:2 majority. It could be argued that the advent of statutory exceptions for criminal exculpatory evidence shows that such a rule does not pose significant threats to client confidence in legal communications, thereby disproving an essential plank of the reasoning of the majority in *Carter*. However it would still be difficult to counter the arguments that these considerations were before the court in *Carter*; that it was a matter within the knowledge and experience of appellate judges, as experienced former practitioners, to determine; and that there is a strong general rule that the mere change in the composition of the High Court bench is no reason to permit the re-argument of settled decisions of that court.

[146] High Court of Australia, transcript, 15 Nov. 1994 at 24.

[147] *Ibid.* at 11–12; *Carter* v. *The Managing Partner, Northmore Hale Davy & Leake* (1995) 183 CLR at 154.

[148] *Carter* v. *The Managing Partner, Northmore Hale Davy & Leake* (1995) 183 CLR at 130–1.

[149] *Ibid.* at 141.

[150] Presumably it would be an even more unusual situation if there were two such clearly exculpatory privileged statements cancelling each other out.

[151] *Carter* v. *The Managing Partner, Northmore Hale Davy & Leake* (1995) 183 CLR at 164–5.

below,[152] as well as in American cases concerning co-accused.[153] It has also been recommended by law reformers.[154] Alternatively, if a fixed rule is required, the *Barton* exception could be held simply not to apply in joint trials. In *R.* v. *Dunbar and Logan* Martin JA cast this as a general exception to the *Barton* rule.[155] In the *Carter* case counsel for the appellant argued that their proposed exception did not apply between co-accused.[156] The legislative *Barton* rule in the Australian Evidence Act 1995 contains an exception for "associated defendants".[157] This follows a recommendation from the Australian Law Reform Commission that the Barton rule may be too wide in its application to joint trials.[158] This fine-tuning of the *Barton* rule is strongly endorsed by McNicol:

> There is little point in protecting the rights of one accused . . . whilst simultaneously invading the rights of other accused persons by denying them full, free and confidential access to their own lawyers without fear of disclosure.[159]

CONCLUSIONS

The ultimate appellate courts in England and Australia have rejected proposed exceptions for criminal exculpatory evidence largely due to a fear of recognising derogations to the supposedly absolute nature of the privilege. However much of the fear driving this result is due to the failure to distinguish between different types of balancing processes. The proposed exception does not necessarily involve resort to case-by-case balancing.

The interest in giving a criminal accused access to all exculpatory evidence is a strong one that has been recognised in the context of a number of different exclusionary evidential rules. The recent refusal of English and Australian courts to give effect to the *in favorem innocentiae* principle is partly based on a misunderstanding of the nature and operation of this rule. The treatment of the proposed new exception is typical of the mis-analysis of the structure of the privilege generally. Appellate courts, particularly in England and Australia, continue to view the privilege with an outdated and unrealistic framework depen-

152 See p. 184 above; *R.* v. *Dunbar and Logan* (1982) 138 DLR (3d) 221 and *R.* v. *Ataou* [1988] QB 798 (CA) both involved co-accused, though in *Ataou* one of the co-accused pleaded guilty and gave evidence for the prosecution.

153 E.g. *State* v. *Cascone* 487 A.2d 186 (Conn. SC 1985).

154 New Zealand Law Commission, n. 82 above, 192–3.

155 *R.* v. *Dunbar and Logan* (1982) 138 DLR (3d) at 251–2. Note that while this was cast as an exception to the *Barton* rule which should be decided by *ad hoc* balancing, it could equally be decided on the basis of a fixed rule.

156 High Court of Australia, transcript 15 Nov. 1994 at 13–14.

157 Defined as someone currently being prosecuted for matters arising from the same events, though not necessarily in a joint trial.

158 Australian Law Reform Commission, *Evidence*, Report No. 38 (Australian Law Commission, 1987) 114 para. 196.

159 S.B. McNicol, n. 43 above 104.

dant on incorrect assumptions concerning the timing of states of knowledge and the patterns of individual decision-making. Where other derogations from the privilege, such as waiver or the crime-fraud rule, are concerned, this mis-analysis has led mainly to problematic categorisations of rules and undue inflexibility in the law. Where the *in favorem innocentiae* principle is concerned, the mis-analysis has led to the rejection of an important value in the system of criminal law, and the assertion of a dubious priority of values.

The Canadian Supreme Court has consistently advocated an innocence exception in its dicta, and it is only a matter of time until it does so in ratio decidendi. It is yet to be seen what approach other Commonwealth jurisdictions, particularly New Zealand and South Africa, will take. There is a first instance unreserved civil decision of the Hong Kong High Court in which the judge ordered disclosure on the ground that the client could not have had any "residual interest that is necessary to be protected".[160] However this decision was made without the benefit of authority and with little argument or consideration. It is unlikely to stand as broad authority. Mathieson states that the *Carter* and *Derby Magistrates* cases will be followed in New Zealand at least.[161] However this is by no means certain.[162] New Zealand, Canada and South Africa all have a recent history of determining issues of criminal procedure in terms of constitutional rights, a history which was lacking in both England and Australia in 1995.

Although the future of an innocence exception in the Commonwealth looked bleak in 1995, five years on the outlook is quite different. It can be stated with some confidence that the exception is already law in Canada. There are good reasons to believe that the *Derby Magistrates* case will have to be reconsidered once the Human Rights Act 1998 comes into force in the United Kingdom.[163] Human rights legislation may also lead to similar results in New Zealand and South Africa. It is quite possible that once the appropriate cases have found their way through the different common law jurisdictions, most of the Commonwealth will recognise the innocence exception, and only the Australian common law[164] will be left, isolated by their High Court's decision in the *Carter* case.

[160] *Longines Investments Limited* v. *JSM*, unreported Hong Kong High Court, 19 Feb. 1997 (discussed in C. Passmore, "Spending Privilege", *NLJ Practitioner*, 20 Mar. 1998 at 408).

[161] Mathieson (1998) 415–2: "The privilege is not defeated by the accused's need to use the privileged material to establish his innocence. . . . The authority of New Zealand decisions to the contrary must now be questionable."

[162] It may be worth noting that the leading New Zealand authority on this issue (*R.* v. *Craig* [1975] 1 NZLR 597) was decided by the same judge that gave the leading opinion in *R.* v. *Uljee* [1982] 1 NZLR 561, which declined to follow long-established English authority on another point of privilege law.

[163] See the discussion of this case in Chap. 3 above.

[164] As opposed to those cases covered by the federal Evidence Act 1995.

10

Loss of Privilege Based on Intent and Disclosure (Waiver)

INTRODUCTION

Traditional formulations of the privilege describe it as being absolute except for the doctrine of waiver. Waiver provides the only circumstance in which parties may lose the benefit of the privilege they could previously claim. In theory it is the only circumstance in which a party can impart information under the expectation of confidentiality but then have that expectation frustrated by a legal rule.[1] Thus the boundaries of the doctrine of waiver are extremely important to the structure of the privilege rule.[2] It is not possible to overestimate the degree to which this exception controls the rule itself.

However the use of the doctrine of waiver in privilege law presents many analytical problems. It is an extremely vague and imprecise term.[3] It is an arbitrary doctrine introduced to prevent a person from taking up two inconsistent positions.[4] A leading exposition of the meaning of waiver defines it by reference to three elements: (1) a distinct act (2) that is intentional and is (3) made with knowledge.[5] Though as will be shown below, "waiver" in privilege law may possess none of these elements.

The traditional analysis of cases dealt with as "waiver" is inadequate. The cases currently dealt with under the broad category of implied or imputed waiver need to be re-categorised according to their underlying bases. In reality there are three groups of justifications for these exceptions to the privilege: true implied intent,[6] confidentiality considerations and fairness considerations. The

[1] This may be compared to the theoretical explanation for the operation of the crime-fraud rule, which holds that if a communication is tainted by a desire to perpetrate a crime or fraud, then no legal relationship arises, and hence no legal privilege either.

[2] S.B. McNicol, *Law of Privilege* (Law Book Co., Sydney, 1992) 13 ("fundamental . . . central to the whole concept (of privilege)"; R.L. Marcus, "The Perils of Privilege: Waiver and the Litigator" (1986) 84 *Mich LR* 1605 ("waiver . . . casts a long shadow"); also see *In re Martin Marietta Corp* v. *United States* 856 F.2d 619 at 623 (4th Cir. 1988).

[3] J.S. Ewart, *Waiver Distributed* (Harvard University Press, Cambridge, Mass., 1917) 5 ("the word is used indefinitely to cover for vague uncertain thought"); A.K. Turner, *Estoppel by Representation* (3rd edn., Butterworths, London, 1977) 320 ("not capable of exact definition").

[4] *Pilcher* v. *Rawlins* (1872) 7 Ch App 259 at 268, *per* James LJ (CA).

[5] *Craine* v. *Colonial Mutual Fire Insurance Co Ltd* (1920) 28 CLR 305 at 327 (HCA), *per* Isaacs J; also see cases cited in A.E. Turner, *Estoppel by Representation* (3rd ed., Butterworths, London, 1977), 320.

[6] In contrast to the fictitious or notional implied intent currently used as a basis for waiver.

first two of these categories are dealt with in this chapter, and the third category, fairness-based loss of privilege, is discussed separately in the next chapter.

The first group of cases are those in which waiver is dealt with as a matter of the privilege holder's intention. This will be referred to as "intent-based loss of privilege", or "true implied waiver". The role of intent in the operation of this rule will be analysed and it will be shown that these cases may not actually turn on intent, but are more influenced by actual disclosure. This may be due to considerations external to the lawyer–client relationship and the limits of confidentiality. In light of this, it should be questioned whether it is appropriate to continue to recognise and give effect to any form of intent-based waiver whatsoever.

The cases based on fairness considerations should be viewed as a number of separate exceptions to the privilege. If intent is not relevant to these cases, then it should not be a factor in the reasoning. Some cases previously dealt with under the rubric of implied waiver do not raise fairness issues, and it must be questioned whether these should continue to be recognised as grounding exceptions to the privilege. Cases concerning selective disclosure and "limited waiver" are normally also dealt with as implied waiver. However these cases do not raise issues of fairness and possibly do not involve any element of intention either. This whole category of cases should be subsumed under the consideration of confidentiality as a substantive requirement. There are important differences between an exception to privilege and the absence of a substantive requirement, such that this error of classification cannot be brushed aside.

Once the cases traditionally dealt with as "waiver" are reviewed in this fashion, it will become clear that there are actually a number of different exceptions to the privilege, most of which have nothing to do with an intention to abandon the privilege. The current classification greatly obscures the proper bases for exceptions to the privilege and hence obscures the nature of the privilege itself. The analysis of the waiver doctrine below should show that the privilege is a flexible and balanced rule which is often overridden by competing considerations. This accords with the conclusions reached elsewhere in this book concerning other derogations.

SECTION I: INTENT BASED LOSS OF PRIVILEGE

Role of Intention

This section will deal with situations in which loss of privilege occurs directly as a result of some act or decision taken by the party claiming privilege, and where it can properly be said that that party had an intention to waive the privilege. This covers both express intent to waive[7] and implied intent in a narrower sense

[7] Express intent to waive is rare: see J.H. Wigmore and J.T. McNaughton, *Evidence in Trials at Common Law* (Little, Brown & Co., Boston, 1961) viii 636; R.L. Marcus, n. 2 above, 1618.

than that usually used in relation to the privilege: that is, where the actions of a party evince an unexpressed but actual intention to waive the privilege.[8]

There has always been some doubt about the precise role intention should play in determining loss of the privilege. In most Commonwealth countries the terminology is framed in terms of an "intention", however fictional that concept may be in practice. American academics have been divided on this issue since the start of this century. Wigmore argued for a long time that intent was largely irrelevant. Morgan, on the other hand, argued that waiver should depend on intent and knowledge. Morgan's view prevailed in the drafting of the Model Code and the Uniform Rules of Evidence, but was then rejected by the draughtsmen of the Californian Code on grounds of its inconsistency with the existing law.[9] An advisory committee on a later edition of the Uniform Rules of Evidence accepted the Californian model and, while its rule was not adopted federally,[10] many states followed its pattern.[11] Thus in the United States the most common test used is voluntariness rather than intent.[12]

Even for the cases where loss of privilege is rationalised as a matter of intent, intent may not be the decisive or dictating factor. As a starting point it may be useful to ask the question whether intent alone could be sufficient to ground a waiver. If parties decide they will waive the privilege and communicate this, will they be fixed with an effective disclosure at that point? There is a strong policy reason why such an expressed intention may be enforced. This is the policy interest in the maintenance of the certainty of actions; if the privilege has been waived, or purports to have been waived, then other parties should be entitled to act on the basis that the (non-privileged) status of that material will remain.[13]

However there are two closely related types of cases which suggest that intent alone is not sufficient to lead to loss of the privilege. The first are cases of contractual waiver. This is where a party to a contract states a positive intention to disclose privileged communications or contracts not to claim the privilege.[14] Some writers argue that such a waiver should be upheld as a matter of the law of contract.[15] There appears to be strong support for this view in the United

[8] The description "intent to waive the privilege" is not here meant to convey the precise mental state which gives rise to this conclusion. There are a number of possible mental states from which intention to waive the privilege could be inferred, such as intention to disclose the information to particular parties, intention to abandon confidentiality altogether and intention not necessarily to abandon confidentiality, but to do acts which show that lawyer–client communications in the instant case are not dependent on an expectation of confidentiality.

[9] C. Wright, and K. Graham, *Federal Practice and Procedure* (West Publishing, St Paul, Minn., 1992) xxvia, 538–9.

[10] It is now Rejected Rule 511.

[11] E.g. see C. Wright and K. Graham, n. 9 above, 539 n. 31.

[12] Comment, "Developments in the Law—Privileged Communications" (1985) 98 *Harv LR* 1450 at 1629 n. 1.

[13] E.g. see *Meltend Pty Ltd* v. *Restoration Clinics of Australia Pty Ltd* (1997) 145 ALR at 406.

[14] C. Wright and K. Graham, n. 9 above, 550 n. 4.

[15] R.A. Sedler and J.J. Simeone, "The Realities of Attorney–Client Confidences" (1963) *Ohio St LJ* 1 at 46; Comment, "Limitations on Californian Professional Privileges" (1976) 9 *UCDLR* 477 at 492.

States,[16] particularly in relation to insurance contracts.[17] However the better view is that a contractual term stipulating waiver should not, without more, lead to loss of the privilege.[18] If the secrecy on which the privilege is based has not been frustrated, protection should remain. Intent should not be controlling on the issue of waiver. This may be compared with the privilege against self-incrimination, where contractual waivers may perhaps not be given effect to.[19]

The second and closely related category of cases concerns the finality of waiver. The issue here is partly whether courts will allow parties to change their minds with regard to their intent to disclose privileged communications.[20] American courts are unlikely to enforce even a voluntary and knowing waiver if the privilege-holder has changed his mind before actual disclosure.[21] While the authority is limited, it seems a party can withdraw consent to disclose,[22] although much of the discussion of the issue in the United States relates to statutory medical privileges.[23] The same result would probably be reached in England, following comments made by the Court of Appeal in *Goldman* v. *Hesper*.[24] However the position in other Commonwealth jurisdictions is uncertain.[25] The answer may be, as suggested in *Goldman* v. *Hesper*, that the waiver

[16] Comment, n. 15 above, at 492.

[17] See C. Wright, and K. Graham, *Federal Practice and Procedure* (West Publishinhg, St Paul, Minn., 1989) xxv, 403–4 for a detailed discussion of waiver of attorney–client privilege as a term in insurance contracts.

[18] See C. Wright and K. Graham, n. 9 above, 550 n. 5.

[19] The position in both England and America is in some doubt: see *Mirror Group Newspapers* v. *Maxwell* [1993] Ch 1 (CA); *Morgan* v. *Thomas* 448 F 2d 1356 (5th Cir. 1971). For a thorough and insightful analysis of this issue see K.D. Grevling, "Contracting Out of the Privilege Against Self-Incrimination" in F.D. Rose (ed.), *Consensus Ad Idem* (Sweet & Maxwell, London, 1996).

[20] Note that this refers to an intention formed after the communications have come into existence. If there is an intention to disclose a document, such as an expert's report, to the other side and this intention is expressed before the report has been commissioned, then the issue will probably be one of whether the document was ever intended to be confidential in the first place. This was the case in *Marlborough Hotel Co Ltd* v. *Parkmaster (Canada) Ltd* (1959) 17 DLR 2d 720 (Man. CA).

[21] *United States* v. *Aronoff* 466 F.Supp. 855 at 858 (DC NY 1979) (concentrating on actual disclosure and dismissing an estoppel-type argument); *Natlee Draft Horse Co* v. *Cripe & Co* 135 SW 292 (Kentucky CA 1911) (allowing a straight withdrawal after a clear express waiver).

[22] *Lohman* v. *Superior Court* 146 Cal. Rptr 171 at 174 (Cal. CA 1978); *Driskell* v. *State* 659 P.2d 343 (Oklahoma CCA 1983).

[23] E.g. see W.R. Peterson, "The Patient–Physician Privilege in Missouri" (1952) 20 *UKCLRev* 122 at 128; S. Jacobs, "Privileged Communications Between Physician and Patient in California" (1932) 20 *Calif LR* 302 at 311.

[24] [1988] 3 All ER 97. The defendant signed a form of consent written by the plaintiff which waived the defendant's privilege over certain documents and allowed the plaintiff to inspect them. Before inspection had taken place the defendant, on advice, withdrew the waiver. The plaintiff argued that the defendant could not go back on the initial waiver. Taylor LJ, rejecting this contention for the Court of Appeal, held that "no action had been taken on the letter of waiver . . . nothing had been done and nothing was spoiled. The pass had not been sold, and in my judgment the defendant was perfectly entitled, on taking advice, to withdraw the waiver and her withdrawal was effective" (*ibid*., at 98).

[25] The New Zealand Court of Appeal would probably uphold the privilege after such a change of mind. This may be surmised from its generous approach to maintenance of the privilege despite limited disclosure. E.g. see *R.* v. *Uljee* [1982] 1 NZLR 561 and *C-C Bottlers Ltd* v. *Lion Nathan* [1993] 2 NZLR 445 (HC). The same leniency possibly may not be shown in Australia, where a strict view of detriment may be taken. In *Argyle Brewery Pty Ltd* v. *Darling Harbourside* (1994) 120 ALR

can be withdrawn unless and until the other party has taken some action in reliance on it, usually by inspecting the relevant documents.

Therefore it seems that intention alone is insufficient to enforce a waiver of the privilege.[26] Importance is placed on the actuality of disclosure. It is necessary to ask why this is a relevant and important consideration.

Actual Disclosure

There are a number of reasons why actual disclosure may be an important issue in determining whether the privilege has been lost, such as:

(1) because the actual disclosure has destroyed the confidential nature of the communication such that there is nothing left to protect;
(2) because the disclosure evinces the lack of need for confidence for the communication to have been made in the first place;
(3) because the disclosure causes some detriment to the opponent; and
(4) because to uphold the privilege despite the disclosure may bring the integrity of the judicial system and its method of fact-finding into disrepute.

These reasons may be taken roughly in turn.

Perhaps the most obvious reason why an actual disclosure should be recognised as leading to a loss of the privilege is that, once confidence is lost, there may be nothing left to protect.[27] The first point that should be made in relation to this is that a distinction should be drawn between disclosures destroying confidentiality which occur before and after the communication of the information between lawyer and client. Where disclosure occurs beforehand the issue is one relating to the existence of the privilege in the first place. It is only where the disclosure occurs after the communication has been passed between lawyer and client that any issue of loss of the privilege arises.

Given this latter circumstance, one must question the basis upon which a party claiming privilege is, because of the disclosure, not allowed to maintain its

537 (Fed. Ct.) Argyle, during negotiations, produced a document which they described as a "draft" writ, and this was placed on the table. They also claimed it was ready to be filed the next day if necessary. Beaumont J, for the Federal Court, held there was a waiver on grounds of unfairness. Argyle's actions were calculated to give them a bargaining advantage. However there was no indication on the facts of the case that Argyle would have let their opponents see the document if they had attempted to pick it up. If Argyle had said that they had a writ ready in the next room this would presumably not have led to a waiver. It is difficult to see the relevant difference between the two scenarios.

[26] "The privilege . . . should be regarded as sacred. It is not to be whittled away by means of specious argument that it has been waived. Least of all should courts seize upon slight and equivocal circumstances as a technical reason for destroying the privilege": *People* v. *Kor* 277 P.2d 94 at 100 (DCA Cal. 1974). For similar sentiments see *Sullivan* v. *Superior Court* 105 Cal. Rptr 241 (Cal. CA 1972) and *Lohman* v. *Superior Court* 146 Cal. Rptr at 174.

[27] This rationale is made in many writings on the subject. For a typical example of the use of this reasoning in case law see *United States* v. *Kelsey-Hayes Wheel Co* 15 FRD 461 at 464 (DC Mich. 1954).

claim. It is clear that the client may still value the privilege even after a disclosure of the communication has occurred.[28] Even if the only motivation for claiming the privilege is the forensic advantage gained by it, this is still something which the privilege ought to protect. In fact, this is the very concern the privilege ought to safeguard. The privilege operates narrowly to protect information from disclosure via compulsion to a judicial or administrative body. It is an important part of the rationale for the rule that it encourages disclosure on the basis that the communication will not later be used against the disclosing party in court or by an investigative body. However by preventing this compulsion the privilege removes only one of the threats to the confidentiality of the communication. It does not remove, and was never capable of removing, all of the threats to confidentiality.[29] Conversely, even if the communication has been disclosed in one realm, the continued insistence that it may not be used in another (and usually more detrimental) realm actively promotes the purpose and effect of the privilege. Thus even where actual disclosure to the world has occurred, maintenance of the privilege for pure forensic advantage only is still justifiable and within the rationale of the privilege. The final section of this chapter will further examine the possible meaning and explanation of the privilege if it is accepted that it can continue to exist despite the actual disclosure of the material.

There are already some rules which allow for the continued operation of the privilege even when the material has been disclosed, such as in the American "eavesdropper rule",[30] or the alternative negligence standard for inadvertent disclosures,[31] or in cases holding that inadvertent disclosure resulting from some illegal or unethical act will not lead to loss of the privilege.[32] Putting the privilege to one side for the moment, the fact that information is publicly available does not necessarily make it admissible in evidence. For example, evidence excluded under provisions relating to unlawful searches may not be introduced despite being widely known. Inadmissible confessions may be in a similar position. However much of the criticism of these rules may stem from this very feature.

[28] Note, "The Attorney–Client Privilege After Attorney Disclosure" (1980) 78 *Michigan LR* 927 at 936–8.

[29] *Ibid.* at 935.

[30] The third party eavesdropper is even allowed to testify about what he heard in the trial in which privilege is maintained: *United States* v. *Olmstead* 7 F Supp. 760 at 763 (1925), affirmed in 277 US 438; *Clark* v. *State* 261 SW 2d 339 at 341–3 (Texas CCA 1953). However this rule does not fit easily with other waiver principles and may not be the best precedent for the continued operation of the privilege in circumstances of disclosure.

[31] E.g. *Mendenhall* v. *Barber-Greene Co.* 531 F Supp. 951 at 955 (DC Illinois 1982).

[32] E.g. *ITC Film Distributors Ltd* v. *Video Exchange Ltd* [1982] Ch 431 (Ch.); *Schetter* v. *Schetter* 239 So. 2d 51 at 52 (DCA Florida 1970) (disclosure resulting from lawyer's own breach of client confidentiality); *In re Grand Jury Proceedings Involving Berkley & Co.* 466 F. Supp. 863 at 869 (DC Minn. 1979). Note that there is a strong counter-argument on this point that if the effects of inadvertent disclosure were allowed to be taken back, then the normal incentive to screen out material would be withdrawn and there may be uncertainty about whether privilege would actually be asserted over items produced in discovery: R.L. Marcus, n. 2 above, 1636.

The answer may be that it is not the lack of confidentiality *per se* that leads to the privilege being lost upon a disclosure of the communication, but rather that there are other values associated with the disclosure that support this effect. For example a commonly used argument for loss of privilege following disclosure is that the disclosure shows that the communication was not made in reliance on an expectation of confidentiality. Wright and Graham[33] argue that waiver is not just about the lack of concern for privacy of itself, but rather that by abandoning secrecy the client has shown that he did not need the privilege in order to reveal secrets to his lawyer. The same authors also argue that this may explain many waiver rules,[34] such as why disclosure grounding waiver must be non-coerced[35] and why knowledge of the privilege is irrelevant.[36]

The main problem with this justification for loss of privilege following disclosure is that it fits only the theoretical framework for disclosures that occur prior to lawyer–client communications. The same reasoning cannot be applied where the disclosure happens after the communication has taken place. In this latter scenario the client may indeed have relied on an expectation of confidentiality as a basis for the original disclosure. The most that could be said is that the disclosure illustrates that the client no longer holds an interest in the continued confidentiality of that communication. However this sort of argument formed the basis of the recognised interest exception cases which were expressly overruled by the House of Lords in the *Derby Magistrates* case and criticised by the High Court of Australia in the *Carter* case.[37]

We have seen that the two justifications for the importance of actual disclosure that are most often expressed, namely the lack of confidentiality and the lack of reliance on confidentiality, are insufficient to explain the rule fully. This raises the question whether there may be further factors at play. One unarticulated rationale for the rule may be a concern that to uphold the privilege despite the fact of a disclosure may bring the integrity of the judicial system and its method of fact-finding into disrepute. Simply stated, it would appear to be irrational and artificial if the law insisted that a fact-finder must not take cognisance of a communication which is known to many people already.[38] The real concern may be to avoid what has been termed "systemic embarrassment".[39] The gap between common sense and the legal rule is too great to bear. This argument has been used to explain other principles of evidence law, such as hearsay.[40]

33 n. 9 above, at 519–20.

34 *Ibid.* at 520; also see Note, n. 29 above, 935.

35 C. Wright and K. Graham, n. 9 above, at para. 5726.

36 *Ibid.* at para. 5728.

37 Although it is not certain that this reasoning has been completely abandoned in Australia, as discussed in the previous chapter. The doctrine may still be used in New Zealand.

38 "[A] result that not only suppresses the truth but threatens to make justice a mockery": R.L. Marcus, n. 2 above, 1636.

39 Comment, n. 12 above, 1661.

40 C. Nesson, "The Evidence or the Event? On Judicial Proof and the Acceptability of Verdicts" (1985) 98 *Harv LR* 1357 at 1373. However this theory has been convincingly refuted by R. Park,

When analysed properly this factor is a poor justification for this type of waiver. The privilege by its very nature seeks to withhold relevant and potentially valuable and exculpatory evidence. It is motivated by a rationale which is justifiable only when applied as a general rule. The utilitarian rationale makes far less sense when applied on an individual basis, as is effectively the case here. However, despite the inadequacy of this factor as a principled justification for the rule, it still remains one of the main true motivations for the rule. Perhaps it is because judges have failed to face up to this as an express reason behind waiver that the actual merits of this logic have not been properly tested.

Finally, it may be worth mentioning that the possibility of detriment being caused to a party is also a reason for placing the emphasis on actual disclosure, though obviously the evaluation of detriment will be different in each case, and may well be absent altogether. Therefore the existence of detriment to a party can at most amount to a factor to be considered only where it applies.

There is some difficulty in justifying the continued recognition of intent-based waiver. Even if a party expresses an intention to disclose privileged information, it is hard to see why that party should not be able to change its mind before the information is released, where such a change of mind causes no detriment to another party. The fact of lack of confidentiality or the shown lack of reliance on confidentiality does not adequately explain the emphasis on actual disclosure. Therefore it is hard to escape the conclusion that the recognition of express waiver is at least in part due to concerns external to the lawyer–client relationship and the rationale for the privilege.

A concern for the integrity of the justice system is an inadequate reason for maintaining the rules that form intent-based loss of privilege. Parties should be able to change their minds and effectively withdraw a waiver. The only limit to this is where the actions of the privilege-holder in re-asserting the privilege may prejudice the opponent, in the sense that the opponent is put in a worse position than he otherwise would have been in had the privilege holder asserted privilege throughout.[41] There is a significant case to be made for the abolition of intent-based loss of privilege altogether and concentration on unfairness as the only ground for loss of privilege.

SECTION II: DISCLOSURE BASED LOSS OF PRIVILEGE

Disclosure of privileged communications may be either deliberate or inadvertent. The following section will examine inadvertent disclosure and two of the main types of deliberate disclosure: the rules commonly termed "selective dis-

"The Hearsay Rule and the Stability of Verdicts: A Response to Professor Nesson" (1986) 70 *Minn LR* 1057.

[41] One example may be where an opponent has developed his litigation strategy in reliance upon the disclosed material, as in *In re Grand Jury Investigation of Ocean Transportation* 604 F 2d 672 at 675 (DC Cir. 1979).

closure" and "limited waiver". It will be argued that these rules are not based on fairness considerations, as the rules discussed below relating to partial disclosure and putting in issue are. Rather, the rules relating to selective disclosure and limited waiver have arisen out of concerns for the continued confidentiality of the communications. Because of this the place of these rules within the privilege needs to be re-assessed.

Deliberate Selective Disclosure

Selective disclosure refers to disclosure to a limited group of people that does not necessarily destroy the privilege in relation to the rest of the world. Most Commonwealth jurisdictions have embraced the rule, but this often depends on whom the disclosure is to.[42] For example, it has been held that disclosure may not lead to loss of the privilege where it is to a party with a common interest in the litigation,[43] to an associate or confidant unconnected with the proceedings[44] or to members of a team of advisers including lawyers, accountants and bankers all together.[45] New Zealand courts have been particularly generous in allowing selective disclosure without loss of the privilege.[46]

There seems to be a frequent misconception about the reason underlying this rule. Many of the cases discussed above present selective disclosure as a head of implied or imputed waiver, and therefore proceed to deal with it as an issue of fairness.[47] However selective disclosure does not raise issues of fairness at all. If party A cannot gain access to materials no unfairness is caused by the fact that those materials have been disclosed to third party B, where party A never had any right to those materials anyway.[48] The act of selective disclosure does not

[42] E.g. Toohey J in *Goldberg* v. *Ng* (1996) 185 CLR 83 at 106–9 (HCA); *C-C Bottlers Ltd* v. *Lion Nathan* [1993] 2 NZLR at 448–9.

[43] E.g. *Buttes Gas and Oil Co* v. *Hammer (No.3)* [1981] QB 223 (CA), but note that in this case the same solicitor was used in any case; *Guiness Peat Properties Ltd* v. *Fitzroy Robinson Partnership* [1987] 2 All ER 716; *Gotha City* v. *Sotheby's* [1998] 1 WLR 114 at 122 (CA); *Farrow Mortgage Services* v. *Webb* (1996) 39 NSWLR 601 at 609–12 (NSW CA).

[44] *Harbour Inn Seafoods Ltd* v. *Switzerland General Insurance* [1990] 2 NZLR 381 at 384 (HC); *C-C Bottlers Ltd* v. *Lion Nathan* [1993] 2 NZLR 445 (disclosure to financial advisers).

[45] *Nederlandse Reassurantie Groep Holding NV* v. *Bacon & Woodrow (a firm)* [1995] 1 All ER 976 (QBD).

[46] See n. 44 above.

[47] Selective disclosure has also been rationalised on the basis of intention. E.g. see *Woollahra Municipal Council* v. *Westpac Banking Corp.* (1994) 33 NSWLR 529 at 539D (NSW SC) and *Harbour Inn Seafoods Ltd* v. *Switzerland General Insurance* [1990] 2 NZLR at 384. Such a rationale is doubtful: see *Thomason* v. *Council of the Municipality of Campbelltown* (1939) 39 SR (NSW) 347 at 355 (NSW SC) ("The mere fact that a person on some one occasion chooses to impart to another or others advice which he has received from his solicitor indicates no intention on his part to waive his right to refuse to disclose in evidence"). In any case this would be subject to the same criticisms made above in relation to intent-based loss of privilege.

[48] R.L. Marcus, n. 2 above, 1639. Marcus cites the very useful example of *In re Supboenas Duces Tecum to Fulbright and Jaworski* 738 F 2d 1367 (DC Cir. 1984). There materials were disclosed to the Securities and Exchange Commission (SEC). Private plaintiffs sought access to these documents and were granted it on the basis that submission to the SEC was a testimonial use of the

of itself cause a party any greater detriment than that otherwise resulting from their initial inability to gain access to the evidence.[49] Put simply, selective disclosure does not put a party in any worse a position. As Giles J explained in *Woollahra Municipal Council* v. *Westpac Banking Corp*:

> disclosure to a third party . . . does not mean that fairness requires disclosure to anyone else with a reason for seeing the documents, other than in the general sense that it would be unfair for the person entitled to the privilege to assert it when the privilege had been lost by the disclosure. The loss of the privilege would found the unfairness, not the other way around.[50]

Rather than fairness considerations, selective disclosure raises the issue of confidentiality. It is wrong to impose a rule that any disclosure leads to loss of the privilege as this confuses confidentiality with the values it is designed to protect.[51] The goals promoted by confidentiality often are not harmed by allowing some selective disclosure.

Deliberate Purposive Disclosure ("Limited Waiver")

The rule sometimes termed "limited waiver" refers to the deliberate disclosure of materials for a specific and limited purpose.[52] For example, in *British Coal Corporation* v. *Dennis Rye Ltd (No.2)*[53] a disclosure for criminal proceedings did not constitute a waiver for later civil proceedings.[54] Similarly, in *Goldman* v. *Hesper*[55] there was no waiver as a result of seeking a taxation of the bill of costs.[56] And in *Bourns Inc* v. *Raychem Corp*[57] disclosure for the purposes of taxation proceedings did not lead to a waiver in respect of disclosure sought by a foreign court. One may seek to reject the generality of a limited waiver rule and restrict *British Coal Corporation* v. *Dennis Rye Ltd (No.2)* to its particular facts and the overriding public interest in encouraging co-operation with prosecuto-

materials. This is wrong. The mistake arises from confusing the rationales for partial and selective disclosure, and applying them to the wrong parties. While the truth-garbling rationale may have justified some disclosure to the SEC, this did not apply in relation to the private plaintiffs.

49 Comment, n. 12 above, 1645; *Teachers Insurance & Annuity Association of America* v. *Shamrock Broadcasting Co* 521 F Supp 638 at 645 (DC NY 1981).

50 (1994) 33 NSWLR at 539.

51 Comment, n. 12 above, 1644.

52 *Goldberg* v. *Ng* (1996) 185 CLR at 106.

53 [1988] 1 WLR 1113 (CA).

54 *Quaere* though whether this decision was based on fairness or on an objective assessment of a lack of intent to waive.

55 [1988] 3 All ER 97.

56 Note though that the case was decided in the context of a statutory regime for taxations, which included a statutory requirement to disclose privileged documents and a duty on the taxing officer to maintain the privilege as far as possible. The same result was reached in *Bourns Inc* v. *Raychem Corp*, *The Times*, 26 Nov. 1998 (Ch). Compare the different result in *Giannarelli* v. *Wraith* (1991) 98 ALR 1 (HCA).

57 [1999] 1 All ER 908 at 920–1 (Ch. D).

rial authorities.[58] However such a restrictive reading may not square with the plain language of the judgment and the clear role of the abovementioned public policy as a supplementary factor only.[59]

Australian courts are divided on whether to apply the English rule of limited waiver. The English cases were applied in *Network Ten Ltd* v. *Capital Television Holdings Ltd*,[60] *Optus Communications Pty Ltd* v. *Telstra Communications Ltd*[61] and *State Bank of South Australia* v. *Smoothdale Ltd (No. 2)*,[62] as well as by Kirby P in *Goldberg* v. *Ng*.[63] However the rule was expressly rejected by McHugh J in *Gianarelli* v. *Wraith (No. 2)*[64] and by Clarke JA in *Goldberg* v. *Ng*.[65] When the latter case came before the High Court, Toohey and Gummow JJ expressly approved of the limited waiver rule. The majority joint judgment of Deane, Dawson and Gaudron JJ held that such a result might be possible, though effectively rendered such a possibility irrelevant where the disclosure occurred in one proceeding and the material was sought in a related proceeding. This case is dealt with in more detail below.

The limited waiver rule has been largely rejected in the United States. There is a vast body of case law and academic discussion there concerning the subsequent use of materials disclosed to the Securities and Exchange Commission. Initially it was thought that privilege in such documents could be maintained. The landmark case holding that disclosure to the SEC waives the privilege once and for all is *Permian Corporation* v. *United States*,[66] and this is referred to as "the Permian Rule". This rule squarely raises and expressly rejects the concept of limited waiver.[67] The reason given for the rejection of the limited waiver rule is that the legal privilege is a privilege to keep secrets, and if a client deliberately reveals secrets for his own ends, there is little justification for permitting him to require other fora to adhere to the secrecy. McCormick argues that this stated reason masks the true reason: that allowing a subsequent claim of privilege would unfairly disadvantage the opponent who has reasonably assumed the evidence would be available.[68]

[58] E.g. C. Passmore, Privilege (CLT, Sutton Coldfield, 1998) 179–80.

[59] For the clear and broad terms of the principle, see [1988] 1 WLR at 1121D–E. For the supplementary nature of the public policy consideration, see *ibid.* at 1122A.

[60] (1995) 16 ACSR 138 at 147 (NSW SC).

[61] Federal Court, 27 Apr. 1995, Lockhart J.

[62] 64 SASR 224 at 227–9.

[63] (1994) 33 NSWLR 639 at 654.

[64] (1991) 171 CLR 592 at 606–7. The Full Court in *State Bank of South Australia* v. *Smoothdale Ltd (No. 2)* and Kirby P in *Goldberg* v. *Ng* held that McHugh J had not foreclosed this issue with his judgment in *Gianarelli* v. *Wraith (No. 2)*.

[65] (1994) 33 NSWLR at 676.

[66] 665 F.2d 1214 (DC Cir. 1981).

[67] See *ibid.* at 1220–1. Also see: *In re Supboenas Duces Tecum to Fulbright and Jaworski* 738 F 2d at 1369–70; *Maryville Academy* v. *Loeb Rhoades & Co* 559 F Supp 7 at 9 (DC Ill. 1982); *In re Penn Central Commercial Paper Litigation* 61 FRD 453 at 464 (DC NY 1973) and extensive authorities cited therein at n. 26.

[68] J.W. Strong *et al.* (eds.), *McCormick on Evidence* (4th edn., West Publishing, St Paul, Minn., 1992), 132–3.

Despite the criticisms levelled at it, the English rule is a good one. As with selective disclosure, such actions rarely visit any unfairness on an opponent.[69] Use in a prior proceeding causes the information-deprived party in the subsequent proceeding no actual detriment. "The loss of the privilege would found the unfairness, not the other way around."[70] Fairness is not an appropriate issue to be considering in the context of limited waiver, which turns, if anything, on issues of confidentiality alone.

However fairness considerations are often mistakenly included in the calculus of exceptions such as the limited waiver rule. This can lead to problems in applying the rule. A good example of this is the leading Australian case of *Goldberg* v. *Ng*, where unfairness in one proceeding was held to have carried over and led to disclosure in another proceeding. The case concerned two proceedings, a disciplinary investigation and a civil claim against a solicitor; both actions arising out of the same incident. The solicitor under investigation produced privileged documents to the Law Society for the purpose of the disciplinary investigation, but attempted to assert privilege over those documents in the civil action. The majority of the High Court held that the two actions were so closely tied up that any unfairness caused by not disclosing documents in the disciplinary proceedings would carry over to the civil action.

The majority decision in *Goldberg* v. *Ng* is wrong. The issue in the case was not unfairness caused in the civil claim, but simply one of continued confidentiality. In any case, if any unfairness existed, it had its effect in the first proceeding only. The two proceedings cannot be linked in this way. The dissenting judgment of Toohey J is to be preferred. He recognised that limited waiver does not depend on unfairness, but rather an imputation based on an objective assessment of conduct. He decided the case on the basis that the circumstances of this particular disclosure militated against any implied or imputed waiver.

It is still possible to explain selective disclosure cases other than by reference to confidentiality. For example, *British Coal Corporation* v. *Dennis Rye Ltd (No.2)* could be explained as a case where an actual waiver by voluntary disclosure was overridden by a greater public policy requiring the maintenance of confidentiality. There is undoubtedly a valid public policy being served by encouraging people to assist in criminal investigations. However the more immediate concern, and the one motivating the judgments in *Dennis Rye*, was the effect of the disclosure on the parties.

[69] *Goldberg* v. *Ng* (1996) 185 CLR at 109.

[70] *Woollahra Municipal Council* v. *Westpac Banking Corporation* (1994) 33 NSWLR 529 at 539, *per* Giles J (NSW SC).

Inadvertent Disclosure of Copies

The issue of inadvertent disclosure, and the approach of courts to granting relief when it occurs, will be considered in detail in Chapter 12 below.[71] One issue that may be more conveniently dealt with in this chapter is the question whether, in circumstances where copies of privileged material have been disclosed inadvertently, such disclosure leads to a loss of privilege in the original documents.[72] This raises the question whether confidentiality is an ongoing requirement for the privilege, and whether loss of confidentiality necessarily results in loss of the privilege.

When discussing the problem of copy documents, attention usually focuses on the status of the copy. For example, in the leading case of *Calcraft* v. *Guest*[73] both the status of the original and the status of the copy were discrete subjects for consideration before the Court of Appeal. However when dealing with the status of the original documents, Lord Lindley MR says only:

> if there are any documents which were protected by the privilege . . . that privilege has not been lost. I take it that, as a general rule, one may say once privileged always privileged. I do not mean to say that privilege cannot be waived, but that the mere fact that documents used in previous litigation are held and have not been destroyed does not amount to a waiver of the privilege.[74]

The issue Lord Lindley MR fails to address is whether the fact that the documents have been seen by the opponent leads to a loss of confidentiality and loss of the privilege. Perhaps this was implicit in his judgment. Note though that this matter was expressly addressed by counsel.[75] Similarly in *Ashburton* v. *Pape*[76] the issue of the status of the original documents was neither raised nor discussed. However in this case it was not an issue in the appeal.

Recent English cases on accidental disclosure show a division on this point which may need to be resolved by the House of Lords. In *Webster* v. *James Chapman & Co* Scott J held that "[i]f the document has been disclosed, be it by trickery, accident or otherwise, the benefit and protection of legal privilege will have been lost".[77] However it seems that in this case waiver was not put forward by the party seeking disclosure.[78] A similar strict view was taken in *Guiness Peat*

[71] Note also that the issue may be resolved differently under the Evidence Act 1995 (Aust.): see K. Smark, "Privilege Under the *Evidence Acts*" (1995) 18 *UNSWLJ* 95 at 100–1.

[72] For a discussion of this issue from an American perspective, see J.M. Grippando, "Attorney–Client Privilege: Implied Waiver Through Inadvertent Disclosure of Documents" (1985) 39 *Uni Miami LR* 511; Note, "Inadvertent Disclosure of Documents Subject to Attorney–Client Privilege" (1983) 82 *Mich LR* 598.

[73] [1898] 1 QB 759 (CA).

[74] *Ibid.* at 761–2.

[75] *Ibid.* at 761, *per* Cripps QC for the respondent: "nor is the privilege destroyed because the solicitor has wrongfully handed over the document to the other side".

[76] [1913] 2 Ch 469 (CA).

[77] [1989] 3 All ER 939 at 946 (Ch.).

[78] This point is made by Vinelott J in *Derby* v. *Weldon (No.8)* [1991] 1 WLR 73 at 83 (Ch.).

Properties Ltd v. *Fitroy Robinson Partnership*.[79] Slade LJ, for the Court of Appeal, first pointed out that in the present case there was clearly no intention to abandon the privilege. Then, adopting an argument of counsel, approved the following principles:

> privilege is essentially privilege from compulsory disclosure . . . once a privileged document has not only been disclosed but also inspected in the course of discovery, it is too late to put the clock back: the privilege is lost . . .
> . . . Ordinarily, in my judgment, a party to litigation who sees a particular document referred to in the other side's list, without privilege being claimed, and is subsequently permitted inspection of that document, is fully entitled to assume that any privilege which might otherwise have been claimed for it has been waived. Let there be no doubt about that.[80]

It seems clear then that Slade LJ, who was speaking for the Court of Appeal, was advocating an extremely strict waiver rule, to the effect that inadvertent disclosure made during discovery will automatically lead to a loss of the privilege. And in *Black & Decker* v. *Flymo*[81] Hoffman J held that once a document passed into the hands of an opponent pursuant to an exchange of witness statements, the question was no longer one of privilege, but of admissibility. Thus there could be no privilege once the information had been disclosed in an exchanged witness statement.

As well as significant judicial support, the automatic loss of privilege argument has significant academic support. Andrews emphatically states that "the law is clear . . . inadvertent disclosure by the privilege holder causes privilege to lapse".[82] Toulson and Phipps state that the bounds of confidence and privilege are the same, as "confidentiality is a pre-requisite of . . . privilege".[83] Dr Newbold also strongly advocates the view that any disclosure will lead to loss of the privilege. She completely rejects Professor Heydon's argument[84] that privilege should continue despite inadvertent disclosure, saying:

> If [confidential information] has been disclosed the issue is simply whether it can be used or not and this will depend on the equitable jurisdiction to restrain breach of confidence. It has nothing to do with whether it would be privileged if compelled. Therefore, it is not a question of privilege "continuing" as Professor Heydon seems to think. Privilege cannot "continue". It is inapplicable to the voluntary disclosure situation.[85]

As far as Dr Newbold is concerned, there is not even any issue whether inadvertent disclosure leads to loss of the privilege.

[79] [1987] 2 All ER 716.
[80] *Ibid.* at 729–30.
[81] [1991] 1 WLR 753 at 755 (Ch.).
[82] J.A. Andrews (1989) 623.
[83] R.G. Toulson and C.M. Phipps, *Confidentiality* (Sweet & Maxwell, London, 1996) 184; but compare *ibid.* at 211–12.
[84] J.D. Heydon, "Legal Professional Privilege and Third Parties" (1974) 37 *MLR* 601 at 609.
[85] A.L.E. Newbold, "Inadvertent Disclosure in Civil Proceedings" (1991) 107 *LQR* 99 at 112.

The better view is that privilege may still exist despite some disclosure. This is a simple and, until *Guiness Peat* and *Webster* v. *Chapman,* quite unremarkable proposition. This has been expressly recognised by Australian[86] and New Zealand[87] courts. Canadian courts have always been quite clear that inadvertent disclosure will not necessarily constitute waiver.[88] The approach in the United States favours maintenance of the privilege the most.[89]

Within the rule of legal professional privilege confidentiality is a substantive requirement in the sense that the communication must originally be made under circumstances of confidence. This can be seen in Wigmore's much-quoted definition of the requirements of the privilege,[90] and is to be found in all other standard definitions of the privilege.[91] Looking at the matter from first principles, it makes sense that if confidentiality is to be a substantive requirement of the privilege, the issue should be whether confidentiality existed at the time the legal communication was made, as this is the time the relevant communications became privileged. There are categories of cases which call into question this substantive requirement, such as the eavesdropper cases.[92] However after the legal communication is made under circumstances which bring the communication within the privilege rule, then anything that may occur after that point to call into question the privileged status of those communications is a matter of waiver.[93] This accords with the basic structure of the privilege rule. Substantive requirements are those which arise, by definition, at the time of the communication. After the communication has been invested with privileged status, this status can be removed only by an overriding exception to the privilege rule. The result of this is that any issue of disclosure of privileged communications is an issue of waiver, not an issue of loss of confidentiality as a substantive requirement.[94]

[86] E.g. *Goldberg* v. *Ng* (1994) 33 NSWLR 639 at 675 (NSW CA) (note that the issue was not raised on the appeal to the High Court); *Woollahra Municipal Council* v. *Westpac Banking Corporation* (1994) 33 NSWLR at 539; *Meltend Pty Ltd* v. *Restoration Clinics of Australia* Pty Ltd (1997) 145 ALR 391 (Fed. Ct.); *Hooker Corp* v. *Darling Harbour Authority* (1987) 9 NSWLR 538 at 541 (NSW SC); *DPP* v. *Kane* (1997) 140 FLR 468; also see R.J. Desiatnik, *Legal Professional Privilege in Australia* (Prospect Media, Sydney, 1999) 109–13.

[87] E.g. *National Insurance Co Ltd* v. *Whirlybird Holdings Ltd* [1994] 2 NZLR 513 (CA); *Spicers Paper (NZ) Ltd* v. *Whitcoulls Group Ltd* [1996] 1 NZLR 72 (HC).

[88] E.g. *Western Canada Investment Co* v. *McDiarmid* (1922) 66 DLR 457 (Sask. CA); *Re Stevens and Prime Minister of Canada* (1997) 144 DLR (4th) at 566–7.

[89] E.g. see Note, "Inadvertent Disclosure of Documents Subject to Attorney–Client Privilege" (1983) 82 *Mich LR* 598; Note, n. 28 above, 929–39; J.M. Grippando, "Attorney–Client Privilege: Implied Waiver Through Inadvertent Disclosure of Documents" (1985) 39 *Uni Miami LR* 511.

[90] J.H. Wigmore and J.T. McNaughton, n. 7 above, 554.

[91] E.g. C. Tapper, *Cross and Tapper on Evidence* (8th ed., Butterworths, London, 1995) 474.

[92] E.g. *R.* v. *Braham and Mason* [1976] VR 547, discussed above.

[93] Anything that calls into question the communication's privileged status by virtue of the fact of disclosure or possible loss of confidentiality, that is. Of course events may occur that raise the possible application of other exceptions to the privilege. E.g., the communications might later be used in furtherance of a crime or fraud.

[94] Compare R.J. Desiatnik, n. 86 above, 113, who says, relying on the passage from Lord Lindley MR's judgment in *Calcraft* v. *Guest* quoted above, that loss of privilege through inadvertent disclosure "is not a waiver of legal professional privilege, [though] the privilege is just as effectively ended".

Loss of privilege through waiver, as discussed in this and the next chapter, depends on more than just the fact of disclosure. It may be determined by other factors, such as considerations of fairness. Thus privilege can continue to exist despite the fact that disclosure has occurred and confidentiality has to some extent been lost, where such other factors that are taken into account militate against a finding of waiver. This was effectively the situation in *Ashburton, Goddard* v. *Nationwide Building Society* and *Derby* v. *Weldon (No.8)*.[95] The judgments in *Guiness Peat* and *Webster* v. *Chapman*, and the academic commentary to the contrary, should be questioned on this point.

SECTION III: MEANING OF PRIVILEGE WHERE IT EXISTS DESPITE DISCLOSURE

The conclusion just reached that loss of confidentiality does not automatically dictate loss of the privilege is firmly entrenched in the case law on waiver. However it does raise an interesting issue of theory. If it is possible to have privilege over confidence-breached material, then what does it mean to say that the privilege applies in such circumstances? Put another way, in what sense does the privilege still operate when confidentiality has been breached?

In order to examine this issue, it may be useful to ask another question. Can documents ever change from being privileged to unprivileged, and then back to being privileged again? It seems that in a case such as *Calcraft*, they can. In *Calcraft* privileged documents were first held by the rightful owners.[96] The documents were then accidentally disclosed and held by the opponent. Copies were made and the originals were returned. It was held that privilege existed over the original documents, but not the copies. However at the point when the opponent had possession of the original documents, could it be said that these original documents were privileged? If the documents were so privileged, then how is this possible? How can a litigant still have privilege when his opponent has possession of the relevant document? The owner of the "privileged" document could not resist disclosure as the document had already been disclosed. On the other hand, if we say the document is not privileged[97] then does it change status throughout? That is, it is first privileged, then when disclosed not privileged, then when handed back to the owner it is privileged again.

One possible answer may be to say that the document is privileged throughout, but that privilege means a bar to disclosure only while the documents are in the owner's possession. So in *Calcraft* the original document moved in and out

[95] [1991] 1 WLR 73.

[96] More accurately a predecessor in title.

[97] As seems to be the strong view of J.A. Andrews, n. 82 above, 611: "[a] second reason for regretting the reliance placed in *Calcraft* upon the primary/secondary evidence distinction is that it might imply that the privilege holder can prevent primary evidence (the original document) being adduced even if is held at the material time by the other party. It is important to note that in fact privilege at common law can never be asserted as a sword".

of possession of the owner, but its privileged status remained. This may be what was meant by Andrews when he said:

> the common law privilege gives control only so long as material is in the privilege holder's possession . . . A distinction can be drawn between the mere loss of information and loss of juridical rights in, or in respect of, that information. When an opponent gains *de facto* access to privileged material, he should not gain complete freedom to use that information. To suppose otherwise would involve confusing the mere fact that he has possession of the information with its ownership.[98]

A slightly different explanation may be that privilege is the ability to bar disclosure at the time disclosure is compelled, which may be some time in the future.[99] Thus at the time documents are being held by an opponent, the owner does not have the present ability to bar disclosure, but does have the potential to bar it in the future if he can manage to get the documents returned first. This is effectively saying that even if your opponent has your legal communications, those communications are still privileged because you have the ability to get them back and then prevent disclosure by asserting the privilege.

CONCLUSION

In determining how much disclosure is required before the privilege will be lost, some judges and writers have suggested applying the principles used in equitable breach of confidence.[100] However it would be wrong to do this. Privilege and equitable confidentiality are based on fundamentally different concerns.[101] The privilege is primarily concerned with behavioural consequences: the effect of lack of client trust on lawyer–client communications. Equitable confidentiality is not at all concerned with behavioural consequences. Rather, it is concerned with the interest a person has in keeping a matter private as against the rest of the world. Thus any disclosure to the world, however small and whoever to, affects in some small way the interest which equitable confidentiality seeks to protect.

In comparison, the privilege is concerned only with disclosure to the court or other investigative body. Leaving aside conclusions to be drawn in chapter 12 below, this is the privilege's only area of operation. Thus if there is a disclosure

98 *Ibid.* at 612, 628–9.

99 *Quaere* whether this is what J.A. Andrews, n. 82 above, 611 means when he says: "[t]he reason the [recipient of accidentally disclosed communications] will not usually be able to produce the original document is that it will have returned to the privileged party's control and, at that point, the privilege can be invoked at common law once more".

100 E.g. C. Passmore, n. 58 above 173–4. The analogy has also been used both in England (*Gotha City* v. *Sotheby's* [1998] 1 WLR at 118) and in Australia (*Woollahra Municipal Council* v. *Westpac Banking Corp.* (1994) 33 NSWLR at 540B–C, discussing *Goldberg* v. *Ng* at first instance).

101 Discussed in chapter 12 below. Also see *Hartogen Energy* v. *Australian Gas Light Co* (1992) 109 ALR 177 at 185–6 (Fed. Ct.).

to a group of people, the privilege may still be serving an important purpose by withholding this information from the court, as doing so will go some way to maintaining client confidence in the protection afforded to communications with lawyers, with all the important behavioural consequences this brings. Thus the scope of waiver arising from selective disclosure should not be aligned with the equitable confidentiality doctrine.

Confidentiality should be considered only as a factor at the time the legal communication is made. After that it should hardly ever be taken into account in determining whether communications should no longer be considered privileged.[102] The only limits may be where disclosure has been made to an agent or representative of the opponent, and the practical workability of withholding from a court a communication the contents of which are widely known.[103]

[102] Even if the privileged communication is published to almost all the world, if the privilege can still be effectively maintained before a court or other investigative body, then there is little reason not to continue to bolster candid legal communications (*contra* C. Tapper, n. 91 above, 474 and C. Passmore, n. 58 above, 174; also see *Chandris Lines* v. *Wilson & Horton Ltd* [1981] 2 NZLR 600 (HC), where this was actually the case). Witholding privileged communications from a court will have this effect, even if the information is known to the rest of the world. In fact the privilege may serve its purpose more effectively if more people are already aware of the contents of the communication. Refusing to admit into evidence publicly known communications highlights the strength of the rule, and hence may promote even more favourable behaviour as a result.

[103] As in *Harbour Inn Seafoods Ltd* v. *Switzerland General Insurance* [1990] 2 NZLR at 384.

11

Fairness-based Loss of Privilege (Waiver)

INTRODUCTION

The rules relating to partial disclosure and putting in issue, which form the core of the doctrine of "implied waiver", are generally regarded as based on a combination of implied intention and fairness considerations together.[1] Alternatively the fairness considerations are somehow seen as arising out of the intention to waive. However these cases have nothing to do with intention.[2] If anything there is an inverse relationship between the concepts. Fairness dictates that the privilege holder's intention be overridden.

The continued categorisation of these cases under the heading "waiver" leads to the misplaced use of intent-type analyses where they really have no place, as well as a failure to give proper credit to broader fairness considerations. For example in *Causton* v. *Mann Egerton (Johnsons) Ltd*[3] the majority ignored legitimate fairness considerations and upheld the privilege on the basis that they could find no implication of waiver.[4] Lord Denning's dissent shows the difficulty involved in trying to fit such cases into the traditional waiver framework when what is thought to be at issue are really basic views on what is fair between the parties.[5]

The first two sections of this chapter will examine the rules relating to partial disclosure and putting in issue. Attention will be focused on the precise role of intention and fairness considerations in the formulation of these rules. The remaining sections will examine the role and place of fairness as a consideration or criterion for loss of the privilege, and the effect that this may have on the continued operation and efficacy of the doctrine.

[1] E.g. see J.H. Wigmore and J.T. McNaughton, *Evidence in Trials at Common Law* (Little, Brown & Co., Boston, 1961) viii 635.

[2] S.B. McNicol, *Law of Privilege* (Law Book Co., Sydney, 1992) 27; C. Wright and K. Graham, *Federal Practice and Procedure* (West Publishing, St Paul, Minn., 1992) xxiv, 514; Comment, "Developments in the Law—Privileged Communications" (1985) 98 *Harv LR* 1450 at 1629.

[3] [1974] 1 All ER 453 (CA); discussed further at p. 223 below.

[4] *Ibid.* at 458f, 460g–h.

[5] Especially see *ibid.* at 458a–c.

PARTIAL DISCLOSURE

The general rule for privilege is that the parties are free to decide the extent of their waiver.[6] Loss of privilege due to partial disclosure occurs where a party introduces into evidence part of a larger body of privileged material, while not affirmatively abandoning its claim to privilege over the remainder of the information.[7] The claim for further disclosure may be of another part of the same document[8] or of different documents considered to be part of the same transaction or subject matter.[9] However this principle applies only to the use of documents at trial, and not to disclosure made on discovery.[10] It is also possible that privilege may be lost over a document by mere reference to it in an expert's report or witness statement.[11] The rule of partial disclosure may also be the rea-

[6] *Lyell* v. *Kennedy* (1884) 27 Ch.D 1 at 24 (CA); *General Accident Fire and Life Assurance Corp Ltd* v. *Tanter* [1984] 1 WLR 100 at 114F (QB).

[7] Partial disclosure without waiver of the remainder of the communication is recognised under the Evidence Act 1995 (Aust.): see *Adelaide Steamship Co Ltd* v. *Spalvins* (1998) 152 ALR 418 at 426 (Fed. Ct.); *Towney* v. *Minister for Land* (1997) 147 ALR 402 (Fed. Ct.).

[8] E.g. *Great Atlantic Insurance Co* v. *Home Insurance Co* [1981] 2 All ER 485 (CA).

[9] E.g. *General Accident Fire and Life Assurance Corp Ltd* v. *Tanter* [1984] 1 WLR at 115 ("the extent of the waiver relates to the transaction to which that evidence goes. The extent of the transaction has to be determined"); *R.* v. *Secretary of State for Transport, ex p. Factortame Ltd, The Times*, 11 Sept. 1997 (DC) (although the Court held there was no loss of privilege as the two sets of documents related to different time periods and there was no unfairness resulting). Note that in *General Accident Fire and Life Assurance Corp Ltd* v. *Tanter* Hobhouse J said the test for the extent of waiver in relation to a particular conversation was not the subject matter test. Where documents are concerned the fairness test will usually lead to a consideration of whether the documents concern the same subject matter. The possibly different approach in Canada may be to look at all the circumstances of the case to determine whether the conduct is misleading: see *Lowry* v. *Canadian Mountain Holidays Ltd* (1984) 59 BCLR 137 at 142–3 (BC SC); *Stevens* v. *Canada (Privy Council)* (1997) 144 DLR (4th) 553 at 568 (Fed. Ct.). S. 126 of the Evidence Act 1995 (Aust.) states a different test, which is that disclosure of the connected documents be "reasonably necessary to enable a proper understanding of the communication or document". For the legislative history and comments on this provision, see *Towney* v. *Minister for Land* (1997) 147 ALR at 408–9, 412–14. This provision is different from the common law test: *ibid.* at 413.

[10] *Curlex Manufacturing Pty Ltd* v. *Carlingford Australia General Insurance Ltd* [1987] 2 Qd R 335 (Qld. SC); *G.E. Capital Group Ltd* v. *Bankers Trust Co* [1995] 1 WLR 172 at 175 (CA); *The "Sagheera"* [1997] 1 Lloyd's Rep 160 (QB); *Stevens* v. *Canada (Privy Council)* (1997) 144 DLR (4th) at 567.

[11] Under r. 31.14 of the Civil Procedure Rules 1998 a party may inspect documents referred to in another party's statement of case, witness statement, witness summary, affidavit or expert's report (but see r. 35.10(4) in relation to instructions referred to in experts' reports). Under the Rules of the Supreme Court there was some difference of opinion whether this amounted to waiver: see *Clough* v. *Tameside and Glossop Health Authority* [1998] 2 All ER 971 (QB) (waiver); *Vista Maritime Inc* v. *Sesa Goa*, Mance J, 24 Oct. 1997 (no waiver); for an analysis of the pre-CPR position see I.R. Scott, "Legal Professional Privilege in 'Connected' Documents" (1998) 17 *CJQ* 365. The filing and serving of witness statements in Australia does not lead to loss of the privilege in them under the regime of s. 122 of the Evidence Act 1995 (Aust.): see *Akins* v. *Abigroup Ltd* (1998) 43 NSWLR 539 (NSW CA), and the cases cited therein; *Nilson Industrial Electronics Pty Ltd* v. *Nationale Semiconductor Corp* (1994) 48 FCR 337; *contra Complete Technology Pty Ltd* v. *Toshiba (Australia) Pty Ltd* (1994) 53 FCR 125; also see R.J. Desiatnik, Legal Professional Privilege in Australia (Prospect Media, Sydney 1999) 105–6. For the purposes of waiver under the Evidence Act 1995 (Aust.) a mere reference to legal advice in a public statement will probably not suffice as waiver: *Ampolex Ltd* v. *Perpetual Trustee Co (Canberra) Ltd* (1996) 40 NSWLR 12 at 24 (NSW SC),

son why English courts have found that the privilege is waived when lawyers disclose their reasons for advising their criminal accused clients to remain silent in response to police questioning.[12] However in relation to this last category of cases, the courts have not expressly stated whether or not this is the actual reason for the waiver in this type of situation.[13]

The rationale for this exception to the privilege is not the fact of loss of confidentiality over the disclosed part of the communications.[14] There is no necessary reason why loss of confidentiality over one part of a group of privileged materials should be considered to have the same effect in relation to confidentiality over the rest of the materials. For similar reasons the rationale is also unlikely to be that the partial disclosure evinces an intention to abandon confidentiality. For example, in *Great Atlantic Insurance Co* v. *Home Insurance Co*[15] the considerations relating to truth-garbling discussed below were sufficient to lead to loss of the privilege despite a clear intent not to lose privilege over the remaining communications. The Australian case of *Attorney-General (N.T.)* v. *Maurice*[16] similarly did not depend on an intent of any sort. The better rationale for this exception to privilege is fairness and consistency.[17] As Hobhouse J expressed the matter in *General Accident Fire and Life Assurance Corp Ltd* v. *Tanter*, "[t]he underlying principle is one of fairness in the conduct of the trial and does not go further than that".[18] It may be misleading and therefore unfair to allow one party to present only part of a privileged communication.[19] This rationale has gained wide acceptance in all common law jurisdictions and appears to be a sound one.[20]

137 ALR 28 at 34 (HCA). Nor will the mere calling of an expert witness or the insubstantial reference to his instructions lead to loss of the privilege over those instructions: *Tirango Nominees Pty Ltd* v. *Dairy Vale Foods Ltd* (1998) 156 ALR 364 (Fed Ct); *Australian Competition and Consumer Commission* v. *Australian Safeways Stores Pty Ltd* (1998) 153 ALR 393 at 434 (Fed Ct.); also see the cases cited in Desiatnik, above, 126. However the relevant statutory provision requires disclosure of the "substance of the evidence" in any case. For another useful example of this broad principle in a different context, see *Towney* v. *Minister for Land* (1997) 147 ALR at 414.

12 R. v. *Condron and Condron* [1997] 1 WLR 827; R. v. *Bowden* [1999] 1 WLR 823.

13 See J. Auburn, "Implied Waiver and Adverse Inferences" (1999) 115 *LQR* 590.

14 Comment, n. 2 above, 1633.

15 [1981] 1 WLR 529.

16 (1986) 161 CLR 475.

17 *Ibid.* at 481, 487–8, 492–3; *Duplan Corp* v. *Deering Milliken Inc* 397 F Supp 1146 at 1161–2 (DC Sth Carolina 1975); *Burnell* v. *British Transport Commission* [1956] 1 QB 187 at 190 (CA); R. v. *Secretary of State for Transport, ex p. Factortame Ltd, The Times*, 11 Sept. 1997 ("I can see no unfairness to the applicants").

18 [1984] 1 WLR at 114.

19 E.g. see J.H. Wigmore and J.T. McNaughton, n. 1 above, 635; *Great Atlantic Insurance Co* v. *Home Insurance Co* [1981] 2 All ER at 492; *Nea Katerina Maritime Co Ltd* v. *Atlantic & Great Lakes Steamship Corp* [1981] Comm LR 138 (QB); *Derby & Co Ltd* v. *Weldon (No. 10)* [1991] 1 WLR 660 at 669 (Ch.); *Re Königsberg (a bankrupt)* [1989] 3 All ER 289 (Ch.).

20 Australian courts have held that the test for loss of privilege under s. 122 of the Evidence Act 1995 (Aust.), which provides for loss of the privilege where the "substance of the evidence" has been disclosed, is a purely quantitative one: *Adelaide Steamship Co Ltd* v. *Spalvins* (1998) 152 ALR at 426; *Towney* v. *Minister for Land* (1997) 147 ALR at 412–14; *Telstra Corp* v. *BT Australasia Pty Ltd*

It should be noted that there is a tendency in the case law to assume that this is the *only* category of fairness-based waiver. This tendency can be seen among both text writers[21] and judges[22] alike. Another problem is the danger of partial disclosure developing into a formalised category divorced from its underlying rationale: that is, that courts will simply look to whether there has been a partial disclosure and fail to ask the essential question whether the partial disclosure has actually led to unfairness or prejudice.[23] This has already happened in a number of American cases in which waiver has been found even though there seems to be a lack of apparent detriment. Sometimes this is explicitly recognised,[24] however usually it is done more as a matter of oversight.[25] There are some signs of this tendency in Commonwealth cases as well. For example, in *Harbour Inn Seafoods Ltd* v. *Switzerland General Insurance*[26] the Court stated the rule that partial disclosure leads to waiver, with no mention of whether the disclosure actually caused unfairness or not.[27] In the foundation case of *Great Atlantic Insurance Co* v. *Home Insurance Co*[28] the only issue discussed was whether a partial disclosure occurred. Detriment was assumed. Fortunately, though, many cases in the Commonwealth stay closer to an investigation of the actual unfairness of the disclosure.[29] There may well be an argument for restricting the partial disclosure rule by imposing a direct requirement of unfairness or detriment.[30]

(1998) 156 ALR 634 (Fed. Ct.). This result is not necessarily dictated by the terms of the statutory provision. What amounts to the "substance of the evidence" may not be capable of simple objective assessment in isolation from the context. Also see *Ampolex Ltd* v. *Perpetual Trustee Company (Canberra) Ltd* (1996) 40 NSWLR 12 at 18–19 (SC) and R.J. Desiatnik, n. 11 above, at 159–60.

21 E.g. see J.H. Wigmore and J.T. McNaughton, n. 1 above, 635.

22 E.g. *Attorney-General (N.T.)* v. *Maurice* (1986) 161 CLR at 481, *per* Gibbs CJ and at 487–88 per Mason and Brennan JJ; but compare Deane J's apparently broader notion of fairness.

23 Note that there should be no force in the complaint that a test of actual prejudice introduces an element of *ad hoc* assessment, as opposed to the essentially fixed-rule oriented nature of the privilege. This is because the partial disclosure doctrine already assumes loss of privilege from an event occurring after the client has reposed confidence in the lawyer and in circumstances where the client would often not be aware of the danger of loss of the privilege.

24 E.g. *Nye* v. *Sage Products Inc* 98 FRD 452 at 453 (DC Ill. 1982): "[t]he papers submitted on this motion do not demonstrate that plaintiff's partial disclosure will result in some specific prejudice to the defendants . . . In defining the extent of a party's waiver of the privilege, a court is not required to determine whether the party has gained any particular tactical advantage by its partial disclosure".

25 E.g. *R.J. Hereley & Son Co* v. *Stotler & Co* 87 FRD 358 (DC Ill. 1980).

26 [1990] 2 NZLR at 383.45.

27 But compare the same judgment, *ibid.* at 384.25, possibly taking fairness into account.

28 [1981] 1 WLR 529.

29 E.g. see *Attorney-General (N.T.)* v. *Maurice* (1986) 161 CLR at 489–90, finding partial disclosure but no prejudice.

30 As can be seen in a number of American cases, such as *First Wisconsin Mortgage Trust* v. *First Wisconsin Corp* 86 FRD 160 at 174 (DC Wisc. 1980) ("fairness in this case does not require that their privilege should cease, and the Court will not require it"); *United States* v. *Aronoff* 466 F Supp at 863 ("the Government has not alleged any prejudice resulting from Aronoff's assertions about privileged communications . . . Consequently, their legal effect is to let a whisker out of the bag, but not the whole cat").

PUTTING IN ISSUE AND RELATED RULES

English civil procedure rules now provide that parties can require production of documents referred to in pleadings (now called "statements of case").[31] This may be similar to the state of the law in Australia.[32] Other Commonwealth countries may have some form of compromise whereby a party can mention a document in a pleading without losing the privilege over it; however if that party quotes from the document or otherwise relies on it they then lose the privilege.[33] "Putting in issue" refers to the situation where pleadings, although not necessarily mentioning privileged documents expressly, place a privileged communication at issue in the proceedings.

The institution of civil proceedings by a client against his solicitor constitutes an implied waiver of privilege in some jurisdictions, notably England[34] and Australia.[35] However it is difficult to find support for such a rule outside these two countries[36] and it is particularly contentious in the United States.[37] In England the rule may need to be re-assessed once the Human Rights Act 1998 comes into force.[38] Where the exception exists, it should be seen as an application of the putting in issue rule. By instituting proceedings against his lawyer the client has put in issue all materials relating to the professional conduct of that relationship. Over the last several years English courts have extended this principle[39] even to

[31] See r. 31.14 of the Civil Procedure Rules 1998.

[32] R.J. Desiatnik, n. 11 above, at 108 n. 79 states that "in Australia, a reference to the effect of a document may well be sufficient to constitute a waiver of any privilege maintained for it".

[33] *C-C Bottlers Ltd* v. *Lion Nathan* [1993] 2 NZLR at 448; *Equiticorp Industries Group Ltd* v. *Hawkins* [1990] 2 NZLR 175 at 180–1 (HC).

[34] *Lillicrap* v. *Nalder & Son (a firm)* [1993] 1 All ER 724 (CA); *Paragon Finance Plc & Ors* v. *Freshfields (a firm)* [1999] 1 WLR 1170 (CA); see J. Auburn, "Evidential Issues in Professional Negligence Litigation" (1999) 115 *LQR* 590.

[35] *Goldberg* v. Ng (1996) 185 CLR 83; *Wardrope* v. *Dunne* [1996] 1 Qd R 224 (Qld. SC).

[36] E.g. Canada or South Africa.

[37] See C. Wright and K. Graham, n. 2 above, at 516–17 (DC Conn. 1976); *People* v. *Lines* 531 P.2d 793 (Cal. SC 1975). One case supporting the rule is *Sedco International SA* v. *Cory* 683 F 2d 1201 at 1206 (8th Cir. 1982).

[38] The claimant/former client may argue that his Art. 8 right to private communications would be infringed by disclosure. In this regard see the interesting case of *MS* v. *Sweden* (1997) 3 BHRC 248, where a person who had brought a personal injury action effectively resisted disclosure of her own medical records on this basis. On the other hand the defendant/former legal representative will argue that his Art. 6(1) right to a fair hearing would be infringed by the denial of access to such evidence. It is likely that the law will remain largely unchanged. Disclosure of such evidence is necessary for a fair hearing and, to the extent that it is a derogation from Art. 8, is a necessary one and is not disproportionate to the aim it seeks to accomplish, particularly as the defendant/former legal representative previously did have access to that material, and the disclosure for the purposes of the professional negligence litigation would be circumscribed by the rule limiting use of the material outside those proceedings.

[39] *Lillicrap* v. *Nalder & Son (a firm)* [1993] 1 All ER 724 (CA) (files relating to other matters in which the same firm solicitors acted for the plaintiff); *Kershaw* v. *Whelan* [1996] 1 WLR 358 (QB) (files of another firm of solicitors who had acted for the plaintiff, these files being in the possession of the defendant firm).

the situation where the defendant is not a lawyer at all, the privileged material sought being necessary to determine a claim put in issue by the plaintiff.[40] However in *Paragon Finance Plc & Ors* v. *Freshfields (a firm)*[41] the Court of Appeal pruned back some of these developments and restricted the client–lawyer litigation putting in issue rule to the files of the defendant firm of solicitors. Finally, where the exception operates, there is often no intention to abandon privilege and no deliberate act of abandonment.[42] The scope of the loss of privilege is dependent on considerations of fairness, and often no attempt is made to evaluate intention.[43]

Another example of waiver by putting in issue is where a party pleads insufficient or inadequate legal advice.[44] In Canada[45] and the United States[46] pleadings of inadequate legal advice in various contexts have automatically led to waiver of the privilege relating to the legal advice at issue. This also commonly occurs in applications for permission to proceed with an action despite the expiration of the statutory limitation period.[47] In determining such an application the court must have regard to the steps taken to receive legal advice and the nature of such advice. Thus privileged communications are necessarily put in issue.[48] This form of waiver is used extensively in the United States.[49]

Whether the putting in issue rule is a general rule applying to any type of pleading that may put legal communications in issue is a contentious matter. It is probably seen as such a general rule in United States federal jurisdictions,[50] and in Australian common law,[51] and possibly even under the Australian fed-

[40] *Hayes* v. *Dowding* [1996] PNLR 578 (Ch D).

[41] [1999] 1 WLR 1170.

[42] E.g. *Goldberg* v. *Ng* (1996) 185 CLR at 96.

[43] *Lillicrap* v. *Nalder & Son (a firm)* [1993] 1 All ER at 729f; *Nederlandse Reassurantie Groep Holding NV* v. *Bacon & Woodrow (a firm)* [1995] 1 All ER at 986.

[44] E.g. *Nowak* v. *Sanyshyn* (1979) 23 OR (2d) 797 (Ont. HC), where the plaintiff, an elderly lady with poor English, sought to have a mortgage declared void on the basis of insufficient legal advice. The very pleading itself was sufficient to waive privilege over her legal communications relating to the transaction (*ibid.* at 800).

[45] E.g. *Harich* v. *Stamp* (1979) 27 OR (2d) 395 (Ont. CA); *Lev* v. *Lev (No 2)* (1990) 64 Man R (2d) 306 (Man. Ct. of QB); *Souter* v. *375561 B.C. Ltd.* (1995) 130 DLR (4th) 81 at 85–6 (BC CA).

[46] E.g. *Hunt* v. *Blackburn* 128 US 464, 9 S Ct 125 (1888); *United States* v. *Woodall* 438 F.2d 1317 at 1324 (5th Cir. 1970).

[47] As allowed under s. 2D of the Limitation Act 1939 (UK).

[48] *Jones* v. *G.D. Searle & Co* [1979] 1 WLR 101 (CA); see C. Passmore, *Privilege* (CLT, Sutton Coldfield, 1998) 198–200.

[49] E.g. *Byers* v. *Burleson* 100 FRD 436 at 440 (DC Cir. 1983).

[50] See cases in nn. 66–7 below.

[51] *Wardrope* v. *Dunne* [1996] 1 Qd R at 226 stands as clear authority for the proposition, holding that "when the contents of a privileged communication become the subject of a legitimate and reasonable issue in the litigation, then the privilege is lost". Also see other Australian cases cited therein, as well as the more recent cases of *Adelaide Steamship Co Ltd* v. *Spalvins* (1998) 152 ALR at 426–7, 429–30, in which the Full Federal Court doubted whether this head of waiver amounts to more than examples of partial disclosure or implied consent waiver, and *Southern Equities Corp Ltd (in liq.)* v. *Arthur Anderson and Co* (1997) 70 SASR 166 at 176, 189–93 (FC) (detailed investigation of whether pleadings put in issue a party's corporate state of mind in relation to the transactions at issue and whether legal advice contributed to that state of mind).

eral Evidence Act 1995.[52] English authority was divided on this issue.[53] However most recently the Court of Appeal has come out strongly against a generalised rule.[54] Certainly more than mere relevance to an issue in the case must be necessary to overturn the privilege, as the privilege is premised on the withholding of relevant evidence.[55] And, as stated by Bleby J in *Southern Equities Corp Ltd (in liq.)* v. *Arthur Anderson and Co*, "it is not sufficient merely to demonstrate that a party's state of mind or knowledge is in issue . . . If that were the case, privilege would almost always be waived in cases of misrepresentation, negligence and misleading and deceptive conduct where questions of a plaintiff's reliance or state of mind was in issue . . . There must be something more from which it can be shown that the legal advice in question was relevant in the formation of that state of mind or belief or that the advice itself in some way becomes an issue in the action".[56]

The rationale for the putting in issue rule is not completely clear. It should not be that such actions show an absence of the need for confidentiality,[57] because reliance on the facts conveyed by a confidential communication is not a disclosure of the communication itself.[58]

A better justification for the rule is the ground of fairness; that putting a communication in issue raises the same fairness consideration as partial disclosure, though in the pre-trial context. That is, allowing a party to mention or rely on privileged communications in pleadings but keep them privileged from production may hinder effective trial preparation and distort settlement values.[59] Further, where a party bears the burden of proof on an issue and can discharge

[52] In *New South Wales* v. *BT Australasia Pty Ltd*, Federal Court, 24 July 1998 a majority of the Full Federal Court held that the putting in issue rule may come within s. 122(1) of the Act: see the unreported judgment of Branson J at 7. Also see *Telstra Corp Ltd* v. *BT Australasia Pty Ltd* (1998) 156 ALR 634 at 648 (Fed Ct).

[53] Colman J in *Nederlandse Reassurantie Groep Holding NV* v. *Bacon & Woodrow (a firm)* [1995] 1 All ER at 987 was firmly against such a rule. He expressly rejected the application of American cases in England as "a fundamental inroad into the scope of legal professional privilege". However Jonathan Parker J in *Hayes* v. *Dowding* [1996] PNLR 578 cast doubt on that case and interpreted *Lillicrap* v. *Nalder* as authority for a broad putting in issue rule: see *Hayes* v. *Dowding* [1996] PNLR at 589D–E. He also approved of American and Australian cases which set out a broad rule, and said that the law in all three jurisdictions was "substantially the same" (*ibid.* at 594A). Also see *Muller* v. *Linsley & Mortimer (a firm)*, *The Times*, 8 Dec. 1994 (CA), a case concerning without prejudice privilege in which the Court of Appeal found the privilege waived when the plaintiff put the reasonableness of his own conduct in issue by pleading that the settlement which actually occurred was a reasonable mitigation of damage.

[54] *Paragon Finance Plc & Ors* v. *Freshfields (a firm)*[1999] 1 WLR 1170. This aspect of the case is discussed in J. Auburn, "Generalised Rules of Fairness in Evidence Law" (2000) 63 *MLR* 104.

[55] See the discussion of the American rule at p. 221 below.

[56] (1997) 70 SASR at 193.

[57] Compare J.H. Wigmore and J.T. McNaughton, n. 1 above, 855 para. 2389.

[58] This seems to be one of the reasons given by the authors of Comment, n. 2 above, 1637 n. 33. The relevance of their other reason that clients frequently discuss with their lawyers the very subject matter of litigation is doubtful.

[59] Comment, n. 2 above, 1639. In *Sicpa North America Inc* v. *Donaldson Enterprises Inc* 430 A.2d 262 (NJ Superior Ct. 1981) the court acted on a concern that a disclosure of privileged communications may have unfairly distorted settlement negotiations.

that burden only by adducing evidence of a privileged nature, then waiver may be warranted at the discovery stage.[60] While the party seeking disclosure could wait until the trial to seek to enforce waiver, this would have the detriments listed above, as well as the issue of surprise.[61]

However these explanations are not completely convincing. The party seeking disclosure is not in a worse position in terms of the information he possesses simply by virtue of knowing that the privileged material exists. Settlement values are distorted only if that party makes unfounded assumptions about the importance of the undisclosed material. It may be argued that any problems relating to the hindering of effective trial preparation and surprise should be dealt with through better civil procedure rules, rather than by manipulating and perhaps distorting evidential rules. As with partial disclosure, a requirement of actual detriment may restrict loss of privilege in this category of cases to those which truly warrant such a result.

Marcus complains that this is an inflexible application of the rule used to rob a party of the privilege as the price for raising a particular issue, irrespective of the fairness or unfairness resulting from the actual use of privileged information.[62] In support of this position it could be argued that the content of legal communications may well serve useful forensic functions in a huge variety of types of litigation, and the contribution of such information is always a matter of degree. Further, it may be noted that the privilege rule assumes the relevance of the privileged communications to the forensic process as if the material were not relevant, it could always be excluded on this basis, without resort to the privilege. Thus the use of particular pleadings alone should never lead to the loss of the privilege.

Another important argument against the putting in issue rule is that it may pervert the waiver doctrine because it rests on the unfairness of having the privilege, rather than the unfairness of the act relied upon.[63] It has been argued that if, as here, the real issue is that the existence of the privilege itself is unfair, then "distorting waiver analysis is not a promising solution"[64] and that it is better to adjust the pleading burdens or standards of proof to remedy this unfairness. This argument is misplaced. If the problem is that the existence of the privilege itself is unfair, this is the very circumstance in which the privilege should be overturned and an exception to it established.

The same writers argue that if such an exception were recognised it would not be possible to contain the logic of this reasoning.[65] This may be true of the position in the United States, where the putting in issue rule has been extended too

[60] Comment, n. 2 above, 1639.

[61] Such a rationale for putting in issue was most clearly articulated in *Nowak* v. *Sanyshyn* (1979) 23 OR (2d) at 799.

[62] See generally R.L. Marcus, "The Perils of Privilege: Waiver and the Litigator" (1986) 84 *Mich LR* 1605, 1628–33.

[63] *Ibid.* at 1630–3; Comment, n. 2 above, 1641–3.

[64] R.L. Marcus, n. 62 above, 1632.

[65] Comment, n. 2 above, 1641–2.

far. For example, in two of the leading American cases on putting in issue, *Hearn* v. *Rhay*[66] and *United States* v. *Exxon Corp*,[67] privileged communications were relevant to affirmative defences put forward, but were by no means the only evidence available. Critics are correct to describe the result in *Exxon* as "outrageous".[68] The legal communications at issue were certainly relevant to the affirmative defence raised, but the pleading itself did not squarely require their production in order to resolve the issue raised. There is a valid distinction to be drawn here between privileged communications being no more than relevant and even important to the issue pleaded, and when the issue in a pleading cannot be resolved without recourse to privileged information.

A final problem with the exception described above is that, depending on the way it is framed, it may depend on a case-by-case balancing approach.[69] However an exception which turns on the criterion of a particular pleading should surely be susceptible to rule balancing.

ANALYSIS OF THE FAIRNESS RATIONALE

One issue that applies to all exceptions is whether there is a requirement of an actual act of unfairness. Cases decided under the rules dealt with above often proceed on the assumption that unfairness can arise only from an act.[70] Some writers claim that such a requirement exists, and it has also been suggested that it is this that prevents the fairness test from getting out of control.[71] However there is no reason why the unfairness cannot come from the inherent situation or system. One possible example may be putting in issue cases. As the problem arises simply from the basic institution of a claim, it stems from the inherent unfairness of having the privilege available in such causes of action.

The tendency in some case law to assume that all unfairness within the waiver rule is act-induced rather than systemic may be due to the continued invocation of the language, if not the principles, of waiver. Waiver is closely associated with volition, whether this be the act of disclosing the privileged communications themselves, or some other voluntary act from which an intention to abandon confidentiality is implied. It is impossible to fit systemic unfairness into a waiver

[66] 68 FRD 574 (DC Wash. 1975). In this case a prisoner brought a civil claim against two prison officers for violation of constitutional civil rights. The prison officers pleaded an affirmative defence of good faith, which can be overcome by a plaintiff only if the plaintiff proves the defendants knew they were violating the plaintiff's civil rights at the time. The defendants admitted taking legal advice prior to acting, but asserted legal privilege over that advice. The court acted on what it saw as a clear case of unfairness and found a waiver of the privilege by use of the particular pleading.

[67] 94 FRD 246 (DC Cir. 1981), where Exxon defended claims of overcharging by pleading reliance on a particular governmental interpretation of the prevailing regulations.

[68] Comment, n. 2 above, 1642.

[69] See Comment, n. 2 above, 1640–1 for a detailed criticism of the rule on this basis.

[70] E.g. see *Harbour Inn Seafoods Ltd* v. *Switzerland General Insurance* [1990] 2 NZLR 381, discussed above.

[71] R.L. Marcus, n. 62 above, 1650.

analysis. The fact that exceptions to the privilege can arise from situations inherent in the litigation system heightens the need to get away from the language of waiver. This concept offers us no analytical tools with which to deal with systemic unfairness.[72]

Many writers argue against the use of fairness as a factor in determining exceptions to the privilege. Wright and Graham favour a straight test of voluntariness on the ground that this would make privilege law more predictable and efficient, albeit at the cost of sometimes being unfair.[73] They criticise the notion of a fairness test as an inherently value-ridden and political concept. However Wright and Graham's criticisms are mostly made in the context of the core waiver situation of a positive election to waive. They almost concede the relevance of fairness to cases dealt with under the broader head of implied waiver.

Another problem with using unfairness as the touchstone for the bulk of privilege exceptions may be the difficulty of distinguishing the unfairness grounding a privilege exception from the unfairness inherent in all cases where privilege is claimed and parties are deprived of relevant evidence. In both situations (unfairness which does and does not result in loss of privilege) the party asserting the privilege has chosen to make use of some information and deny the court other information. This problem is heightened if inherent or systemic unfairness is recognised as sufficient to lead to loss of the privilege. Further, it should be noted that there are a number of costs associated with broad waiver rules, such as the increased spending of resources on safeguards to reduce the risk of waiver,[74] increased litigation costs,[75] the judicial burden of administering the rule[76] and most importantly the undermining of confidence in the privilege, particularly among those not wealthy enough to pursue adequate waiver-avoidance strategies.[77]

Perhaps the most that can be said in opposition to this valid criticism of the unfairness test is that fairness is always a matter of degree, and that this should not prevent courts from making decisions about the levels of unfairness which will and will not be tolerated for the sake of other goals in the justice system. There is no natural dividing line distinguishing unacceptable impediments to truth-finding. It is easy to label any decision reached as arbitrary.

Fairness may be an essential element in exceptions to the privilege. It is difficult to justify the removal[78] of privilege as a result of the use of privileged communications where that use causes no unfairness to any of the parties. Some see unfairness as the only rationale and as the underlying basis for all waiver.[79]

[72] *Ibid.* at 1652.

[73] C. Wright and K. Graham,n. 2 above, 522.

[74] R.L. Marcus, n. 62 above, 1606.

[75] *Ibid.* at 1609–13.

[76] *Ibid.* at 1614–15.

[77] *Ibid.* at 1606, 1615.

[78] As opposed to the non-recognition.

[79] E.g. R.L. Marcus, n. 62 above, 1607, committing the common error of not splitting waiver up into its specific rules.

Given that unfairness is clearly a requirement in most exceptions to the privilege, it may be worth considering whether it could be possible to use a generalised fairness test as an all-encompassing exception to and limit on the privilege.[80] This would overcome the danger of failure to recognise different types of unfairness. For example, in *Causton* v. *Mann Egerton (Johnsons) Ltd*[81] a non-binding understanding was reached between the parties for exchange of experts' reports. After the plaintiffs produced their reports to the defendant the defendant refused to reciprocate. The case did not fit into any of the existing categories of waiver and so the privilege was upheld. However the case could have been dealt with on the basis of unfairness. The privilege could have been overturned on the ground that its continued assertion by the defendant was unfair in the circumstances.

However if fairness is used as a broad touchstone for all such privilege exceptions then this may either introduce an element of *ad hoc* balancing into the privilege or strain the distinction between *ad hoc* and rule balancing. This distinction is not clear-cut. A rule which purports to depend upon *ad hoc* balancing but is strongly guided or confined by reference to set factors may provide greater certainty of operation than a fixed test which utilises a vague standard such as that of general fairness between the parties. And conversely, the use of a broad test such as that of general fairness can, by the accumulation of precedent, develop into numerous sub-rules detailing the requirements of fairness across specific circumstances. The body of law so developed may in effect be a set of rule-balanced rules, whether the underlying test is formally described as being determined on an *ad hoc* or on a rule-balanced basis.

EFFECT ON ABSOLUTENESS OF THE PRIVILEGE

The current rule of implied waiver seriously undermines the absoluteness and predicability of the privilege. This is because many of the possible circumstances which may give rise to implied waiver cannot be known or defined in advance. A ready example may be found in a recent leading case on waiver, *Goldberg* v. *Ng*,[82] discussed above. In that case the client[83] objected to disclosing documents to an inquiry as he was keen to retain confidentiality in them. He agreed to submit the documents on the basis that confidentiality and the privilege would be retained. Privilege was later found to have been waived by the disclosure of the documents to the inquiry. The result meant that a clear expectation of confidentiality had been disappointed, despite the fact that the disclosure was made only in reliance on that expectation. Many similar examples can be given.

80 I.e. just have two exceptions to privilege—true implied waiver and unfairness.

81 [1974] 1 All ER 453.

82 (1996) 185 CLR 83; see p. 206 above.

83 Actually a lawyer being sued by his own client.

It should however be possible to predict the application of the rules discussed above in the majority of situations. Parties should be able to see in advance when they are putting privileged communications in issue in a proceeding, or that their partial disclosure of some material may threaten the continued secrecy of other related information. These rules are usually triggered by an active decision of a party, and a vigilant lawyer should be alert to such effects. One immediate problem of advance prediction of the operation of these rules is that some exceptions may turn on inherent or systemic unfairness in the litigation. A wider and more serious problem is that, even though most of these exceptions must be triggered by a specific voluntary act of a party, people other than the party may have authority to perform the act which leads to loss of the privilege. The lawyer has wide power to perform acts which deprive his client of the privilege. Lawyers have ostensible authority to bind their clients in any matter arising in or incidental to litigation, and this may lead to loss of the privilege even though the express wishes of the client are that privilege be maintained.[84] The courts seem very keen to uphold the principle of ostensible authority, and place great importance on the need for parties to litigation to be able to rely on representations made by their opponent's solicitors. However the importance placed on this consideration may seem odd given the absence of any requirement of actual reliance.

As well as loss of privilege caused by a party's lawyer, there are other circumstances in which the safe operation of the privilege is beyond the control or even knowledge of the privilege-holding party. For example, in some cases representatives such as the trustee in bankruptcy,[85] liquidator[86] or personal representative of an estate[87] may cause the party he is representing to lose its privilege. Such possibilities must diminish the expectation a client holds of the confidentiality of his communications. Finally, with the danger of a largely *ad hoc* and improperly articulated fairness test, there is a risk that courts may simply order disclosure because the material is important.[88] An example of this may be the tendency of some courts to find waiver due to partial disclosure without insisting on actual detriment,[89] as discussed above.

[84] E.g. as in *Causton* v. *Mann Egerton (Johnsons) Ltd* [1974] 1 All ER 453 at 457 and *Great Atlantic Insurance Co* v. *Home Insurance Co* [1981] 2 All ER at 492.

[85] *Re Königsberg (a bankrupt)* [1989] 3 All ER 289.

[86] *Re Stanhill Consolidated Ltd* [1967] VR 749 (Vic. SC); *Commissioner for Corporate Affairs (WA)* v. *Eastoe* (1989) 15 ACLR 694 (WA SC); *Re Dallhold Investments Pty Ltd* (1994) 130 ALR 287.

[87] *Chant* v. *Brown* (1849) 7 Hare 79, 68 ER 32; *Doe d. Marriott* v. *Hertford* (1849) 19 LJQB 526.

[88] R.L. Marcus, n. 62 above, 1649.

[89] E.g. *Nye* v. *Sage Products Inc* 98 FRD at 453; *R.J. Hereley & Son Co* v. *Stotler & Co* 87 FRD 358 (DC Ill. 1980); *Harbour Inn Seafoods Ltd* v. *Switzerland General Insurance* [1990] 2 NZLR at 383.45.

THE EFFECTS OF WAIVER: TOTAL OR PARTIAL ABROGATION

The final issue that needs to be dealt with relates to the effects of waiver on the privilege. Does it remove only some of the effects of the privilege, or does it remove all of them? It may seem obvious that waiver, or the different rules traditionally categorised under that name, should operate totally to destroy legal professional privilege, leaving the relevant communication in the same position, and with the same effect, as if no privilege had arisen in the first place.[90] As one writer describes it: "perpetual extinction of a privilege holder's common law and equitable rights".[91]

Thus it may come as some surprise to see that a leading Australian evidence text, the Australian Cross on Evidence, says simply that waiver "does not render the privileged communication unprivileged".[92] McNicol's *Law of Privilege* explains this apparent contradiction.[93] She says that legal professional privilege is a rule that leads to numerous distinct consequences, and that waiver operates on certain consequences only. She cites a number of cases in support of these propositions, most of which are Australian. For convenience this will be referred to as the "Australian view" of privilege and waiver, although obviously not all Australian writers and judges would subscribe to this view. This view was also used as an argument by the *amicus curiae* in the *Derby Magistrates* case[94] as a reason for allowing disclosure.

The Australian view of the effect of waiver should be rejected. Privilege is an all or nothing status. If it applies, it carries with it all the consequences of the rule. If it does not apply, none of the consequences of the rule apply. There is no middle ground. However, given the eminence of the texts which have endorsed the Australian view, it may be necessary to take some time to examine the bases for their conclusions, and the logical steps involved.

Much of the impetus behind the Australian view of waiver comes from the Victorian case of *Re Stanhill Consolidated Ltd.*[95] Section 367 of the state companies legislation[96] provided that companies inspectors shall not require lawyers to give evidence of "privileged communications". The issue before the

[90] Although there is still a relevant theoretical difference between an exception and the absence of a substantive rule; the former may induce disclosures with the promise of confidentiality.

[91] N.H. Andrews, "The Influence of Equity Upon the Doctrine of Legal Professional Privilege" (1989) 105 *LQR* 608 at 623.

[92] D. Byrne and J.O. Heydon, *Cross on Evidence: Fourth Australian Edn.* (Butterworths, Sydney, 1991) 688.

[93] S.B. McNicol, n. 2 above, 33 ff.

[94] "The order for disclosure does not mean that the privilege has come to an end: it could be cited in any related civil proceedings": *R.* v. *Derby Magistrates' Court, ex p. B* [1996] 1 AC at 494E, *per* Mr Stephen Richards as *amicus curiae*. If a judge were to take this step the better explanation would be that the disclosure had destroyed the privilege; however it nonetheless remained open for the judge to impose conditions on the future use of that information.

[95] [1967] VR 749 (Vic. SC).

[96] Companies Act 1961 (Vict.).

court was whether waiver of the privilege by the liquidator meant the communication was no longer privileged for the purpose of section 367: in other words, whether privilege-waived communications could still be described as "privileged" for the purpose of section 367.

Menhennitt J held that privileged communications are communications passing on a privileged occasion and that waiver does not take the communication out of this category, but merely affects certain consequences that would otherwise flow from the fact that the communication is privileged. On this basis he decided that waiver has no application to the operation of section 367. The other consequence still to flow from privilege-waived communications, according to Menhennitt J, is that they cannot be used to ground a defamation claim. An important case relied on by him is *Minter* v. *Priest*.[97] In that case Lord Atkin held that privilege still applies to a communication to protect it from grounding a defamation claim, even once the privilege is waived.[98] Lord Buckmaster makes a clear statement to the same effect.[99] *Gatley on Libel and Slander* asserts the opposite, saying that privilege-waived communications do not benefit from qualified privilege.[100] However there is no reasoning offered by *Gatley* and the authority it relies upon is vague.[101] This issue is quite separate from the debate in the case on whether legal communications benefit from absolute or qualified privilege from defamation.[102]

The result reached in *Minter* v. *Priest* was correct. However the interpretation of the meaning of the judgment in *Re Stanhill* is not. *Minter* v. *Priest* dealt with the requirements and effects of qualified privilege. Menhennitt J in *Re Stanhill* misinterprets this as discussing legal professional privilege as well. This mistake is then picked up by McNicol, who uses it to base a broader theory which not even Menhennitt J fully expounded.

Privilege-waived communications can still attract some of the effects of qualified privilege from defamation, but this has nothing whatsoever to do with legal professional privilege. Much of the problem in this area comes from the confusing of the two privilege rules, legal professional privilege and qualified privilege from defamation. This confusion is not helped by a lack of clarity at times within the judgments themselves. For example there is significant reference to

[97] *Minter* v. *Priest* [1930] AC 558 (HL); for the use made of this in *Re Stanhill Consolidated Ltd* see Menhennitt J in [1967] VR at 751–2.

[98] [1930] AC at 579–80.

[99] *Ibid*. at 570. Note though that the real issue in *Minter* v. *Priest* may have been whether the privilege was actually waived, rather than the effect of any waiver. There were two recipients of the communication in issue. The privilege may have been waived with respect to only one of these recipients. It is possible therefore that the privilege was effectively not waived as the other recipient could still claim it (see *ibid*. at 568).

[100] P.S. Lewis, *Gatley on Libel and Slander* (8th edn., Sweet & Maxwell, London, 1981) para. 1212 n. 56; also see R.L. McEwen and P.S. Lewis, *Gatley on Libel and Slander* (7th edn., Sweet & Maxwell, London, 1974) para. 1131 n. 47.

[101] It is difficult to find any direct authority supporting this proposition.

[102] *More* v. *Weaver* [1928] 2 KB 520 (CA) held that it was absolutely privileged, but *Minter* v. *Priest* effectively overruled it and held that the privilege was qualified.

"privilege" *simpliciter* without distinguishing between the two. It seems to have been assumed that the two go together.[103]

Qualified privilege in defamation operates completely separately and has a different basis from legal professional privilege. One category of qualified privilege is composed of relationships considered to require such treatment, such as judicial communications or parliamentary communications. This has nothing to do with the rule of legal professional privilege, but operates side-by-side with it and is dependant on similar conditions.[104] The issue of qualified privilege in defamation arises only after legal professional privilege has been waived.[105] If legal professional privilege is not waived then the client may prevent his lawyer from disclosing a professional and potentially defamatory communication.[106]

The second main support cited by Menhennitt J in *Re Stanhill Consolidated Limited* for the proposition that privilege-waived communications are still privileged is the concept of partial waiver. Partial waiver has been discussed above. Menhennitt J's argument is that the existence of partial waiver shows that waiver does not destroy all the consequences of privilege.[107] However Menhennitt J's argument is flawed. The effect of partial waiver is that part of a communication remains privileged while another part does not. The privilege itself still has all-or-nothing status. For those parts of the communication where the privilege has been waived, there are no remaining effects of the lost privilege.

Menhennitt J's decision and reasoning was considered by Sackville J, of the Australian Federal Court in *Re Dallhold Investments Pty Ltd*.[108] This case also concerned a purported waiver by a liquidator of the company's privilege. Sackville J followed *Re Stanhill* and interpreted Menhennitt J's decision as purely turning on the construction of the relevant statutory provision in that case, stating that:

> Menhennitt J construed s. 367 as laying down its own rule concerning communications which were privileged at the time they took place. The section simply said . . . that no inspector should require disclosure of such communications. In the learned

[103] Only Lord Atkin dealt with this well. He said that there are two separate protections over lawyer–client communications, which arise from "entirely distinct rights".

[104] Qualified privilege in defamation may in some respects be broader. E.g. it concentrates on the fact that a lawyer and a client were involved and it is not necessary that the content of the communication relate to legal advice.

[105] E.g. see *Minter* v. *Priest* [1930] AC at 579–80, *per* Lord Atkin.

[106] *Ibid.* at 584, *per* Lord Atkin: if "the evidence is admissible, then the contest as to protection from disclosure is over". One interesting question posed but not answered by Lord Warrington in *Minter* v. *Priest* is the extent to which a litigant can prevent the disclosure of professional communications where such communications do not benefit from qualified privilege due to the existence of express malice. The answer is straightforward. If the express malice does not amount to a crime or fraud, then the communication is still privileged. The potentially higher standard of propriety for assertion of qualified privilege in defamation cannot be used as a means of raising the standard in evidence law.

[107] *Re Stanhill Consolidated Limited* [1967] VR at 752.

[108] (1994) 130 ALR 287 (Fed. Ct.).

judge's view, no subsequent waiver of legal professional privilege could affect the fact that the communications were privileged at the time they took place.[109]

However this is wrong. The provision at issue in *Re Stanhill* can be read this way only if one pretends that there is no common law waiver rule. The word "privileged" in the provision must be taken to include within it all of the rules that go to make up the privilege, including the rules relating to waiver. There is also no reason to read into the relevant provision a narrow temporal limit.

Perhaps the most worrying reason advanced for the divisible nature of the privilege is, it is claimed, that the privilege offers protection not just from disclosure in court, but also from disclosure to anyone in any circumstance. Therefore, it is argued, privilege-waived communications still benefit from this latter protection. This is completely wrong. Subject, of course, to what will be said below in relation to inadvertent disclosure, legal professional privilege protects communications from legal compulsion only. It does not offer any further protection. The latter effect cited comes from other principles, including equity and ethical rules. It has nothing to do with legal professional privilege.

The last support for the concept of a divisible privilege is the "once privileged, always privileged" rule. McNicol cites both McHugh J in *Gianarelli* v. *Wraith*[110] and Stevenson J in *Hobbs* v. *Hobbs and Cousens*[111] in support of her thesis, and seems to be arguing that once a communication is privileged waiver does not take away all of the consequences of this privileged status, just some of them. This is, like the others above, a seriously flawed argument. The "once privileged, always privileged" rule has nothing to do with whether or not there are any residuary effects imposed by privilege-waived communications. The former rule just refers to the effect of the privilege, and goes some way to defining the circumstances in which the privilege will not be lost. This rule in no way detracts from the all-or-nothing nature of the privilege. If the privilege is waived, the "once privileged, always privileged" rule is irrelevant as there is nothing for it to operate on.

The cases cited by McNicol in no way advance her argument. In *Hobbs* v. *Hobbs and Cousens* the "once privileged, always privileged" rule is used only to establish that a party cannot disclose a communication to a taxing officer and still withhold it from an opponent. This is really just a restatement of the basic waiver rule. And in *Gianarelli* v. *Wraith*, McHugh J just uses *Hobbs* v. *Hobbs and Cousens* and the "once privileged, always privileged" rule to find that as a general rule, legal professional privilege applies in proceedings before taxing officers.[112] He was not indicating that there is any residuary privilege left after a waiver has occurred.

It seems clear that the theory of divisible privilege propounded in Australia is wrong in both principle and authority. Some of the confusion may have arisen

109 *Ibid*. at 292.
110 (1991) 98 ALR 1.
111 [1960] P 112.
112 *Gianarelli* v. *Wraith* (1991) 98 ALR at 7.

from the use of the traditional concept of waiver. It is hoped that once this area is re-categorised as "loss of privilege" there will be no room for argument about the effect of the operation of these rules.

CONCLUSION

The term "waiver" is unhelpful and should be discarded. There are many different meanings which could be ascribed to it, none of which accurately describes what binds together the rules contained within it, and what separates these rules from other privilege derogations not so described. Currently there are three broad groups of rules dealt with as "waiver" of the privilege: true intent-based rules, non-intent confidentiality-based rules and non-intent fairness-based rules. It is questionable whether the first group, true intent-based rules, should continue to be recognised at all. The second group, non-intent confidentiality-based rules, should be abolished as privilege exceptions and subsumed under the substantive requirement of confidentiality. This leaves only the middle category of non-intent fairness-based rules.

Therefore it is possible to say that there is no such thing as "waiver" in privilege law. Instead there are numerous different exceptions to privilege which depend on different fairness considerations such as partial disclosure, problems arising from putting in issue and related rules such as the rule dealing with client–lawyer litigation. All of these are separate, though in some cases similar, rules which have nothing to do with the affirmative relinquishment or abandonment of a right.

The current system of classifying cases under waiver leads to the intrusion of spurious intent-based arguments and makes it difficult to give proper recognition and effect to systemic unfairness caused by the privilege. Most importantly, it obscures the true scope and bounds of the privilege and leads to a mistaken view of its fundamental nature. Once the waiver doctrine is re-evaluated in the manner described above it will become apparent that legal professional privilege is not an absolute rule which may never be derogated from. Rather it is a complex system of rules with numerous exceptions and significant flexibility.

The rule of privilege bears little relation to its exception of waiver. The two rules have different purposes and structures and to some extent undermine each another. The only link is that they operate in respect of the same material. That is, waiver concerns situations in which the privilege is displaced. The privilege itself is concerned with maintaining the faith of clients in the sanctity of their legal communications. Because of this the substantive rule emphasises predictability of operation and seeks to achieve this through inflexible criteria. Waiver on the other hand is a bundle of rules that usually arise from basic notions of fairness, as illustrated above. Being grounded in first principles fairness, it is more flexible in its operation, and therefore its application cannot be predicted with the same certainty. Needless to say, this partly defeats the purpose of the substantive rule. Other exceptions to the privilege rule do not suffer from this problem.[113] However while this may seem illogical, the inconsistency between the rule and its exception serves a valuable purpose. It allows the strictness of the privilege to be upheld in theory at least, thereby preserving clients' expectations, while using the exception to ameliorate the harshness of the substantive rule. This is, to a certain extent, living a lie. But it is a lie that seems to keep everyone happy.

[113] E.g., the rationale for the crime-fraud exception is traditionally stated as being that a communication between a client and a lawyer for the purpose of furthering a crime or fraud is not a communication made for the purpose of seeking legal advice, and hence outside the scope of the privilege's protection. By adopting this rationale the goals of the substantive rule and the exception are not seen to be in irreconcilable conflict.

12

Inadvertent disclosure

INTRODUCTION

This chapter will discuss the admissibility of inadvertantly disclosed privileged communications. There are at least three sub-issues which arise in considering this problem: first, whether there is or should be a loss of privilege over the original privileged documents on their disclosure to an opponent or on the opponent possessing or having possessed a copy of the document (this is generally regarded as an issue of waiver of privilege over the original documents, and was discussed in Chapter 10 above); secondly, the status of copies of privileged documents in the hands of an opponent and whether those documents are privileged or otherwise inadmissible; thirdly, the possible means of restricting use of documents already disclosed.

Much of the discussion will relate to the inadvertent disclosure of documents. However it should be noted at the outset that the term "inadvertent disclosure" is used in many different ways.[1] Further, this chapter will not look at the converse situation of whether copies of unprivileged documents sent to a lawyer for the purpose of legal advice are privileged.[2] Finally, unfortunately there is no space in the present discussion for an analysis of the effect of the rule of hearsay on the admissibility of secondary evidence of privileged documents.[3]

It should also be noted that in England an important opportunity to resolve this vexed area of law may recently have been missed. The original draft of the new Civil Procedure Rules provided that privileged documents inadvertently disclosed could not be used if the solicitor receiving the documents should have realised, having regard to the manner and circumstances of the disclosure, that a mistake had occurred.[4] However the revised draft rules removed this

[1] See C. Wright and K. Graham, *Federal Practice and Precedent* (West Publishing, St Paul, Minn, 1992) xxvia, 542–3. For an interesting description of the way these issues usually arise in large-scale commercial litigation, see S. Zindel, "Waiver and Legal Professional Privilege: *Derby* v. *Weldon*" [1991] NZLJ 132, written by one of the practitioners responsible for organising the discovery which gave rise to the inadvertent disclosures in the *Derby* v. *Weldon* litigation.

[2] R. v. *Board of Inland Revenue, ex p. Goldberg* [1988] 3 All ER 248 (QBD); discussed in A.A.S. Zuckerman, "Evidence" (1988) *All ER Annual Review* 135; *Dubai Bank* v. *Galadari* [1989] 3 All ER 769 (CA); *Australian Federal Police* v. *Propend Finance* (1997) 141 ALR 545.

[3] In *Bell* v. *David Jones Ltd* (1948) 49 SR (NSW) 223 at 227, the New South Wales Court of Appeal held that, while in the ordinary case failure to answer a subpoena to produce documents will not entitle the party who issued the subpoena to adduce secondary evidence, where the refusal was on grounds of privilege secondary evidence may be admissible.

[4] See M. Hemsworth, "Disclosure Under the New Civil Procedure Rules" [1998] *New LJ* 1300 at 1331.

provision. The final form of the rule is rule 31.20 of the Civil Procedure Rules 1998, which provides that:

> Where a party inadvertently allows a privileged document to be inspected, the party who has inspected the document may use it or its contents only with the permission of the court.

This leaves the issue completely to the discretion of the court, with nothing to guide its exercise other than the general factors guiding the exercise of all discretion under the Rules.[5] The Practice Direction accompanying Part 31 does not expand upon rule 31.20. Thus in England there is little alternative but to look at the pre-existing case law for some clues about the way the issue may now be resolved in that jurisdiction under the new Rules. In any case the early indications are that the pre-existing rules will largely remain. In *Breeze* v. *John Stacey & Sons Ltd*[6] the Court of Appeal applied the same developed principles to a case of inadvertant disclosure arising under the Civil Procedure Rules and effectively rejected a submission that the priorities of the new regime should lead to a result more favourable to the continued maintenance of the privilege.

This book concerns derogations from the privilege. Specifically it seeks to analyse the conditions under which derogations from the privilege may be recognised. The admission of secondary evidence of privileged communications is a literal derogation from the privilege: the rule allows in evidence of the contents of the privileged communication. The accepted thinking in this area is that the privilege is powerless to prevent this derogation, but that relief can be obtained from the separate rule of equitable breach of confidence. However it will be argued in this chapter that much of the relief granted over secondary evidence of privileged communications cannot be derived from the equitable rule. Rather, it must stem from the privilege itself. The privilege may be much stronger than previously thought.

SECTION I: THE UNRESOLVED PROBLEM

Calcraft v. *Guest* and *Ashburton* v. *Pape*

The position established by the two leading cases of *Calcraft* v. *Guest*[7] and *Ashburton* v. *Pape*[8] is well set out in evidence texts[9] and need not be described in detail here. In the simplest terms possible, the law following these cases is as follows:

[5] I.e. the overriding objective in r. 1.
[6] *The Times*, 8 July 1999.
[7] [1898] 1 QB 759.
[8] [1913] 2 Ch 469.
[9] E.g. C. Tapper, *Cross and Tapper on Evidence* (8th edn., Butterworths, London, 1995) 481–3.

(i) if a party has in his possession a copy of a privileged document belonging to the other party, the holder of the copy may use it in evidence despite the fact that the original is privileged (*Calcraft* v. *Guest*);
(ii) however the copy, as well as being a copy of a privileged document, is also a document obtained in breach of the equitable rule of confidence, and as such the owner of the original (legally privileged) document may apply to a court for an injunction to prevent use of the document obtained through breach of confidence (*Ashburton* v. *Pape*).[10]

This latter action is taken under the equitable doctrine and is entirely independent of the privilege rule. Two separate and distinct rules coincidentally apply to the same document. Relief sought under the equitable doctrine just happens to have an effect which greatly serves the purpose of the privilege rule by effectively filling a gap in the application of the privilege.

The two cases establishing this state of the law are themselves not enormously complex. However as certain key facts and conclusions have become the subject of controversy, which has then impacted on the differing views of the state of the law, it may be useful briefly to describe the cases.

The documents in issue in *Calcraft* v. *Guest*[11] related to a previous action a century ago involving substantially the same issue as that being presently litigated. After judgment was given in the present action, the unsuccessful defendant came into possession of the documents from the previous action, which had belonged to the predecessor in title of the present plaintiff. Copies were made and the originals were ultimately returned. On appeal from the decision that had been made in the court below without knowledge of or reference to the then undiscovered documents, two separate issues were argued before the Court of Appeal: first, whether the original documents, having fallen into the hands of the opponent but then recovered, were still privileged; secondly, if the originals were privileged and so could not be disclosed, whether the defendant was entitled to produce the copies in evidence. The Court of Appeal held that the originals were still privileged, but that the copies could be produced in evidence.

In *Ashburton* v. *Pape*[12] privileged documents belonging to Lord Ashburton, the plaintiff in a pending bankruptcy action, were obtained by Pape, the defendant in the same action. Pape copied the documents and returned the originals. The trial judge ordered that Pape return all originals of privileged documents and restrained him from using any of the copies or information contained therein, *except* for the purpose of the present bankruptcy proceedings. Lord Ashburton appealed on the ground that the exception in the trial judge's injunction was wrong and should be removed. The validity of the main part of the

[10] Query though whether the same result would be achieved in Scots law. Professor Black says that in Scots law an enforceable obligation of confidence could probably not be forced on the recipient of confidential information against his will, and that such an obligation would require the consent of the obligor: see R. Black, "A Question of Confidence" [1982] *J. Law Soc Scotland* 299 at 300.

[11] [1898] 1 QB 759.

[12] [1913] 2 Ch 469.

injunction was not challenged or discussed before the Court of Appeal, and counsel for Pape did not even argue the appeal at all. Thus there was no dispute whether the original documents were privileged, or whether Lord Ashburton was entitled to recover possession of the copies.

It is important to realise that *Ashburton* v. *Pape* was decided with full awareness of the meaning and implication of *Calcraft* v. *Guest*. As Tapper points out,[13] Cozens-Hardy appeared in both cases.[14] This fact is significant[15] as it reinforces the falsity of the claimed clash between the cases. *Ashburton* v. *Pape* was decided as a deliberate limit on the effect of *Calcraft* v. *Guest*. The latter case played a major part in both the argument and decision in the former case.[16]

Matthews interprets *Ashburton* v. *Pape* as holding only that the fact that material is admissible evidence is no bar to the grant of an injunction, and not that injunctions may have an effect at trial.[17] This is certainly the impression conveyed by the Law Reports headnote to the case,[18] as well as part of the judgment of Swinfen Eady LJ.[19]

However this limited reading of the case does not match its essential facts. The exception at issue on appeal was as follows: "except for the purpose of the pending proceedings in the defendant . . . Pape's bankruptcy and subject to the direction of the Bankruptcy Court". The point of the appeal was to extend the injunction to the litigation and despite any court order. The Law Reports headnote is slightly misleading in this respect. The proper meaning of the issue being decided was best expressed by Cozens-Hardy MR, when he stated the issue as follows:

> Now, the question is raised that that exception is wrong, and that the injunction ought to go to the full extent *until the trial of the action*, namely, from publishing or making use of any of the copies of letters or information contained therein.[20]

Thus the case was concerned with the proper limits to, and effect of, injunctive relief, rather than with whether injunctive relief could apply over material that also happened to be admissible.

[13] C. Tapper, "Privilege and Confidence" (1972) 35 *MLR* 83 at 85.

[14] As counsel arguing *Calcraft* v. *Guest* and as the Master of the Rolls deciding *Ashburton* v. *Pape*.

[15] *Contra* A.L.E. Newbold, "Inadvertent Disclosure in Civil Proceedings" (1991) 107 *LQR* 99 at 113 ("Mr Tapper thinks it unlikely that Lord Cozens-Hardy would 'wittingly have subverted' *Calcraft*. It is rather strange to attribute to counsel arguing a case on behalf of a client the views which he submits on behalf of the client's cause. The fact that he argues a certain proposition on behalf of a client is no indication that he 'believes' in it").

[16] *Ashburton* v. *Pape* [1913] 2 Ch at 471 (argument) and 473, 474 (judgments); also see *Derby & Co. Ltd* v. *Weldon (No. 8)* [1991] 1 WLR at 77–8, *per* Vinelott J.

[17] P. Matthews, "Breach of Confidence and Legal Privilege" (1981) 1 *Legal Studies* 77 at 87–8.

[18] "It is no answer . . . to say that the copies . . . will be wanted in pending proceedings".

[19] *Ashburton* v. *Pape* [1913] 2 Ch at 477: "[t]he fact, however, that a document, whether original or copy, is admissible in evidence is no answer".

[20] *Ibid*. at 472.

Before leaving *Ashburton* v. *Pape* it is worth noting that there has been some dispute over the meaning of a particular passage in the judgment of Cozens-Hardy MR. The passage is as follows:

> It seems to me that, although Pape has had the good luck to obtain a copy of these documents which he can produce without a breach of this injunction, there is no ground whatever in principle why we should decline to give the plaintiff the proper protection which in my view is his right as between him and Pape.[21]

Commentators have in the past had trouble with this passage.[22]

However the difficulty caused by this passage has been overstated.[23] This particular passage is not crucial to an understanding of the ratio of the case. The other two judges were perfectly clear about the relationship between the case before them and *Calcraft* v. *Guest*. These other judgments make the same point in unambiguous terms.[24]

The passage quoted above would be perfectly clear if one were to excise the words "without a breach of this injunction". In any case, the passage must be read in light of the previous half-page of the same judgment. It seems clear from this that Cozens-Hardy MR is doing no more than reconciling the present relief with the rule in *Calcraft*, and that "this injunction" is simply a sloppy reference to the order of Neville J. That is, Cozens-Hardy MR is simply saying that Pape's good luck in having possession of copies means he could produce them in the bankruptcy proceedings pursuant to the trial judge's order, that order being deliberately made in conformity with the rule in *Calcraft* v. *Guest*; but that is no reason for the Court of Appeal to stop there, as this court (the Court of Appeal) can still grant the relief asked for without infringing upon the principle in *Calcraft* v. *Guest*.

The explanation of this passage offered by Andrews[25] is curious. Andrews says that Pape did actually get the copied documents into evidence in the bankruptcy proceedings, thereby frustrating Ashburton's legal victory. Therefore, Andrews says, the quoted passage should be read only as saying that Ashburton has the right to the injunction as a matter of law, but then noting that in this case Pape has had the good fortune of getting the material into evidence before relief was ordered. However there is no indication of this from the report of the case, which makes absolutely no suggestion that the copies went into evidence before the granting of the injunction. The tenor of the other two judgments, both of which could also have been revised afterwards in accordance with the practice

[21] *Ibid.* at 473.

[22] E.g. see C. Tapper, n. 13 above, at 86; J.A. Andrews (1989) 616–17; J.D. Heydon, *Evidence Cases and Materials* (2nd edn., Butterworths, London, 1984) 408; P. Matthews, n. 17 above, at 86–7.

[23] E.g. J.A. Andrews, n. 22 above, 618 says that the entire issue of copy documents was "delphically discussed in *Ashburton*".

[24] Particularly the judgment of Kennedy LJ, [1913] 2 Ch at 474.

[25] J.A. Andrews, n. 22 above, 616–18.

of the Law Reports,[26] makes clear that the copied documents never got into evidence.

Subsequent Debate

Following *Ashburton* v. *Pape* the matter seemed settled. It was considered that two separate doctrines were at play. If the remedies sought were not within those associated with the privilege, relief may be sought under the rule governing breach of confidence. While there may possibly be overlap, there was thought to be no conflict of doctrines.

Over the last two decades there has been significant debate over the nature of the jurisdiction under which relief is granted in this area. This is much more than a semantic debate about jurisdiction. If the relief sought is solely equitable it may not be capable of application to all of the disclosures. Further, if the equitable jurisdiction can apply, it will do so only on certain terms. That is, there are some factors associated with the grant of an equitable injunction that are very difficult to exclude. However if the ground for granting relief is some ancillary non-equitable jurisdiction to support the legal rule of privilege, then the scope of the relief may be significantly wider, and the factors governing the granting of relief may be different. Alternatively, if the basis for relief is a common law rule of fairness, then the principles governing relief may be different again.

Two recent cases seem to have fused the equitable doctrine with the rule of legal professional privilege to create a single ground of relief, stronger than each of the individual components. In *Goddard* v. *Nationwide Building Society*,[27] Nourse LJ seems to have rested the injunction granted on both the equitable doctrine and the privilege. He said that "the equitable jurisdiction . . . can prevail over the rule of evidence only in cases where privilege can be claimed".[28]

Andrews interprets Nourse LJ's statement as meaning that the equitable jurisdiction in such cases bars evidence at trial. Andrews describes Nourse LJ as having decided that "[e]quity will enable the privilege holder . . . to restrain a person from adducing this information as evidence".[29] Thus the equitable rule appears to meld together with the legal (privilege) rule. This view has been the subject of severe criticism, which will be discussed in the next section below. However Andrews' interpretation of Nourse LJ's judgment is wrong. Nourse LJ is not saying that the equitable jurisdiction operates to restrain the adducing of

[26] J.A. Andrews, n. 22 above, at 617–618 says that "[p]erhaps one should explain the fact that the Master of the Rolls made this point in conclusive terms in the Law Reports, but equivocally in the other reports, by recalling that his revision of the Law Reports' proofs would have occured much later than the hearing of the appeal. By the stage of proof-reading, it might have become clear that in fact Pape had precisely this good fortune".

[27] [1986] 3 All ER 264 (CA), noted in T.R.S. Allan, "Privilege and Confidentiality: Secondary Evidence and Third Parties" [1987] CLJ 43.

[28] [1986] 3 All ER at 271.

[29] J.A. Andrews, n. 22 above, 619–20.

evidence in court. This can be seen in a crucial sentence shortly after the one quoted earlier, in which he says:

> I do not believe that equity would restrain a litigant who already had a record of such a communication in his possession from using it for the purposes of his litigation. It cannot be the function of equity to accord a de facto privilege to communications in respect of which no privilege can be claimed.[30]

What Nourse LJ may really be saying in this crucial passage in his judgment is that the party asserting privilege will obtain fully effective relief only when he employs the equitable jurisdiction coupled with the application of legal professional privilege. The importance of this view will be discussed below.[31] However Nourse LJ described the entire solution sought by the privilege holder as an assertion of "the equitable jurisdiction".[32]

The apparent fusion of equitable and legal rules by Nourse LJ has an important effect on the rule which results. Nourse LJ held that the right to relief does not depend in any way on the conduct of the recipient of the document.[33] This factor has in other cases been seen as an important consideration in the granting of equitable relief.[34] Further, he also held that relief under this jurisdiction is not discretionary.[35] This issue will be dealt with in the separate section on remedies.[36]

In *English & American Insurance Ltd* v. *Herbert Smith*[37] Browne-Wilkinson V-C first stated his opinion that *Ashburton* v. *Pape* and *Goddard* were correctly decided,[38] then went on to say:

> I therefore hold that I am bound by the decisions in *Lord Ashburton* v. *Pape* and *Goddard* v. *Nationwide Building Society* to grant the relief sought against both defendants. I confess that it is a result which gives me some satisfaction. Legal professional privilege is an important safeguard of a man's legal rights. It is the basis on which he and his advisers are free to speak as to matters in issue in litigation and otherwise without fear that it will subsequently be used against him. In my judgment, it is most undesirable if the security which is the basis of that freedom is to be prejudiced by mischances which are of everyday occurrence leading to documents which have escaped being used by the other side.

It is uncertain whether Browne-Wilkinson V-C was basing the relief which he granted on the equitable doctrine of breach of confidence or on legal professional privilege. His high regard for the decision in *Goddard* and his emphatic statement of the importance of protecting the privilege rule suggest he may have

30 [1986] 3 All ER at 271.
31 See pp. 247–9 below.
32 [1986] 3 All ER at 271.
33 *Ibid.* at 271–2.
34 See pp. 253–5 below.
35 *Ibid.* at 272.
36 See p. 250ff.
37 [1988] FSR 232 (Ch.).
38 *Ibid.* at 236–7, as well as rightly saying that the correctness of those cases was beyond his capacity to question.

been basing relief on both principles together, as Nourse LJ seems to have done in *Goddard*.

Finally, in *Derby & Co. Ltd* v. *Weldon (No. 8)*[39] Vinelott J, in a judgment upheld by the Court of Appeal, rejected an attack on *Goddard* made by Scott J in *Webster v Chapman*,[40] then said that:

> the injunctions granted in *Ashburton*'s and *Goddard*'s cases . . . could not, as I see it, have been founded solely on the ground that the information contained in them had been imparted in confidence. If the injunction is sought, in the words of Nourse LJ "in aid of legal professional privilege", no balancing act is called for.[41]

The decision in *Ashburton* v. *Pape* seemed, from the wording of the judgments, to be drawn solely from the equitable doctrine of confidentiality. Newbold argues that this was the rule as originally established, and that cases subsequent to *Ashburton* v. *Pape* have erred in straying from this original basis. Newbold's argument is perhaps best expressed in her own words:

> There has been, for over a century, a misconception that inadvertent disclosure is connected with, or part of, the law relating to legal professional privilege. In fact, inadvertent disclosure . . . has nothing whatever to do with legal professional privilege. It is covered solely by the law relating to confidentiality.[42]

The issue is not just that the appropriate remedy comes from the equitable doctrine of confidentiality, but also that the legal privilege rule plays no part at all in the relief given. To explain the argument again in Newbold's own words:

> The cases in the area of inadvertent disclosure are extremely problematic precisely because they have failed to appreciate the distinction between legal professional privilege and confidentiality. Modern court decisions have not recognised that inadvertent disclosure is solely a matter of confidentiality. Instead the courts have generally dealt with inadvertent disclosure as a matter of legal professional privilege. This error has never been criticised either in the cases or in the limited literature that exists on legal professional privilege . . . It is not sufficient to understand that there is a distinction between privilege and confidentiality. It must be recognised that these two doctrines apply in two separate and mutually exclusive situations. Once a document is in the hands of a third party, privilege is irrelevant.[43]

Newbold further claims that all cases except for *Webster* v. *Chapman*, and all academics discussing the issue over the last half-century are wrong because of their failure to appreciate the separateness of the rules governing privilege and confidentiality.[44] Newbold's article has been cited by judges across the Commonwealth,[45] and has clearly had a significant effect on the debate in this area.

[39] [1991] 1 WLR 73.
[40] [1989] 3 All ER 939.
[41] [1991] 1 WLR at 84.
[42] A.L.E. Newbold, n. 15 above, 99.
[43] *Ibid.* at 101–2.
[44] *Ibid.*
[45] E.g. *Shaw* v. *Harris (No.1)* (1992) 3 Tas R 153 at 158–9 (Tas SC).

Matthews is of a similar view. He draws the clear distinction between confidence and privilege, saying they operate in "entirely independent" fields, and that there is "no duplication of doctrine involved, and no conflict, because the two doctrines concern quite separate matters".[46] Matthews also says that Tapper and Heydon (in articles discussed above) were both "mistaken" to think otherwise.[47] However Matthews' criticism here is based upon an erroneous characterisation of the arguments of Tapper and Heydon.[48]

Some support for the views of Newbold and Matthews may be found in Scott J's judgment in *Webster v Chapman*,[49] where he rejected the proposition advanced in *Goddard* that the granting of relief was not a matter of discretion. Scott J further emphasised that the principle in *Ashburton* v. *Pape* rests solely on the confidential nature of the communication at issue. *Webster* v. *Chapman* has been doubted in New Zealand,[50] but has received some support in Australia.[51]

The main problem with this approach, as will be shown in the following section, is that it is too simplistic. It provides a neat theoretical division of doctrines which ignores the inevitable complications posed by this issue. The "equity only" approach fails to provide any answers to the most difficult questions, such as on what basis the injunctions issued in previous cases validly seek to cover oral evidence of the contents of originals or copies of privileged documents.

Abolition of *Calcraft* v. *Guest*

The rule in *Calcraft* v. *Guest* has been described as "one of the least satisfactory aspects of Commonwealth law on the topic" of privilege.[52] While it has been applied in Canada[53] and a similar rule exists in the United States,[54] it has been

[46] P. Matthews, n. 22 above, 77, 78.

[47] *Ibid.* at 78.

[48] Contrary to the implication made by Matthews, neither Tapper nor Heydon suggested that confidence may be a ground for refusing to give evidence. E.g., see C. Tapper, n. 22 above, 84.

[49] [1989] 3 All ER at 944.

[50] *National Insurance Co Ltd* v. *Whirlybird Holdings Ltd* [1994] 2 NZLR at 516.

[51] *Hong Kong Bank of Australia* v. *Murphy* [1993] VR 419 (Vic. SC); *Copping* v. *ANZ McCaughan Ltd*, LEXIS, 24 Apr. 1995 at 24–5 (SA FC); *Ulgera Gap Nominees Pty Ltd* v. *Elders Ltd*, LEXIS, 29 Oct. 1996 (SA FC); also see *DPP* v. *Kane*, LEXIS, 29 Apr. 1997 (NSW SC).

[52] G.L. Peiris, "Legal Professional Privilege in Commonwealth Law" (1982) 31 *ICLQ* 609 at 630.

[53] *Pfiel* v. *Zinc* (1984) 60 BCLR 32 (BC SC); *McPherson* v. *Institute of Chartered Accountants* (1988) 32 BCLR (2d) 328 (BC CA); J. Sopinka *et al.*, *The Law of Evidence in Canada* (Butterworths, Toronto, 1992) 672–5. However Canadian courts may be moving away from *Calcraft* v. *Guest*: see *Double-E Inc* v. *Positive Action Tool Western Ltd* (1989) 1 FC 163 at 169–70 (Fed. Ct.); *In re Markovina* (1991) 57 BCLR (2d) 73 at 83–5 (BC SC).The rule was to be abolished in cl. 12 of the Draft Act proposed by the Ontario Law Reform Commission, *Report on the Law of Evidence* (Ministry of the Attorney-General, 1976).

[54] J.H. Wigmore and J.T. McNaughton, *Evidence in Trials at Common Law* (Little, Brown & Co., Boston, 1961) viii 633–4; *Scwartz* v. *Wegner* 124 NW (2d) 489 (Minn. SC 1963); *Dobbins* v. *State* 483 P (2d) 255 (Wyo. SC 1971); *Miller* v. *Anderson* 294 A (2d) 344 (Conn. Ct. of Common Pleas 1972); J.M. Grippando, "Attorney–Client Privilege: Implied Waiver Through Inadvertent Disclosure of Documents" (1985) 39 *U Miami LR* 511.

rejected in New Zealand[55] and its status in Australia is far from clear.[56] In England the rule has received some judicial criticism,[57] but has not yet been challenged in the House of Lords. Similarly, while the Law Reform Committee criticised the rule, it stopped short of recommending its immediate legislative abrogation, instead saying that the matter should be considered by the Criminal Law Revision Committee.[58] When the Criminal Law Revision Committee reported six years later it did not discuss this issue.

The rule has also received significant academic criticism. For example, McNicol, mirroring comments by Heydon,[59] criticises *Calcraft* v. *Guest* on the basis that the rule was:

> developed at a time when eavesdropping techniques were undeveloped . . . the advent of modern listening devices and other eavesdropping techniques call for some drastic reassessment of the need for a rule such as that in *Calcraft* v. *Guest*. A blanket common law rule which admits secondary evidence of a privileged communication *whenever* and *however* that communication comes into the hands of a third party is unacceptable.[60]

She goes on to argue that the equitable remedy is incapable of offering a complete solution and that the only answer is abolition of the principle in *Calcraft* v. *Guest*:

> the equitable right of the privilege-holder to restrain by injunction the use of the information where there has been a breach of confidence will never be adequate to completely counteract anomalies and anachronisms contained in the rule in *Calcraft* v. *Guest*. What is called for is the outright abolition of the rule in *Calcraft* v. *Guest* and

[55] R. v. *Uljee* [1982] 1 NZLR 561.

[56] It was accepted without question in *Bell* v. *David Jones Ltd* (1948) 49 SR (NSW) at 227–8. However S.B. McNicol, *Law of Privilege* (Law Book Co., Sydney, 1992) 85 says that "[a]lthough there has been a paucity of Australian decisions in this area, it appears . . . that the Australian courts' attitude will be to eschew the *Calcraft* v. *Guest* rule either indirectly by finding technical distinctions on the facts or by ingeniously recategorising the fact situations so as to dispense with the need for the *Calcraft* v. *Guest* rule altogether". In *Baker* v. *Campbell* (1983) 153 CLR 52 all judges who mentioned the rule cast doubt upon its application in Australia; however only Brennan J was prepared to go as far as expressly stating that it should not be followed. The Australian Law Reform Commission effectively ignored the *Calcraft* v. *Guest* rule in its recommended statutory formulation of the privilege (see Australian Law Reform Commission, *Evidence*, Report No.38 (Australian Law Reform Commission, 1987) para. 195). In *Shaw* v. *Harris (No.1)* (1992) 3 Tas R at 160 Wright J declined to express a view on the argument that *Calcraft* was no longer good law in Australia. R.J. Desiatnik, *Legal Professional Privilege in Australia* (Prospect Media, Sydney, 1999) 113–14 is certain that the decision represents the law in Australia, though he may be underestimating the opposition to it: *ibid.* at n. 120, citing only *Baker* v. *Campbell*.

[57] In *English & American Insurance Ltd* v. *Herbert Smith* [1988] FSR at 237–7 Browne-Wilkinson V-C responded to an argument that *Ashburton* v. *Pape* was wrongly decided by saying that he did not think there was anything wrong with that case and that "I think that when this or some other case reaches the House of Lords it may well be that the absolute rule laid down in *Calcraft* v. *Guest* is the suspect decision".

[58] Law Reform Committee, Sixteenth Report, Cmnd 3472 (HMSO, London, 1967) paras. 31–33.

[59] J.D. Heydon, "Legal Professional Privilege and Third Parties" (1974) 37 *MLR* 601 at 606–7.

[60] S.B. McNicol, n. 56 above, 91.

the formulation of a new approach to the whole important area of 'disclosure' of privileged documents.[61]

Calcraft v. *Guest* has been criticised as based simply on the doubtful precedent of *Lloyd* v. *Mostyn*[62] and not decided "as a matter of principle".[63] However this overlooks the fact that the case was a logical application of the basic principle that all relevant evidence is admissible unless there is a reason for its inadmissibility or exclusion. The case is more accurately seen as a refusal to extend the privilege into a new area hitherto unrecognised, rather than as some new limit to the scope of the privilege. However the time has now come to re-examine this rule to see whether the protection afforded to the privilege should indeed be extended to cover secondary evidence of privileged communications.

There are a number of strong reasons why the rule in *Calcraft* v. *Guest* should be abolished. First, the same policy consideration which restricts the compellability of privileged communications also supports the exclusion of secondary evidence of such communications.[64] The secondary evidence derogation undermines the instrumental goals of the privilege.[65] Secondly, the rule simply does not reflect current intuitive notions of justice, which may demand that a soundly held expectation of confidentiality should not be defeated by the surreptitious or fortuitous gathering of secondary evidence by the other side, particularly if the only excuse the law can offer for such an injustice is the paucity of remedies available to the law.[66]

The rule in *Calcraft* v. *Guest* is completely inconsistent with the waiver rule governing overheard lawyer–client communications in many jurisdictions.[67] In the Australian case of *R.* v. *Braham and Mason*[68] a discussion between an accused and his solicitor was overheard by a police officer. The test for waiver of the privilege was set out as follows:

> each case must be examined to see whether the communication was one which should be classed as confidential. The fact of the presence of a third party should be examined to see whether that presence indicates that the communication was not intended to be confidential, or whether the presence of the third party was caused by some necessity or some circumstances which did not affect the primary nature of the communication as confidential.[69]

[61] *Ibid.*

[62] (1842) 10 M&W 478, 152 ER 558.

[63] R. v. *Uljee* [1982] 1 NZLR at 563, *per* Cooke J.

[64] *Ibid.* at 572 per Richardson J.

[65] J. Tsalinidis, "Legal Professional Privilege: Its Rationale and Exceptions", unpublished Master's Thesis, Melbourne University Library, 1985, at 65.

[66] J.D. Heydon, n. 59 above, 607: "the client is almost certain to be ignorant of the possibility of losing his privilege. His lawyer will doubtless encourage him to speak by telling him of the privilege, but he is unlikely to tell the client of how it can be lost".

[67] In England and Australia, but not in New Zealand. Note that while eavesdropper cases usually concern the admissibility of direct evidence rather than secondary evidence (see R. v. *Uljee* [1982] 1 NZLR at 573, *per* McMullin J) the issue is substantially the same.

[68] [1976] VR 547.

[69] *Ibid.* at 549.

In the circumstances the privilege was held to be waived. However one wonders what would have happened if in slightly different circumstances it was held that the communication was still intended to be confidential. As the privilege is only a rule of non-compellability, it is hard to see how the court could have given effect to a finding that the privilege still existed over the communications. A separate rule has been developed protecting the confidential nature of documents brought into court.[70] However this applies only to documents brought into court during trial and obtained improperly by the opposition.[71] This doctrine has, or should have, little to do with the privilege.

R. v. *Braham and Mason* reflects the mistaken assumption that if the privilege is found still to exist, then the court can prevent evidence of the communications being adduced. Such an attitude reflects an intuitive sense of justice that unfortunately does not accord with current authority.

The New Zealand Court of Appeal took a different approach in *R.* v. *Uljee*,[72] declining to apply *Calcraft* v. *Guest* and holding that a third party who overhears privileged communications may be restrained from giving such testimony. Cooke J, after a detailed examination of the secondary evidence rule, concluded in simple terms that if it was found that the privilege existed, then "the law should not shrink from the fair and natural consequence"[73] of excluding evidence of those privileged communications being given by a third party. The New Zealand Cross on Evidence adequately summarises the state of the law without *Calcraft* v. *Guest*:

> Once it is found that confidentiality was intended, that is enough. It is then immaterial whether the client and the legal adviser took due precautions to prevent a third party overhearing their conversation. Further, it is immaterial whether the confidential communication was connected with Court proceedings. Therefore, a third party who has overheard a confidential communication, or come into possession of it (if written), should not be allowed to give evidence of it unless the client waives the privilege.[74]

The main complaint raised at the prospect of abolition of the principle in *Calcraft* v. *Guest* is that such a change would convert the privilege from a rule of non-compulsion to a rule of inadmissibility. It is clear from the following section that if secondary evidence of privileged communications is to be kept away from the fact-finder, a rule of inadmissibility is required. It is not enough simply to try to gain possession of the secondary evidence or restrain its use. However

[70] *ITC Film Distributors Ltd* v. *Video Exchange Ltd* [1982] Ch 431; compare *R.* v. *Dunbar and Logan* (1982) 138 DLR (3d) 221.

[71] Cf. *R.* v. *Tompkins* (1977) 67 Cr App R 181 (CA).

[72] [1982] 1 NZLR 561.

[73] *Ibid.* at 570.

[74] D.L. Mathieson, *Cross on Evidence—New Zealand* (Butterworths, Wellington, 1998) 411; Mathieson's statement accurately reflects the position in New Zealand. However this may not be the law in the other Commonwealth jurisdictions he cites authority from.

the entire history of the privilege has been as a rule of non-compulsion, and not as a rule of inadmissibility.[75]

If we look at rules of inadmissibility in evidence law, it can be seen that they generally prevent the revelation of particular information because the information is damaging or unsafe in itself. It is this which justifies the inadmissibility of the information, however it is sought to be adduced. For example, consider the rules of opinion, character and similar fact evidence. In each case it is the underlying information conveyed that is problematic.[76] The rule prohibiting disclosure in the public interest is also a rule of inadmissibility, and the name has changed from "Crown privilege" to "public interest immunity" partly to reflect this. The main basis for this rule is that the revelation of the information would be damaging in itself.

Applying this analysis to legal communications, we see that there is nothing problematic about this information in itself. It was seen above that the privilege is not concerned with reliability. The only concern is for the indirect detrimental effect of compulsion. If the same information were adduced from an entirely different source, it would be completely consistent with the rationale that this information be adduced. For example, if a client tells a friend his legal secrets, and the friend is later compelled to testify, such compulsion does not affect the goal of the privilege, being confidence in legal communications. Thus the privilege's rationale does not support the total inadmissibility of the information at issue.

However the privilege's rationale may support the total inadmissibility of legal communications. A client would be more inclined to consult his lawyer if he knew their confidential communications were covered by a rule of inadmissibility and so could not be used however they came into the hands of the opponent, rather than merely that they could not be forced to disclose them. Only a rule of inadmissibility, not a rule of privilege, can guarantee that confidential communications will never be revealed.

Some writers see no problem in turning the privilege into a rule of inadmissibility. For example, Andrews says the problem partly arises from Parke B's rejection in *Lloyd* v. *Mostyn* of the view that the trial judge can exclude a copy being put in evidence.[77] This has driven litigants to seek injunctions in an attempt to exclude such evidence. He goes on to say that:

> It is certainly regrettable that they should have had to pursue this path. If Parke B. had endorsed the existence of a judicial power to exclude privileged documents held by the opponent, this would have protected the privilege holder more effectively than an injunction.[78]

[75] E.g. see *R.* v. *Tompkins* (1977) 67 Cr App R at 184; *R.* v. *Governor of Pentonville Prison, ex p. Osman* [1989] 3 All ER 701 at 730 (QBD).

[76] But see *Forster* v. *Friedland* LEXIS, 10 Nov. 1992 (England CA), where Hoffmann LJ discusses the difference between legal professional privilege and the protection given to without prejudice communications; the latter being a rule of inadmissibility and the former not being so.

[77] J.A. Andrews, n. 22 above, 613.

[78] *Ibid.*

There are still significant problems with turning the privilege into a rule of inadmissibility. It is not immediately apparent how the waiver rules would fit into such a privilege. However as seen a few paragraphs above in the discussion of the eavesdropper cases, this area of law already possesses some doctrinal inconsistencies.

The Impossibility of *Ashburton* v. *Pape*[79]

If, however, *Calcraft* v. *Guest* is not abolished, we are stuck with the problem of trying to reconcile and justify the orders given in protection of the privilege. The actual orders given in these cases cannot be explained solely by reliance on the equitable doctrine of breach of confidence. This is because the equitable doctrine can operate only to prevent disclosure outside the courtroom and to retrieve possession of inadvertently disclosed documents. It cannot prevent the admission in evidence of other forms of secondary proof of the confidential communications, such as oral testimony of the contents of a privileged or copied document. For example, Hoffmann J notes in *Re Briamore Manufacturing Ltd* that:

> The [defendant's] solicitor had acquired knowledge of their contents and had made notes of what they said. It is accepted that he could give secondary evidence of the contents of those documents, that he could produce the photocopy which he had made and that the liquidator could be cross-examined on them.[80]

What is really sought is the exclusion of evidence conveying the contents of the legal communication. The only mechanism that can properly do this is a rule establishing the inadmissibility of such evidence. However if this is not the case, then the courts' powers arising from the principle in *Ashburton* v. *Pape* will always be too limited to provide the protection sought.

This limitation on the scope of the equitable doctrine is not a mere unfortunate quirk of the historical development of the rule. It is vitally important to the whole nature of the rule. It is this limitation that prevents the equitable rule from becoming a *de facto* privilege. In this regard it should be noted that the scope of the confidence rule is extremely broad, and may cover relations such as doctor–patient or husband–wife.[81] It is important that the rule be kept to its proper limits, otherwise it would turn into an enormous obstacle to the discov-

[79] The problem dealt with here did not start with *Ashburton* v. *Pape*. Important earlier cases include *Beer* v. *Ward* (1821) Jac 77, 37 ER 779 and *Lewis* v. *Smith* (1849) 1 Mac & G 417, 41 ER 1326. For discussion of these cases see C. Tapper, n. 13 above, 86–7 and P. Matthews, n. 17 above, at, 81–3.

[80] [1986] 1 WLR 1429 at 1431 (Ch.).

[81] E.g. see the cases drawing this distinction between confidentiality and privilege in relation to the evidence of journalists: *British Steel Corp* v. *Granada Television Ltd* [1982] AC 1096 (HL); *Attorney-General* v. *Mulholland* [1963] 2 QB 477 (CA).

ery of truth in litigation.[82] It is worth partly repeating a passage from Nourse LJ's judgment in *Goddard:*

> The equitable jurisdiction is well able to extend, for example, to the grant of an injunction to restrain an unauthorised disclosure of confidential communications between priest and penitent or doctor and patient. But these communications are not privileged in legal proceedings and I do not believe that equity would restrain a litigant who already had a record of such a communication in his possession from using it for the purposes of his litigation. It cannot be the function of equity to accord a de facto privilege to communications in respect of which no privilege can be claimed.[83]

Therefore, it is an important principle that mere confidentiality, even when cast as the equitable doctrine of breach of confidence, is ineffective to resist compulsion by a court.[84] The fact that a disclosure has been made in confidence does not, on its own, provide sufficient ground for the withholding of evidence from a court.[85] So if courts have been restricting the use of confidential material in court, this relief cannot have come from the equitable rule of confidentiality, but from some other principle, such as legal professional privilege.

Ashburton v. *Pape* and the cases following it have given the equitable breach of confidence doctrine a status and effect it simply cannot have. The doctrine covers precisely the same type of communications, and is precisely the same form of "confidentiality", which Lord Cross was referring to in *Alfred Crompton Amusement Machines Ltd* v. *Commissioners of Customs and Excise (No.2)*[86] when he said that confidentiality is of itself insufficient to prevent compulsory disclosure by a court. If a confidential communication is susceptible to court compulsion whilst still secret, it is bizarre to suggest that it gains a very powerful protection from disclosure *by virtue of* a breach of that confidentiality. Or, to put it another way, with respect to curial compulsion of confidential communications, protection exists only if confidentiality is breached. Odd as it seems, this appears to be the current state of the law.

A hypothetical situation which raises essentially the same issue is: what is to stop the holder of copies of privileged documents from sending those documents back to the party claiming confidentiality in them, and then seeking discovery of these copies under the normal civil discovery procedure? It would seem that there is little to prevent a discovery order here as the copies are documents in the holder's custody or power, and if *Calcraft* v. *Guest* applies, then no privilege attaches to them.

This scenario seems ridiculous: the only way to obtain the use of certain documents in litigation is by sending them to an opponent. However the problem arises out of the artificial distinction between copies and originals. Under

[82] A similar point was made by Tapper, n. 13 above, 84.
[83] [1986] 3 All ER at 271.
[84] Compare the different position in Quebec: A.L.E. Newbold, n. 15 above, 103.
[85] *Alfred Crompton Amusement Machines Ltd* v. *Commissioners of Customs and Excise* (No. 2) [1974] AC 405 at 433 (HL); *D* v. *NSPCC* [1978] AC at 218, 230, 238–9, 242.
[86] See n. 85 above.

Calcraft and *Ashburton* the two categories of material are subject to completely different treatment. However in reality they will usually be virtually identical. Both convey the same information and both provide almost identical evidence of the relevant communication.

If *Calcraft* stands, then *Ashburton* must either be wrong or somehow rest on the privilege as well as equitable breach of confidence. It cannot rest on the breach of confidence doctrine alone. The trial judge's original injunction in *Ashburton* was neatly framed to accord with the limits of the doctrine of confidentiality. The Court of Appeal decision extended the injunction also to cover pending court proceedings,[87] which is precisely into the area that the equitable rule does not cover.

In *Derby* v. *Weldon (No.8)* Vinelott J makes this point as grounds for concluding that the injunction granted in that case rested on more than equitable breach of confidence.[88] A simpler and perhaps more likely answer is that the Court of Appeal decision in *Ashburton* is wrong. The substantive scope of the original injunction was not in issue in the appeal. The appeal was only concerned with whether the injunction could extend to the pending court proceedings. All three judges rested the application of the injunction in the curial sphere on equitable breach of confidence. It is this which is wrong. It is a pity that a case which developed into important and longstanding authority on an issue as difficult as this one was decided without the benefit of argument by counsel for the respondent.

It may be safest to concede that *Ashburton* is open to conflicting interpretations. The precise meaning and effect of the case may be an issue on which opinions reasonably differ. At the end of the day it may not be possible to say conclusively what the Court of Appeal judges intended from the case. However what may be more important than the intended result of the case is the principle that it has subsequently led to, mainly from its application by the Court of Appeal over the last two decades. It is this *Ashburton* principle which is, without doubt, a logical impossibility.

Despite the error in *Ashburton*, it may be possible to draw from this case the desired result (being injunctive protection for the privilege) and then construct such relief upon foundations which are able to support it. This may be what Vinelott J was attempting to do in *Derby* v. *Weldon (No.8)*. If courts are to grant injunctions to restrain secondary evidence of the contents of privileged or

[87] P. Matthews, n. 17 above, 84 says the trial judge's exception was wrong partly because it was arbitrary: "[i]f Pape had asked to be able to use the copies in Bow Street Magistrates' Court on a charge of being drunk and disorderly, would Neville J have inserted that into the order?" (*ibid.*). The answer should be yes. Neville J's order was not perfect. It may have been better to cast an exception for all judicial compulsion. However Neville J's order was drafted in the context of particular litigation, and that was what Neville J was concerned with. It was a fault, but a small fault, in the order. The same can be said for the fact that Neville J's order effectively allowed the defendant to use the information for the purpose of the present proceedings, whereas a properly drawn order should have directed that the court not so use that evidence.

[88] [1991] 1 WLR at 78–9.

copy documents, and if normal discovery is to be resisted, then we must draw from a principle other than equitable breach of confidence. It seems the only principle available from which to draw from is legal professional privilege.

Filling the Gap Between Confidentiality and Privilege

What then is the precise relationship, as it currently stands at least, between the privilege and the equitable rule? Tapper, in a case note on *Butler* v. *Board of Trade*,[89] described the injunctive relief available in this context as "a massive equitable bolster to the protection afforded by legal professional privilege".[90] One would imagine that this is a fairly accurate description of the current legal position. That is that the equitable rule seeks to provide a further remedy in an area where the protection afforded confidential communications by the privilege rule is felt to be inadequate.

However Newbold disagrees with this. She insists that the two doctrines serve entirely different purposes. After quoting the above passage from Tapper's case note, she says:

> This statement is incorrect. Mr Tapper appears to have misunderstood the effect of the case because he failed to make the distinction between privilege and confidentiality. Deciding that an injunction can be granted to restrain a breach of confidential information is not an "equitable bolster" to legal professional privilege. In fact, as has been stated, it has nothing to do with privilege.[91]

Newbold's attack is misguided, and, in a manner, wrong. The equitable doctrine *is* being used to support the privilege rule. It is churlish to pretend otherwise.

The different ways in which Tapper and Newbold describe the relationship between the privilege and the equitable doctrine are much more than an impractical argument over semantics. There is a very important issue at stake here. The issue is the precise nature of the relationship between the equitable doctrine and the privilege.

As pointed out above, Newbold says that the two principles are entirely separate:

> It is not sufficient to understand that there is a distinction between privilege and confidentiality. It must be recognised that the two doctrines apply in two separate and mutually exclusive situations. Once a document is in the hands of a third party, privilege is irrelevant.[92]

It has already been observed that the principle in *Ashburton* may only apply in respect of copies of documents to which privilege attaches. *Ashburton* and

[89] [1971] Ch 680.
[90] C. Tapper, n. 13 above, 87.
[91] A.L.E. Newbold, n. 15 above, 113.
[92] *Ibid.* at 102.

Goddard both considered the injunction in the context of documents which are privileged. In *Ashburton* Cozens-Hardy MR said "[b]ut that does not seem to me to have any bearing upon a case where the whole subject matter of the action is the right to retain the originals or copies of certain documents *which are privileged*".[93] In *Goddard* Nourse LJ said "the equitable jurisdiction . . . can prevail over the rule of evidence only in cases where privilege can be claimed".[94] Vinelott J in *Derby* v. *Weldon (No.8)* emphasised the way in which the judgment of May LJ in *Goddard* was similarly conditioned.[95]

The reason for this close interconnection between the two principles comes from their practical application, rather than any important identity of theory.[96] If the privilege did not apply to the original documents, even if the equitable rule applied, it would be of no practical use, as the other party could simply obtain discovery of the original documents, not to mention the copies. Thus privilege must still exist for the equitable remedy to be of any practical use.[97]

Note that this is clearly not the view taken by Scott J in *Webster* v. *Chapman*.[98] Scott J held that the privilege had been lost, and then went on to consider the application of the equitable rule to the copy documents.[99] If the original documents were no longer privileged, one wonders why Scott J felt it necessary to wrestle with the status of the copy documents. Surely there was nothing to prevent the admission into evidence of the originals.

Conversely, Andrews is adamant that *Goddard* held that if the privilege is waived, there can no injunction. He says first that: "the decision in *Goddard* makes clear that there can be no injunction after the privilege has been waived".[100] Then later he refers to:

> the categorical statement in Goddard that equity has no further action once waiver has occurred at common law . . . [dealing] with *Goddard*, it will be recalled that the Court of Appeal in that decision declared that once privilege is waived, there can be no injunction.[101]

However *Goddard* does not say this. In that case Nourse LJ said only that the injunction is "granted in aid of the privilege" and that the privilege is absolute until it is waived.[102] The difference between what Nourse LJ says, and what Andrews says Nourse LJ says, is subtle but important. The fate of the two prin-

93 [1913] 2 Ch at 473 (emphasis added).

94 [1986] 3 All ER at 271.

95 [1991] 1 WLR at 79.

96 Compare R.G. Toulson and C.M. Phipps, Confidentially (1996, Sweet & Maxwell, London) 206–7, criticising this aspect of *Goddard* on doctrinal grounds.

97 Of course, as discussed above, the equitable rule may still be of little practical use, as it is powerless to prevent the reception of oral evidence of the contents of the document or of discovery of the copy.

98 [1989] 3 All ER 939.

99 *Ibid.* at 946–7.

100 J.A. Andrews, n. 22 above, 610.

101 *Ibid.* at 627.

102 [1986] 3 All ER at 271.

ciples is, as a matter of practicality, intertwined. However this does not mean that the principles themselves are fused.

Hock Lai Ho argues for a resolution of the issue of inadvertent disclosure of privileged documents by means of a different principle, which is neither the privilege, nor the equitable doctrine.[103] Ho says that *Ashburton* v. *Pape* should be seen as the manifestation of a larger principle of fairness. Under this general principle, where a party could have resisted disclosure if compulsion had been sought, his opponent will be prevented from tendering admissible evidence where this would be unfair. Ho outlines two sources of unfairness: first, where there is no impropriety but the disclosure was against the will of the client; secondly, where there is unconscionable conduct such as trickery or exploitation of an obvious mistake. This will not be the case where the disclosure was inadvertent and the recipient unaware of the mistake.

Ho's principle is different from the privilege. He describes it as "a larger principle that is wider than and which exists alongside the privilege".[104] Later he makes this even clearer:

> we ought not to be led to believe that the reason why we intervene is because of the evidential privilege. In truth, we are concerned with a separate principle concerning fairness in the use of evidence in litigation.[105]

Under this principle the court would also have the power to exclude or expunge evidence even where it has already been tendered. This issue will be discussed in the section on remedies below.

Ho's principle has the advantage of awareness of and faith in the limits of existing doctrines; a quality that has at times been sadly lacking in this area of law. However, while his fairness principle may be tenable in Malaysia, Singapore or even possibly Australia, it is probably not a realistic option in England, where there is a very strong stream of case law setting out the common law admissibility of wrongfully obtained evidence. Despite English precedent there are many reasons of principle why such an approach should not be followed. Cases developed in the context of criminal trials and for the express purpose of protecting criminal accused do not necessarily transfer well to the different priorities of civil litigation. Further, if this principle is to be applied by means of a discretion turning on the conduct of the parties, then how different is it from the equitable doctrine anyway? Finally, Ho's principle may go against the rationale for the privilege. Why should the privilege's operation be dependant on an assessment of the comparative fault of litigants? The privilege is concerned only with maintaining a client's expectation of confidentiality.

[103] H.L. Ho, "Admissibility, Privilege and the Expunging of Evidence" (1994) 6 *Singapore Academy LJ* 146 at 150ff.

[104] *Ibid.* at 150.

[105] *Ibid.* at 158.

SECTION II: PRINCIPLES GROUNDING RELIEF

Potential Remedies

Much of the difficulty in unravelling the problem of accidental disclosure boils down to the appropriate remedy to be applied to restrict the damage done by such disclosures. There are many possible remedies which may be useful for this purpose. The most common orders sought are for the delivery up of the original[106] and copies of the inadvertently disclosed documents, and an injunction to enforce the privileged status of the communications before a court. Additional remedies may include an injunction to restrain the use and disclosure of the material outside court, including an injunction to prevent the making of copies,[107] a declaration as to the status of documents or their evidential use,[108] or an application to strike out pleadings made in reliance on the relevant information.[109]

Note that whatever orders are granted it is impossible to expunge the knowledge of the contents of the documents from the minds of people who have accidentally read them. However it may be possible for the trial judge to restrict questioning clearly based on the knowledge gained from inadvertently disclosed documents which have been returned pursuant to court order.[110] One English judge has taken the extreme step of granting an injunction requiring the solicitors who have read the documents in issue to cease to act in the litigation.[111] Bar ethics rules may already prevent barristers from continuing to act in such circumstances where doing so would not prejudice their lay client.[112]

The most theoretically difficult and contentious remedy at issue is the injunction designed to enforce the privileged status of the communications before a court. Such an injunction may attempt to prevent the disclosure of non-privileged copies of privileged documents to a court, or prevent an opponent from testifying to his knowledge of the contents of privileged documents or copies of them. There is some difference of opinion over the extent to which

[106] Note that, as pointed out by J.A. Andrews, n. 22 above, 612, it was not possible until 1978 for the privilege holder to recover the original document, if this document was still held by its opponent. This was remedied by s. 3(2) of the Torts (Interference with Goods) Act 1977 (UK), which allowed for specific delivery on an action for conversion. Previously the remedy had been in damages only.

[107] E.g. as in *ITC Film Distributors Ltd* v. *Video Exchange Ltd* [1982] Ch 431.

[108] This was used in *Butler* v. *Board of Trade* [1971] Ch 680 because an injunction could not be issued as interlocutory relief against a department of the Crown.

[109] E.g. as sought in *Goddard* v. *Nationwide Building Society* [1986] 3 All ER 264.

[110] See *National Insurance Co Ltd* v. *Whirlybird Holdings Ltd* [1994] 2 NZLR 513.

[111] *Ablitt* v. *Mills & Reeve*, *The Times*, 25 Oct. 1995 (Ch.). 7 files had been sent in error to the opposing party's solicitors. The solicitors receiving the files followed then currrent Law Society guidance and sought instructions from the client, who instructed the solicitors to read the files before handing them back.

[112] General Council of the Bar of England and Wales, *Code of Conduct of the Bar of England and Wales* (General Council of the Bar of England and Wales) Annex H, para. 7; J.A. Andrews and D.M. Hirst, *Criminal Evidence* (3rd edn., Sweet & Maxwell, London, 1997) 390.

such relief is discretionary, and the importance of the knowledge of the recipient of inadvertently disclosed documents of the privileged status of the documents. These issues will be addressed in the section below, along with other issues relating to the granting of remedies to relieve against the effects of accidental disclosure.

Discretion

There is some confusion and difference of opinion over the nature of injunctive relief available in this area. In *Goddard* Nourse LJ held that the granting of an injunction under the principles in *Ashburton* is in some respect not a matter of discretion. He held that:

> once it is established that a case is governed by *Lord Ashburton* v. *Pape*, there is no discretion in the court to refuse to exercise the equitable jurisdiction according to its view of the materiality of the communication, the justice of admitting or excluding it or the like. The injunction is granted in aid of the privilege which, unless and until it is waived, is absolute.[113]

However Nourse LJ then went on to say:

> I do not intend to suggest that there may not be cases where an injunction can properly be refused on general principles affecting the grant of a discretionary remedy, for example on the ground of inordinate delay.[114]

In *Webster* v. *Chapman* Scott J rejected Nourse LJ's view that the remedy may somehow not be discretionary. Scott J held that the remedy arises solely from confidentiality and not in any way from the privilege, and was therefore dependant on the normal conditions for such relief. [115] However it has been shown above that there are good reasons to doubt Scott J's view that the remedy arises solely from confidentiality and not from the privilege.

In *Derby* v. *Weldon (No. 8)* Vinelott J held that Scott J in *Webster* v. *Chapman* was wrong to regard the *Goddard* principles (including the one quoted above) as dicta. Vinelott J went on to hold that:

> If the injunction is sought, in the words of Nourse LJ 'in aid of legal professional privilege', no balancing act is called for . . . The balancing act has already been done by the making of the rule of legal professional privilege; and to do what counsel for the respondents submitted should be done in subsequent litigation would be to deny, in effect, the existence of that rule.[116]

In *Pizzey* v. *Ford Motor Co*[117] the trial judge, after conducting a balancing exercise, refused an injunction. Mann LJ, for the Court of Appeal, held that the

[113] [1986] 3 All ER at 272.
[114] *Ibid.*
[115] [1989] 3 All ER at 945.
[116] [1991] 1 WLR at 84.
[117] LEXIS, 26 Mar. 1993; *The Times*, 8 Mar. 1993; *Independent*, 10 Mar. 1993 (CA).

trial judge was wrong to conduct a balancing exercise to determine the application of injunctive relief. Mann LJ held that *Webster* v. *Chapman* was wrong on this issue, and that *Goddard* and *Derby* v. *Weldon (No. 8)* were correct. In determining the application of injunctive relief, no balancing process is called for.

Discretion may be relevant to injunctive relief for inadvertent disclosure either:

(i) by use of a discretion to determine the application of the substantive right grounding relief (in this case either breach of confidence or privilege); and/or
(ii) by use of a discretion to determine, given the presence of a right, whether relief should be granted (i.e. the discretionary factors circumscribing equitable relief).

If it is accepted that the injunction sought following inadvertent disclosure of privileged materials is an equitable injunction granted in the auxiliary equitable jurisdiction to protect common law rights, it should be clear that the nature of the discretion involved here is as follows. First, with respect to the right grounding relief, there is no discretionary element. Privilege is either recognised or it is not. Recognising the existence of the privilege is not a matter in which discretion enters into. Secondly, at the remedy stage of the analysis, the discretion involved here is the discretion inherent in the application of all equitable remedies.

When Nourse LJ says that relief may be refused on the "general principles affecting the grant of a discretionary remedy",[118] this is correct as long as it is a reference to the principles governing equitable remedies. Nourse LJ's statement, quoted above, that there is no "discretion in the court to refuse to exercise the equitable jurisdiction"[119] because the privilege is absolute may seem odd. The "absoluteness" of the privilege should have nothing to do with the decision to grant a remedy. However this may be the point that Nourse LJ, in a slightly cryptic fashion, was making.[120] That is, he was saying that there is no discretion, at the stage of determining the right, to refuse to consider application of the remedy. This is because the right stems from the privilege, which involves no general discretion at point of recognition, and not from the discretionary right of equitable breach of confidence.

If this is the true meaning of Nourse LJ's judgment, then Scott J in *Webster* v. *Chapman* was wrong to reject it. Scott J used balancing terminology in describing the nature of the discretion employed here, saying the court must "balance on the one hand the legitimate interests of the plaintiff in seeking to keep the confidential information suppressed and on the other hand the legitimate inter-

[118] [1986] 3 All ER at 272.

[119] *Ibid.*

[120] Nourse LJ's judgment may be easier to understand if we knew precisely what arguments he was addressing in this part of his judgment.

ests of the defendant in seeking to make use of the information".[121] This balancing is used to determine application of the right, not the remedy. The right being claimed here is the one arising from the equitable breach of confidence doctrine. As has been shown above, the right being enforced when a party seeks an injunction following inadvertent disclosure of privileged material partly arises from the privilege itself, and not from the equitable breach of confidence doctrine alone. Given this, Scott J's balancing test may have no application. This is what Vinelott J meant when he said, in *Derby* v. *Weldon (No. 8)*, that "[i]f the injunction is sought, in the words of Nourse LJ 'in aid of legal professional privilege', no balancing act is called for".[122]

Knowledge of the Recipient

A difficult issue is the extent to which courts should consider the knowledge of the recipients of the disclosure. It may seem odd that a privilege holder is in a worse position by virtue of the equitable discretion. Under the privilege rule, the knowledge of the recipient is irrelevant to the granting of relief. However under the breach of confidentiality doctrine, the knowledge of the recipient may be an important factor with regard to the discretion.

In *Goddard* Nourse LJ held that:

> the right of the party who desires the protection to invoke the equitable jurisdiction does not in any way depend on the conduct of the third party into whose possession the record of the confidential communication has come . . . This view seems to give effect to the general rule that equity gives relief against all the world, including the innocent, save only a bona fide purchaser for value without notice. It is directly in point in the present case and our decision necessarily affirms it.[123]

In *English & American Insurance Ltd* v. *Herbert Smith* Browne-Wilkinson V-C expressly rejected the submission that exercise of the equitable jurisdiction may depend on the knowledge of the recipient of the disclosure.[124] He also expressly approved the above passage from *Goddard* and rejected any attempt to restrict *Ashburton* and *Goddard* to the situation where the recipient of the disclosure is partially implicated in wrongdoing.[125] Similarly, in *Def American Inc* v. *Phonogram Ltd*[126] Lindsay J in the Chancery Division rejected knowledge of the recipient as a factor in injunctive relief, saying the matter had been put beyond doubt by *Goddard*.

121 [1989] 3 All ER at 945.
122 [1991] 1 WLR at 84.
123 [1986] 3 WLR at 745.
124 [1988] FSR at 237.
125 *Ibid*. Note that this was in the context of a submission that *Ashburton* and *Goddard* were wrongly decided and therefore, although Browne-Wilkinson V-C had no power to overrule these cases, he should greatly restrict their application by reference to this consideration.
126 LEXIS, 29 July 1994 (Ch.), also reported in *The Times*, 16 Aug. 1994.

However in contrast to these cases, Slade LJ in *Guiness Peat* strongly emphasised the knowledge of the recipient as an important factor justifying injunctive relief, holding that, if the other party realises an obvious mistake has been made, the court "should ordinarily intervene" by granting an injunction.[127] The manner in which the reasoning is framed suggests that knowledge of the recipient is elevated to the status of a criterion grounding equitable relief. Slade LJ also expressed this in the form of a general principle for all such cases.[128] Curiously, Slade LJ, in setting out this criterion of knowledge of the recipient, twice expressly claimed to be describing the "injunction in exercise of the equitable jurisdiction exemplified by the *Ashburton, Goddard* and *Herbert Smith* cases".[129] He did not acknowledge the inconsistency between his own principle and the judgments he purported to be following.

English courts now consistently use the likely knowledge of the recipient as a factor grounding relief.[130] This is on an objective test of whether a reasonable person in the position of the recipient would have thought that the privilege had been waived. So in a recent case it was held that the fact that some of the recipients were litigants in person made it even less likely that they would have realised a mistake had been made.[131] The use of the recipient's knowledge as a factor has so far survived the change from the Supreme Court Rules to the Civil Procedure Rules. In *Breeze* v. *John Stacey & Sons Ltd*[132] Peter Gibson LJ for the Court of Appeal held that the "well established" test for inadvertant disclosure would remain under the new Rules. The English approach has been adopted in Australia[133] and New Zealand[134]; however the position in Canada is unclear.[135]

In *Derby* v. *Weldon (No. 8)* both Vinelott J at first instance and Dillon LJ for the Court of Appeal expressly approved of knowledge of the recipient as a valid factor. This had an important effect in the case, as it led Vinelott J to analyse each of the disputed documents to determine whether the recipient would have realised that each was inadvertently disclosed. The Court of Appeal acknowledged the inconsistent treatment of this issue described above, and approved of

127 [1987] 2 All ER at 731.

128 *Ibid.* at 730.

129 *Ibid.* at 730b and 731c.

130 E.g. *Hayes* v. *Dowding* [1996] PNLR at 597–8; also see the case in nn. 131–2. below.

131 "A&O fails to get injunction after faxed evidence blunder", *The Lawyer*, 2 June 1998, 48 (Lindsay J Ch D).

132 *The Times*, 8 July 1999.

133 E.g. *Meltend Pty Ltd* v. *Restoration Clinics of Australia* (1997) 145 ALR 391 at 396 (Fed. Ct.) (document so "patently privileged . . . [recipient solicitors] must have known or realised that the letter had been included . . . by mistake"); *DPP* v. *Kane* (1997) 140 FLR 468 at 485 (Fed. Ct.) ("the privilege is not lost if the hypothetical reasonable person with the qualities of the actual recipient would have so realised"); also see R.J. Desiatnik, *Legal Professional Privilege in Australia* (Prospect Media, Sydney, 1999) 109–13.

134 E.g. *National Insurance Co Ltd* v. *Whirlybird Holdings Ltd* [1994] 2 NZLR 513 at 517 (CA); *Spicers Paper (NZ) Ltd* v. *Whitcoulls Group Ltd* [1996] 1 NZLR 72 (HC).

135 The position taken by Rothstein J in *Re Stevens and Prime Minister of Canada* (1997) 144 DLR (4th) at 566–7 is unclear.

Guiness Peat over *Goddard* and *Herbert Smith*, also stating that the court was in any case bound by *Guiness Peat.*

Both the trial judge and the Court of Appeal in *Derby* v. *Weldon (No. 8)* seem to have confused the issue of waiver with the issue of injunctive relief. Vinelott J extensively analyses the effect of knowledge of the recipient on the ostensible authority of the legal adviser.[136] This analysis is clearly directed towards the issue of waiver. Dillon LJ, for the Court of Appeal, distinguishes both the *Goddard* and *Herbert Smith* cases on the ground that there was no issue of waiver in those cases.[137] Thus when he later discusses the importance of knowledge of the recipient as a factor, he may be doing so in the context of the factors determining waiver. Similar confusion has beset some academic commentators,[138] and the use of knowledge of the recipient as a factor in determining waiver appears to have the support of at least one Australian case.[139]

The confusion between waiver principles and principles grounding the injunction is unfortunate. It should be relatively clear that knowledge of the recipient may be a valid factor in determining waiver. It is wrong to think that waiver is purely concerned with the intention of the privilege holder. As was shown in the previous chapter, this is just one part of the doctrine (or doctrines). There are other waiver rules which depend on fairness-based considerations, in which reference to the knowledge of the recipient would not be out of place.

However this says nothing about whether the recipient's knowledge should be relevant to the granting of injunctive relief. If the remedy is based on the courts' auxiliary equitable jurisdiction to protect the common law privilege rule, or is based on the equitable breach of confidence doctrine, then one would think that the remedy is governed by the equitable principles usually grounding such relief. The law of breach of confidence does not normally restrict relief by reference to such a factor.[140]

Timing: When is It Too Late?

The next issue concerning injunctive or other relief following inadvertent disclosure of secondary evidence is how far should courts be prepared to go in remedying the effects of such disclosures. The Court of Appeal in *Goddard* seemed to draw the line at the point where evidence is introduced at trial. Relief was granted even though the recipient of the disclosure had already used the evidence to compile his pleadings. The pleadings drawn up in reliance on the inadvertently disclosed evidence were struck out. Nourse LJ held that "the party

136 [1991] 1 WLR at 87.

137 *Ibid.* at 95.

138 E.g. J.A. Andrews, n. 22 above, 629 ("it is regrettable that Slade LJ in *Guiness Peat* has made consideration of the recipient's state of mind and conduct an ingredient in the analysis of waiver").

139 *DPP* v. *Kane*, LEXIS, 29 Apr. 1997 (NSW SC).

140 Cf. R.G. Toulson and C.M. Phipps, *Confidentiality* (Sweet & Maxwell, London, 1996) 208–9; though it may be relevant to a claim based on change of position.

who desires protection must seek it before the other party has adduced the confidential communication in evidence or otherwise relied on it at trial".[141]

Andrews suggests that the effect of *Goddard* is that it is too late only if evidence has been introduced, or perhaps, if the case formulated in pleadings has been presented during opening speeches at trial.[142] This aspect of *Goddard* was followed and applied in *Def American Inc* v. *Phonogram Ltd*,[143] where Lindsay J drew a sharp distinction between pre-trial and trial disclosure.

Such a rule would accord well with the analogous issue of the subsequent use of documents disclosed for the purpose of proceedings. Rule 31.22 of the Civil Procedure Rules 1998 provides that such documents disclosed for the purpose of proceedings may not be disclosed for any other purpose, except where, inter alia, the document has been read or referred to at a public hearing.[144]

However cases decided after *Goddard* appear to set the limit on remedies at an earlier point in time, holding that some forms of pre-trial disclosure may bar a remedy. In *Pizzey* v. *Ford Motor Co*[145] Mann LJ, for the Court of Appeal, held that once inspection had taken place then it was too late for the court to intervene. Similarly, in *Black & Decker* v. *Flymo* Hoffmann J held that if privileged material had been inadvertently disclosed in an exchange of witness statements, then it would be too late for the court to seek to remedy the situation. He held that once a document had passed into the hands of the opposition the question was no longer one of privilege, but of admissibility. The Court of Appeal in *Breeze* v. *John Stacey & Sons Ltd*[146] affirmed the rule as stated in *Pizzey* that, once inspection had taken place, the court would not intervene; and also held that this remained the case under the Civil Procedure Rules 1998.

Australian courts seem more willing to offer relief where pre-trial disclosure has occurred. In *Kabwand Pty Ltd* v. *National Australia Bank*[147] privileged material was inadvertently included in the bundle of documents for inspection, and inspection occurred. The recipient of the inadvertent disclosure then requested copies of the privileged documents and, when this was refused, he sought a court order allowing him to copy the documents. Although it was held that the privilege had been waived, and that the recipient had acquired some knowledge of the documents, the order for copies was still refused, on the ground that there is still a valid difference between seeing a document during inspection and possessing a copy of it.[148] Although the Court professed to be following principles set out by the English cases discussed above, the result of

[141] [1986] 3 All ER at 271g.

[142] J.A. Andrews, n. 22 above, 620.

[143] LEXIS, 29 July 1994; *The Times*, 16 Aug. 1994.

[144] The other circumstances are where the court gives permission or the relevant parties agree to disclosure.

[145] LEXIS, 26 Mar. 1993; *The Times*, 8 Mar. 1993; *Independent*, 10 Mar. 1993.

[146] *The Times*, 8 July 1999.

[147] (1987) 81 ALR 721 (Fed Ct).

[148] *Ibid.* at 723. Also see *Key International Drilling Co Ltd* v. *TNT Bulk Ship Operations* [1989] WAR 280 (WA SC).

the case was much more favourable for the holder of privileged documents than would have been the case for the holder of such documents in England. In *Hong Kong Bank of Australia* v. *Murphy*[149] inspection had taken place and inadvertently disclosed documents had already been copied. However the court was still willing to countenance the making of orders to protect the privilege if it had found the privilege still to exist. In *Hooker Corp* v. *Darling Harbour Authority*[150] relief was granted after inspection but before the relevant cross-examination which would have dealt with the disclosed material;[151] although later courts have attempted to distinguish or restrict this case.[152] However there is no complete consensus on this issue in Australia. In *Meltend Pty Ltd* v. *Restoration Clinics of Australia Pty Ltd*[153] Goldberg J effectively held that no relief could be granted following inspection, on the ground that allowing parties to "change their mind" after inspection "has the potential to become unworkable".[154]

An alternative approach may be to focus on the effect of the disclosure, rather than its strict timing. In the law of breach of confidence it has been suggested that injunctions should not be issued if the defendant has acted in good faith and changed his position in reliance on the disclosure.[155] A similar rule could perhaps be employed in the area of injunctions in support of legal professional privilege.

The simplest and ultimately most honest approach may be to say that the only limit is the courts' capacity to provide an effective remedy. Glimpses of this can be seen in the cases already discussed. For example, in *Guiness Peat* Slade LJ said that the court could intervene to protect the privilege "save where it is too late to restore the status quo", and then later saying that in the present case "it is not too late to put the clock back".[156] It may be that the bounds of what the court considers are possible remedies may be changing, and that over time the Court of Appeal may increasingly feel that it can do more to protect the privilege.

The most powerful remedy imaginable may be the expunging or retracting of evidence already admitted. Resort to such a remedy may be unthinkable in England; however it has been done in at least one Commonwealth jurisdiction.

In the Malaysian case of *Dato' Au Ba Chi*[157] the plaintiff obtained a copy of

149 [1993] VR 419 (Vic. SC).

150 (1987) 9 NSWLR 538.

151 Compare *Re Illawarra County Council (General Conditions of Employment) Award*, New South Wales Industrial Relations Commission, 17 June 1992, Glynn J, where no relief was granted as cross-examination based on the disclosed material had already taken place.

152 E.g. see *Meltend Pty Ltd* v. *Restoration Clinics of Australia Pty Ltd* (1997) 145 ALR at 398, 404; *Doran Constructions Pty Ltd* v. *University of Newcastle*, New South Wales Supreme Court, 12 Dec. 1997, Rolfe J at 14.

153 (1997) 145 ALR 391.

154 *Ibid.* at 406. The characterisation of a party "changing its mind" seems odd in the context of inadvertent disclosure.

155 F. Gurry, *Breach of Confidence* (Clarendon Press, Oxford, 1984) 405–7.

156 [1987] 2 All ER at 731.

157 [1989] 3 MLJ 445 (HC).

the defendant's privileged document. The plaintiff then included the document in an agreed bundle, and the plaintiff's witness referred to it at trial. The defendant successfully obtained an order expunging the document from the agreed bundle and also expunging all references to it by a witness in the notes of evidence. Oddly, the issue of remedies does not appear to have been the subject of much argument or analysis before the court.

It has been argued that such a remedy could be justified as an extension of the criminal law discretion to exclude admissible evidence where its reception would be unfair to the accused.[158] However, apart from the fact that such a discretion probably does not exist in civil cases,[159] the expunging of evidence already admitted is very different from the exclusion of evidence not yet disclosed to the fact-finder. In terms of the exclusion of evidence for countervailing policy reasons, English law has always drawn quite a clear line at the point at which the evidence is adduced to the fact-finder. A closely analogous example is the waiver rule in *Great Atlantic Insurance Co* v. *Home Insurance*.[160] While not clearly articulated, an important reason for this rule may be practicability. Once evidence has been disclosed to the people charged with determining the truth in the trial, it is difficult then to expect those people to put such evidence out of their minds.

CONCLUSION

This whole area urgently needs to be reviewed by the House of Lords. When that court does deal with the issue, it will find that while the actual decisions in *Calcraft* v. *Guest* and *Ashburton* v. *Pape* may be reconcilable on their facts, the broad values which underpin the two cases are not. The broad value behind *Calcraft* v. *Guest* is the interest in the reception of all relevant evidence which is not rendered inadmissible or excluded by any rule of evidence. The broad value behind *Ashburton* v. *Pape* is the desire to protect legal communications from use in court, even after some disclosure has occurred, in order to maintain the faith of clients in the protection afforded to legal communications. The courts want to give the privilege greater protection than it actually has, but also do not want to alter their existing legal doctrines in order to achieve this change.

The first change that should be made is to abandon reliance on doctrinal purity and abolish the rule in *Calcraft* v. *Guest*. This will have the effect of extending the scope of privilege protection beyond its previous limits. However such a change would be entirely justified by and consistent with the goals of the privilege. The sense of dissatisfaction with this area of the privilege stems from the apparent unfairness caused by adducing secondary evidence of privileged

[158] H.L. Ho, n. 103 above, 150.

[159] E.g. *Helliwell* v. *Piggott-Sims* [1980] FSR 356 at 357 (CA).

[160] [1981] 2 All ER at 493; also see *General Accident Fire and Life Assurance Ltd* v. *Tanter* [1984] 1 WLR 100.

documents. This sense of unfairness should be tackled at its source, rather than accepting the rule and then trying to evade its immediate consequences.

If the rule in *Calcraft* v. *Guest* is to remain, the answer does not lie in the equitable breach of confidence doctrine. The rule in *Ashburton* v. *Pape* is like a plaster that has been applied over a bad shotgun wound, the plaster then being blamed when the victim does not recover. *Ashburton* v. *Pape* is a separate principle that has been used to try to fill a gap in the privilege where both the logic of the privilege and an intuitive sense of justice demand that a remedy be given. It is now clear that the gap in the privilege doctrine is larger than first thought.

The equitable doctrine, while sound in itself, has obscured the real problem in the privilege, which is the fact that the scope of the privilege and the remedies available to enforce it are not strong enough to supply the degree of protection that would be appropriate. Seen in this way, the real problem arises with thinking that *Ashburton* v. *Pape* can provide a useful answer to the whole issue.

13

Past and Future Directions

Commonwealth judges usually assume the privilege to be sacrosanct, or present it as such. This book has attempted to challenge this assumption. The reality is that it is not as important to maintain a near-absolute privilege and restrict the derogations as judges and practitioners usually claim it is. Clients are not aware of, or greatly under-estimate, the existence and scope of privilege derogations. It is impossible for a client to know at the time of requesting legal advice whether his legal communications will remain privileged or not. There is an unavoidable element of uncertainty in the operation of the rule as it currently exists. The scope of the privilege is determined on nothing more than a basic assessment of competing policy interests, and this is done on a rule balanced basis.

The claims of the privilege have in the past been overstated. As explained in this book, American empirical data on this issue are not ambiguous. They clearly show that the privilege is more robust than previously thought. Specifically, as it is dependant on client expectations of confidentiality for its continued functioning, rather than on the reality of such confidentiality, it is capable of accommodating changes in the scope of the privilege, while still fulfilling its essential function.

All this is not to say that the privilege is undeserving of protection; rather, that we should be more sceptical of the claims made for the privilege, and more willing to challenge its application in specific areas where this application appears to be producing unjust results. In approptiate circumstances more weight should be accorded to the values underlying the disclosure of evidence.

There are three discernible trends in the development of the privilege over the last two decades: first, the expansion of the range of application of the privilege beyond curial compulson to a variety of forms of executive compulsion, from search warrants to the opening of prison mail; secondly, the common law's maintenance of a high degree of protection for the privilege. This has come from wide interpretations of the rule's substantive scope, restrictive interpretations of its derogations (with some obvious exceptions such as the broadening of the crime-fraud rule in England and issue waiver in Australia) and the refusal in many jurisdictions to recognise new common law derogations. Thirdly, while human rights legislation has been introduced in most Commonwealth jurisdictions in this time, these new regimes have not made a significant impact on the substantive rules of the common law privilege.

It has been argued in this book that the recent history of the privilege displays an over-estimation of the demands of confidentiality and an under-estimation of the need for disclosure of evidence. It would be nice to think that in the future there will be a more realistic evaluation of the extent of "absoluteness" required by the privilege, along the lines of that undertaken in Chapters 4 and 5. However in reality it is doubtful that this will happen. Judges in Commonwealth courts seem wedded to a particular view of the operation of legal communications, and the role of the privilege within the lawyer–client relationship. This attitude is unlikely to change quickly. Judges will not examine the American studies; and if examined they would most likely be rejected out of hand as this is simply not a form of analysis judges in Commonwealth courts are traditionally amenable to.

The upshot is that the numerous inconsistencies in the doctrine will remain. For example, lawyers claim that any recognition of new or extended derogations would pose a fundamental threat to client confidence, yet ignore the facts that clients are clearly not aware of existing derogations, and no lawyer would contemplate warning them about possible privilege derogations at the first consultation. The only hope may be that human rights legislation forces a more taxing examination of the demands of disclosure. For example, if the *Derby Magistrates* case is viewed through the lens of the European Convention on Human Rights, it is highly likely that a different result will be reached. This is because the Convention demands a more careful assesment of the purposes sought to be achieved by rules impinging upon the privilege, and the means by which the privilege is impinged, as well as a greater weight on the values underlying disclosure of evidence.

Index